MW01706962

About Pearson

Pearson is the world's learning company, with presence across 70 countries worldwide. Our unique insights and world-class expertise comes from a long history of working closely with renowned teachers, authors and thought leaders, as a result of which, we have emerged as the preferred choice for millions of teachers and learners across the world.

We believe learning opens up opportunities, creates fulfilling careers and hence better lives. We hence collaborate with the best of minds to deliver you class-leading products, spread across the Higher Education and K12 spectrum.

Superior learning experience and improved outcomes are at the heart of everything we do. This product is the result of one such effort.

Your feedback plays a critical role in the evolution of our products and you can contact us - reachus@pearson.com. *We look forward to it.*

CLASS 6

Pearson IIT Foundation Series

Mathematics

CLASS

6

Pearson IIT Foundation Series

Mathematics

Trishna Knowledge Systems

Pearson

Photo Credits

All Chapter Openers: Poznyakov. Shutterstock
Icons of Practice Questions: graphixmania. Shutterstock
Icons of Answer Keys: Viktor88. Shutterstock
Icons of Hints and Explanation: graphixmania. Shutterstock

Senior Editor—Acquisitions: Nandini Basu
Senior Editor—Production: G. Sharmilee

ISBN 978-93-528-6740-0

First Impression

Published by Pearson India Education Services Pvt. Ltd, CIN: U72200TN2005PTC057128.

Head Office: 15th Floor, Tower-B, World Trade Tower, Plot No. 1, Block-C, Sector-16, Noida 201 301, Uttar Pradesh, India.
Registered Office: 4th Floor, Software Block, Elnet Software City, TS-140, Block 2 & 9, Rajiv Gandhi Salai, Taramani, Chennai 600 113, Tamil Nadu, India.
Fax: 080-30461003, Phone: 080-30461060
Website: in.pearson.com, Email: companysecretary.india@pearson.com

Compositor: SRS Global, Puducherry.
Printer in India at India Binding House, Noida.

Brief Contents

Contents

Preface

Pearson IIT Foundation Series has evolved into a trusted resource for students who aspire to be a part of the elite undergraduate institutions of India. As a result, it has become one of the best-selling series, providing authentic and class-tested content for effective preparation—strong foundation, and better scoring.

The structure of the content is not only student-friendly but also designed in such a manner that it motivates students to go beyond the usual school curriculum, and acts as a source of higher learning to strengthen the fundamental concepts of Physics, Chemistry, and Mathematics.

The core objective of the series is to be a one-stop solution for students preparing for various competitive examinations. Irrespective of the field of study that the student may choose to take up later, it is important to understand that Mathematics and Science form the basis for most modern-day activities. Hence, utmost effort has been made to develop student interest in these basic blocks through real-life examples and application-based problems. Ultimately, the aim is to ingrain the art of problem-solving in the mind of the reader.

To ensure high level of accuracy and practicality, this series has been authored by a team of highly qualified teachers with a rich experience, and are actively involved in grooming young minds. That said, we believe that there is always scope for doing things better and hence invite you to provide us with your feedback and suggestions on how this series can be improved further.

Chapter Insights

REMEMBER

Before beginning this chapter, you should be able to:

- Recall digits and numbers
- Perform addition, subtraction, multiplication and division of numbers

Remember section will help them to memorize and review the previous learning on a particular topic

Key points will help the students to identify the essential points in a chapter

KEY IDEAS

After completing this chapter, you should be able to:

- Define even numbers, odd numbers, prime numbers, sphenic numbers, composite numbers, twin prime, co-primes
- Understand highest common factor (HCF)

INTRODUCTION

We have come across the concept of 'fraction' in previous classes. In this section, we shall learn about the types of fractions, ordering of fractions and the basic arithmetic operations in fractions, etc.

Imagine that you have invited five friends to your birthday party. You have cut the cake into six equal pieces. Each person gets one piece out of a total of six pieces. In other words, each person gets one-sixth of the cake. We know that 1/6 is a fraction. Here, cake is considered as whole and a piece is a part. 3/4, 4/5, 4/9 and 21/2 are some examples of fractions.

Text: Concepts are explained in a well structured and lucid manner

Note boxes are some add-on information of related topics

NOTE

If there is a set of two unlike fractions with same numerators, then the fraction with the smaller denominator will be the greater fraction. For example, between 4/9 and 4/6, 4/6 will be greater.

EXAMPLE 2.9

Find the smallest number which is divisible by 18, 15 and 12.

SOLUTION

The objective is to find the smallest common multiple of 18, 15 and 12.

(LCM of 12, 15, 18)

$12 = 2^2 \times 3$; $15 = 3 \times 5$

$18 = 3^2 \times 2$

$\therefore$ LCM $= 2^2 \times 3^2 \times 5 = 180$

Examples are given topic-wise to apply the concepts learned in a particular chapter

Illustrative examples solved in a logical and step-wise manner

TEST YOUR CONCEPTS

Very Short Answer Type Questions

Direction for questions from 1 to 5: Fill in the blanks.

1. The number of factors of 24 is ______.
2. The greatest 2-digit multiple of 8 is ______.
3. The greatest common factor of 9 and 15 is ______.
4. The number of prime factors of 48 is ______.
5. The greatest pair of twin primes of 2-digit numbers is ______.

Direction for questions from 6 to 10: Select the correct alternative from the given choices.

6. Which of the following is a prime number?
 (a) 87 (b) 69 (c) 57 (d) 97

Direction for questions from 12 to 16: Fill in the blanks.

12. The number of common multiples of 6 and 15 is ______.
13. The least common multiple of two co-primes is ______.
14. LCM $(a, b) \times$ HCF (a, b) = ______.
15. The largest 3-digit number divisible by 9 is ______.
16. The smallest 4-digit number divisible by 11 is ______.

Direction for questions from 17 to 22: Select the correct alternative from given choices.

Different levels of questions have been included in the *Test Your Concepts* as well as on *Concept Application* which will help students to develop the problem-solving skill

'Test Your Concepts' at the end of the chapter for classroom preparation

CONCEPT APPLICATION

1. If P is a 3-digit number and Q is the number formed by reversing the digits of P, then find the difference between the place value of the digits in the tenth place.
 (a) 1 (b) 9
 (c) 0 (d) Cannot say
2. A shopkeeper brought 12 dozen eggs out of which 2 dozen eggs are sold and 9 eggs are damaged. After removing the damaged eggs, 8 eggs are replaced. Find the remaining number of eggs with the shopkeeper finally.
 (a) 8 dozen (b) 119
 (c) 10 dozen (d) 121
3. If A, B, C and D represents $\times$, $\div$, $+$ and $-$ respectively, then find the value of $90B3A5D3C9$.
 (a) 12 (b) 24
 (c) 156 (d) 30

'Concept Application' section with problems divided as per complexity.

32. Converting kg into gm:

$3 \text{ kg} = 3000 \text{ gm}$

$2.6 \text{ kg} = 2600 \text{ gm}$

$2 \text{ kg} = 2000 \text{ gm}$

HCF of 3000, 2600, 2000 is

$3000 = 3 \times 2^3 \times 5^3$

$2600 = 2^3 \times 5^2 \times 13$

$2000 = 2^4 \times 5^3$

$\text{HCF} = 2^3 \times 5^2 = 8 \times 25 = 200 \text{ gm}$

$\therefore$ The minimum number of pieces that Bhavagna get from the three cakes

$$= \frac{3000}{200} + \frac{2600}{200} + \frac{2000}{200} = 15 + 13 + 10 = 38$$

33. LCM of 30, 75, 120:

$30 = 2 \times 3 \times 5;\ 75 = 3 \times 5^2$

$120 = 2 \times 2 \times 2 \times 3 \times 5 = 2^3 \times 3 \times 5$

$\text{LCM} = 2^3 \times 3 \times 5^2 = 600$

Hints and Explanation for key questions along with highlights on the common mistakes that students usually make in the examination

Series Chapter Flow

Class 6

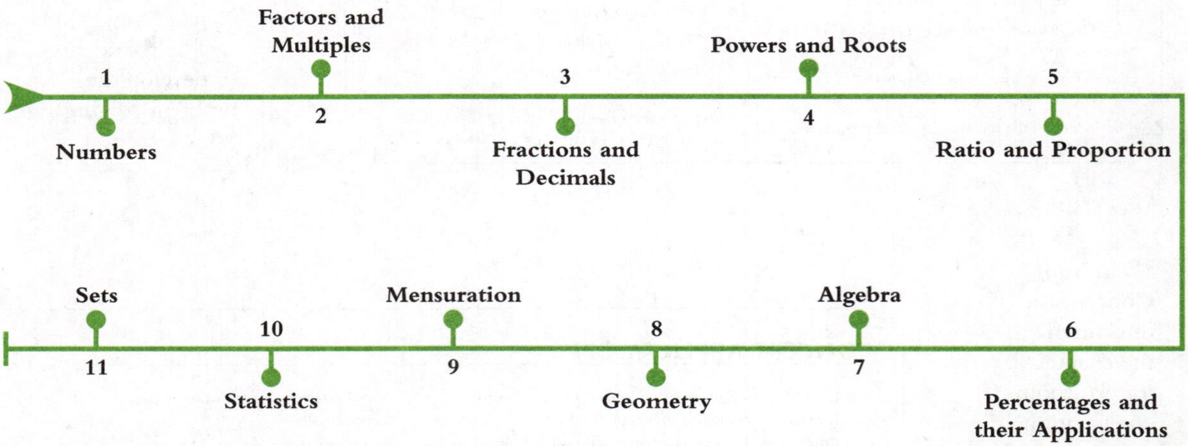

Class 8

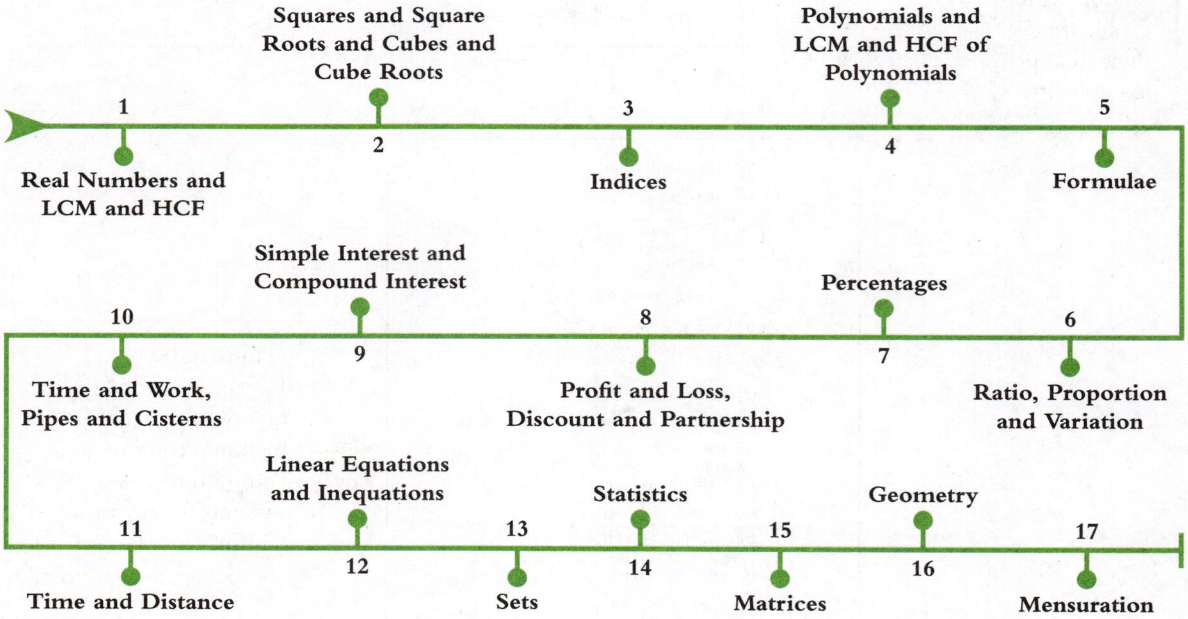

Class 7

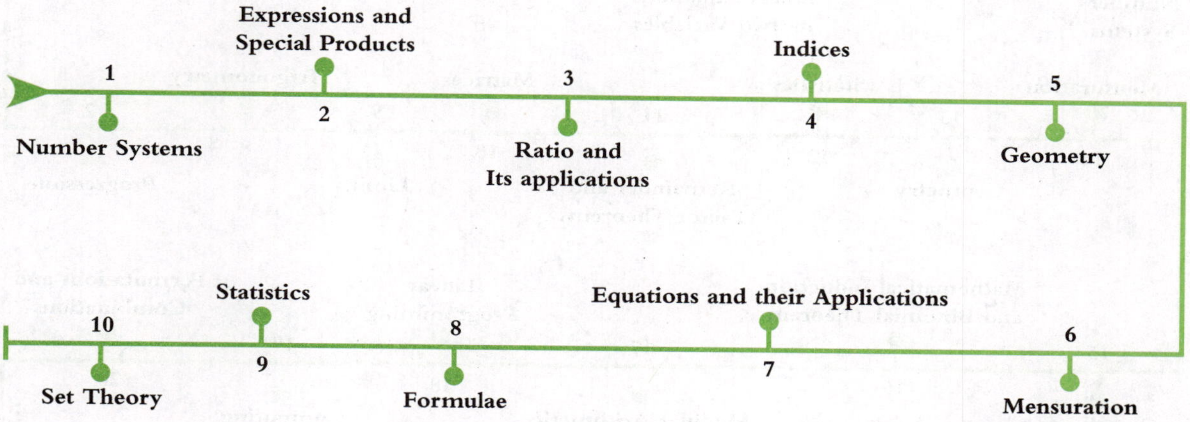

Class 9

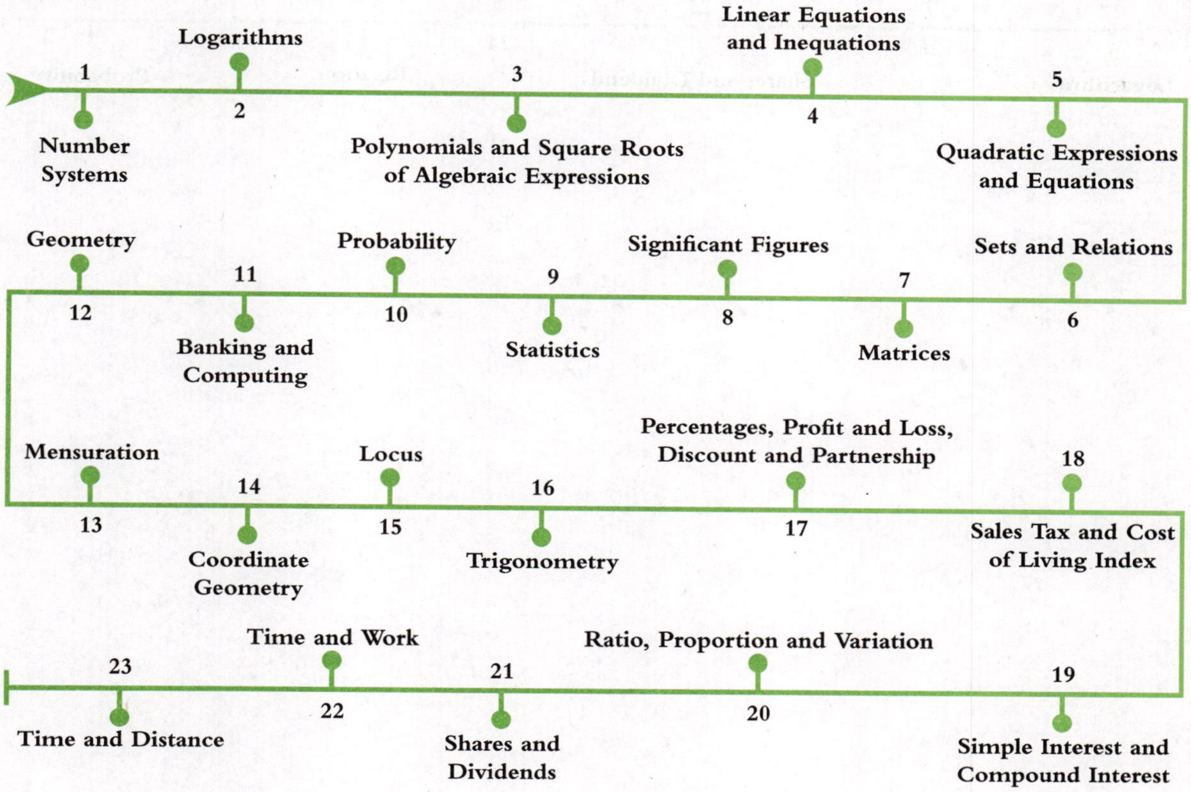

Class 10

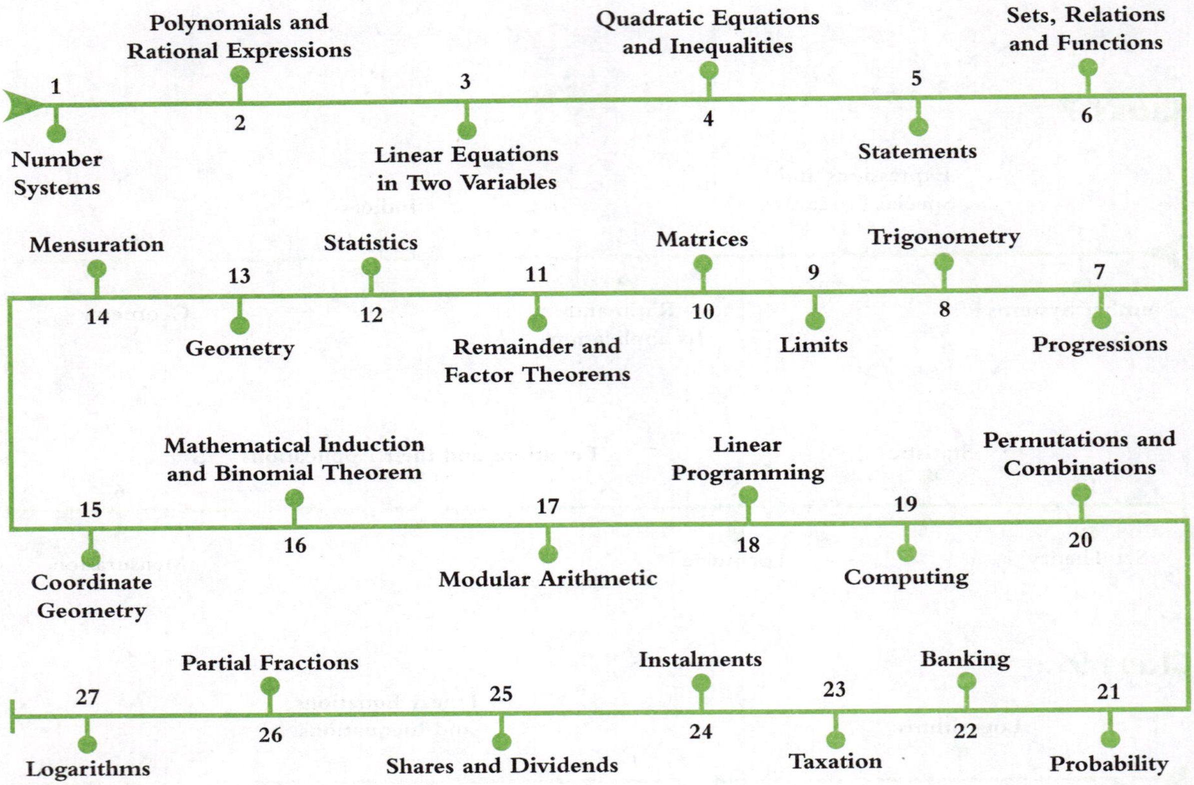
1 Number Systems
2 Polynomials and Rational Expressions
3 Linear Equations in Two Variables
4 Quadratic Equations and Inequalities
5 Statements
6 Sets, Relations and Functions
7 Progressions
8 Trigonometry
9 Limits
10 Matrices
11 Remainder and Factor Theorems
12 Statistics
13 Geometry
14 Mensuration
15 Coordinate Geometry
16 Mathematical Induction and Binomial Theorem
17 Modular Arithmetic
18 Linear Programming
19 Computing
20 Permutations and Combinations
21 Probability
22 Banking
23 Taxation
24 Instalments
25 Shares and Dividends
26 Partial Fractions
27 Logarithms

Chapter 1

Numbers

REMEMBER

Before beginning this chapter, you should be able to:

- Recall digits and numbers
- Perform addition, subtraction, multiplication and division of numbers

KEY IDEAS

After completing this chapter, you should be able to:

- Understand Hindu-Arabic system
- Describe face value and place value of digits
- Work on integers
- Describe properties of numbers and perform operations on numbers
- Apply BODMAS rule

INTRODUCTION

In lower classes, we have studied numbers, addition, subtraction, multiplication and division of numbers. In this chapter, we shall study a system of numbers, integers and operations on numbers. Before we begin the study of numbers in detail, let us look at the numerals ranging from small to large numbers as shown in table given below.

Info Box!

The concept of zero as a digit was discovered in India.

TABLE 1.1 Use of 10 digits from 0 to 9 to describe all numbers

Place Name	Numeral	No. of Digits
Ten Crores	10,00,00,000	9 digits
Crores	1,00,00,000	8 digits
Ten Lakhs	10,00,000	7 digits
Lakhs	1,00,000	6 digits
Ten Thousands	10,000	5 digits
Thousands	1,000	4 digits
Hundreds	100	3 digits
Tens	10	2 digits
Ones	1	1 digit

Hindu–Arabic System

As we know, we use 0, 1, 2, 3, 4, 5, 6, 7, 8 or 9 to write any number. The system where we use 0, 1, 2, ..., 9 to write any number is known as Hindu–Arabic System.

Notation and Numeration

Notation is the representation of a number in figures. Numeration is the representation of number in words.

TABLE 1.2 Notation and Numeration

Number	Number in Words
23,576	Twenty three thousand, five hundred and seventy six.
5,48,907	Five lakh, forty eight thousand nine hundred and seven.
12,00,50,056	Twelve crore, fifty thousand and fifty six.

Expanded Form

When we write any number, for example, 123, what it actually displays is 100 + 20 + 3. In simple words, '100 + 20 + 3' is an expanded form of 123. When we expand a number, we show the value of each digit. This is called its expanded form.

EXAMPLE 1.1

Expand 23,579.

SOLUTION

23,579 = 2(10000) + 3(1000) + 5(100) + 7(10) + 9(1) = 20000 + 3000 + 500 + 70 + 9

FACE VALUE AND PLACE VALUE OF DIGITS

The actual value of a digit in a number is called face value of the number. The place value of a digit of a number is the digit times the value of the place.

Example: The face value and place value for 20,980 are given below.

TABLE 1.3 Face and place values of digits

Digit	Face Value	Place Value
2	2	2(10000) = 20,000
9	9	9(100) = 900
8	8	8(10) = 80

NOTE

The place value of a digit is based on the position of the digit, whereas the face value of a digit remains same irrespective of the places of the digit.

Numbers to be Remembered

1. 1 Googol = 10^{100}
2. 1 Googolplex = 10^{googol}
3. 1 Arab = 10^{9}
4. 1 Kharab = 10^{11}
5. 1 Vrinda = 10^{22}
6. 1 Padma = 10^{32}
7. 1 Samudra = 10^{52}

Info Box!

Name of the popular search engine 'Google' came from the misspelling of the word 'googol'.

International System of Numeration

This system is same as the Indian system up to five digits. The smallest 6-digit number 100000 is called one hundred thousand. The comma is placed to mark ones and thousands. Hence, it is written as 100,000.

TABLE 1.4 International system of numeration

100,000,000 9 digits	Hundred millions	Millions
10,000,000 8 digits	Ten millions	Millions
1,000,000 7 digits	Millions	Millions
100,000 6 digits	Hundred thousands	Thousands
10,000 5 digits	Ten thousands	Thousands
1,000 4 digits	Thousands	Thousands
100	Hundreds	Ones
10	Tens	Ones
1	Ones	Ones

COMPARISON OF NUMBERS

To understand the concept of comparison of numbers, following points must be kept in mind:

1. For a given number the numbers lying on the right hand side of the number are greater.
2. Among the given numbers, the number which has more number of digits is the greatest number.
3. If the number of digits of different numbers is same, than we shall compare the left most digits of the numbers. The number which has greater digit in the same place is the greatest number.

Successors and Predecessors

The successor of a number is the number that is 1 more than the given number, whereas predecessor of a number is the number which is 1 less than the given number.

Example: The successor of 9,00,000 is 9,00,001 and the predecessor of 9,00,003 is 9,00,002.

EXAMPLE 1.2

Compare 21,342 and 9,876.

SOLUTION

21,342 has five-digits and 9,876 has four-digits. Therefore, 21,342 is greater than 9,876.

EXAMPLE 1.3

Compare 57,986 and 58,320.

SOLUTION

The given numbers have same number of digits. If we compare the left most digits, the digits which are in the ten thousands place are equal.

Now let us compare the digits which are in thousands place. As 8 is greater than 7, we conclude that 58,320 is greater than 57,986.

EXAMPLE 1.4

Find the number of all the three-digit numbers in Hindu–Arabic System.

SOLUTION

The greatest three-digit number is 999. The greatest two-digit number is 99.

The number of all the three-digit numbers = 999 – 99 = 900.

EXAMPLE 1.5

List out all the three-digit numbers formed by using the digits 2, 7 and 9.

SOLUTION

Hundreds Place	Numbers
2	279 and 297
7	729 and 792
9	927 and 972

INTEGERS

In the lower classes, we have studied natural numbers and whole numbers. In this chapter, we shall learn what integers are and also we shall learn the properties of integers and operations on integers.

1. **Natural numbers:** All counting numbers are natural numbers.

   1, 2, 3, 4, ... are natural numbers.

2. **Whole numbers:** Zero and natural numbers together are called whole numbers.

NOTE

The other name for zero is cipher.

3. **Integers:** All the numbers .... –3, –2, –1, 0, 1, 2, 3, ... are integers.

Integers as Directed Numbers

We come across many situations, where we use integers in opposite sign.

Let us see some situations where we use integers in opposite sign.

1. If the distance above sea level is represented by positive number, then the distance below sea level is represented by negative integer.
   For example: 65 m above sea level is represented by +65 m and 33 m below sea level is represented by –33 m.
2. If the temperature above freezing point is represented by positive number, then the temperature below freezing point is represented by negative integer.
   For example: 13°C above freezing point is represented by +13°C and 15°C below freezing point is represented by –15°C.
3. If profit made on selling an article is represented by a positive number, then loss incurred on selling an article is represented by a negative number.
   For example: ₹45 profit is represented by ₹+45 and ₹36 loss is represented by ₹–36.

Representation of Integers on the Number Line

A line on which numbers are represented is known as the number line. Some integers are represented on the number line given aside.

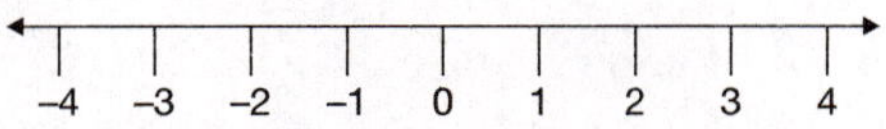

FIGURE 1.1 Number Line

We observe the following about the number line.

1. As we move from left to right, the integers are in the ascending order.
   $-4 < -3 < -2 < -1 < 0 < 1 < 2 < 3$.......
   As we move from right to left, the integers are in the descending order.
2. When we add a positive integer, the result obtained is to the right of the given integer.
   For example: $0 + 2 = 2$, 2 is to the right of 0. $2 + 1 = 3$, 3 is to the right of 2. $1 + 4 = 5$, 5 is to the right of 1.
3. When we add a negative integer to a given integer, the result obtained is to the left of the given integer.
   For example: $2 + (-3) = -1$, -1 is to the left of 2. $4 + (-3) = 1$, 1 is to the left of 4.
4. When we subtract a positive integer, from a given integer, the result obtained is to the left of the given integer.
   For example: $3 - 2 = 1$, 1 is to the left of 3. $3 - 2 = 1$, 1 is to the left of 2.
5. When we subtract a negative integer from a given integer, the result obtained is to the right of the given integer.
   For example: $3-(-4) = 7$ and 7 is to the right of 3.
6. The sum of two positive integers is a positive integer.
   For example: $3 + 5 = 8$; $6 + 5 = 11$
7. The sum of two negative integers is a negative integer.
   For example: $(-5) + (-4) = -8$; $(-5) + (-6) = -11$
8. The sum of a positive integer and a negative integer may be positive, negative or zero.
   For example: (i) $6 + (-3) = 3$; (ii) $5 + (-7) = -2$; (iii) $6 + (-6) = 0$

Let us learn the addition and subtraction of integers with the help of the following examples.

EXAMPLE 1.6

Arrange the following in ascending order: $-3, -8, 10, -2, 7, 15, -12, 6$.

SOLUTION

$-12, -8, -3, -2, 6, 7, 10, 15$.

EXAMPLE 1.7

Add 5 to -3 and show the addition on the number line.

SOLUTION

When a positive integer is added, we should move towards the right on the number line.

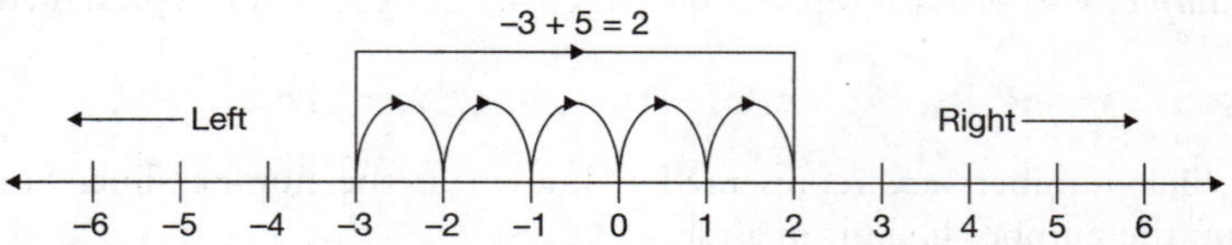

EXAMPLE 1.8

Find the value of 4 + (–5).

SOLUTION

When a negative integer is added, we should move towards the left on the number line.

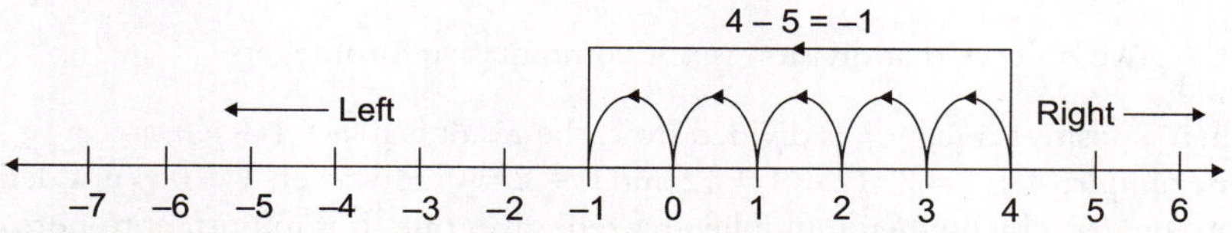

EXAMPLE 1.9

Evaluate: 86 – 72 + 33 – 48 + (–14) – (–26)

SOLUTION

86 – 72 + 33 – 48 + (–14) – (–26) = 86 – 72 + 33 – 48 – 14 + 26

= 86 + 33 + 26 – 72 – 48 – 14 = 145 – 134 = 11

Multiplication of Integers

1. The product of two positive integers p and q is also a positive integer.
   For example: 4 × 5 = 20 and 6 × 4 = 24.
2. The product of a positive integer and a negative integer is negative.
   For example: 5 × (–6) = –30 and (–8) × 6 = –48.
3. The product of two negative integers is a positive integer.
   For example: (–7) × (–2) = 14 and (–6) × (–7) = 42.
4. The product of three negative integers is a negative integer.
   For example: (–3) × (–5) × (–2) = (15 × –2) = –30.
5. The product of four negative integers is a positive integer.
   For example: (–1) × (–2) × (–3) × (–6) = 36.

Division of Integers

We know that 2 (4) = 8. We can write that as 8 ÷ 4 = 2 or 8 ÷ 2 = 4. Thus, we can say that division is an inverse operation of multiplication.

1. When we divide a positive integer by another positive integer, we get a positive number, which need not be an integer.

   For example: $7 \div 5 = \frac{7}{5}$ or $1\frac{2}{5}$. We observe that division is not closed for integers.
2. When a negative integer is divided by a positive integer, we get a negative number.
   For example: –12 ÷ 4 ⇒ –12/4 = –3. When 12 is divided by 4, the quotient is 3 and we get a negative sign before 3.

when divison you rite the number as a fraction and write – in front of the fraction

3. When a positive integer is divided by a negative integer, we get a negative number.
For example: $30 \div (-10)$ can be written as $-(30/10) = -3$.

4. When a negative integer is divided by a negative integer, we get a positive number.
For example: $(-40) \div (-4)$ can be written as $(40/4) = 10$.

5. For two integers p and q, $(p \div q) \neq (q \div p)$.
For example: $3 \div 1 = 3$ and $1 \div 3 = 1/3$.
$3 \neq \frac{1}{3}$. We observe that division is not commutative for integers.

6. When a positive integer p is divided by 1, the result is p. $p \div 1 \div p$.
For example: $3 \div 1 = 3$, $12 \div 1 = 12$ and $0 \div 2 = 0$. However, $1 \div 0$ is not defined. There is no integer which when multiplied by zero gives one. It is important to note that $0 \div 0$ is not defined. Any integer (or any number) when multiplied by zero gives zero.

EXAMPLE 1.10

Evaluate: **(I)** $4752 \div 132$ **(II)** $3564 \div 22$

SOLUTION

(I) $4752 \div 32 \Rightarrow \frac{4752}{132} = \frac{1188}{3} = \frac{108}{3} = 36$

(II) $3564 \div 22 \Rightarrow \frac{3564}{2} = \frac{324}{2} = 162$

EXAMPLE 1.11

Abhi covers a certain distance in 120 minutes. He covers half of the distance in 2/3 of the time. Find the time taken to cover the remaining distance.

SOLUTION

Total time taken = 120 minutes

Time taken to cover the remaining distance = $\left(1-\frac{2}{3}\right)120 = \left(\frac{1}{3}\right)120 = 40$ minutes

EXAMPLE 1.12

Malini and Manoj visited Kulu Manali. They observed the temperature of the place as follows. Initially there was 10°C later there was a 4° fall in the temperature. Again there was 2° rise, 5° fall, 6° rise and 3° fall. Find the status of the temperature at the end.

SOLUTION

The above situation can be represented by the following numerical expression:

$10° - 4°C + 2°C - 5°C + 6°C - 3°C = 18°C - 12°C = 6°C$

Absolute Value of an Integer

The absolute value of an integer is the numerical value regardless of its sign (+ or –). The absolute value of an integer x is denoted by $|x|$. $|-13| = 13$; $|13| = 13$; $|0| = 0$.

SIMPLIFICATION

To simplify arithmetic expressions, which involve various operations like brackets, multiplication, addition, etc., a particular sequence of operations has to be followed. For example: $2 + 3 \times 4$ has to be calculated by multiplying 3 with 4 and the result is 12. Now, 12 is added to 2 to produce an output result of 14. This is because in arithmetic operations, multiplication should be done first before addition is taken up.

The hierarchy of arithmetic operations is given by a rule called BODMAS rule. The operations have to be carried out in the following order, in which they appear in the word BODMAS, where different letters of the word BODMAS stand for the following operations:

B Brackets

O Of

D Division

M Multiplication

A Addition

S Subtraction

There are four types of brackets:

1. **Vinculum:** This is represented by a bar on the top of the numbers.

   For example: $2 + 3 - \overline{4+3}$. Here, the figures under the vinculum have to be calculated as 4 + 3 first and the 'minus' sign before 4 is applicable to 7. Thus the given expression is equal to 2 + 3 – 7 which is equal to –2.

2. **Simple Brackets:** These are represented by ( )
3. **Curly Brackets:** These are represented by { }
4. **Square Brackets:** These are represented by [ ]

The brackets in an expression have to be opened in the order of vinculum, simple brackets, curly brackets and square brackets, i.e., $[\ \{\ (\overline{\quad})\ \}\ ]$ to be opened from inside to outwards.

After brackets is O in the BODMAS rule that stands for 'of' which means multiplication.

Example: 1/2 of 4 will be equal to $1/2 \times 4$ which is equal to 2.

After O, the next operation is D it stands for division. This is followed by M which stands for multiplication. After multiplication, A that stands for addition will be performed. Then, S meant for subtraction is performed.

EXAMPLE 1.13

Simplify: $4 \times 3 - 2 + 16 \div 8$

SOLUTION

$4 \times 3 - 2 + 16 \div 8 = 4 \times 3 - 2 + 2 = 12 - 2 + 2 = 12$

EXAMPLE 1.14

Simplify: 12 ÷ 4 – 3 × 6 + 7

SOLUTION

12 ÷ 4 – 3 × 6 + 7 = 3 – 3 × 6 + 7 = 3 – 18 + 7 = 10 – 18 = –8

FEXAMPLE 1.15

Simplify: 92 – [18 + 16 ÷ 4{26 – (14 – 7 – 3)}]

SOLUTION

$92 - [18 + 16 \div 4\{26 - (14 - \overline{7 - 3})\}]$

= 92 – [18 + 16 ÷ 4 {26 – (14 – 4)}] = 92 – [18 + 16 ÷ 4 {26 – 10}]

= 92 – [18 + 16 ÷ 4 × 16] = 92 – [18 + 4 × 16]

= 92 – [18 + 64] = 92 – [82] = 10

EXAMPLE 1.16

If P means multiplication, Q means division, R means addition and S means subtraction, then find the value of $36P48Q16R15S23$.

SOLUTION

$36P48Q16R15S23$

= 36 × 48 ÷ 16 + 15 – 23 = 36 × 3 + 15 – 23 = 108 + 15 – 23 = 100

TEST YOUR CONCEPTS

Very Short Answer Type Questions

Direction for questions from 1 to 5: Fill in the blanks.

1. The number of digits in the Hindu-Arabic number system is ______.
2. The local value (place value) of the digit '3' in the number 2356 is ______.
3. The digit whose place value is always the same regardless of its position or place in a given number is ______.
4. The difference between the place value and face value of the digit '6' in the number 9867 is ______.
5. The number of 4-digit numbers in the Hindu-Arabic system is ______.

Direction for questions from 6 to 10: Select the correct alternative from given choices.

6. The number of 3-digit numbers that can be formed using the digits 3, 5 and 7 without repetition is ______.
   (a) 3 (b) 4
   (c) 5 (d) 6
7. The sum of the successor and the predecessor of 100 is ______.
   (a) 198 (b) 199
   (c) 200 (d) 201
8. The difference between the greatest and the smallest numbers formed by all the digits 2, 3, 5, and 7 is $XYZX$, where X, Y, Z are digits, then X is ______.
   (a) 5 (b) 8
   (c) 9 (d) 10
9. The number of digits in the successor of the greatest 4-digit number is ______.
   (a) 4 (b) 5
   (c) 3 (d) 6
10. A is a 3 digit number and B is the number formed by reversing the digits of A. The face value of the digit in the tens place of $A - B$ is ______. $(B < A)$
   (a) 9
   (b) 1
   (c) 0
   (d) 2

Direction for question 11: Match the Column A with the Column B.

11.

	Column A			Column B
(a)	Arab	( )	(p)	10^9
(b)	Mahasamudram	( )	(q)	10^{11}
(c)	Kharab	( )	(r)	10^{52}
(d)	Googol	( )	(s)	10^{100}

Direction for questions from 12 to 15: Fill in the blanks.

12. The absolute value of –36 is ______.
13. $|-7| - |-8| =$ ______.
14. $4 + (-8) - 7 =$ ______.
15. The sum of two integers is –6 and one of them is 7, then the other is ______.

Direction for questions from 16 to 19: Select the correct alternative from given choices.

16. Which of the following statement is true?
   (a) The product of two negative integers is negative.
   (b) The sum of a negative integer and a positive integer is always positive.
   (c) The product of two positive and two negative integers is positive.
   (d) The product of any number of negative integers is negative.
17. Which of the following is true?
   A: $-12 + (-15)$ B: $-16 - (12)$ C: $-14 - (-12)$
   (a) $B > C > A$ (b) $A + B > C$
   (c) $C > A > B$ (d) $A < B < C$
18. Which of the following properties are true?
   (A) $(14) \div (-2) = 7$
   (B) $(-14) \div 2 = -7$
   (C) $(-14) \div (-2) = 7$
   (a) A, B (b) B, C
   (c) A, C (d) A, B, C
19. Which of the following statements is true?
   (a) If there is a drop of 4°C from –10°C, the result is –6°C

(b) 525 m above sea level is denoted as –525 m

(c) $|-5| - |-3| = |-8|$

(d) The absolute value of an integer is never less than the integer itself.

Direction for question 20: Match the Column A with Column B.

20.

Column A		Column B
(a) (–2) (–3) (–5)	( )	(p) –30
(b) 6 (–2) (–3)	( )	(q) –36
(c) (–15) (–2)	( )	(r) 30
(d) (–9) (–2) (–2)	( )	(s) 36

Direction for questions from 21 to 24: Fill in the blanks.

21. $\overline{8-3} - 2 =$ _______.

22. $6 \div 3 + 3 =$ _______.

23. $5 \times 2 + 4 =$ _______.

24. $9 \times (-13) - 13 =$ _______.

Direction for questions from 25 to 28: Select the correct alternative from given choices.

25. $15 \div 3 \times 5 - 10 =$ _______.

(a) 15 (b) –9 (c) –3 (d) 20

26. $5 \div 5 \div 5 =$ _______.

(a) 5 (b) $\frac{1}{5}$

(c) 25 (d) $\frac{1}{25}$

27. Which of the following is false?

(a) $2 \times 7 - 7 = 0$ (b) $2 + 3 \times 2 = 10$

(c) $16 \div 8 + 8 = 1$ (d) All of these

28. Which of the following is true?

(a) $4 \div 4 + 1 = 2$ (b) $5 - 2 \times 3 = 9$

(c) Both (a) and (b) (d) None of these

Direction for question 29: Match the Column A with the Column B.

29.

Column A		Column B
(a) $3 \times 2 - 8 \div 4$	( )	(p) 14
(b) $4 \div 2 + 3 \times 4$	( )	(q) 12
(c) $18 - 9 \div 3 \times 5$	( )	(r) 4
(d) $72 - 15 \times 20 \div 5$	( )	(s) 3

Short Answer Type Questions

30. Write the following numbers in words.

(i) 5,00,78,90,500 (ii) 1,01,00,17,000

(iii) 90,00,09,050

31. Write the following in figures.

(i) Six crore six lakh and six thousand

(ii) Seven arab five crore three hundred and one

(iii) Eighty eight crore ninety nine lakh fifty five thousand and seventy four

32. Find the difference between the place values of the two 5's in 895435.

33. Write all the possible three-digit numbers using the digits 5, 0 and 7 without repetition of the digits.

34. *X* is the number of two-digit numbers formed by 3, 5, or 7, when the repetition is allowed. *Y* is the number of two-digit numbers formed by 3, 5, or 7, when the repetition is not allowed. Find by how much *X* exceeds *Y*.

35. Write all the possible 4-digit even numbers using the digits 5, 8, 9 and 4 when the repetition is not allowed.

36. Find the difference between the greatest 5-digit number and the greatest 4-digit number formed using the digits 7, 6, 2, 5, 1 when the repetition is not allowed.

37. *A* and *B* are two numbers. The non-zero digit in the crore's place of *A* is 3 less than the digit in the hundreds place of *B*. The non-zero digit in 10's place of *B* is 2 less than the number in 10's place of *A*. If both the numbers have equal number of digits and all the remaining digits are equal but not zeros, then find the least possible difference between *A* and *B*.

38. Write the expanded form of twenty four lakh seventy five thousand and fifty six.

39. How many whole numbers are there between 321 and 543 which do not change, when the order of the digits is reversed?

40. Represent the following as integers.
(a) Gain of ₹28
(b) Loss of ₹48
(c) 36 m below sea level
(d) 12°C rise in temperature
(e) 5°C fall in temperature

41. Arrange the following integers in ascending order.
(i) 3, –5, 0, –2, –7, –1, 4
(ii) –15, –12, 11, –13, 10, 5, –9

42. Write the following in descending order.
(i) –8, 6, –9, 13, –23, 14, –16, 25
(ii) 42, –43, 64, –86, 120, –115

43. Write the statements given below in symbols and list the elements.
(i) Integers lying between –15 and –8.
(ii) Integers greater than –5 and less than 1.
(iii) If A and B are the number of elements in the sets (i) and (ii), respectively, then find the value of $|-(A - B)|$.

44. Find the value of
(i) $|-15| + |12|$ (ii) $-|13| - |-7|$
(iii) $|17| - |-9|$

45. X is an integer in m representing '16 m below sea level'. Y is an integer in ₹ representing withdrawal of ₹24. Z is an integer in ₹ representing a gain of ₹32. Find the following.
(i) $|X| - |Z|$ (ii) $||Y| - |Z||$
(iii) $|X| + |Y|$

46. A is neither positive nor negative $B = -|-8|$, C is the absolute value of –12.
(i) $A + B + C$ (ii) $|B + C|$
(iii) Compare $2B$, A and $3C$

47. Do the following simplification and show it on the number line.
3 + 5 – 6 – 4

48. Evaluate:
(i) 14625 ÷ 25 (ii) 15120 ÷ 144

49. An integer P is added to another integer Q, then the result is R. If R is –12 more than P, then find Q. Also find R when P is 42.

50. A basket contains 120 fruits from which 15 are sold and 42 are spoiled. After removing the spoiled fruits, 36 new fruits are placed in the basket. Find the number of fruits in the basket finally.

Direction for questions from 10 to 19: Simplify the following.

51. $45 - 26 \div 13 \times 6 + 10$

52. $65 \div 5 - 15 \times 3 + 27 \div 9 \times 3 - 24 \div 8 + 7$

53. $[\{12 - \overline{14 - 8} + 7\} - 15]$

54. $52 - [48 \div 12 \times 6\ \{6 - (8 \times 3 - \overline{6 - 4})\}]$

55. $242 - [360 - 248 \div \{180 + 7 \times (2 - \overline{26 - 16})\}]$

56. $25 + [14 - 18 + \{12 \text{ of } 5 - (16 \div 4 \times 3 - 2)\}]$

57. $[78 - \{75 - (76 - \overline{72 - 75})\}]$

58. $\{16 - (4 + 18 \div 6 - \overline{7 - 5}) \times 5]$

59. $[3077 - 85\{32 \div 8 \times (24 - \overline{36 - 18})\}]$

60. $4940 \div [\{12 + 16\ (48 - (8 - \overline{15 + 6}))\}]$

61. If P, Q, R and S represents '×', ÷, + and – respectively, then find the value of $60Q15P35S25R45$.

62. Which integer should be placed in the place of x in $11 + 48 \div (14 - x) + 5 \times [-3]$ such that the result is zero?

CONCEPT APPLICATION

1. If P is a 3-digit number and Q is the number formed by reversing the digits of P, then find the difference between the place value of the digits in the tenth place.
(a) 1 (b) 9
(c) 0 (d) Cannot say

2. A shopkeeper brought 12 dozen eggs out of which 2 dozen eggs are sold and 9 eggs are damaged. After removing the damaged eggs, 8 eggs are replaced. Find the remaining number of eggs with the shopkeeper finally.
(a) 8 dozen (b) 119
(c) 10 dozen (d) 121

3. If A, B, C and D represents ×, ÷, + and – respectively, then find the value of $90B3A5D3C9$.
(a) 12 (b) 24
(c) 156 (d) 30

4. The cost of a pen is the largest two-digit number (in ₹). The cost of a text book and geometry box respectively are the successor and predecessor of the cost of the pen. Find the sum of the costs of the text book and geometry box (in ₹).
   (a) 197 (b) 198
   (c) 200 (d) 201

5. P is neither positive nor negative, $Q = -|-9|$ and R is the absolute value of -13.
   Which of the following is the value of $P + Q + R$?
   (a) 21 (b) 22
   (c) 4 (d) −4

ASSESSMENT TEST

1. Write the expanded form of the following and write in words.
   (i) 32,008 (ii) 7,00,050 (iii) 9,01,020
2. Write the following numbers in figures.
   (i) Seventy nine crore seven hundred and seven
   (ii) Eighty nine lakh sixty four thousand and two
   (iii) Four arab thirty two crore sixty eight lakh thirty four thousand and seventy three
3. Write all the possible 2-digit numbers using the digits 3, 4 and 5 without repeating any digit.
4. Find the difference between the greatest and the smallest four-digit numbers formed by using all the digits 8, 6, 7 and 4.
5. How many six-digit numbers are there in Hindu-Arabic system?
6. Simplify and show it on the number line: $-5 + 4 - 3 - 2 + 7$
7. Evaluate: $35 - 28 + 6 - (-4)$
8. Evaluate: (i) $27225 \div 55$ (ii) $44616 \div 156$
9. Simplify: $3 + 2 - 6 \div 3 \times 7$
10. Simplify: $37 - 24$ of $4 \div 16 \times 5$
11. Simplify: $36 - 369 \div [-72 \div 24 \times 5 + 2(17 - \overline{7 - 18})]$
12. Which integer should be placed in the box such that the result is 2?
    $[\{(20 - 18 - \square) + 2\} \times 4] \div 14$
13. How many 4-digit even numbers can be formed using the digits 5, 6, 7 and 8 without repeating any digit?
14. Write 13,78,54,632 in the expanded form.
15. Arrange the digits 6, 7, 8 and 9 to make the greatest 4-digit number.
    (i) if repetition of digits is not allowed
    (ii) if repetition is allowed

PRACTICE QUESTIONS

CROSSWORD

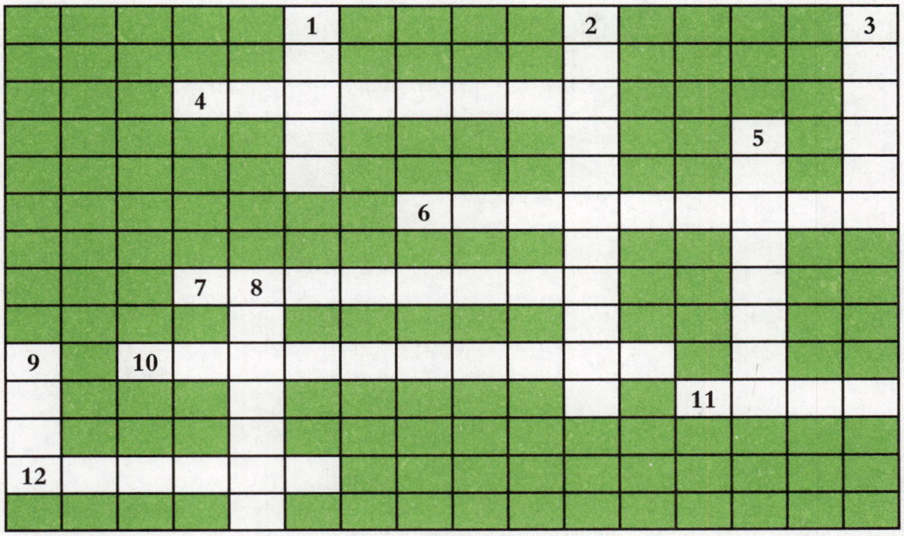

Across

4. The sign of integers less than zero
6. A number that comes just after another
7. The whole numbers and negative natural numbers together
10. Expressing a number in words
11. An integer which is neither positive nor negative
12. The order of operations

Down

1. Each of the symbols in a number system
2. A number that comes just before another
3. It is another name of zero
5. Integers greater than zero
8. Representation of a number by digits
9. Hundred crores

TEST YOUR CONCEPTS

Very Short Answer Type Questions

1. ten
2. 300
3. 0
4. 54
5. 9000
6. (d)
7. (c)
8. (a)
9. (b)
10. (a)
11. (a) → (p) (b) → (r)
    (c) → (q) (d) → (s)
12. 36
13. –1
14. –11
15. –13
16. (c)
17. (c)
18. (b)
19. (d)
20. (a) → (p) (b) → (s)
    (c) → (r) (d) → (q)
21. 7
22. 5
23. 14
24. –130
25. (a)
26. (b)
27. (d)
28. (a)
29. (a) → (r) (b) → (p)
    (c) → (s) (d) → (q)

Short Answer Type Questions

31. (i) 6,06,06,000
    (ii) 7,05,00,00,301
    (iii) 88,99,55,074
32. 4995
33. 507, 705, 750, 570
34. 3
36. 68,869
37. 280
39. 22
40. (a) ₹+28 (b) ₹–48
    (c) –36 m (d) 12°C (e) –5°C
41. (i) –7, –5, –2, –1, 0, 3, 4.
    (ii) –15, –13, –12, –9, 5, 10, 11.
42. (i) 25, 14, 13, 6, –8, –9, –16, –23.
    (ii) 120, 64, 42, –43, –86, –115.
43. (i) –14, –13, –12, –11, –10, –9
    (ii) –4, –3, –2, –1, 0
    (iii) 1
44. (i) 27, –20, 8
45. (i) –16 (ii) 8 (iii) 40
46. (i) 4 (ii) 4 (iii) $2B < A < 3C$
47. (i) –2
48. (i) 585 (ii) 105
49. 30
50. 99
51. 43

ANSWER KEYS

52. –19
53. –2
54. 436
55. –116
56. 71
57. 82
58. –9
59. 1037
60. 5
61. 160
62. 2

CONCEPT APPLICATION

1. (c)
2. (b)
3. (c)
4. (b)
5. (c)

ASSESSMENT TEST

3. six
4. 4086
5. 9,00,000
6. 1
7. 17
8. (i) 495 (ii) 286
9. –9
10. 7
11. 27
12. 3
13. 12

CROSSWORD

Across

4. Negative
6. Successor
7. Integers
10. Numeration
11. Zero
12. BODMAS

Down

1. Digit
2. Predecessor
3. Cipher
5. Positive
8. Numeral
9. Arab

TEST YOUR CONCEPTS

Very Short Answer Type Questions

1. 0, 1, 2, 3, 4, 5, 6, 7, 8 and 9 are the ten-digits used in the Hindu–Arabic number system.
2. The local value or the place value of 3 in 2356 is $3 \times 100 = 300$.
3. The place value of the digit '0' is always '0'.
4. 9867: Place value of '6' is $6 \times 10 = 60$

   Face of the digit is 6.

   Difference of the two $= 60 - 6 = 54$
5. The number of 4-digit numbers $= 9999 - 999$

   $= 9000$
6. 357, 375, 537, 573, 735, 753. Therefore, '6' three-digit numbers can be formed.

   Hence, the correct option is (d).
7. The required sum $= 101 + 99 = 200$.

   Hence, the correct option is (c).
8. $XYZX = 7532 - 2357 = 5175$

   $\therefore x = 5$

   Hence, the correct option is (a).
9. The greatest 4–digit number is 9999 and its successor is 10000 a 5 digit number.

   Hence, the correct option is (b).
10. Let A be 854

    $= 854 - 458 = 396.$

    $\therefore$ The required face value = 9

    Hence, the correct option is (a).
11. (a) 1 Arab = 100 crores $= 100 \times 10^7 = 10^9$

    (b) 1 Mahasamudram $= 10^{52}$

    (c) 1 Kharab = Ten thousand crores $= 10^4 \times 10^7$

    $= 10^{11}$

    (d) 1 Googol $= 10^{100}$

    (a) → (p), (b) → (r), (c) → (q), (d) → (s).
12. $|-36| = 36$
13. $|-7| - |-8| = 7 - 8 = -1$
14. $4 + (-8) - 7$

    $= 4 - 8 - 7 = -11$
15. The other number is $-6 - 7 = -13$
16. Since, $-2 \times -3 = 6$

    $2 \times 3 = 6$

    Choice (c) follows.

    Hence, the correct option is (c).
17. $A = -12 - 15 = -27$

    $B = -16 - 12 = -28$

    $C = -14 + 12 = -2$

    $B < A < C.$

    Hence, the correct option is (c).
18. (B) and (C) are true.

    Hence, the correct option is (b).
19. The absolute value of an integer is always greater than or equal to the integer itself.

    Hence, the correct option is (d).
20. (a) $(-2)(-3)(-5) = -30 \rightarrow$ (p)

    (b) $6(-2)(-3) = 36 \rightarrow$ (s)

    (c) $(-15)(-2) = 30 \rightarrow$ (r)

    (d) $(-9)(-2)(-2) = -36 \rightarrow$ (q)

    The correct match is as follows:

    (a) → (p), (b) → (s), (c) → (r), (d) → (q)
21. $8 - \overline{3 - 2}$

    $= 8 - 1 = 7$
22. $6 \div 3 + 3 = 2 + 3 = 5$
23. $5 \times 2 + 4 = 10 + 4 = 14$
24. $9 \times (-13) - 13$

    $= -117 - 13 = -130$
25. $15 \div 3 \times 5 - 10$

    $= 5 \times 5 - 10 = 15$

    Hence, the correct option is (a).

26. $5 \div 5 \div 5 = 1 \div 5 = \frac{1}{5}$

Hence, the correct option is (b).

27. All the given statements are false.

Hence, the correct option is (d).

28. $4 \div 4 + 1 = 1 + 1 = 2$

Hence, the correct option is (a).

29. (a) $3 \times 2 - 8 \div 4 = 6 - 2 = 4$

(a) → (r)

(b) $4 \div 2 + 3 \times 4 = 2 + 12 = 14$

(b) → (p)

(c) $18 - 9 \div 3 \times 5 = 18 - 3 \times 5 = 18 - 15 = 3$

(c) → (s)

(d) $72 - 15 \times 20 \div 5 = 72 - 15 \times 4 = 72 - 60 = 12$

(d) → (q)

Short Answer Type Questions

30. 5,00,78,90,500

(i) Five arab seventy eight lakh ninety thousand and five hundred.

(ii) 1,01,00,17,000

One arab one crore seventeen thousand.

(iii) 90,00,09,050

Ninety crores nine thousand and fifty.

31. (i) 6,06,06,000 (ii) 7,05,00,00,301

(iii) 88,99,55,074

32. 895435

One of the two 5's is in units place and the other is in thousands place.

Their place values are 5000 and 5.

∴ The difference of the two values is 5000 – 5 = 4995.

33. 5, 0, 7 are the three-digits (given). The possible 3–digit numbers are: 507, 705, 750, 570.

34. The two-digit numbers with repetitions of the digits 3, 5, 7 are 33, 55, 77.

∴ The required numbers of numbers = 3

35. The given digits are 5, 8, 9 and 4.

Four-digit even numbers using the given digits.

(i) Ending with 4 are: 5894, 5984
9584, 9854
8954, 8594

(ii) Ending with 8 are: 5498, 5948
4958, 4598
9548, 9458

36. The given digits are 5, 2, 1, 7, 6.

The greatest 5 digit number is 76521.

The greatest 4 digit number is 7652.

∴ Difference of two numbers = 76521 – 7652 = 68869.

37. A and B are having equal number of digits and the difference should be the least.

Let the crores place of A be 1 and the hundreds place of B be 4.

Let the tens place digit of B be 1 and that of A be 3.

∴ Let A = 1, 11, 11, 411

B = 1, 11, 11, 131

∴ Their difference = 280

38. 2475056

= 2000000 + 400000 + 70000 + 5000 + 0 + 50 + 6

39. From 321 to 543 the numbers which cannot be changed when the order of digits reversed are 323, 333, 343, 353, 363, 373, 383, 393; 404, 414, 424, 434, 444, 454, 464, 474, 484, 494, 505, 515, 525, 535.

∴ The total combination is 22.

40. (a) Gain of ₹28 → ₹+28

(b) Loss of ₹48 → ₹–48

(c) 36 m below sea level → –36 m

(d) 12°C rise in temperature → +12°C

(e) 5°C fall in temperature → –5°C

41. (i) Ascending order: –7, –5, –2, –1, 0, 3, 4

(ii) Ascending order: –15, –13, –12, –9, 5, 10, 11

42. (i) Descending order: 25, 14, 13, 6, –8, –9, –16, –23

(ii) Descending order: 120, 64, 42, –43, –86, –115

43. (i) –14, –13, –12, –11, –10, –9

(ii) –4, –3, –2, –1, 0

(iii) $A = 6, B = 5$

$|-(A - B)| = |-(6 - 5)| = |-1| = 1$

44. (i) $|-15| + |12| = 15 + 12 = 27$

$-|13| - |-7| = -13 - 7 = -20$

$|17| - |-9| = 17 - 9 = 8$

45. $X = -16$

$Y = -24$

$Z = +32$

(i) $|X| - |Z|$

$= |-16| - |32| = 16 - 32 = -16$

(ii) $|Y| - |Z|$

$= |-24| - |32| = 24 - 32 = -8$

$\Rightarrow ||Y| - |Z|| = |-8| = 8$

(iii) $|X| + |Y|$

$= |-16| + |-24| = 16 + 24 = 40$

46. $A = 0, B = -|-8| = -8$

$C = |-12| = 12$

(i) $A + B + C = 0 + (-8) + 12 = 4$

(ii) $|B + C| = |-8 + 12| = 4$

(iii) $2B = 2 \times (-8) = -16$

$A = 0, 3C = 3 \times 12 = 36$

$2B < A < 3C$

47. $3 + 5 - 6 - 4 = 8 - 10 = -2$

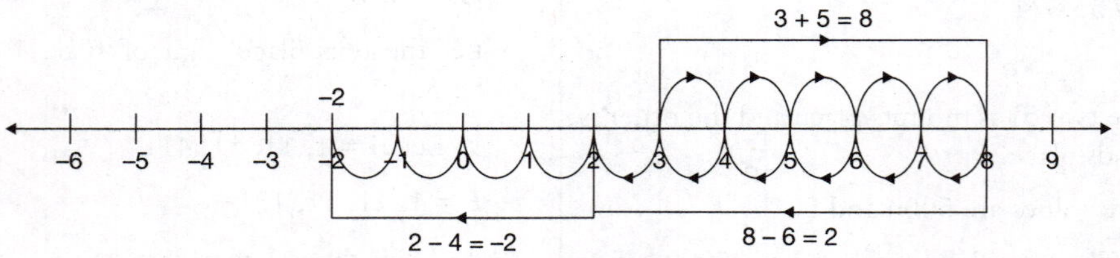

48. (i) 14625 ÷ 25

$$\frac{14,625}{25} = \frac{2925}{5} = 585$$

(ii) 15120 ÷ 144

$$\frac{15,120}{144} = \frac{3780}{36} = \frac{420}{4} = 105$$

49. $P + Q = R$

$P + Q = P + (-12)$

$Q = -12$

If $P = 42$, $R = P + Q = 42 + (-12)$

$= 30$

50. The following numerical expression represents the situation explained in the problem.

$= 120 - 15 - 42 + 36$

$= 156 - 57$

$= 99$

∴ Finally, there are 99 fruits in the basket.

51. $45 - 26 \div 13 \times 6 + 10$

$= 45 - 2 \times 6 + 10 = 45 - 12 + 10 = 55 - 12 = 43$

52. $65 \div 5 - 15 \times 3 + 27 \div 9 \times 3 - 24 \div 8 + 7$

$= 13 - 15 \times 3 + 3 \times 3 - 3 + 7 = 13 - 45 + 9 - 3 + 7$

$= 22 - 48 + 7 = -19$

53. $[\{(12 - \overline{14 - 8}) + 7\} - 15]$

$= [\{12 - 14 + 8) + 7\} - 15] = [\{6 + 7\} - 15]$

$= [13 - 15] = -2$

54. $52 - [48 \div 12 \times 6 \{6 - (8 \times 3 - \overline{6 - 4})\}]$

$= 52 - [4 \times 6 \{6 - (24 - 6 + 4)\}]$

$= 52 - [24.\{6 - 22\}] = 52 - [24 \times (-16)]$

$= 52 + 384 = 436$

55. $242 - [360 - 248 \div \{180 + 7 \times (2 - \overline{26 - 16})\}]$

$= 242 - [360 - 248 \div \{180 + 7 \times (2 - 10)\}]$

$= 242 - [360 - 248 \div \{180 + (7)(-8)\}]$

$= 242 - [\{360 - 248 \div \{180 - 56\}]$

$= 242 - [360 - 248 \div 124]$

$= 242 - [360 - 2] = 242 - [358] = -116$

56. $25 + [14 - 18 + \{12 \text{ of } 5 - (16 \div 4 \times 3 - 2)\}]$

$= 25 + [-4 + \{60 - (4 \times 3 - 2)\}]$

$= 25 + [-4 + \{60 - 10\}] = 25 + [-4 + 50]$

$= 25 + 46 = 71$

57. $[78 - \{75 - (76 - \overline{72 - 75})\}]$

$= [78 - \{75 - (76 - 72 + 75)\}]$

$= [78 - \{75 - (76 + 3)\}]$

$= [78 - \{75 - 79\}] = [78 - \{-4\}] = 78 + 4$

$= 82$

58. $\{16 - (4 + 17 \div 6 - \overline{7 - 5}) \times 5\}$

$= \{16 - (4 + 3 - 2) \times 5\} = \{16 - (7 - 2) \times 5\}$

$= \{16 - 25\} = -9$

59. $[3077 - 85 \{32 \div 8 \times (24 - \overline{36 - 18})\}]$

$= 3077 - 85 \{32 \div 8 (24 - 18)\}]$

$= [3077 - 85 \{(32 \div 8 \times 6)\}]$

$= [3077 - 85 \{4 \times 6\}] = [3077 - 85 \times 24]$

$= 3077 - 2040 = 1037$

60. $4940 \div [12 + 16 \{(48 - (8 - \overline{15 - 6})\}]$

$= 4940 \div [12 + 16 \{48 - (8 - 21)\}]$

$= 4940 \div [12 + 16 \{48 + 13\}]$

$= 4940 \div [12 + 16 \{61\}]$

$= 4940 \div [12 + 976] = 4940 \div 988 = 5$

61. $60\ Q\ 15\ P\ 35\ S\ 25\ R\ 45$

$= 60 \div 15 \times 35 - 25 + 45$

$= 4 \times 35 + 20 = 140 + 20 = 160.$

62. $11 + 48 \div (14 - x) + 5 \times (-3) = 0$

$48 \div (14 - x) + 5 \times (-3) = -11$

$48 \div (14 - x) - 15 = -11$

$48 \div (14 - x) = 4 \Rightarrow (14 - x) = 12$

$\Rightarrow x$ must be 2.

CONCEPT APPLICATION

1. Let the 3-digit numbers be xyz, the 3-digit number after reversing the digits of xyz is zyx.

The difference between the place values of tenth digits $= 10y - 10y$

$= 0$

Hence, the correct option is (c).

2. Number of eggs brought by the shopkeeper = 12 dozen = 144

Number of eggs sold by the shopkeeper = 2 dozen = 24

Number of eggs with the shopkeeper finally = 144 − 24 − 9 + 8

= 119

Hence, the correct option is (b).

3. $90B3A5D3C9 = 90 \div 3 \times 5 - 3 + 9$

$= 150 + 6$

Hence, the correct option is (c).

4. The largest 2-digit number = 99

Therefore, the cost of a pen = ₹99

The successor and predecessor of 99 are 100 and 98.

The sum of the costs of the text book and the geometry box = 98 + 100

= ₹198

Hence, the correct option is (b).

5. $P = 0,\ Q = -9,\ R = 13$

$P + Q + R = 0 - 9 + 13 = 4$

Hence, the correct option is (c).

ASSESSMENT TEST

1. (i) 32,008

$= 3 \times 10000 + 2 \times 1000 + 0 + 0 + 8 \times 1$

$= 30000 + 2000 + 8$

In words: Thirty two thousand and eight

(ii) 7,00,050

$= 7 \times 100000 + 0 + 0 + 0 + 5 \times 10 + 0$

$= 700000 + 50$

In words: Seven lakh and fifty.

(iii) 9,01,020

$= 9 \times 100000 + 0 + 1 \times 1000 + 0 + 2 \times 10 + 0$

$= 900000 + 1000 + 20$

In words: Nine lakh one thousand and twenty.

2. (i) 79,00,00,707 (ii) 89,64,002

(iii) 4,32,68,34,073

3. We are given 3 digits.

We can make three 2-digit combinations.

Digits	3, 4	4, 5	5, 3
	34	45	53
	43	54	35

∴ There exist six 2-digit numbers.

4. The greatest 4-digit number formed with the given digits is 8764.

The smallest 4-digit number formed with the given digits is 4678.

∴ The difference between the two numbers

$8764 - 4678 = 4086$

5. The largest 6-digit number is 9,99,999.

The largest 5-digit number is 99,999.

∴ The number of 6-digit numbers is

9,99,999 – 99,999 = 9,00,000

6. $-5 + 4 - 3 - 2 + 7 = 11 - 10 = 1$

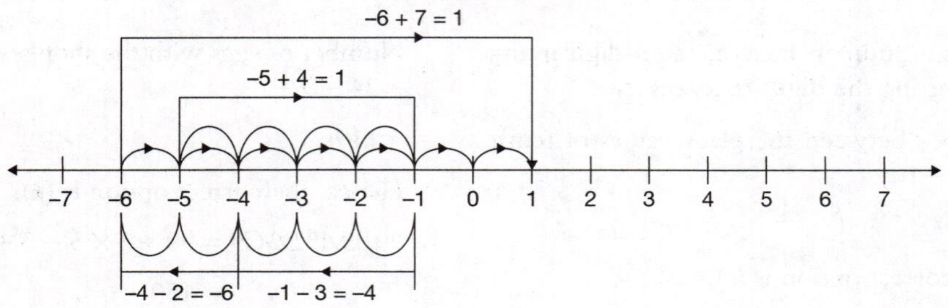

7. $35 - 28 + 6 - (-4)$

$= 35 - 28 + 6 + 4 = 35 - 28 + 10$

$= 45 - 28 = 17$

8. (i) $27225 \div 55$

$$\frac{27225}{55} = \frac{5445}{11} = 495 = 495$$

(ii) $44616 \div 156$

$$\frac{44616}{156} = \frac{3432}{12} = 286 = 286$$

9. $3 + 2 - 6 \div 3 \times 7$

$= 3 + 2 - 2 \times 7 = 3 + 2 - 14 = 5 - 14 = -9$

10. $37 - 24$ of $4 \div 16 \times 5$

$= 37 - 96 \div 16 \times 5 = 37 - 6 \times 5 = 37 - 30 = 7$

11. $36 - 369 \div [-72 \div 24 \times 5 + 2\,(17 - \overline{7 - 8})]$

$= 36 - 369 \div [-72 \div 24 \times 24 \times 5 + 2\,(17 - 7 + 18)]$

$= 36 - 369 \div [-72 \div 24 \times 5 + 2(28)]$

$= 36 - 369 \div [-3 \times 5 + 56] = 36 - 369 \div [41]$

$= 36 - 9 = 27$

12. $[\{(20 - \overline{18 - \square}) + 2\} \times 4] \div 14 = 2$

$[\{20 - \overline{18 - \square}) + 2\} \times 4] = 28$, since $\frac{28}{14} = 2$

$\{(20 - \overline{18 - \square})) + 2\} = 7$, since $7 \times 4 = 28$

$(20 - \overline{18 - \square})) = 5$, since $5 + 2 = 7$

$\overline{18 - \square} = 15$, since $20 - 15 = 5$

$\Rightarrow \square = 3$, since $18 - 15 = 3$

$\therefore$ 3 should be there in the box.

13. Let the 4-digit number is ending with 6.

			6

The remaining three places can be filled using the three-digits 5, 7, 8.

5786, 5876, 857, 7586, 7856, 8576, 8765

Similarly, the number if 4-digit numbers ending with eight is 6.

Hence, we get twelve, 4-digit even combinations with the given digits.

14. 10,00,00,000 + 3,00,00,000 + 70,00,000 + 8,00,000 + 50,000 + 4,000 + 600 + 30 + 2

15. (i) 9876

(ii) 9999

Chapter 2

Factors and Multiples

REMEMBER

Before beginning this chapter, you should be able to:

- Recall multiplication tables
- Perform multiplication and division of tables

KEY IDEAS

After completing this chapter, you should be able to:

- Define even numbers, odd numbers, prime numbers, sphenic numbers, composite numbers, twin prime, co-primes
- Understand highest common factor (HCF)
- Understand least common multiple (LCM)
- Describe relationship between LCM and HCF
- Apply test of divisibility

INTRODUCTION

The study of Mathematics involve numbers and various operations performed on them. While discussing operations such as multiplication and division, we often come across terms, such as, factors and multiples. These two terms are directly connected to one another. It is important to know how they are related and differentiated from each other.

FACTORS AND MULTIPLES

When two or more natural numbers are multiplied, then the product obtained is called the multiple of either of the numbers. Each of those numbers is called a factor of the product.

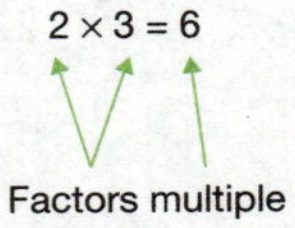

Example: For instance, 2(3) = 6. Here, 6 is a multiple of 2 and 3. Also, 2 and 3 are two factors of 6.

X	1	2	3	4	5	6	7	8	9	10
1	1	2	3	4	5	6	7	8	9	10
2	2	4	6	8	10	12	14	16	18	20
3	3	6	9	12	15	28	21	24	27	30
4	4	8	12	16	20	24	28	32	36	40
5	5	10	15	20	25	30	35	40	45	50
6	6	12	18	24	30	36	42	48	54	60
7	7	14	21	28	35	42	49	56	63	70
8	8	16	24	32	40	48	56	64	72	80
9	9	18	27	36	45	54	63	72	81	90
10	10	20	30	40	50	60	70	80	90	100

FIGURE 2.1 Multiplication Chart

EXAMPLE 2.1

Find the factors of 12 and 14.

SOLUTION

$12 = 1 \times 12 = 2 \times 6 = 3 \times 4$

∴ The factors of 12 are 1, 2, 3, 4, 6 and 12.

$14 = 1 \times 14 = 2 \times 7$

∴ The factors of 14 are 1, 2, 7 and 14.

EXAMPLE 2.2

Find the first five multiples of 5.

SOLUTION

$5 \times 1 = 5$; $5 \times 2 = 10$; $5 \times 3 = 15$; $5 \times 4 = 20$; $5 \times 5 = 25$.

∴ 5, 10, 15, 20 and 25 are the first five multiples of 5.

Even Numbers

Integers which are divisible by 2 are called even numbers.

Examples: 0, 2, 4, 6, 8, 10, 12, ... are even numbers.

1	2	3	4	5	6	7	8	9	10
11	12	13	14	15	16	17	18	19	20
21	22	23	24	25	26	27	28	29	30
31	32	33	34	35	36	37	38	39	40
41	42	43	44	45	46	47	48	49	50
51	52	53	54	55	56	57	58	59	60
61	62	63	64	65	66	67	68	69	70
71	72	73	74	75	76	77	78	79	80
81	82	83	84	85	86	87	88	89	90
91	92	93	94	95	96	97	98	99	100

FIGURE 2.2 Sieve of Eratosthenes

Odd Numbers

Integers that are not divisible by 2 are called odd numbers.

Examples: 1, 3, 5, 7, 9, 11, 13, ... are odd numbers.

> **Info Box!**
>
> Sieve of Eratosthenes is used to find first 25 prime numbers by first listing out numbers between 1 and 100 in a 10×10 grid and by removing only multiples of 2, 3, 5, and 7.

Prime Numbers

The natural numbers which has exactly two factors are called prime numbers.

Examples: 2, 3, 5, 7 are some prime numbers.

Sphenic Numbers

A positive integer which is the product of three distinct prime factors is called a sphenic number.

Example: $30 = 2 \times 3 \times 5$

Composite Numbers

The natural numbers which have more than two factors are called composite numbers.

Examples: 4, 6, 8, 9, 10 are some composite numbers.

Twin Primes

Prime numbers differing by 2 are called twin primes.

Examples: 5 and 7 are twin prime numbers.

Co-primes

Every pair of two natural numbers having no common factor other than 1 is called a pair of co-primes.

Examples: Consider the numbers 16 and 15.

The common factors of 16 and 15 is 1 only. Hence, they are relative primes.

GREATEST COMMON DIVISOR OR HIGHEST COMMON FACTOR

The highest common factor (HCF) of two or more natural numbers is the largest factor in the set of common factors of those numbers. In other words, the HCF or greatest common divisor (GCD) of two or more numbers is the largest number that divides each of them exactly.

Prime Factorization Method

When the numbers whose GCD has to be found are relatively small, this is the best method. Here, we resolve the given numbers into their prime factors and find out the product of common factors of given numbers. This method can be easily applied to any number of numbers.

> **Info Box!**
>
> Knowledge of prime factors is applied in Cryptography (study of solving codes).

EXAMPLE 2.3

Write all the prime factors of the following.

(I) 18 **(II)** 124

SOLUTION

(I)

$$\begin{array}{r|l} 2 & 18 \\ \hline 3 & 9 \\ \hline & 3 \end{array}$$

$18 = 2 \times 3 \times 3$

$\therefore$ The prime factors of 18 are 2 and 3.

(II)

$$\begin{array}{r|l} 2 & 124 \\ \hline 2 & 62 \\ \hline & 31 \end{array}$$

$124 = 2 \times 2 \times 31$

$\therefore$ The prime factors of 124 are 2 and 31.

EXAMPLE 2.4

Find the HCF of 12 and 56 by prime factorization method.

SOLUTION

$12 = 2 \times 6$ $\quad$ $56 = 2 \times 28$

$= 2 \times 2 \times 3$ $\quad$ $56 = 2 \times 2 \times 14$

$= 2^2 \times 3^1$ $\quad$ $56 = 2^3 \times 7^1$

$\therefore$ HCF $= 2^2 = 4$ (Product of all common prime factors with their least exponents)

Division Method

When the numbers whose GCD has to be found are very large, it is time consuming to use prime factorization method.

In this case, we use the method of 'Long Division'. This method was proposed by Euclid and the following steps are involved in it.

Step 1: Divide the larger number by the smaller number. If the remainder is zero, then the divisor is the GCD, otherwise not.

Step 2: Let the divisor in step 2 be the dividend now and the remainder of step 1 becomes the divisor of step 2. If the remainder is zero, then the divisor is HCF. Otherwise, step 2 has to be repeated.

EXAMPLE 2.5

Find the HCF of 120, 320 and 420.

SOLUTION

Let $A = 120$, $B = 320$, $C = 420$

HCF of 120, 320

```
120) 320 (2
     240
     ----
      80) 120 (1
          80
          ---
          40) 80 (2
              80
              --
               0
```

∴ HCF of 120, 320 is 40

```
40) 420 (10
    400
    ---
    20) 40 (2
        40
        --
         0
```

HCF of 40, 420 is 20

∴ HCF of 120, 320 and 420 is 20.

LEAST COMMON MULTIPLE

The least common multiple (LCM) of two or more natural numbers is the least of their common multiples. In other words, the LCM of two or more numbers is the least number which can be divided exactly by each of the given numbers.

Info Box!

LCM is always greater than or equal to the largest number of the set.

Prime Factorization Method

The given numbers are expressed as a product of prime factors. We select the common prime factors having the highest exponent. Then we multiply all such common factors with the prime factors which are not common. The product obtained is the LCM.

EXAMPLE 2.6

Find the LCM of 12 and 15 by prime factorization method.

SOLUTION

$12 = 4 \times 3 = 2^2 \times 3^1$

$15 = 3 \times 5 = 3^1 \times 5^1$

LCM $(12, 15) = 2^2 \times 3^1 \times 5^1 = 60$

2	12
2	6
	3

3	15
	5

EXAMPLE 2.7

Find the LCM of 24 and 40.

SOLUTION

∴ The LCM of 24 and 40

$= 2 \times 2 \times 2 \times 3 \times 5$

$= 120$

2	24, 40
2	12, 20
2	6, 10
	3, 5

Relationship between LCM and GCD

The LCM and GCD of two given numbers are related to the given numbers by the following relationship.

The product of two numbers = The product of their LCM and GCD

Where, LCM denotes the LCM of the given numbers and GCD denotes the GCD of the given numbers.

> **Info Box!**
>
> If a product is divisible by two factors, then it is also divisible by the product of those two factors.

EXAMPLE 2.8

LCM of two numbers is 378 and their HCF is 9. If one of the numbers is 63, then find the other number.

SOLUTION

We know that LCM × HCF = The product of two numbers

Let the products of two numbers be N_2

$378 \times 9 = 63 \times N_2$

$378 = 7N_2$

$N_2 = \frac{378}{7} = 54$

∴ The other number is 54.

EXAMPLE 2.9

Find the smallest number which is divisible by 18, 15 and 12.

SOLUTION

The objective is to find the smallest common multiple of 18, 15 and 12.

(LCM of 12, 15, 18)

$12 = 2^2 \times 3$; $15 = 3 \times 5$

$18 = 3^2 \times 2$

∴ LCM $= 2^2 \times 3^2 \times 5 = 180$

DIVISIBILITY

Consider two natural numbers *a* and *b*. When *a* is divided by *b*, if a remainder of zero is obtained, we say that *a* is divisible by *b*.

Example: 12 is divisible by 3 because when 12 is divided by 3, the remainder is zero. Also, we say that 12 is not divisible by 5, because 12 when divided by 5 leaves a remainder 2.

Tests of Divisibility

Test of divisibility lets us know whether a number is divisible by another or not without doing the calculations. We now study the methods to test the divisibility of natural numbers with 2, 3, 4, 5, 6, 8, 9 and 11 without performing actual division.

Test of Divisibility by 2

A natural number is divisible by 2, if its units digit is divisible by 2, i.e., the units place is either 0, 2, 4, 6 or 8.

Example: The numbers 4096, 23,548 and 34,052 are divisible by 2 as they end with 6, 8 and 2, respectively.

Test of Divisibility by 3

A natural number is divisible by 3, if the sum of its digits is divisible by 3.

Example: Consider the number 21,43,251. The sum of the digits of 21,43,251 is (2 + 1 + 4 + 3 + 2 + 5 + 1), i.e., 18. As 18 is divisible by 3, the number 21,43,251 is divisible by 3.

Test of Divisibility by 4

A natural number is divisible by 4, if the number formed by its last two-digits in the same order (ten's digit and unit's digit) is divisible by 4.

Example: 4096, 53,216, 548 and 4000 are all divisible by 4 as the numbers formed by taking the last two-digits in each case is divisible by 4.

Test of Divisibility by 5

A natural number is divisible by 5, if its unit's digit is either 0 or 5.

Example: The numbers 4095 and 235060 are divisible by 5 as they have 5 and 0 in their respective units' places.

Test of Divisibility by 6

A number is divisible by 6, if it is divisible by both 2 and 3.

Example: Consider the number 7,53,618. Since its units digit is 8, it is divisible by 2. Also its sum of digits is 7 + 5 + 3 + 6 + 1 + 8 = 30. As 30 is divisible by 3, 7,53,618 is divisible by 3. Hence, 7,53,618 is divisible by 6.

Test of Divisibility by 8

A number is divisible by 8, if the number formed by its last three-digits in the same order (hundreds, tens and units digits) is divisible by 8.

Example: 15,840, 5432 and 7096 are all divisible by 8 as the numbers formed by the last three-digits in each case are divisible by 8.

Info Box!

If the digits at ones, tens and hundreds place is 0, then the number is divisible by 1000.

Test of Divisibility by 9

A natural number is divisible by 9, if the sum of its digits is divisible by 9.

Example: Consider the number 1,25,847. The sum of digits = 1 + 2 + 5 + 8 + 4 + 7 = 27. As 27 is divisible by 9, the number 1,25,847 is divisible by 9.

Test of Divisibility by 11

A number is divisible by 11, if the difference between the sum of the digits in odd places and the sum of the digits in even places of the number is either 0 or a multiple of 11.

Example: Consider the number 95,82,540. Now, (the sum of digits in odd places) – (the sum of digits in even places) = (9 + 8 + 5 + 0) – (5 + 2 + 4) = 11, which is divisible by 11.

Hence, 95,82,540 is divisible by 11.

TEST YOUR CONCEPTS

Very Short Answer Type Questions

Direction for questions from 1 to 5: Fill in the blanks.

1. The number of factors of 24 is ______. 8
2. The greatest 2-digit multiple of 8 is 96______.
3. The greatest common factor of 9 and 15 is ______. 3
4. The number of prime factors of 48 is ______. 2^4
5. The greatest pair of twin primes of 2-digit numbers is ______ 71 and 73

Direction for questions from 6 to 10: Select the correct alternative from the given choices.

6. Which of the following is a prime number?
(a) 87 (b) 69 (c) 57 (d) 97
7. Which of the following is not a sphenic number?
(a) 30 (b) 42 (c) 60 (d) 70
8. Which of the following is a composite number?
(a) 37 (b) 47 (c) 57 (d) 67
9. The HCF of which of the following pairs of composite numbers is different from that of the others? (Odd man out)
(a) 12, 18 (b) 24, 30
(c) 18, 30 (d) 18, 45
10. Which of the following is the greatest measure that can be used to measure the quantities 68 m, 102 m and 119 m?
(a) 34 (b) 51
(c) 13 (d) 17

Direction for question 11: Match the Column A with the Column B.

11.

Column A			Column B
(a) Prime number	( )	(p)	Divisible by only three prime numbers.
(b) Sphenic number	( )	(q)	'2' must be its factor.
(c) Composite number	( )	(r)	It has at least three factors.
(d) Even number	( )	(s)	It has only two factors.

Direction for questions from 12 to 16: Fill in the blanks.

12. The number of common multiples of 6 and 15 is ______.
13. The least common multiple of two co-primes is ______.
14. LCM $(a, b) \times$ HCF (a, b) = ______.
15. The largest 3-digit number divisible by 9 is ______.
16. The smallest 4-digit number divisible by 11 is ______.

Direction for questions from 17 to 22: Select the correct alternative from given choices.

17. The LCM of a and b is 220. Which of the following can be the HCF of a and b?
(a) 33 (b) 15 (c) 20 (d) 12
18. Which of the following pairs of numbers have their LCM 144?
(a) 18, 36 (b) 16, 96
(c) 24, 48 (d) 9, 16
19. The HCF of the two numbers a and b is 12. Which of the following can be the LCM of a and b?
(a) 44 (b) 65 (c) 76 (d) 96
20. Which of the following is divisible by 8, 15 and 6?
(a) 60 (b) 96 (c) 180 (d) 240
21. Which of the following is not divisible by 9?
(a) 345672 (b) 278901
(c) 46938 (d) 96435
22. Which of the following is divisible by 8?
(a) 7248882 (b) 836486
(c) 92304 (d) 726436

Direction for question 23: Match the Column A with the Column B.

23.

Column A			Column B
(a) 6, 8, 12	( )	(p)	72
(b) 8, 12, 18	( )	(q)	180
(c) 12, 18, 30	( )	(r)	288
(d) 18, 24, 32	( )	(s)	24

Short Answer Type Questions

24. List out all the common factors of the following pairs of numbers.
   (a) 120 and 160 (b) 52 and 32
25. List out all the 2-digit prime numbers which are greater than 50.
26. Express the following as the product of prime numbers.
   (a) 36 (b) 75
27. List out all the 2-digit twin primes.
28. Find the HCF of the following numbers by prime factorization method.
   (a) 24, 60 (b) 48, 64, 80
29. Find the HCF of 72, 140, 256 by division method.
30. Find the greatest number that divides 160, 264 leaving a remainder 4 in each case.
31. Find the greatest number that divides 80 and 115 leaving remainders 8 and 7 respectively.
32. On her birthday, Jyothsna received three different cakes of weight 3 kg, 2.6 kg and 2 kg from her father, mother and sister respectively. She cut the three cakes into pieces of equal weights without any remainder. Find the minimum number of pieces that she can get from the three cakes.
33. Find the LCM of 30, 75 and 120 by prime factorization method.
34. Find the LCM of 48, 60 and 280 by synthetic division method.
35. The product of two numbers is 1680 and the LCM of two numbers is 420. Find their HCF.
36. Find the greatest 3-digit number which is divisible by 16, 18 and 24.
37. Find the smallest number greater than 2 which gives a remainder 2 when divided by 16, 18 and 24.
38. Find the smallest number which when added by 6 is exactly divisible by 9 and 33.
39. Find the greatest 3-digit number which is a common multiple of 6, 15, and 21.
40. Rishitha and Lohitha are twins. They play a game, in which they open a page of a text book printed in English. From the first letter of the page, Rishitha strikes every 12th letter and Lohitha strikes every 18th letter. If they strike the same letter 17 times in the page, then find the minimum number of letters in the page selected.
41. Bhavagna celebrates her birthday every year. The number of chocolates that she distributes every year is the greatest 3-digit common multiple of all the prime factors of the number representing that year. How many chocolates should Bhavagna distribute in the year 2016?

CONCEPT APPLICATION

1. There are three empty drums which can hold 384 litres, 576 litres and 288 litres of water. Each of them is to be filled by using a measuring jar, a whole number of times. What is the largest possible capacity of the measuring jar with which we can fill all the three drums?
   (a) 96 litres (b) 24 litres
   (c) 72 litres (d) 36 litres
2. The dimensions of a hall are 6048 cm × 2440 cm. What is the minimum number of identical square shaped tiles that is required to furnish the hall?
   (a) 2320 (b) 1061
   (c) 1240 (d) 2320
3. A father gave equal amount of money to his three daughters Simron, Cinderella and Sreya to purchase some items for his birthday party. Simron brought puffs which costs ₹18 each, Cinderella bought cakes which costs ₹24 each and Sreya bought cool drinks which costs ₹30 each. If they spent their money completely on these items, then find the minimum number of cakes that Cinderella bought.
   (a) 12 (b) 16
   (c) 24 (d) 15
4. Miss Sumitha has three drumsticks in her kitchen which are 72 cm, 90 cm and 84 cm, respectively. She wanted to cut them into equal size of pieces. Find the minimum number of pieces that she can cut.

PRACTICE QUESTIONS

(a) 41 (b) 58
(c) 48 (d) 54

5. There are 72 green colour, 144 red colour and 234 orange colour chairs in an auditorium. A boy want to put the chairs in rows such that each row is of the same coloured chairs and the number of chairs is equal in each row. Find the minimum number of rows of chairs in the auditorium.
(a) 30 (b) 25
(c) 15 (d) 45

ASSESSMENT TEST

1. List out all the common factors of 64 and 96.
2. Write all the common prime factors of 720 and 140.
3. Find the HCF of 126 and 144 by prime factorization method.
4. Find the HCF of 84 and 112 by division method.
5. Find the least common multiple of 8, 15 and 20 by prime factorization method.
6. Find the least common multiple of 24, 40 and 60 by synthetic division.
7. The LCM of two numbers is 112 and their HCF is 2. If one of the numbers is 14, then find the other number.
8. A number *P* is divisible by 5, 4, 8 and 9. If *p* is a 3-digit number, then find all the possible values for *P*.
9. Aakruthi and Prakruthi are playing skipping-rope. Aakruthi skips 30 times in a minute and Prakruthi skips 20 times in a minute. Both of them start skipping at 4.50 p.m. and continue till 5 p.m. without any interruption. How many times do they skip the rope simultaneously after 4.50 p.m.?
10. Write the first three multiples of 48.
11. Write three factors of 48.
12. Which of the following pairs are co-prime?
    2, 3; 8, 9; 21, 22
13. Which of the following numbers are divisible by 5, 55, 556, 50058, 85501?
14. Is 199 a prime number?
15. Two bags of sugar contain 26 and 39 kg of sugar, respectively. What is the greatest weight that can be used to measure the weight in each bag an exact number of times? How many times will it take to weigh all the sugar in the two bags using this weight?

CROSSWORD

Across

4. The natural numbers having more than two factors
8. The units digit of an odd number which is divisible by 5
9. The number of common factors of co-primes other than 1
11. All the even numbers are divisible by

Down

1. The name of divisor when the remainder is 0
2. The natural numbers having exactly two factors
3. The greatest, among the common factors of given numbers
5. The minimum number of factors of a composite number
6. The least among the common multiples of given numbers
7. A number which is divisible by 2 and 3, it is also divisible by
10. The HCF of two co-primes is

TEST YOUR CONCEPTS

Very Short Answer Type Questions

1. 8
2. 96
3. 3
4. 2
5. (71, 73)
6. (d)
7. (c)
8. (c)
9. (d)
10. (d)
11. (a) → (s), (b) → (p), (c) → (r), (d) → (q)
12. infinite
13. their product
14. $a \times b$
15. 999
16. 1001
17. (c)
18. (d)
19. (d)
20. (d)
21. (c)
22. (c)
23. (a) → (s), (b) → (p), (c) → (q), (d) → (r)

Short Answer Type Questions

24. (a) 1, 2, 4, 5, 8, 10, 20, 40
    (b) 1, 2, 4
25. 53, 59, 61, 67, 71, 73, 79, 83, 89 and 97
26. (a) $2^2 \times 3^2$ (b) 3×5^2
28. (a) 12 (b) 16
29. 4
30. 52
31. 36
32. 38
33. 600
34. 1680
35. 4
36. 864
37. 146
38. 93
39. 840
40. 612
41. 966

CONCEPT APPLICATION

1. (a)
2. (b)
3. (d)
4. (a)
5. (b)

ASSESSMENT TEST

1. 1, 2, 4, 8, 16, 32
2. 2 and 5
3. 18
4. 28
5. 120
6. 120
7. 16
8. 360 and 720
9. 100

CROSSWORD

Across

4. Composite
8. Five
9. Zero
11. Two

Down

1. Factor
2. Prime
3. HCF
5. Three
6. LCM
7. Six
10. One

TEST YOUR CONCEPTS

Very Short Answer Type Questions

1. $24 = 1 \times 24 = 2 \times 12 = 3 \times 8 = 4 \times 6$

   There are 8 factors.

2. $8 \times 12 = 96$

   96 is the greatest 2-digit multiple of 8.

3. $3 \times 3 = 9$, $3 \times 5 = 15$

   3 is the greatest factor of 9 and 15.

4. $48 = 2 \times 2 \times 2 \times 2 \times 3$

   2 and 3 are the prime factors of 48.

   ∴ The number of prime factors = 2

5. (71, 73) is the greatest pair of twin primes of the two-digit primes.

6. Choice (d) follows.

   Hence, the correct option is (d).

7. $30 = 2 \times 3 \times 5$; $42 = 2 \times 3 \times 7$; $60 = 2 \times 3 \times 5 \times 2$

   $70 = 2 \times 5 \times 7$

   Hence, the correct option is (c).

8. 57 is divisible by 3.

   Hence, the correct option is (c).

9. HCF (12, 18) = 6

   HCF (24, 30) = 6

   HCF (18, 30) = 6

   HCF (18, 45) = 9

   Hence, the correct option is (d).

10. Given: 68, 102, 119

    $68 = 17 \times 4$; $102 = 17 \times 6$; $119 = 17 \times 7$

    Hence, the correct option is (d).

11. (a) Prime number has only 2 factors → (s)

    (b) Sphenic number should have only 3 prime factors → (p)

    (c) Composite number should have at least 3 factors → (r)

    (d) '2' must be a factor of an even number → (q)

    The correct match is as follows:

    (a) → (s), (b) → (p), (c) → (r), (d) → (q)

12. infinite

13. their product

14. $a \times b$

15. 999

16. When 1000 is divided by 11, the reminder is 10.

    ∴ 1001 is the smallest 4-digit number divisible by 11.

17. The HCF must be a factor of LCM.

    Hence, the correct option is (c).

18. Here, 9 and 16 are co-primes.

    Hence, the LCM = $9 \times 16 = 144$

    Hence, the correct option is (d).

19. The HCF is the factor of LCM.

    Choice (d) follows.

    Hence, the correct option is (d).

20. LCM of 8, 15, 6:

2	8, 15, 6
3	4, 15, 3
	4, 5, 1

    ∴ LCM = 120

    All the multiples of 120 are divisible by 8, 15 and 6.

    ∴ Choice (d) follows.

    Hence, the correct option is (d).

21. Going by options: 46938

    $4 + 6 + 9 + 2 + 8 = 30$ is not divisible by 9.

    Hence, the correct option is (c).

22. 92304, the number formed by the last 3 digits (304) is divisible by 8.

    Hence, the correct option is (c).

23. (a) 6, 8, 12

    $6 = 2 \times 3$; $8 = 2^3$; $12 = 2^2 \times 3$;

    LCM = $2^3 \times 3 = 24$ → (s)

(b) 8, 12, 18

$8 = 2^3; 12 = 2^2 \times 3; 18 = 3^2 \times 2$

$\text{LCM} = 2^3 \times 3^2; = 72 \rightarrow$ (p)

(c) 12, 18, 30

$12 = 2^2 \times 3; 18 = 2 \times 3^2; 30 = 2 \times 3 \times 5$

$\text{LCM} = 2^2 \times 3^2 \times 5 = 180 \rightarrow$ (q)

(d) 18, 24, 32

$18 = 3^2 \times 2; 24 = 3 \times 2^3; 32 = 2^5$

$\text{LCM} = 2^5 \times 3^2 = 288 \rightarrow$ (r)

The correct match is as follows:

(a) → (s), (b) → (p), (c) → (q), (d) → (r)

Short Answer Type Questions

24. (a)

$120 = 1 \times 120$	$160 = 1 \times 160$
$= 2 \times 60$	$= 2 \times 80$
$= 3 \times 40$	$= 4 \times 40$
$= 4 \times 30$	$= 5 \times 32$
$= 5 \times 24$	$= 8 \times 20$
$= 6 \times 20$	$= 10 \times 16$
$= 8 \times 15$	
$= 10 \times 12$	

The common factors of 120 and 160 are {1, 2, 4, 5, 8, 10, 20, 40}.

(b)

$52 = 1 \times 52$	$32 = 1 \times 32$
$= 2 \times 26$	$= 2 \times 16$
$= 4 \times 13$	$= 4 \times 8$

The common factors of 52, 32 are {1, 2, 4}.

25. The 2-digit prime numbers greater than 50 are 53, 59, 61, 67, 71, 73, 79, 83, 89 and 97.

26. (a) $36 = 2^2 \times 3^2$

(b) $75 = 3 \times 5^2$

27. (11, 13), (17, 19), (29, 31), (41, 43), (59, 61), (71, 73)

There are 6 twin primes which are of two-digits.

28. (a) $24 = 2^3 \times 3; 60 = 2^2 \times 3^1 \times 5^1$

$\text{HCF} = 2^2 \times 3 = 12$

(b) 48, 64, 80

$48 = 2^4 \times 3; 64 = 2^6; 80 = 2^4 \times 5$

$\text{HCF} = 2^4 = 16$

29. The HCF of 72, 140, 256:

```
72) 140 (1
    72
    68) 72 (1
        68
         4) 68 (17
            68
             0
```

∴ The HCF of 72 and 140 is 4.

```
4) 256 (64
   24
    16
    16
     0
```

∴ The HCF of 72, 140, 256 is 4.

30. $160 - 4 = 156$

$264 - 4 = 260$

HCF of 156, 260÷

```
156) 260 (1
     156
     104) 156 (1
          104
           52) 104 (1
               104
                 0
```

∴ The HCF of 260 and 156 is 52.

∴ The required number is 52.

31. The required number is the HCF of (80 – 8) and (115 – 7), i.e., HCF (72, 108)

```
72) 108 (1
    72
    36) 72 (2
        72
         0
```

∴ The required number is 36.

32. Converting kg into gm:

3 kg = 3000 gm

2.6 kg = 2600 gm

2 kg = 2000 gm

HCF of 3000, 2600, 2000 is

$3000 = 3 \times 2^3 \times 5^3$

$2600 = 2^3 \times 5^2 \times 13$

$2000 = 2^4 \times 5^3$

HCF $= 2^3 \times 5^2 = 8 \times 25 = 200$ gm

∴ The minimum number of pieces that Bhavagna get from the three cakes

$= \frac{3000}{200} + \frac{2600}{200} + \frac{2000}{200} = 15 + 13 + 10 = 38$

33. LCM of 30, 75, 120:

$30 = 2 \times 3 \times 5$; $75 = 3 \times 5^2$

$120 = 2 \times 2 \times 2 \times 3 \times 5 = 2^3 \times 3 \times 5$

LCM $= 2^3 \times 3 \times 5^2 = 600$

34. LCM of 48, 60, 280:

48, 60, 280

```
2 | 48, 60, 280
2 | 24, 30, 140
2 | 12, 15, 70
3 | 6, 15, 35
5 | 2, 5, 35
    2, 1, 7
```

LCM $= 2 \times 2 \times 2 \times 3 \times 5 \times 2 \times 7 = 1680$

35. Let the two numbers be a and b.

We know that:

LCM × HCF $= a \times b$

420 × HCF = 1680

HCF $= \frac{1680}{420} = 4$

36. Let us find the LCM of 16, 18 and 24.

```
2 | 16, 18, 24
2 | 8, 9, 12
2 | 4, 9, 6
3 | 2, 9, 3
    2, 3, 1
```

LCM $= 2 \times 2 \times 2 \times 3 \times 2 \times 3 = 144$

All multiples of 144 are also divisible by 16, 18 and 24.

∴ $144 \times 6 = 864$ is the required 3-digit number.

37. The required number is the least common multiple of (16, 18, 24) + 2.

```
2 | 16, 18, 24
2 | 8, 9, 12
2 | 4, 9, 6
3 | 2, 9, 3
    2, 3, 1
```

LCM $= 2 \times 2 \times 2 \times 3 \times 2 \times 3 = 144$

∴ The required number is 144 + 2 = 146

38. The required number is LCM (9, 33) – 6.

```
3 | 9, 33
    3, 11
```

LCM $= 3 \times 3 \times 11 = 99$

∴ The required number is 99 – 6 = 93

39. LCM 6, 15, 21:

```
3 | 6, 15, 21
    2, 5, 7
```

LCM $= 3 \times 2 \times 5 \times 7 = 210$

∴ The required number is $210 \times 4 = 840$

40. LCM of 12, 18:

```
2 | 12, 18
3 | 6, 9
    2, 3
```

∴ Both of them strike every 36th letter of the page.

LCM $= 2 \times 3 \times 2 \times 3 = 36$

Since both of them strike 17 times, the page should contain at least $36 \times 17 = 612$ letters.

41. LCM of 2016:

$$\begin{array}{r|l} 2 & 2016 \\ \hline 2 & 1008 \\ \hline 2 & 504 \\ \hline 2 & 252 \\ \hline 2 & 126 \\ \hline 3 & 63 \\ \hline 3 & 21 \\ \hline & 7 \end{array}$$

∴ The prime factors of 2016 are 2, 3, 7.

LCM of 2, 3, 7 is = 42

$42 \times 10 = 420$

$42 \times 20 = 840$

$42 \times 23 = 966$

∴ The number of chocolates that Bhavagna distributed in the year 2016 is 966.

CONCEPT APPLICATION

1. The HCF of 384, 576 and 288 is 96.

Hence, the greatest possible size of the measuring vessel is 96 litres.

Hence, the correct option is (a).

2. The HCF of 6048 and 2440 is 8.

Therefore the number of tiles required

$$= \frac{(6048 + 2440)}{8}$$

$$= \frac{8488}{8} = 1061$$

Hence, the correct option is (b).

3. The LCM of 18, 24, 30 is 360.

Hence, the amount given to each daughter is ₹360

Therefore, the number of cakes bought by cinderella $= \frac{360}{24} = 15$

Hence, the correct option is (d).

4. The HCF of 72, 90 and 84 is 6.

The number of pieces of drumsticks

$$= \frac{(72 + 90 + 84)}{6} = \frac{246}{6} = 41$$

Hence, the correct option is (a).

5. The HCF of 72, 144, 234 is 18.

The total number of rows

$$= \frac{(72 + 144 + 234)}{18} = \frac{450}{18} = 25$$

Hence, the correct option is (b).

ASSESSMENT TEST

1. $64 = 1 \times 64 = 2 \times 32 = 4 \times 16 = 8 \times 8$

$F_{64} = \{1, 2, 4, 8, 16, 32, 64\}$

$96 = 1 \times 96 = 2 \times 48 = 3 \times 32 = 4 \times 24 = 6 \times 16 = 8 \times 12$

$F_{96} = \{1, 2, 3, 4, 6, 8, 12, 16, 24, 32, 48, 96\}$

∴ The common factors are

$= \{1, 2, 4, 8, 16, 32\}$

2. Common prime factors of 720 and 140:

$$\begin{array}{r|l} 2 & 720 \\ \hline 2 & 360 \\ \hline 2 & 180 \\ \hline 3 & 90 \\ \hline 3 & 30 \\ \hline 5 & 10 \\ \hline & 2 \end{array} \qquad \begin{array}{r|l} 2 & 140 \\ \hline 2 & 70 \\ \hline 5 & 35 \\ \hline & 7 \end{array}$$

The prime factors of 72 are 2, 3, 5.

The prime factors of 140 are 2, 5, 7.

∴ The common prime factors are 2 and 5.

3. HCF of 126 and 144:

$126 = 2 \times 63$ $\quad$ $144 = 2 \times 72$

$= 2 \times 3 \times 21$ $\quad$ $= 2 \times 2 \times 36$

$= 2 \times 3 \times 3 \times 7$ $\quad$ $= 2 \times 2 \times 2 \times 18$

$= 2^1 \times 3^2 \times 7^1$ $\quad$ $= 2^4 \times 3^2$

∴ HCF (126, 144) $= 2 \times 3^2$

$= 18$

4. Division method:

```
84) 112 (1
    84
    28) 84 (3
        84
         0
```

∴ HCF of 84, 112 is 28

5. LCM of 8, 15, 20 by prime factorization method:

$8 = 2^3$; $15 = 3 \times 5$; $20 = 2^2 \times 5$

LCM $= 2^3 \times 3 \times 5 = 120$

6. LCM of 24, 40, 60 by synthetic division method:

2	24, 40, 60
2	12, 20, 30
2	6, 10, 15
5	3, 5, 15
3	3, 1, 3
	1, 1, 1

LCM $= 2 \times 2 \times 2 \times 3 \times 5 = 120$

7. LCM = 112, HCF = 2; $A = 14$

LCM × HCF = The product of two numbers

$112 \times 2 = 14(B)$

$8 \times 2 = B$

$B = 16$

∴ The other number is 16.

8. P is the common multiple of 5, 4, 8, 9.

2	5, 4, 8, 9
2	5, 2, 4, 9
	5, 1, 2, 9

LCM $= 2 \times 2 \times 5 \times 2 \times 9 = 360$

$360 \times 1 = 360$

$360 \times 2 = 720$

$360 \times 3 = 1080$ is a 4 digit number

∴ P can be 360 and 720.

9. Time taken by Aakruthi to skip the rope for 1 time

$= \frac{60}{30} = 2$ seconds

Time taken by Prakruthi to skip the rope for 1 time

$= \frac{60}{30} = 3$ seconds

∴ Time taken by them to skip the rope simultaneously

= LCM (2, 3) = 6 seconds

∴ For every 6 seconds, they skip the rope simultaneously.

⇒ They skip the rope 10 times for every minute.

∴ In the given time, i.e., 10 minutes, they skip the rope simultaneously $= 10 \times 10 = 100$ times.

10. Multiply 48 with first three natural numbers

48×1, 48×2, and 48×3

Hence, the first three multiples of 48 are 48, 96 and 144.

11. 48 can be represented as product of two numbers in the following ways:

1×48, 2×24, 16×3, 12×4, 8×6.

Factors of 48 are 1, 2, 3, 4, 6, 8, 16, 24, 48.

Any three factors 48 can be 1, 2 an 3

12. All of the pairs are co-primes.

13. For a number to be divisible by 5, the digit at the units place should be either 0 or 5.

Out of the given numbers, only 5 is divisible by 5.

14. 199 would be a prime number if it were not divisible by any prime number other than itself.

It can be obtained that 199 is not divisible by 2, 3, 5, 7, 11, 13. Hence, it is a prime number.

15. 13 kg, 5 times

Chapter

3

Fractions and Decimals

REMEMBER

Before beginning this chapter, you should be able to:

- Recall representation of fractions
- Perform multiplication and division of numbers

KEY IDEAS

After completing this chapter, you should be able to:

- Know types of fractions
- Understand comparison of fractions
- Perform operations on fractions
- Describe decimal numbers
- Understand comparison of decimals and work on decimals operations

INTRODUCTION

We have come across the concept of 'fraction' in previous classes. In this section, we shall learn about the types of fractions, ordering of fractions and the basic arithmetic operations in fractions, etc.

Imagine that you have invited five friends to your birthday party. You have cut the cake into six equal pieces. Each person gets one piece out of a total of six pieces. In other words, each person gets one-sixth of the cake. We know that 1/6 is a fraction. Here, cake is considered as whole and a piece is a part. 3/4, 4/5, 4/9 and 21/2 are some examples of fractions.

FRACTIONS

A number of the form a/b, where a, b are whole numbers and $b \neq 0$ is a fraction. The number a is the numerator and b is the denominator. There are three types of fractions.

1. **Proper fraction:** A fraction that represents a part of whole is a proper fraction. The numbers 1/2, 3/4, 5/6, 0/7 are some examples of proper fractions. In a proper fraction, the numerator is less than the denominator. The whole number 0 can be expressed as a proper fraction.
2. **Improper fraction:** A fraction that represents a combination of a whole and a part of the whole is an improper fraction. The numbers 5/4, 8/3, 20/9, 7/7 are some examples of improper fractions. In an improper fraction, the numerator is greater or equal to its denominator. All natural numbers can be expressed as improper fractions.

> **Info Box!**
>
> Fractions with same denominators are called like fractions!

3. **Mixed fraction:** When an improper fraction is written as an integer followed by a proper fraction, it is written as a mixed fraction.

   Example: The fraction 5/4 can be written as 1 + 1/4. Here, 1 is a whole and 1/4 is a part.

Comparison of Fractions

A set of fractions can be compared by using the following steps.

1. First, convert the given fractions into like fractions.
2. Second, the fraction which has the greater numerator will be the greater fraction.

> **NOTE**
>
> If there is a set of two unlike fractions with same numerators, then the fraction with the smaller denominator will be the greater fraction. For example, between 4/9 and 4/6, 4/6 will be greater.

Let us learn this with the help of examples.

EXAMPLE 3.1

Compare $\frac{2}{5}$ and $\frac{13}{25}$.

SOLUTION

$\frac{2}{5}$ can be written as $\frac{2 \times 7}{5 \times 7} = \frac{14}{35}$. Now $\frac{14}{35} > \frac{13}{35} \Rightarrow \frac{2}{5} > \frac{13}{35}$

EXAMPLE 3.2

Convert $\frac{13}{9}$ into a mixed fraction.

SOLUTION

Here, 13 is divided by 9, the quotient is 1 and the remainder is 4.

$\therefore \frac{13}{9} = 1\frac{4}{9}$

EXAMPLE 3.3

Convert $8\frac{2}{5}$ into a improper fraction.

SOLUTION

$$8\frac{2}{5} = \frac{(8 \times 5) + 2}{5} = \frac{40 + 2}{5} = \frac{42}{5}$$

Addition of Fractions

Let us understand the addition of fractions with the help of following points.

1. **A fraction and an integer:** The integer is expressed as a fraction with the same denominator as the fraction and the numerators are added.

   Example: $\frac{3}{8} + 2 = \frac{3}{8} + \frac{16}{8} = \frac{19}{8}$

2. **Two or more fractions:** All the fractions in the expression are expressed with a common denominator and the numerators are added.

   Example: $\frac{2}{3} + \frac{3}{5} = \frac{2(4)}{3(4)} + \frac{3(3)}{4(3)} = \frac{10}{15} + \frac{9}{15} = \frac{19}{15}$

Multiplication of Fractions

We shall now learn how to multiply fractions.

1. **A fraction and an integer:** First let us consider the multiplication of a proper fraction with a whole number.

   Example: $2\left(\frac{1}{2}\right) = \frac{2(1)}{2} = 1$

2. **Multiplication of a mixed fraction by a whole number:**

   Example: $2\left(5\frac{1}{3}\right) = 2\left(\frac{16}{3}\right) = \frac{32}{3}$

3. **Multiplication of a fraction by a fraction:**

   $$\text{The product of two fractions} = \frac{\text{The product of their numerators}}{\text{The product of their denominators}}$$

   Example: $\frac{3}{5}\left(\frac{3}{4}\right) = \frac{9}{20}$

Info Box!

Product of a fraction and its reciprocal is 1.

Division of Fractions

We shall now learn how to divide fractions with the help of following points.

1. **Whole number by a fraction:** We find that the division sign is replaced by a multiplication sign and the fraction a/b is replaced by the fraction b/a.

   For example, $5 \div 1/2 = 5(2/1) = 10$.

NOTE

The multiplicative inverse of 1/5 is 5 and that of 1/4 is 4. The multiplicative inverse of a number is also known as its reciprocal. The product of a number and its reciprocal is one. When the product of two non-zero numbers is one, each of them is the reciprocal of the other.

2. **Division of a fraction by a whole number:** We multiply the fraction by the multiplicative inverse of the whole number. For example, $\frac{1}{4} \div 3$ can be written as $\frac{1}{4} \div \frac{3}{1} = \frac{1}{4}\left(\frac{1}{3}\right) = \frac{1}{12}$.

3. **Division of a fraction by another fraction:** We multiply the first fraction by the multiplicative inverse of the second. For example, $\frac{3}{2} \div \frac{6}{8} = \frac{3}{2} \times \frac{8}{6} = 2$.

EXAMPLE 3.4

Simplify: $\frac{1}{2} + \frac{4}{3} + \frac{5}{2}$

SOLUTION

$$\frac{1}{2} + \frac{4}{3} + \frac{5}{2} = \frac{3+8+15}{6} = \frac{26}{6} = \frac{13}{3}$$

EXAMPLE 3.5

Simplify: $\frac{4}{9} + \frac{1}{3} - \frac{3}{4}$

SOLUTION

$$\frac{4}{9} + \frac{1}{3} - \frac{3}{4} = \frac{16+12-27}{36} = \frac{1}{36}$$

EXAMPLE 3.6

Simplify: $1\frac{1}{11} \times 3\frac{1}{11} \div 4\frac{7}{11}$

SOLUTION

$$1\frac{1}{11} + 3\frac{1}{11} \div 4\frac{7}{11} = \frac{12}{11} \times \frac{34}{11} \div \frac{51}{11} = \frac{12}{11} \times \frac{34}{11} \times \frac{11}{51} = \frac{12}{11} \times \frac{2}{3} = \frac{4}{11} \times 2 = \frac{8}{11}$$

DECIMAL NUMBERS

Consider the fractions 1/2, 1/4 and 1/8.

$\frac{1}{2}$ can be written as $\frac{1(5)}{2(5)} = \frac{5}{10}$ and 5/10 can be written as 0.5.

Similarly, $\frac{1}{4} = \frac{1(25)}{4(25)} = \frac{25}{100}$. This can be written as 0.25.

5/100 can be written as 0.05 and 32/10 can be written as 3.2.

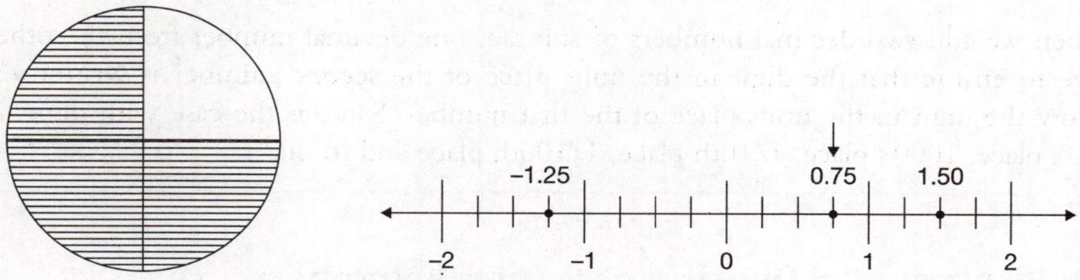

FIGURE 3.1 Three-fourth of a portion

0.5, 0.25, 0.03 and 3.5 are some examples of decimal numbers. A fraction in which the denominator is 10, 100, 1000, ……(i.e., a power of 10) is called a decimal fraction. When the denominator is indicated by placing a point in the numerator, the expression is called a decimal. In lower classes, we learnt about place value, units, tens, hundreds, etc. The place value of the first digit after the decimal point is 1/10 (called TENTHS), that of the second digit is 1/100 (called HUNDREDTHS) and so on. For example: 357.26 can be written in the expanded form as 3(100) + 5(10) + 7(1) + 2(1/10) + 6(1/100).

Comparison of Decimal Numbers

Consider the decimal numbers 32.24 and 32.41. Which of the two is greater?

Initially, we have to compare the digits on the left hand side of the decimal point, starting from the left most digits. In the given two numbers, 32 is common. Now the first digit after the decimal has to be considered. In 32.41, 4 is the first digit to the right of the decimal (the digit in the tenths place) and in 32.24, 2 is the first digit to the right of the decimal (the digit in the tenth place). As in this case, 4 > 2, 32.41 > 32.24.

TABLE 3.1 Common fractions and their decimal numbers

Fractions	Decimals
1/100	0.01
1/20	0.05
1/10	0.1
1/5	0.2
1/4	0.25
1/3	0.33
1/2	0.5
3/4	0.75

Addition and Subtraction of Decimals

Decimal numbers are added and subtracted one from the other in the following way.

(i)
$$\begin{array}{r} 23.43 \\ +34.25 \\ \hline 57.68 \\ \hline \end{array}$$

(ii)
$$\begin{array}{r} 24.56 \\ -12.23 \\ \hline 12.33 \\ \hline \end{array}$$

> **NOTE**
>
> When we add two decimal numbers or subtract one decimal number from the other, we have to ensure that the digit in the units place of the second number is written exactly below the digit in the units place of the first number. Same is the case with digits in the 100's place, 1000's place, 1/10th place, 1/100th place and so on.

Multiplication and Division of Decimal Numbers

We shall begin with simpler examples.

(i) $(0.3)\ (0.7) = \left(\frac{3}{10}\right)\left(\frac{7}{10}\right) = \frac{21}{100} = 0.21$

(ii) Divide 12.4 by 0.4. 12.4 ÷ 0.4 can be written as $\left(\frac{124}{10}\right) \div \left(\frac{4}{10}\right)$

$$= \frac{124}{10} \times \frac{10}{4} = \frac{124}{4} = 31$$

EXAMPLE 3.7

Find the sum of 1.4 and 2.23.

SOLUTION

1.4 + 2.23 = 3.63

EXAMPLE 3.8

Find the difference of 47.16 and 39.17.

SOLUTION

47.16 – 39.17 = 7.99

EXAMPLE 3.9

Convert $\frac{24}{25}$ into a decimal fraction.

SOLUTION

$$\frac{24}{25} \times \frac{4}{4} = \frac{96}{100} = 0.96$$

EXAMPLE 3.10

Simplify: 27.47×10

SOLUTION

$$27.47 \times 10 = 274.7$$

EXAMPLE 3.11

Divide 8.4 by 6.

SOLUTION

$$8.4 \div 6 = (84/10) \div 6 = (84/10)(1/6) = \frac{84}{6}\left(\frac{1}{10}\right) = \frac{14}{10} = 1.4$$

TEST YOUR CONCEPTS

Very Short Answer Type Questions

Direction for questions from 1 to 5: Fill in the blanks.

1. 4/3 is a/an _____ (proper/improper) fraction.
2. 5/5 is a/an _____ (proper/improper) fraction.
3. 6/7 is a/an _____ (proper/improper) fraction.
4. Convert 9/2 as a mixed fraction, the answer is _____.
5. The fraction 744/496 in its lowest terms is _____.

Direction for questions from 6 to 10: Select the correct alternative from given choices.

6. If $\frac{3}{4} = \frac{k}{12}$, then k is _____ .
   (a) 3 (b) 4
   (c) 6 (d) 9
7. 7/9 is equivalent to ___________.
   (a) 14/18 (b) 35/45
   (c) 56/72 (d) All of these
8. $13\frac{4}{5}$ = ______________.
   (a) 65/5 (b) 72/5
   (c) 69/5 (d) 17/5
9. What part of the given figure is shaded?

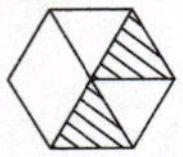

   (a) 2/3 (b) 1/3
   (c) 1/2 (d) 2/5
10. Which of the following is the largest?
   (a) 2/3 (b) 4/7
   (c) 3/5 (d) 1/15

Direction for question 11: Match Column A with Column B.

11.

Column A (Fraction of shaded part)		Column B
(a) $\frac{1}{2}$	( )	(p) 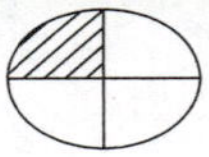
(b) $\frac{1}{3}$	( )	(q) 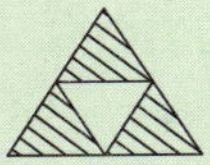
(c) $\frac{1}{4}$	( )	(r) 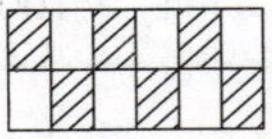
(d) $\frac{3}{4}$	( )	(s) 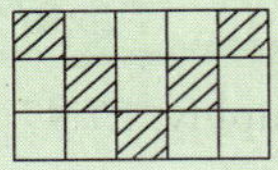

Direction for questions from 12 to 16: Fill in the blanks.

12. $\frac{1}{2} + \frac{3}{4} =$ _________.
13. $\frac{3}{8} \div \frac{2}{3} =$ _________.
14. $\frac{2}{5}$ of $3\frac{4}{7} =$ _________.
15. $\left[\frac{2}{7} + \frac{4}{7}\right] \times \left[4\frac{2}{3}\right] =$ _________.
16. $\left(2\frac{2}{5}\right)\left(1\frac{2}{3}\right) =$ _________.

Direction for questions from 17 to 21: Select the correct alternative from given choices.

17. Sujith travels one-third of a distance. If the distance is 12 km, then find the remaining distance that he would have travelled (in km).
   (a) 2 (b) 4
   (c) 6 (d) 8
18. The total strength of a class is 36 students. If three-fourth of the students is taking an examination from the class, then how many students are not taking the examination?
   (a) 9 (b) 12
   (c) 24 (d) 27
19. Anil travels from place A to place B and Akhil travels from place B to place A. Anil travels one-third of the distance and Akhil travels one-fourth of the distance. The distance travelled by Anil is one kilometre more than the distance travelled by Akhil. What is the distance between place A and place B? (In km)

(a) 9 (b) 10
(c) 12 (d) 18

20. $\frac{1}{2}+\frac{3}{4}+\frac{1}{8}=$ ________.

(a) 1/2 (b) 5/4
(c) 9/8 (d) 11/8

21. $\frac{2}{3}\div\frac{4}{3}\times\frac{2}{3}+1=$ ________.

(a) 7/3 (b) 4/3
(c) 3/10 (d) 6/17

Direction for question 22: Match Column A with Column B.

22.

Column A		Column B
(a) $\left(\frac{1}{2}+\frac{1}{3}\right)$ of 6	( )	(p) $\left(\frac{3}{4}-\frac{1}{3}\right)$ of 12
(b) $\left(\frac{1}{3}+\frac{1}{6}\right)$ of 18	( )	(q) $\left(\frac{5}{2}-\frac{2}{3}\right)$ of 6
(c) $\left(\frac{1}{4}+\frac{1}{3}\right)$ of 12	( )	(r) $\left(\frac{5}{4}-\frac{1}{2}\right)$ of 12
(d) $\left(\frac{1}{5}+\frac{1}{6}\right)$ of 30	( )	(s) $\left(\frac{3}{4}-\frac{1}{6}\right)$ of 12

Direction for questions from 23 to 27: Fill in the blanks.

23. 23.143 + 17.159 = ______.

24. 36.121 – 33.429 = ______.

25. 0.00125 × 200 = ______.

26. 50.2 ÷ 1.255 = ______.

27. 2.3 + 4.4 + 6.9 = ______.

Direction for questions from 28 to 32: Select the correct alternative from the given choices.

28. $\frac{120}{25}=$ ______.

(a) 0.048 (b) 4.8
(c) 48 (d) 4.08

29. 1.36 = ______.

(a) $\frac{24}{25}$ (b) $\frac{14}{25}$
(c) $\frac{32}{25}$ (d) $\frac{34}{25}$

30. 18 – 13.169 = ______.

(a) 3.831 (b) 4.831
(c) 5.831 (d) 2.831

31. 37.23 ÷ 10 = ______.

(a) 372.3 (b) 3.723
(c) 37.23 (d) 0.3723

32. 1.608 ÷ 1.34 = ______.

(a) 3.2 (b) 2.2
(c) 1.2 (d) 4.2

Direction for question 33: Match Column A with Column B.

33.

Column A		Column B
(a) 0.456 × 0.3	( )	(p) 0.1468
(b) 0.734 × 0.2	( )	(q) 0.1368
(c) 0.0739 × 2	( )	(r) 0.1478
(d) 0.0689 × 2	( )	(s) 0.1378

Short Answer Type Questions

34. List out the proper and improper fractions from the following.

(a) 7/2 (b) 3/4 (c) 5/2
(d) 11/13 (e) 7/15 (f) 17/13
(g) 72/21 (h) 81/87 (i) 16/15
(j) 20/29

35. Compare:

(i) 27/40 and 31/50
(ii) 4/5 and 7/8

36. Arrange the following fractions in ascending order and descending order.

(i) $\frac{7}{9},\frac{13}{15},\frac{23}{27},\frac{20}{21}$

(ii) $\frac{4}{5},\frac{11}{20},\frac{11}{15},\frac{22}{25}$

37. Convert 6/5 and 12/7 as mixed fractions?

38. Convert (i) $1\frac{3}{4}$ and (ii) $3\frac{4}{5}$ as improper fractions.

39. Reduce 1562/1846 and 924/1188 in lowest terms.

40. Three friends *A*, *B* and *C* have some money. If *A* has 3/10 of the total money, *B* has 7/15 of the total money and *C* has 7/30 of the total money. Who has the biggest share of the money? If the total money is ₹1500, then how much money does *A* have?

41. There are 125 balls in a basket. Out of which, 15 are white, 25 are brown, 35 are green, and the remaining are pink in colour. Find the share of the balls for each colour in the basket.

42. What should be added to the sum of 1/8 and 1/7 so that the sum is 5/14?

43. What should be subtracted from the sum of $\frac{1}{12}$ and $\frac{1}{8}$ so that the difference is $\frac{1}{18}$?

44. Simplify: $\frac{1}{2} \div \frac{4}{3} \times \frac{2}{3} \div \frac{1}{2} + \frac{3}{4} - \frac{5}{2} + \frac{2}{3} \times \frac{9}{4} \div \frac{2}{3}$

45. Simplify:

$$2\frac{1}{2} - \left[2 \div \left\{\frac{1}{9}\left[\frac{1}{2} + \frac{1}{2} + \frac{1}{2}\right] + \frac{1}{2}\right\} \times 3\right] \div 2\frac{1}{4} \times \frac{2}{3}$$

46. Simplify: $1\frac{2}{15} + 2\frac{2}{15} + 3\frac{2}{15} + \ldots + 100\frac{2}{15}$

47. Simplify: $1\frac{1}{11} + 2\frac{2}{11} + 3\frac{3}{11} + \frac{4}{11} + \frac{5}{11} + \frac{6}{11}$

48. Joshna and Vijay have some chocolates. The number of chocolates with Joshna is two-third of the number of chocolates with Vijay. If Vijay gives five chocolates to Joshna, then both will have equal number of chocolates. How many chocolates does Joshna have?

49. Priyanka spends 2/15 of her income on clothes, 1/9 of her income on entertainment, 4/15 of her income on rent, 1/3 of the income on food and she saves the remaining amount of ₹10,500. What is the income of Priyanka?

50. A rope of length $18\frac{1}{2}$ m is cut into equal pieces of $1\frac{7}{30}$ m each. Find the number of pieces.

51. Convert 7/20 into a decimal fraction.

52. Convert 0.425 into a fraction.

53. Simplify: 128.364 + 10.08 – 132.16 + 9.8

54. Simplify:
$0.9 + 0.9 \times 0.9 \div 0.9 - 0.9 + 0.9 \div 0.9 \times 0.9$

55. What should be added to 1.834 so that the sum is 5?

56. What should be subtracted from the sum of 1.48 and 1.368 so that the difference is 1?

57. By how much is the sum of 44.44 and 32.03 greater than their difference?

58. How many glasses of water is required to fill one litre water bottle, if one glass of water is 25 mL?

59. Ram purchased 3 notebooks that each costs ₹20.75 and 4 pencils that each costs ₹4.25. Ram gave ₹100 to the shopkeeper. How much money should Ram get back from the shopkeeper?

CONCEPT APPLICATION

1. Mr Perfect earns ₹54000 per month. He spends $\frac{2}{15}$ of his earnings on house rent, $\frac{4}{9}$ of his earnings on other household items and saves the remaining. What fraction of amount is the savings in his earnings?

   (a) $\frac{19}{45}$ (b) $\frac{17}{45}$
   (c) $\frac{13}{24}$ (d) $\frac{11}{25}$

2. The cost of one dozen oranges is ₹$43\frac{1}{2}$. Find the cost of $2\frac{1}{3}$ dozen of oranges (in ₹).

   (a) 203 (b) $\frac{203}{2}$
   (c) $\frac{101}{2}$ (d) $100\frac{1}{2}$

3. A water bottle is $\frac{3}{5}$ full and $\frac{1}{7}$ of the water is drawn. How much water is remaining in the bottle?

   (a) $\frac{16}{35}$ (b) $\frac{17}{35}$
   (c) $\frac{8}{17}$ (d) $\frac{2}{35}$

PRACTICE QUESTIONS

4. The length of a rope is 23.25 m. If two pieces of lengths 6.42 m and 3.09 m are cut, then find the length of the remaining rope.
(a) 12.74 (b) 13.64
(c) 13.74 (d) 14.54

5. The weight of a piece of gold is 0.2354 kg and the cost of gold is ₹2875.50 per gram. If 9.56 gm is separated for an ornament, then find the cost of the remaining gold?
(a) 646577.42
(b) 646627.42
(c) 646587.42
(d) 649402.92

ASSESSMENT TEST

1. Compare $\frac{2}{3}$ and $\frac{4}{5}$.
2. Compare $2\frac{3}{4}$ and $2\frac{19}{25}$.
3. Arrange $\frac{2}{7}$, $\frac{4}{5}$ and $\frac{3}{4}$ in ascending order.
4. Simplify: (i) $\frac{2}{3}+\frac{4}{5}$ (ii) $\frac{7}{9}+\frac{11}{18}$
5. Simplify: (i) $\frac{7}{2}-\frac{3}{4}$ (ii) $\frac{8}{11}-\frac{2}{3}$
6. Simplify: $4\frac{1}{6}\left[\frac{1}{3}-\left\{\frac{1}{4}-\frac{2}{5}\right\}+\frac{1}{3}\div\frac{25}{24}\right]$
7. (i) 4.2 + 0.27
(ii) 32.45 + 45.69
8. (i) Subtract 9.133 from 13.012.
(ii) Subtract 3.2 from 5.15.
9. (i) Find the value of 1.238 × 10.
(ii) Find the value of 1.32 × 1.2.
10. Reduce 480/840 to its simplest form.
11. Arrange the following fractions in ascending order.
2/5, 3/5, 4/5, 5/5, 6/5
12. Arrange the following in descending order.
5/2, 5/3, 5/4, 5/5, 5/6
13. By how much is the difference of 18.89 and 11.21 less than that of their sum?
14. What should be added to 6.77 to get 7?
15. What should be added to the difference of 6.88 and 4.25 to get 5?

CROSSWORD

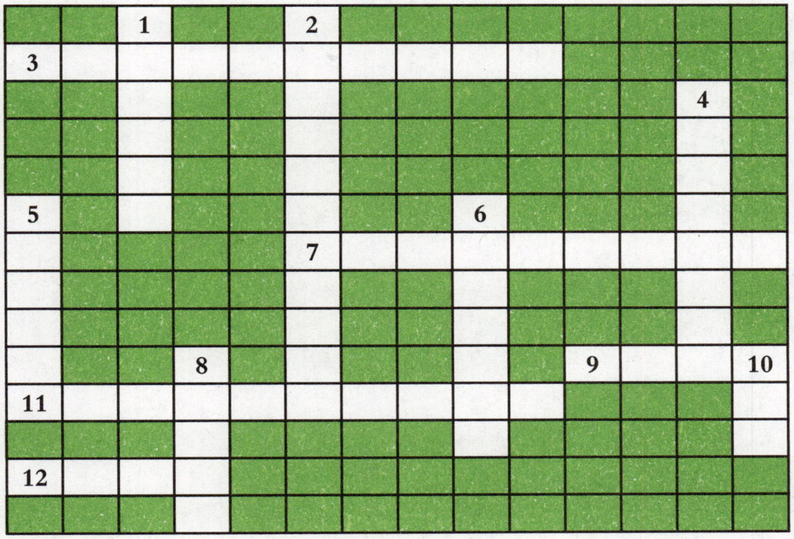

Across

3. The second place to the right hand side of the decimal point
7. In x/y, x is called
9. The sum of $-17/5$ and $17/5$ is
11. x/y and y/x are said to be ___ to each other.
12. Fractions whose denominators are same.

Down

1. Fractions whose denominators are different
2. In x/y, y is called
4. A fraction whose denominator is less than the numerator.
5. A fraction whose denominator is more than the numerator.
6. A fraction whose denominator is 10, 100, 1000 ___.
8. A fraction which is a combination of a whole number and a proper fraction.
10. The product of $3/8$ and $8/3$.

TEST YOUR CONCEPTS

Very Short Answer Type Questions

1. improper
2. improper
3. proper
4. $4\frac{1}{2}$
5. $\frac{3}{2}$
6. (d)
7. (d)
8. (c)
9. (b)
10. (a)
11. (a) → r; (b) → s; (c) → p; (d) → q
12. $\frac{5}{4}$
13. $\frac{9}{16}$
14. $1\frac{3}{7}$
15. 4
16. 4
17. (d)
18. (a)
19. (c)
20. (d)
21. (b)
22. (a) → p; (b) → r; (c) → s; (d) → q
23. 40.302
24. 2.692
25. 0.25
26. 40
27. 13.6
28. (b)
29. (d)
30. (b)
31. (b)
32. (c)
33. (a) → q; (b)→ p; (c) → r; (d) → s

Short Answer Type Questions

35. (i) $\frac{27}{40} > \frac{31}{50}$; (ii) $\frac{4}{5} < \frac{7}{8}$
36. (i) $\frac{7}{9} < \frac{23}{27} < \frac{13}{15} < \frac{20}{21}$; $\frac{20}{21} > \frac{13}{15} > \frac{23}{27} > \frac{7}{9}$
    (ii) $\frac{11}{20} < \frac{11}{15} < \frac{4}{5} < \frac{22}{25}$; $\frac{22}{25} > \frac{4}{5} > \frac{11}{15} > \frac{11}{20}$
37. (i) $1\frac{1}{5}$ (ii) $1\frac{5}{7}$
38. (i) $\frac{7}{4}$ (ii) $\frac{19}{5}$
39. (i) $\frac{11}{13}$ (ii) $\frac{7}{9}$
40. *B*; ₹450
41. $\frac{3}{25}, \frac{1}{5}, \frac{7}{25}, \frac{2}{5}$
42. $\frac{5}{56}$
43. $\frac{11}{72}$
44. 1
45. $-\frac{1}{6}$
46. $5063\frac{1}{3}$
47. $7\frac{10}{11}$
48. 20
49. ₹67, 500
50. 15
51. 0.35

52. $\frac{17}{40}$
53. 16.084
54. 1.8
55. 3.166
56. 1.848
57. 64.06
58. 40
59. ₹20.75

CONCEPT APPLICATION

1. (a)
2. (b)
3. (a)
4. (c)
5. (d)

ASSESSMENT TEST

1. $\frac{2}{3} < \frac{4}{5}$
2. $2\frac{3}{4} < 2\frac{19}{25}$
3. $\frac{2}{7} < \frac{3}{4} < \frac{4}{5}$
4. (i) $\frac{22}{15}$ (ii) $\frac{25}{18}$
5. (i) $\frac{11}{4}$ (ii) $\frac{2}{33}$
6. $\frac{241}{72}$
7. (i) 4.47 (ii) 78.14
8. (i) 3.879 (ii) 1.95
9. (i) 12.38 (ii) 1.584

CROSSWORD

Across

3. Hundredths
7. Numerator
9. Zero
11. Reciprocal
12. Like

Down

1. Unlike
2. Denominator
4. Improper
5. Proper
6. Decimal
8. Mixed
10. One

TEST YOUR CONCEPTS

Very Short Answer Type Questions

1. an improper fraction (Numerator > Denominator)
2. an improper fraction
3. a proper fraction (Numerator < Denominator)
4. $\frac{9}{2} = 4\frac{1}{2}$
5. $\frac{744}{496} = \frac{3}{2}$
6. $\frac{3}{4} = \frac{k}{12} \Rightarrow \frac{3(3)}{4(3)} = \frac{k}{12} \Rightarrow k = 9$

   Hence, the correct option is (d).
7. $\frac{7}{9} = \frac{14}{18} = \frac{35}{45} = \frac{56}{72}$

   Hence, the correct option is (d).
8. $13\frac{4}{5} = \frac{(13 \times 5) + 4}{5} = \frac{65 + 4}{5} = \frac{69}{5}$

   Hence, the correct option is (c).
9. $\frac{2}{6} = \frac{1}{3}$

   Hence, the correct option is (b).
10. Given that: $\frac{2}{3}, \frac{4}{7}, \frac{3}{5}$

    LCM of 3, 7, 5 is 105.

    $\frac{2}{3} \times \frac{35}{35} = \frac{70}{105}; \frac{4}{7} \times \frac{15}{15} = \frac{60}{105}$

    $\frac{3}{5} \times \frac{21}{21} = \frac{63}{105}; \frac{7}{15} \times \frac{7}{7} = \frac{49}{105}$

    $\therefore \frac{70}{105}$, i.e., $\frac{2}{3}$ is the largest fraction.

    Hence, the correct option is (a).
11. (a) $\frac{1}{2} = \frac{6}{12} \rightarrow$ (r)

    (b) $\frac{1}{3} = \frac{5}{15} \rightarrow$ (s)

    (c) $\frac{1}{4} \rightarrow$ (p)

    (d) $\frac{3}{4} \rightarrow$ (q)

    Therefore, the correct match is:

    $\therefore$ (a) $\rightarrow$ (r); (b) $\rightarrow$ (s); (c) $\rightarrow$ (p); (d) $\rightarrow$ (q)
12. LCM of 2, 4 is 4.

    $\frac{1}{2} \times \frac{2}{2} = \frac{2}{4}$

    $\frac{3}{11} + \frac{3}{11} = \frac{2}{4} + \frac{3}{4} = \frac{5}{4}$
13. $\frac{3}{8} \div \frac{2}{3} = \frac{3}{8} \times \frac{3}{2} = \frac{9}{16}$
14. $\frac{2}{5}$ of $3\frac{4}{7} = \frac{9}{10} \times \frac{25}{7} = \frac{10}{7} = 1\frac{3}{7}$
15. $\left[\frac{2}{7} + \frac{4}{7}\right] \times \left[4\frac{2}{3}\right] = \frac{9}{10} \times \left[\frac{14}{3}\right] = 4$
16. $\frac{9}{5}\left(1\frac{2}{3}\right) = \left(\frac{12}{5}\right)\left(\frac{5}{3}\right) = 4$
17. Required distance $= \left(\frac{2}{3}\right)$ of 12 km $= \frac{2}{3} \times 12 = 8$ km.

    Hence, the correct option is (d).
18. Required number of students $= \left(\frac{1}{4}\right)(36) = 9$

    Hence, the correct option is (a).
19. Let the distance between place A and place B be 'd'.

    $\frac{d}{3} = \frac{7}{8} + 1$

    $\frac{12.5}{12.5} = \frac{d+4}{4}$

    $4d = 3d + 12 \Rightarrow d = 12$

    The distance between the place A and place B is 12 km.

    Hence, the correct option is (c).
20. $\frac{1}{2} + \frac{3}{4} + \frac{1}{8} = \frac{(1 \times 4) + (3 \times 2) + (1 \times 1)}{8}$

    $= \frac{4 + 6 + 1}{8} = \frac{11}{8}$

    Hence, the correct option is (d).

21. $\frac{2}{3} \div \frac{4}{3} \times \frac{2}{3} + 1 = \frac{\left(\frac{2}{3}\right)}{\left(\frac{4}{3}\right)} \times \frac{2}{3} + 1$ (BODMAS)

$= \frac{1}{2} \times \frac{2}{3} + 1 = \frac{1}{3} + 1 = \frac{4}{3}$

Hence, the correct option is (b).

22. (a) $\left(\frac{1}{2}+\frac{1}{3}\right)$ of $6 = \left(\frac{3+2}{6}\right) \times 6 = \frac{5}{6} \times 6 = 5$

(b) $\frac{7}{9}$ of $18 = \left(\frac{2+1}{6}\right) \times 18 = 9$

(c) $\left(\frac{1}{4}+\frac{1}{3}\right)$ of $12 = \left(\frac{3+4}{12}\right) \times 12 = 7$

(d) $\left(\frac{1}{5}+\frac{1}{6}\right)$ of $30 = \left(\frac{6+5}{30}\right) \times 30 = 11$

(p) $\left(\frac{3}{4}-\frac{1}{3}\right)$ of $12 = \left(\frac{9-4}{12}\right) \times 12 = 5$

(q) $\left(\frac{5}{2}-\frac{2}{3}\right)$ of $6 = \left(\frac{15-4}{6}\right) \times 6 = 11$

(r) $\left(\frac{5}{4}-\frac{1}{2}\right)$ of $12 = \left(\frac{5-2}{4}\right) \times 12 = 9$

(s) $\left(\frac{3}{4}-\frac{1}{6}\right)$ of $12 = \left(\frac{9-2}{12}\right) \times 12 = 7$

Therefore, the correct match is:

(a) → (p); (b) → (r); (c) → (s); (d) → (q)

23. $23.143 + 17.159 = 40.302$

24. $36.121 - 33.429 = 2.692$

25. $0.00125 \times 200 = 0.25$

26. $\frac{50.2}{1.255} = \frac{50200}{1255} = 40$

27. $2.3 + 4.4 + 6.9 = 13.6$

28. $\frac{120}{25} = \frac{120}{25} \times \frac{4}{4} = \frac{480}{100} = 4.8$

Hence, the correct option is (b).

29. $1.36 = \frac{136}{100} = \frac{34}{25}$

Hence, the correct option is (d).

30. $18 - 13.169 = 4.831$

Hence, the correct option is (b).

31. $37.23 \div 10 = \frac{37.23}{10} = 3.723$

Hence, the correct option is (b).

32. $\frac{1.608}{1.34} = 1.2$

Hence, the correct option is (c).

33. (a) $0.456 \times 0.3 = 0.1368 \rightarrow$ (q)

(b) $0.734 \times 0.2 = 0.1468 \rightarrow$ (p)

(c) $0.0739 \times 2 = 0.1478 \rightarrow$ (r)

(d) $0.0689 \times 2 = 0.1378 \rightarrow$ (s)

Therefore, the correct match is:

(a) → q; (b) → (p); (c) → (r); (d) → (s)

Short Answer Type Questions

34. Proper fractions

$\frac{3}{4}, \frac{11}{13}, \frac{7}{15}, \frac{81}{87}, \frac{20}{29}$

Improper fractions

$\frac{7}{2}, \frac{5}{2}, \frac{17}{13}, \frac{72}{21}, \frac{16}{15}$

35. (i) Given $\frac{27}{40}$ and $\frac{31}{50}$.

LCM of 40 and 50 is 200.

$\frac{27}{40} = \frac{27}{40} \times \frac{5}{5} = \frac{135}{200}; \frac{31}{50} = \frac{31}{50} \times \frac{4}{4} = \frac{124}{200}$

$\frac{135}{200} > \frac{124}{200}; \Rightarrow \frac{27}{40} > \frac{31}{50}$

(ii) Given $\frac{4}{5}$,and $\frac{7}{8}$. LCM of 5, and 8 are 40.

$\frac{4}{5} = \frac{4}{5} \times \frac{8}{8} = \frac{32}{40}; \frac{7}{8} = \frac{7}{8} \times \frac{5}{8} = \frac{35}{40}$

$\frac{32}{40} < \frac{35}{40} \Rightarrow \frac{4}{5} < \frac{7}{8}$

36. (i) Given, $\frac{7}{9}, \frac{13}{15}, \frac{23}{27}, \frac{20}{21}$.

LCM of 9, 15, 27 and 21 is 945.

$\frac{7}{9} = \frac{7}{9} \times \frac{105}{105} = \frac{735}{945}; \frac{13}{15} = \frac{13}{15} \times \frac{63}{63} = \frac{819}{945}$

$\frac{23}{27} = \frac{23}{27} \times \frac{35}{35} = \frac{805}{945}; \frac{20}{21} = \frac{20}{21} \times \frac{45}{45} = \frac{900}{945}$

$$\frac{735}{945} < \frac{805}{945} < \frac{819}{945} < \frac{900}{945} \Rightarrow \frac{7}{9} < \frac{23}{27} < \frac{13}{15} < \frac{20}{21}$$

Descending Order: $\frac{20}{21} > \frac{13}{15} > \frac{23}{27} > \frac{7}{9}$

(ii) $\frac{4}{5}, \frac{11}{20}, \frac{11}{15}, \frac{22}{25}$.

LCM of 5, 20, 15 and 25 is 300.

$$\frac{4}{5} = \frac{4}{5} \times \frac{60}{60} = \frac{240}{300}; \frac{11}{20} = \frac{11}{20} \times \frac{15}{15} = \frac{165}{300}$$

$$\frac{11}{15} = \frac{11}{15} \times \frac{20}{20} = \frac{220}{300}; \frac{22}{25} = \frac{22}{25} \times \frac{12}{12} = \frac{264}{300}$$

$$\frac{165}{300} < \frac{220}{300} < \frac{240}{300} < \frac{264}{300} \Rightarrow \frac{11}{20} < \frac{11}{15} < \frac{4}{5} < \frac{22}{25}$$

Descending Order: $\frac{22}{25} > \frac{4}{5} > \frac{11}{15} > \frac{11}{2}$

37. (i) $\frac{6}{5} = 1\frac{1}{5}$

(ii) $\frac{12}{7} = 1\frac{5}{7}$

38. (i) $1\frac{3}{4} = \frac{(4 \times 1) + 3}{4} = \frac{4+3}{4} = \frac{7}{4}$

(ii) $3\frac{4}{5} = \frac{(5 \times 3) + 4}{5} = \frac{15+4}{5} = \frac{19}{5}$

39. (i) $\frac{1562}{1846} = \frac{11 \times 142}{13 \times 142} = \frac{11}{13}$

(ii) $\frac{924}{1188} = \frac{7 \times 132}{9 \times 132} = \frac{7}{9}$

40. Given that:

A has $\frac{3}{10}$, B has $\frac{8}{15}$ and C has $\frac{7}{30}$ of the total money.

LCM of 10, 15, and 30 is 30.

$$\frac{3}{10} = \frac{3}{10} \times \frac{3}{3} = \frac{9}{30}; \frac{7}{15} = \frac{7}{15} \times \frac{2}{2} = \frac{14}{30}; \frac{7}{30} = \frac{7}{30}$$

$\therefore$ B has the biggest share among the three.

If the total money is ₹1500, then A has $\frac{9}{30} \times$ ₹1500 = ₹450.

41. The number of pink balls = 125 – (15 + 25 + 35)

= 125 – 75 = 50

Share of the different coloured balls in the total number of balls			
White	**Brown**	**Green**	**Pink**
$\frac{15}{125} = \frac{3}{25}$	$\frac{25}{125} = \frac{1}{5}$	$\frac{35}{125} = \frac{7}{25}$	$\frac{50}{125} = \frac{2}{5}$

42. Given:

$$\frac{1}{8} + \frac{1}{7} = \frac{7+8}{56} = \frac{15}{56}$$

The required fraction $= \frac{5}{14} - \frac{15}{56} = \frac{20-15}{56} = \frac{5}{56}$

$\therefore$ $\frac{5}{56}$ should be added to the sum $\frac{7}{8}$ and $\frac{1}{9}$ to get $\frac{5}{14}$.

43. $\frac{1}{12} + \frac{1}{8} = \frac{2+3}{24} = \frac{4}{5}$

The required fraction $= \frac{5}{24} - \frac{1}{18}$

$$= \frac{3 \times 5 - 4 \times 1}{72} = \frac{15-4}{72} = \frac{11}{72}$$

$\therefore$ $\frac{11}{72}$ should be subtracted from the sum of $\frac{1}{12}$ and $\frac{1}{8}$ to get $\frac{1}{18}$.

44. $\frac{1}{2} \div \frac{4}{3} \times \frac{2}{3} \div \frac{1}{2} + \frac{3}{4} - \frac{5}{2} + \frac{2}{3} \times \frac{9}{4} \div \frac{2}{3}$

$$= \frac{1}{2} \times \frac{3}{4} \times \frac{2}{3} \times 2 + \frac{3}{4} - \frac{5}{2} + \frac{2}{3} \times \frac{9}{4} \times \frac{3}{2}$$

$$= \frac{1}{2} + \frac{3}{4} - \frac{5}{2} + \frac{9}{4} = \frac{12}{4} - \frac{4}{2} = 1$$

45. $2\frac{1}{2} - \left[2 \div \left\{\frac{1}{9}\left(\frac{1}{2} + \frac{1}{2} + \frac{1}{2}\right) + \frac{1}{2}\right\} \times 3\right] \div 2\frac{1}{4} \times \frac{2}{3}$

$$= \frac{5}{2} - \left[2 \div \left\{\frac{1}{9}\left(\frac{3}{2}\right) + \frac{1}{2}\right\} \times 3\right] \div \frac{9}{4} \times \frac{105}{140}$$

$$= \frac{5}{2} - \left(2 \div \left(\frac{1}{6} + \frac{1}{2}\right) \times 3\right) \div \frac{9}{4} \times \frac{2}{3}$$

$$= \frac{5}{2} - \left[2 \times \frac{6}{4} \times 3\right] \div \frac{9}{4} \times \frac{2}{3} = \frac{5}{2} - \left(9 \div \frac{9}{4}\right) \times \frac{2}{3}$$

$$= \frac{5}{2} - 9 \times \frac{4}{9} \times \frac{2}{3} = \frac{5}{2} - \frac{8}{3} = \frac{15-16}{6} = -\frac{1}{6}$$

46. $1\frac{2}{15} + 2\frac{2}{15} + 3\frac{2}{15} + \ldots\ldots + 100\frac{2}{15}$

(1 + 2 + 3 +....+ 100) + $\left(\frac{2}{15}+\frac{2}{15}+\ldots..+\frac{2}{15}(100\text{ terms})\right)$

((100 + 1) + (99 + 2) + ...+ (50 + 51)) + $\left(\frac{2}{15}\times 100\right)$

= (101 + 101 + ...+ 101)(50 terms) + $\left(\frac{200}{15}\right)$

= (50 × 101) + $\left(\frac{40}{3}\right)$ = 5050 + $13\frac{1}{3}$ = $5063\frac{1}{3}$

47. $1\frac{1}{11} + 2\frac{2}{11} + 3\frac{3}{11} + \frac{4}{11} + \frac{5}{11} + \frac{6}{11}$

$= (1 + 2 + 3) + \frac{1}{11} + \frac{2}{11} + \frac{3}{11} + \frac{4}{11} + \frac{5}{11} + \frac{6}{11}$

$= 6 + \left(\frac{1}{11}+\frac{2}{11}+\frac{3}{11}+\frac{4}{11}+\frac{5}{11}+\frac{6}{11}\right)$

$= 6 + \left(\frac{1+2+3+4+5+6}{11}\right) = 6 + \frac{21}{11} = 6 + 1\frac{10}{11} = 7\frac{10}{11}$

48. Let the number of chocolates with Vijay be x

No. of chocolates with Joshna = $\frac{2}{3}x$

Given, $x - 5 = \frac{2}{3}x + 5 \Rightarrow x = 30$

Number of chocolates with Joshna = $\frac{2}{3} \times 30 = 20.$

49. Let I be the income of Priyanka.

Expenditure of Priyanka

$= \left(\frac{2}{15}+\frac{1}{9}+\frac{4}{15}+\frac{1}{3}\right)$ of I

$= \left(\frac{6+5+12+15}{45}\right) I = \left(\frac{38}{45}\right) I$

Savings = $\left(1-\frac{38}{45}\right) I = ₹10,500$

$\left(\frac{45-38}{45}\right) I = 10500$

$\left(\frac{7}{45}\right) I = 10500$

Income = $10500 \times \frac{45}{7}$

The income of Priyanka is ₹67,500.

50. Required number of pieces = $\dfrac{\left(18\frac{1}{2}\right)}{\left(1\frac{7}{30}\right)}$

$= \dfrac{\left(\frac{37}{2}\right)}{\left(\frac{37}{30}\right)} = \frac{37}{2} \times \frac{30}{37} = 15$

51. $\frac{7}{20} = \frac{7}{20} \times \frac{5}{5} = \frac{35}{100} = 0.35$

52. $0.425 = \frac{425}{1000} = \frac{17}{40}$

53. 128.364 + 10.08 – 132.16 + 9.8

```
 128.364
  10.080
   9.800
 -------
 148.244

 148.244
-132.160
 -------
  16.084
```

∴ 128.364 + 10.8 – 132.16 + 9.8 = 16.084

54. 0.9 + 0.9 × 0.9 ÷ 0.9 – 0.9 + 0.9 ÷ 0.9 × 0.9

$= \frac{9}{10} + \frac{9}{10} \times \frac{9}{10} \div \frac{9}{10} - \frac{9}{10} + \frac{9}{10} \div \frac{9}{10} \times \frac{9}{10}$

$= \frac{9}{10} + \frac{9}{10} \times 1 - \frac{9}{10} + 1 \times \frac{9}{10}$

$= \frac{9}{10} + \frac{9}{10} - \frac{9}{10} + \frac{9}{10}$

$= \frac{18}{10} = 1.8$

55.
```
5.000
1.834
-----
3.166
```

3.166 should be added to 1.834 to get 5.

HINTS AND EXPLANATION

56. Sum:

$$\begin{array}{r} 1.480 \\ +1.368 \\ \hline 2.848 \end{array}$$

Now, 2.848 – 1.000 = 1.848

1.848 should be subtracted from the sum of 1.48 and 1.368 to get 1.

57. Sum: Difference:

$$\begin{array}{r} 44.44 \\ +32.03 \\ \hline 76.47 \end{array} \qquad \begin{array}{r} 44.44 \\ -32.03 \\ \hline 12.41 \end{array}$$

∴ Required quantity:

$$\begin{array}{r} 76.47 \\ -12.41 \\ \hline 64.06 \end{array}$$

58. Quantity of water in one glass = 25 mL

Required number of glasses $= \frac{1000}{25} = 40$

59. Cost of each note book = 20.75

Cost of 3 note books = 3 × 20.75 = ₹62.25

Cost of each pencil = ₹4.25

Cost of 4 pencils = 4 × 4.25 = 17

Total expenditure = 62.25 + 17.00 = 79.25

Balance amount = 100 – 79.25 = ₹20.75

CONCEPT APPLICATION

1. Savings $= 54000 - \left(\frac{2}{15} + \frac{4}{9}\right) = 54000\left(\frac{19}{45}\right)$

Hence, the correct option is (a).

2. Cost of $2\frac{1}{3}$ dozen of orange $= 2\frac{1}{3} \times 43\frac{1}{2}$

$= \frac{7}{3} \times \frac{87}{2} = \frac{203}{2}$

Hence, the correct option is (b).

3. Remaining water in the bottle $= \frac{3}{5} - \frac{1}{7}$

$= \frac{(21-5)}{35} = \frac{16}{35}$

Hence, the correct option is (a).

4. Length of the remaining rope

= 23. 25 – (6.42 + 3. 09)

= 23.25 – (9.51) = 13. 74 m

Hence, the correct option is (c).

5. Weight of the piece of gold = 0.2354 kg

= 235.4 grams

Weight of gold used for ornament = 9.56 gm

Remaining gold = 235.4 – 9.56 = 225.84 gm

Cost of the remaining gold = 225.84 × 2875.50

= 649402.92

Hence, the correct option is (d).

ASSESSMENT TEST

1. $\frac{2}{3}$ and $\frac{4}{5}$

LCM of 3 and 5 is 15.

$\frac{2}{3} \times \frac{5}{5} = \frac{10}{15}; \frac{4}{5} \times \frac{3}{3} = \frac{12}{15}$

$\frac{2}{3} < \frac{4}{5}$

2. $2\frac{3}{4}$ and $2\frac{19}{25} \Rightarrow \frac{11}{4}$ and $\frac{69}{25}$

LCM of 4 and 25 is 100.

$\frac{11}{4} \times \frac{25}{25} = \frac{275}{100}; \frac{69}{25} \times \frac{4}{4} = \frac{276}{100}$

$\frac{275}{100} < \frac{276}{100} \Rightarrow 2\frac{3}{4} < 2\frac{19}{25}$

3. $\frac{2}{7}, \frac{4}{5}$ and $\frac{3}{4}$.

LCM of 7, 5 and 4 is 140.

$\frac{2}{7} = \frac{2}{7} \times \frac{20}{20} = \frac{40}{140}; \frac{4}{5} = \frac{4}{5} \times \frac{28}{28} = \frac{112}{140}$

$\frac{3}{4} = \frac{3}{4} \times \frac{35}{35} = \frac{105}{140}$

$\frac{40}{140} < \frac{105}{140} < \frac{112}{140} \Rightarrow \frac{2}{7} < \frac{3}{4} < \frac{4}{5}$.

4. (i) $\frac{2}{3} + \frac{4}{5} = \frac{10+12}{15} = \frac{22}{15}$

(ii) $\frac{7}{9} + \frac{11}{18} = \frac{14+11}{18} = \frac{25}{18}$

5. (i) $\frac{7}{2} - \frac{3}{4} = \frac{14-3}{4} = \frac{11}{4}$

(ii) $\frac{8}{11} - \frac{2}{3} = \frac{24-22}{33} = \frac{2}{33}$

6. $4\frac{1}{6}\left[\frac{1}{3} - \left\{\frac{1}{4} - \frac{2}{5}\right\} + \frac{1}{3} \div \frac{25}{24}\right]$

$= \frac{25}{6}\left[\frac{1}{3} - \left\{\frac{5-8}{20}\right\} + \frac{1}{3} \times \frac{24}{25}\right]$

$= \frac{25}{6}\left[\frac{1}{3} - \left\{\frac{-3}{20}\right\} + \frac{24}{75}\right] = \frac{25}{6}\left[\frac{100+45+96}{300}\right]$

$= \frac{25}{6} \times \frac{241}{300} = \frac{241}{72}$

7. (i) 4.2 + 0.27 = 4.47

(ii) 32.45 + 45.69 = 78.14

8. (i) 13.012 – 9.133 = 3.879

(ii) 5.15 – 3.2 = 1.95

9. (i) 1.238 × 10 = 12.38

(ii) 1.32 × 1.2 = 1.584

10. 480/840 = 2 × 2 × 2 × 2 × 2 × 3 × 5/2 × 2 × 2 × 3 × 5 × 7 = 4/7

11. 2/5 < 3/5 < 4/5 < 5/5 < 6/5

12. 5/6 < 5/5 < 5/4 < 5/3 < 5/2

13. Difference is 7.68. Sum is 30.10

Sum – difference = 22.42

14. 7.00 – 6.77 = 0.23

15. 6.88 – 4.25 = 2.63

To get 5, we need to add (5 – 2.63) = 2.37

Chapter 4

Powers and Roots

REMEMBER

Before beginning this chapter, you should be able to:

- Perform addition of repeated numbers
- Calculate multiplication of repeated numbers

KEY IDEAS

After completing this chapter, you should be able to:

- Apply laws of exponents
- Understand squares and square roots applications
- Calculate cubes and cube roots

INTRODUCTION

We are familiar with the fact that $a + a + a + a = 4a$. The sum of four instances of a number a is four times of a. Similarly, the sum of n instances of a number a is n times a, it is denoted as na, i.e., multiplication is nothing but repeated addition.

The product of n instances of a number a is denoted as a^n. This is an exponential expression. It can be read as a to the power of n or **a** raised to n. Exponentiation is nothing but repeated multiplication.

So, $a \times a \times a \times \ldots\ldots \times a$ (n times) $= a^n$. In the exponential expression a^n, a is called the **base** and n is called the **exponent** or **index**.

Example: $5 \times 5 \times 5 \times 5 = 5^4$

Info Box!

The term 'power' was first time used by Greek Mathematician Euclid for the square of line.

LAWS OF EXPONENTS

We shall look at some of the laws (properties) pertaining to these exponential expressions. The multiplication and the division of exponential expressions can be derived using the laws, which is simple and easier.

Law 1: $2^3 \times 2^2 = (2 \times 2 \times 2)(2 \times 2) = 2 \times 2 \times 2 \times 2 \times 2 = 2^5 = 2^{3+2}$

We can conclude that $a^m \times a^n = a^{m+n}$, where a, m and n are any three numbers.

Law 2: $2^5 \div 2^2 = (2 \times 2 \times 2 \times 2 \times 2) \div (2 \times 2) = 2 \times 2 \times 2 = 2^3 = 2^{5-2}$

We can conclude that $a^m \div a^n = a^{m-n}$, where $a \neq 0$, m and n are any three numbers and $m \geq n$.

Law 3: $a^0 = 1$, where a is any non-zero number.

EXAMPLE 4.1

Prime factorize the following.

(I) 900 **(II)** 1617

SOLUTION

(I) $900 = 2 \times 450$
$= 2 \times 2 \times 225$
$= 2 \times 2 \times 3 \times 75$
$= 2 \times 2 \times 3 \times 3 \times 25$
$= 2 \times 2 \times 3 \times 3 \times 5 \times 5$
$\therefore 900 = 2^2 \times 3^2 \times 5^2$

(II) $1617 = 3 \times 539$
$= 3 \times 7 \times 77$
$= 3 \times 7 \times 7 \times 11$
$\therefore 1617 = 3^1 \times 7^2 \times 11^1$

EXAMPLE 4.2

Write the bases and exponents of the following.

(I) 8^6 **(II)** 25^{11}
(III) -36^{15} **(IV)** $(-36)^{14}$

SOLUTION

(I) Base = 8; Exponent = 6
(II) Base = 25; Exponent = 11
(III) Base = 36; Exponent = 15
(IV) Base = -36; Exponent = 14

EXAMPLE 4.3

Express the following into the exponential form.

(I) $2 \times 2 \times 2 \times 2 \times 2 \times 2 \times 3 \times 3 \times 3 \times 3$

(II) $5 \times 5 \times 7 \times 7 \times 7 \times 11 \times 11 \times 11 \times 11$

SOLUTION

(I) $2 \times 2 \times 2 \times 2 \times 2 \times 2 \times 3 \times 3 \times 3 \times 3 = 2^6 \times 3^4$

(II) $5 \times 5 \times 7 \times 7 \times 7 \times 11 \times 11 \times 11 \times 11 = 5^2 \times 7^3 \times 11^4$

EXAMPLE 4.4

Simplify the following using suitable laws of exponents.

(I) $7^4 \times 7^5$ **(II)** $5^2 \times 5^3 \times 5^6$ **(III)** $2^4 \times 2^8 \times 3^2 \times 3^5 \times 3^8$

SOLUTION

We have $a^m \times a^n = a^{m+n}$

(I) $7^4 \times 7^5 = 7^{4+5} = 7^9$

(II) $5^2 \times 5^3 \times 5^6 = 5^{2+3+6} = 5^{11}$

(III) $2^4 \times 2^8 \times 3^2 \times 3^5 \times 3^8 = 2^{4+8} \times 3^{2+5+8} = 2^{12} \times 3^{15}$

EXAMPLE 4.5

Simplify the following using suitable laws of exponents.

(I) $3^4 \div 3^2$ **(II)** $[5^7 \times 5^3] \div 5^6$

SOLUTION

We have $a^m \div a^n = a^{m-n}$

(I) $3^4 \div 3^2 = 3^{4-2} = 3^2$

(II) $[5^7 \times 5^3] \div 5^6 = [5^{7+3}] \div 5^6 = 5^{10} \div 5^6 = 5^{10-6} = 5^4$

SQUARES AND SQUARE ROOTS

If a number is multiplied by itself, then the product obtained is said to be the square of that number. A number which is the square of a natural number is called a perfect square.

Examples: (i) $1 \times 1 = 1$ (= 1^2), 1 is the square of 1.
(ii) $2 \times 2 = 4$ (= 2^2), 4 is the square of 2.
(iii) $3 \times 3 = 9$ (= 3^2), 9 is square of 3.

∴ 1, 4, 9, 16, 25, ... are the squares of 1, 2, 3, 4, 5, ... respectively.

TABLE 4.1 List of squares from 1 to 12

1^2	1×1	1
2^2	2×2	4
3^2	3×3	9
4^2	4×4	16
5^2	5×5	25
6^2	6×6	36
7^2	7×7	49
8^2	8×8	64
9^2	9×9	81
10^2	10×10	100
11^2	11×11	121
12^2	12×12	144

Now, $a(a) = a^2$, a^2 is the square of a and a is the square root of a^2.

2 is the square root of 4.

3 is the square root of 9.

We write, $\sqrt{4} = 2$, $\sqrt{9} = 3$, $\sqrt{16} = 4$ and so on.

We use the symbol $\sqrt{\ }$ to denote a square root.

Methods for Finding the Square Root of a Number

Let us learn how to find the square root of a number by two methods described as follows.

Method 1

Step (i): Express the given perfect square number as a product of prime factors.
Step (ii): Pair the factors such that primes in each pair thus formed are equal.
Step (iii): Choose one prime from each pair and multiply all such primes.
Step (iv): The product of these primes is the square root of the given number.

EXAMPLE 4.6

Find the square root of 144.

SOLUTION

Step (i): $144 = 2 \times 2 \times 2 \times 2 \times 3 \times 3$
Step (ii): $144 = (2 \times 2) \times (2 \times 2) \times (3 \times 3)$
Step (iii): Consider, $(2) \times (2) \times (3)$
Step (iv): The product $(2) \times (2) \times (3) = 12$

$\therefore$ 12 is the square root of 144.

Method 2

Step (i): Express the given perfect square as the product of prime factors.
Step (ii): Expand the expression in step (i), as an exponential expression.
Step (iii): The square root is the product obtained by taking half of the exponent with the same base.

EXAMPLE 4.7

Find the square root of 324.

SOLUTION

Step (i): $324 = 2 \times 2 \times 3 \times 3 \times 3 \times 3$

Step (ii): $324 = 2^2 \times 3^4$

Step (iii): $\sqrt{324} = 2^1 \times 3^2 = 2 \times 9 = 18$

$\therefore$ 18 is the square root of 324.

EXAMPLE 4.8

Find the square root of 100.

SOLUTION

$100 = 2 \times 2 \times 5 \times 5 = 2^2 \times 5^2$

$\sqrt{100} = 2 \times 5 = 10$

$\therefore$ 10 is the square root of 100.

NOTES

(1) $\sqrt{x \times y} = \sqrt{x} \times \sqrt{y}$

(2) $\sqrt{\dfrac{x}{y}} = \dfrac{\sqrt{x}}{\sqrt{y}}$

(3) $\sqrt{x + y} \neq \sqrt{x} + \sqrt{y}$

(4) $\sqrt{x - y} \neq \sqrt{x} - \sqrt{y}$

CUBES AND CUBE ROOTS

If a number is multiplied by itself three times, then the product obtained is said to be the cube of that number. That means, when a number a is multiplied by itself three times, (to obtain $a \times a \times a$) the product a^3 is said to be the cube of a. The cube of a natural number is called 'perfect cube'.

Examples: (i) $1 \times 1 \times 1 = 1$ $(= 1^3)$, 1 is cube of 1.
(ii) $2 \times 2 \times 2 = 8$ $(= 8^3)$, 8 is the cube of 2.
(iii) $3 \times 3 \times 3 = 27$ $(= 3^3)$, 27 is the cube of 3.

$\therefore$ 1, 8, 27, 64, 125 .... are the cubes of 1, 2, 3, 4, 5, ... respectively.

Now, $a(a)(a) = a^3$, a^3 is the cube of a and a is the cube root of a^3.

2 is the cube root of 8.

3 is the cube root of 27.

We write, $\sqrt[3]{8} = 2$, $\sqrt[3]{27} = 3$, $\sqrt[3]{64} = 4$ and .... so on.

We use the symbol $\sqrt[3]{\ }$ to denote cube root.

TABLE 4.2 List of cubes from 1 to 12

1^3	$1 \times 1 \times 1$	1
2^3	$2 \times 2 \times 2$	8
3^3	$3 \times 3 \times 3$	27
4^3	$4 \times 4 \times 4$	64
5^3	$5 \times 5 \times 5$	125
6^3	$6 \times 6 \times 6$	216
7^3	$7 \times 7 \times 7$	343
8^3	$8 \times 8 \times 8$	512
9^3	$9 \times 9 \times 9$	729
10^3	$10 \times 10 \times 10$	1000
11^3	$11 \times 11 \times 11$	1331
12^3	$12 \times 12 \times 12$	1728

Methods for Finding Cube Root of a Number

Let us learn how to find the cube root of a number by two methods described as follows.

Method 1

Step (i): Express the given perfect cube as the product of its prime factors.
Step (ii): Group the factors such that the primes in each group thus formed are three equal factors.
Step (iii): Choose one prime from each group and multiply all such primes.
Step (iv): The product of these primes is the cube root of the given number.

EXAMPLE 4.9

Find the square root of 216.

SOLUTION

Step (i): $216 = 2 \times 2 \times 2 \times 3 \times 3 \times 3$

Step (ii): $216 = (2 \times 2 \times 2) \times (3 \times 3 \times 3)$

Step (iii): Consider, $(2) \times (3)$

Step (iv): The product $(2) \times (3) = 6$

$\therefore$ 6 is the cube root of 216.

Method 2

Step (i): Express the given perfect cube number as the product of prime factors.
Step (ii): Expand the expression in step (i) as exponential expression.
Step (iii): The cube root is the product obtained by taking one-third of the exponent with the same base.

EXAMPLE 4.10

Find the cube root of 1000.

SOLUTION

Step (i): $1000 = 2 \times 2 \times 2 \times 5 \times 5 \times 5$

Step (ii): $1000 = 2^3 \times 5^3$

Step (iii): $\sqrt[3]{1000} = 2^1 \times 5^1 = 10$

∴ 10 is the cube root of 1000.

NOTES

(1) $\sqrt[3]{\dfrac{x}{y}} = \dfrac{\sqrt[3]{x}}{\sqrt[3]{y}}$

(2) The cube root of a positive number is always positive.
(3) The cube root of a negative number is always negative.

TEST YOUR CONCEPTS

Very Short Answer Type Questions

Direction for questions from 1 to 5: Fill in the blanks

1. $1^1 + (-1)^2 + 1^3 + (-1)^4 + 1^5 + (-1)^6 + \ldots\ldots\ldots + 1^{99} + (-1)^{100} =$ ________.

2. $(99)^{37} \times (99)^{-14} \times (99)^3 \times (99)^{-26} =$ ________.

3. $[(999)^9 \times (999)^{90} \times (999)^{900}] \div (999)^{998} =$ ________.

4. $(2^2)^3 - (-2^3)^2 =$ ________.

5. $[99^1 + 98^2 + 97^3 + \ldots\ldots\ldots + 3^{97} + 2^{98} + 1^{99}]^0 =$ ________.

Direction for questions from 6 to 10: Select the correct alternative from the given choices.

6. Which of the following is negative?
   (a) $(-2)^4\,(3)^5$ (b) $(-3)^3\,(-2)^5$
   (c) $(-2)^2\,(-3)^3$ (d) $(2)^5\,(-3)^2$

7. Which of the following is the greatest?
   (a) $6^2 - 2^2$ (b) $7^2 - 4^2$
   (c) $8^2 - 6^2$ (d) $9^2 - 8^2$

8. Which of the following is/are true?
   (A) 2^6 (B) 3^4 (C) 3^3
   (D) 4^3 (E) 9^2
   (a) $A = D$ (b) $B = E$
   (c) $B = D$ (d) Both (a) and (b)

9. $3^6 - 3^4 \times 3^2 =$ ________.
   (a) 3^4 (b) 3^4 (c) 1 (d) 0

10. Which of the following is not equal to 4096?
    (a) 2^{12} (b) 4^6 (c) 8^5 (d) 16^3

Direction for question 11: Match Column A with Column B.

11.

Column A		Column B
(a) $[2^9 \times 2^{12}] \div 2^5$	( )	(p) 2^{10}
(b) $[2^{19} \times 2^{14}] \div 2^{20}$	( )	(q) 2^{13}
(c) $[2^{17} \times 2^{18}] \div 2^{16}$	( )	(r) 2^{16}
(d) $[2^6 \times 2^{12}] \div 2^8$	( )	(s) 2^{19}

Direction for questions from 12 to 16: Fill in the blanks

12. The smallest perfect square and the perfect cube other than 1 is ______.

13. The square of the smallest two-digit natural number which has the same digits is ________.

14. The cube of the greatest single digit natural number is ________.

15. The sum of the square roots of all the 2-digit perfect squares is ______.

16. The sum of the cube roots of all the 2-digit perfect cubes is ______.

Direction for questions from 17 to 21: Select the correct alternative from the given choices.

17. The square of a natural number and the cube of the number are same. The number(s) is/are _______.
    (a) 0 (b) 1
    (c) Both (a) and (b) (d) None of these

18. Which of the following is not a perfect square?
    (a) 16 (b) 36 (c) 64 (d) 91

19. Which of the following is/are true?
    (a) $\sqrt{16 + 9} = 7$
    (b) $\sqrt{9 + 7} = 4$
    (c) $\sqrt{64 + 36} = 14$
    (d) Both (a) and (c)

20. $\sqrt[3]{829 - 486} =$ ________.
    (a) 9 (b) 8 (c) 7 (d) 6

21. Which of the following is equal to $\sqrt[3]{3^3 + 4^3 + 5^3}$?
    (a) $\sqrt{36}$ (b) $\sqrt{63}$
    (c) $\sqrt{82}$ (d) $\sqrt{83}$

Direction for question 22: Match Column A with Column B.

22.

Column A		Column B
(a) $\sqrt[3]{2^9 \times 3^{12}}$	( )	(p) $2^6 \times 3^4$
(b) $\sqrt[2]{2^{12} \times 3^8}$	( )	(q) $2^4 \times 3^3$
(c) $\sqrt[3]{2^{12} \times 3^9}$	( )	(r) $2^4 \times 3^6$
(d) $\sqrt[2]{2^8 \times 3^{12}}$	( )	(s) $2^3 \times 3^4$

Short Answer Type Questions

23. Find the base and the exponent of each of the following.
(i) $(72)^{36}$ (ii) $(-8)^4$ (iii) -8^4

24. Prime factorize and also write in exponential form of the following.
(i) 360 (ii) 3675

25. Evaluate the following.
(i) $(-5)^3$ (ii) $(-2)^6$
(iii) $(3/11)^3$ (iv) $(2/3)^1\,(2/3)^2\,(2/3)^3$

26. Find the value of an exponential expression whose exponent is the smallest composite number and base is the smallest odd prime number.

27. Simplify the following.
(i) $(3/11)^5 \times (3/11)^6 \times (3/11)^{13}$
(ii) $[(10)^{14} \times (5)^{17} \times (2)^{20}] \div [(10)^{13} \times (5)^{15} \times (2)^{17}]$

28. Simplify $[3^3 + 4^3 + 5^3]^2$ and express in exponential form.

29. What should be multiplied to $2^4 \times 3^2 \times 5^2$ so that the product is equal to 21600?

30. By what should $3^2 \times 5^5 \times 7^2$ be divided so that the quotient is equal to 13125?

31. Simplify: $2^6 \times 2^3 + 2^{19} \div 2^{13} - 2^{11} \div 2^2$

32. Simplify: $\{7^2 \times 7^3\} \div 7^8 \times 7^2 + 4^2 - 3^2$

33. Find the square root of the following.
(i) 2025 (ii) $(2)^{36} \times (3)^{62} \times (7)^{34}$

34. Find the square root of the following.
(i) $256 \div 289$ (ii) (625)(361)

35. Simplify:
(i) $\sqrt{196} - \sqrt{81}$
(ii) $(\sqrt{484} + \sqrt{64}) \div (\sqrt{400} - \sqrt{121})$

36. Find the cube root of the following.
(i) 27000 (ii) $(2)^{63} \times (3)^{66} \times (7)^{69}$

37. Find the cube root of the following.
(i) $(512) \div 1331$ (ii) (343) (1728)

Direction for questions 38 and 39: Compute the following.

38. (i) $\sqrt{10.24}$ (ii) $\sqrt{0.1225}$

39. (i) $\sqrt[3]{1.728}$ (ii) $\sqrt[3]{0.729}$

40. In a school, there is certain number of classrooms. The number of benches in each classroom is equal to that of classrooms. If the total number of benches in all the classrooms is equal to 196, then find the number of benches in each classroom. (The number of classrooms is the square root of the total number of benches)

41. The total surface area of a solid cube is equal to 6 times the square of the edge of the cube. If the total surface area of the cube is 384 sq. cm. Find the length of the edge of the cube in cm.

42. The volume of a solid dice is equal to the cube of its edge. If the volume of the dice is equal to 125 cubic cm, then find the length of the edge of the cube in cm.

CONCEPT APPLICATION

1. How many natural numbers are there from 10^2 to 20^2?
(a) 299 (b) 300
(c) 301 (d) 400

2. $\sqrt{0.64} - \sqrt{0.0064} + \sqrt{6.4} \div \sqrt{0.064} =$ ________.
(a) 10.88 (b) 9.88
(c) 9.72 (d) 10.72

3. $\sqrt[3]{2\sqrt{0.25}} =$ ________.
(a) 0.5 (b) 0.05
(c) 0.005 (d) 1

4. $\left[\left\{\left(\frac{2}{3}\right)^{-2} \times \left(\frac{256}{625}\right)^{\frac{1}{2}}\right\}^{\frac{-1}{2}} \div \left(\left(\frac{4}{3}\right)^{-2}\right)^{3}\right] \times \left(\frac{1}{0.1}\right)^{-1} =$ ________.
(a) $\frac{4^5}{3^7}$ (b) $\frac{4^5}{3^7}$ (c) $\frac{4^6}{3^5}$ (d) $\frac{3^5}{4^6}$

5. A farmer wants to convert his rectangular field into a square shaped field of the same area. The length and the breadth of the field is 54 m and 24 m, respectively. After conversion, what is the side of the square field?
(a) 24 m (b) 36 m (c) 48 m (d) 54 m

ASSESSMENT TEST

1. Prime factorize the following.
   (i) 480 (ii) 729
2. Evaluate the following using laws of exponents.
   (i) $5^3 \times 5^5$
   (ii) $(-2)^{12} \div (-2)^7$
   (iii) $(2/3)^{35} \times (2/3)^{31}$
   (iv) $(5/7)^{65} \div (5/7)^{32}$
3. Simplify $(15^2 + 20^2)^2$ and express in exponential form.
4. Simplify $5^2 + 5^{13} \div 5^9$ of 5^4.

Direction for questions from 5 to 7: Compute the following.

5. $\sqrt{1296}$
6. $\sqrt{17.64}$
7. $\sqrt[3]{5.832}$
8. The area of a square shaped tile is equal to the square of the length of the side of the tile and it is equal to 1.44 sq. ft. Find the length of the side of the tile in feet.
9. A number, x is a perfect cube. What are the possible digits in the unit's place of x?
10. Determine the exponents of -4 which will make it a positive result.
11. What will be the exponent of 5 which will make the result 625?
12. If a painting of area 144 sq. m covers the area of a square frame, then what is the length of the frame?
13. Find the cube of the following:
    (i) 13 (ii) -13
14. Write the exponent of 4 so that the result is 1024.
15. Identify the base and exponent of the following:
    (i) $-(2)^4$ (ii) $(-2)^4$

CROSSWORD

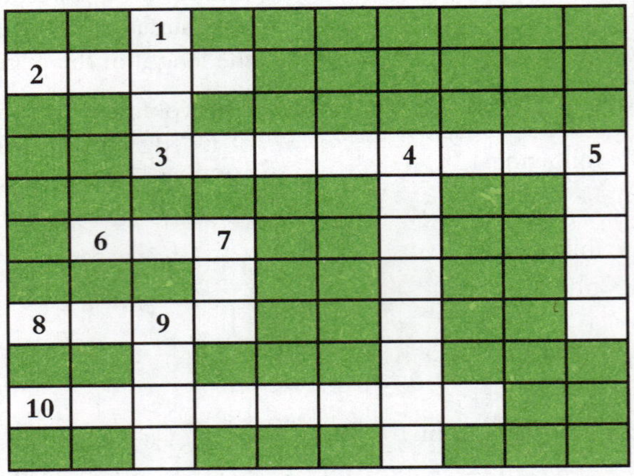

Across

2. The square root of the 'area of a square'
3. In 2^5, the position of 5 is
6. The least number to be multiplied to 18 so that the product is perfect square
8. The result, when a number is multiplied by the square of the number
10. The result, when a negative number is raised to the power of even integer

Down

1. The cube root of the 'volume of a cube'
4. The result, when a negative number is raised to the power of odd integer
5. The least number by which 81 should be divided to get a perfect cube
7. The result, when a rational number is raised to the power of non-negative and non-positive
9. In 2^5, the position of 2 is

TEST YOUR CONCEPTS

Very Short Answer Type Questions

1. 100
2. 1
3. 999
4. 0
5. 1
6. (c)
7. (b)
8. (d)
9. (d)
10. (c)
11. (a) → (r); (b) → (q); (c) → (s); (d) → (p)
12. 64
13. 121
14. 729
15. 39
16. 7
17. (b)
18. (d)
19. (b)
20. (c)
21. (a)
22. (a) → (s); (b) → (p); (c) → (q); (d) → (r)

Short Answer Type Questions

23. (a) Base = 72, Exponent = 36
    (b) Base = –8; Exponent = 4
    (c) Base = 8; Exponent = 4
24. (a) $2^3 \times 3^2 \times 5^1$ (b) $3^1 \times 5^2 \times 7^2$
25. (a) –125 (b) 64
    (c) $\frac{27}{1331}$ (d) $\frac{64}{729}$
26. 81
27. (a) $(3/11)^{24}$ (b) $(5)^3 \times (2)^4$
28. $2^6 \times 3^6$
29. 6
30. 105
31. 2^6
32. $7\frac{1}{7}$
33. (a) 45 (b) $(2)^{18} \times (3)^{31} \times (7)^{17}$
34. (a) 16/17 (b) 475
35. (a) 5 (b) $\frac{10}{3}$
36. (a) 30 (b) $(2)^{21} \times (3)^{22} \times (7)^{23}$
37. (a) $\frac{8}{11}$ (b) 84
38. (a) 3.2 (b) 0.35
39. (a) 1.2 (b) 0.9
40. 14
41. 8
42. 5

CONCEPT APPLICATION

1. (c)
2. (d)
3. (d)
4. (a)
5. (b)

ASSESSMENT TEST

1. (a) $2^5 \times 3 \times 5$ (b) 3^6
2. (a) 5^8 (b) $(-2)^5$
   (c) $(2/3)^{66}$ (d) $(5/7)^{33}$
3. 5^8
4. 26
5. 36
6. 4.2
7. 1.8
8. 1.2
9. 0, 1, 2, 3, 4, 5, 6, 7, 8, or 9

CROSSWORD

Across

2. Side
3. Exponent
6. Two
8. Cube
10. Positive

Down

1. Edge
4. Negative
5. Three
7. One
9. Base

TEST YOUR CONCEPTS

Very Short Answer Type Questions

1. $(-1)^{\text{even}} = 1$

$1^1 + (-1)^2 + 1^3 + (-1)^4 + \dots\dots\dots + 1^{99} + (-1)^{100}$

$= 1 + 1 + 1 + \dots.. + 1$ (100 times) $= 100$

2. $(99)^{37} \times (99)^{-14} \times (99)^3 \times (99)^{-26}$

$= (99)^{37-14+3-26} = (99)^{40-40} = (99)^0 = 1$

3. $[(999)^9 \times (999)^{90} \times (999)^{900}] \div (999)^{998}$

$= [(999)^{9+90+900}] \div (999)^{998}$

$= (999)^{999} \div (999)^{998} = (999)^{999-998} = 999$

4. $(2^2)^3 - (-2^3)^2 = (4)^3 - (-8)^2 = 64 - 64 = 0$

5. $[99^1 + 98^2 + 97^3 + \dots\dots\dots + 3^{97} + 2^{98} + 1^{99}]^0 = 1$, since $a^0 = 1$.

6. Choice (a): $(-2)^4\ (3)^5$ = (positive)(positive) = positive

Choice (b): $(-3)^3\ (-2)^5$ = (negative)(negative) = positive

Choice (c): $(-2)^2\ (-3)^3$ = (positive)(negative) = negative

Choice (d): $(2)^5\ (-3)^2$ = (positive)(positive) = positive

Hence, the correct option is (c).

7. $6^2 - 2^2 = 36 - 4 = 32$

$7^2 - 4^2 = 49 - 16 = 33$

$8^2 - 6^2 = 64 - 36 = 28$

$9^2 - 8^2 = 81 - 64 = 17$

$\therefore$ $7^2 - 4^2$ is the greatest number.

Hence, the correct option is (b).

8. $2^6 = 64 = 4^3$ and $3^4 = 9^2$

Hence, the correct option is (d).

9. $3^6 - 3^4 \times 3^2 = 3^6 - 3^{4+2} = 3^6 - 3^6 = 0$

Hence, the correct option is (d).

10. $2^{12} = 4096$; $4^6 = 4096$; $16^3 = 4096$; $8^5 = 2^{15}$

Hence, the correct option is (c).

11. (a) $[2^9 \times 2^{12}] \div 2^5 = 2^{21} \div 2^5 = 2^{21-5} = 2^{16} \rightarrow$ (r)

(b) $[2^{19} \times 2^{14}] \div 2^{20} = 2^{33} \div 2^{20} = 2^{33-20} = 2^{13} \rightarrow$ (q)

(c) $[2^{17} \times 2^{18}] \div 2^{16} = 2^{35} \div 2^{16} = 2^{35-16} = 2^{19} \rightarrow$ (s)

(d) $[2^6 \times 2^{12}] \div 2^8 = 2^{18} \div 2^8 = 2^{18-8} = 2^{10} \rightarrow$ (p)

Therefore, the correct match is:

(a) $\rightarrow$ (r); (b) $\rightarrow$ (q); (c) $\rightarrow$ (s); (d) $\rightarrow$ (p)

12. The smallest perfect square and perfect cube natural number other than 1 is $64 = 8^2 = 4^3$.

13. The square of the smallest 2-digit natural number, which has same digits, is $11^2 = 121$.

14. The cube of the greatest single digit natural number is $9^3 = 729$.

15. The sum of the square roots of all the 2-digit perfect squares

$= \sqrt{16} + \sqrt{25} + \sqrt{36} + \sqrt{49} + \sqrt{64} + \sqrt{81}$

$= 4 + 5 + 6 + 7 + 8 + 9$

$= 39$

16. The sum of the cube roots of all the 2-digit perfect cubes

$= \sqrt{27} + \sqrt{64}$

$= 3 + 4$

$= 7$

17. $1^2 = 1^3$

Hence, the correct option is (b).

18. 91 is not a perfect square.

Hence, the correct option is (d).

19. $\sqrt{9 + 7} = \sqrt{16} = 4$ is a true statement.

Hence, the correct option is (b).

20. $\sqrt[3]{829 - 486} = \sqrt[3]{343} = \sqrt[3]{7^3} = 7$

Hence, the correct option is (c).

21. $\sqrt[3]{3^3 + 4^3 + 5^3} = \sqrt[3]{27 + 64 + 125} = \sqrt[3]{216}$

$= \sqrt[3]{6^3} = 6 = \sqrt{36}$

Hence, the correct option is (a).

HINTS AND EXPLANATION

Algebra

50. (a) $\sqrt[3]{2^9 \times 3^{12}} = 2^{9/3} \times 3^{12/3} = 2^3 \times 3^4 \to$ (s)

(b) $\sqrt[2]{2^{12} \times 3^8} = 2^{12/2} \times 3^{8/2} = 2^6 \times 3^4 \to$ (p)

(c) $\sqrt[3]{2^{12} \times 3^9} = 2^{12/3} \times 3^{9/3} = 2^4 \times 3^3 \to$ (q)

(d) $\sqrt[2]{2^8 \times 3^{12}} = 2^{8/2} \times 3^{12/2} = 2^4 \times 3^6 \to$ (r)

Therefore, the correct match is:

(a) → (s), (b) → (p), (c) → (q), (d) → (r)

Short Answer Type Questions

23. (a) $(72)^{36}$

∴ Base = 72; Exponent = 36

(b) $(-8)^4$

∴ Base = −8; Exponent = 4

(c) 8^4

∴ Base = 8; Exponent = 4

24. (a) $360 = 2 \times 180$
$= 2 \times 2 \times 90$
$= 2 \times 2 \times 2 \times 45$
$= 2 \times 2 \times 2 \times 3 \times 15$
$= 2^3 \times 3^2 \times 5^1$

(b) $3675 = 3 \times 1225$
$= 3 \times 5 \times 245 = 3 \times 5 \times 5 \times 49$
$= 3 \times 5 \times 5 \times 7 \times 7 = 3^1 \times 5^2 \times 7^2$

25. (a) $(-5)^3 = (-5)(-5)(-5) = -125$

(b) $(-2)^6 = (-2)(-2)(-2)(-2)(-2)(-2) = 64$

(c) $\left(\frac{3}{11}\right)^3 = \left(\frac{3}{11}\right)\left(\frac{3}{11}\right)\left(\frac{3}{11}\right) = \frac{27}{1331}$

(d) $\left(\frac{2}{3}\right)^6 = \left(\frac{2}{3}\right)\left(\frac{2}{3}\right)\left(\frac{2}{3}\right)\left(\frac{2}{3}\right)\left(\frac{2}{3}\right)\left(\frac{2}{3}\right) = \frac{64}{729}$

26. The exponent is the smallest composite number which is 4 and the base is the smallest odd prime number which is 3.

The required expression is $3^4 = 81$.

27. (a) We have $a^m \times a^n = a^{m+n}$

$(3/11)^5 \times (3/11)^6 \times (3/11)^{13} = (3/11)^{5+6+13}$
$= (3/11)^{24}$

(b) We have $a^m \div a^n = a^{m-n}$

$[(10)^{14} \times (5)^{17} \times (2)^{20}] \div [(10)^{13} \times (5)^{15} \times (2)^{17}]$
$= (10)^{14-13} \times (5)^{17-15} \times (2)^{20-17}$
$= (10)^1 \times (5)^2 \times (2)^3 = (5 \times 2) \times (5)^2 \times (2)^3$
$= (5)^{1+2} \times (2)^{1+3} = 5^3 \times 2^4$

28. $[2^3 + 4^3 + 5^3]^2 = [27 + 64 + 125]^2$
$= [216]^2 = [2^3 \times 3^3]^2$
$= [2^3 \times 3^3][2^3 \times 3^3]$
$= 2^{3+3} \times 3^{3+3} = 2^6 \times 3^6$

29. $21600 = (216)(100)$
$= (2^3 \times 3^3)(2^2 \times 5^2) = 2^{3+2} \times 3^3 \times 5^2$
$= 2^5 \times 3^3 \times 5^2$

$21600 = 2^5 \times 3^3 \times 5^2$
$= (2^4 \times 3^2 \times 5^2)(2 \times 3)$
$= (2^4 \times 3^2 \times 5^2)(6)$

The required number = 6

30. $13125 = 3^1 \times 5^4 \times 7^1 = [3^2 \times 5^5 \times 7^2] \div [3 \times 5 \times 7]$
$= [3^2 \times 5^5 \times 7^2] \div 105$

The required number = 105

31. $2^6 \times 2^3 + 2^{19} \div 2^{13} - 2^{11} \div 2^2$
$= 2^6 \times 2^3 + 2^{19-13} - 2^{11-2} = 2^6 \times 2^3 + 2^6 - 2^9$
$= 2^{6+3} + 2^6 - 2^9 = 2^9 + 2^6 - 2^9 = 2^6$

32. $\{7^2 \times 7^3\} \div 7^8 \times 7^2 + 4^2 - 3^2$
$= \{7^{2+3}\} \div 7^8 \times 7^2 + 4^2 - 3^2$
$= 7^5 \div 7^8 \times 7^2 + 4^2 - 3^2$
$= 7^7 \div 7^8 + 16 - 9 = 1 \div 7 + 7$
$= \frac{1}{7} + 7 = 7\frac{1}{7}$

22. $\frac{2x}{3} + 4 = \frac{8}{3}(2x - 6)$

$\frac{2x}{3} + 4 = \frac{16x}{3} - 16 \Rightarrow 4 + 16 = \frac{16x}{3} - \frac{2x}{3}$

$20 = \frac{16 - 2x}{3} \Rightarrow 20 = \frac{14x}{3}$

$20 \times 3 = 14x \Rightarrow 60 = 14x$

$\frac{60}{14} = x \Rightarrow x = \frac{30}{7}$

$\therefore x = \frac{30}{7}$

51. (i) A number is doubled and added to 6, the result is equal to 14.

Let the number be x.

Double the number = $2x$

It is added to 6.

$\Rightarrow 2x + 6$

The result is equal to 14.

$\Rightarrow 2x + 6 = 14$

(ii) Let the number be x.

$\frac{3}{5}$ of the number = $\frac{3x}{5}$

Given that $x + \frac{3x}{5} = 24$

(iii) Let the present age of the man be x years. 20 years ago the age of the man = $(x - 20)$ years

Given that $(x - 20) = \frac{x}{2}$

52. Let the three consecutive natural numbers be $(x - 1)$, (x) and $(x + 1)$.

Given that:

$(x - 1) + (x) + (x + 1) = 90$

$x - 1 + x + x + 1 = 90$

$x = \frac{90}{3}$

$x = 30$

∴ The three numbers are $30 - 1 = 29$, 30 and $30 + 1 = 31$.

∴ The greatest number is 31.

53. Let the breadth of the rectangle be x cm.

Length of the rectangle = $(x + 5)$ cm

Perimeter of the rectangle = $2(\ell + b) = 42$ cm

$2(x + 5 + x) = 42 \Rightarrow 2x + 5 = \frac{42}{2}$

$2x + 5 = 21 \Rightarrow 2x = 21 - 5$

$x = \frac{16}{2} \Rightarrow x = 8$ cm

∴ Length of the rectangle = $x + 5 = 8 + 5 = 13$ cm

54. Let the cost of the burger be ₹x.

The cost of the pizza = $\left(2 + \frac{1}{2}\right)(x) = \frac{5}{2}x$

Given that:

$\frac{5x}{2} + x = 105 \Rightarrow \frac{5x + 2x}{2} = 105$

$\frac{7x}{2} = 105 \Rightarrow x = \frac{105 \times 2}{7}$

$x = 15 \times 2 \Rightarrow x = 30$

∴ The cost of the burger = ₹30.

55. Let the expenditure of Chintu be ₹x.

Savings of Chintu = $\frac{1}{3} \times x = \frac{x}{3}$

Chintu's pocket money = $x + \frac{x}{3}$

$x + \frac{x}{3} = 120 \Rightarrow \frac{3x + x}{3} = 120$

$\frac{4x}{3} = 120$

$4x = 120 \times 3$

$x = \frac{120 \times 3}{4}$

$x = 30 \times 3 = 90$

∴ Savings of Chintu = $\frac{x}{3} = \frac{90}{3} = ₹30$

56. Let the number of chocolates with Rani be x.

Number of chocolates given to her brother = $\frac{2}{5}x$

Number of chocolates given to her sister = $\frac{1}{3}x$

Number of chocolates left with her = 20

ASSESSMENT TEST

1. (a) $480 = 2 \times 240$
$= 2 \times 2 \times 120$
$= 2 \times 2 \times 2 \times 60$
$= 2 \times 2 \times 2 \times 2 \times 30$
$= 2 \times 2 \times 2 \times 2 \times 2 \times 15$
$= 2 \times 2 \times 2 \times 2 \times 2 \times 3 \times 5$
$= 2^5 \times 3 \times 5$

(b) $729 = 3 \times 243$
$= 3 \times 3 \times 81$
$= 3 \times 3 \times 3 \times 27$
$= 3 \times 3 \times 3 \times 3 \times 9$
$= 3 \times 3 \times 3 \times 3 \times 3 \times 3$
$= 3^6$

2. (a) $5^3 \times 5^5 = 5^{3+5} = 5^8$
$(a^m \times a^n = a^{m+n})$

(b) $(-2)^{12} \div (-2)^7 = (-2)^{12-7}$
$= (-2)^5$
$(a^m \div a^n = a^{m-n})$

(c) $(2/3)^{35} \times (2/3)^{31}$
$= (2/3)^{35+31} = (2/3)^{66}$
$(a^m \times a^n = a^{m+n})$

(d) $(5/7)^{65} \div (5/7)^{32} = (5/7)^{65-32}$
$= (5/7)^{33}$
$(a^m \div a^n = a^{m-n})$

3. $(15^2 + 20^2)^2 = (225 + 400)^2$
$= (625)^2 = (5^4)^2 = (5^4)(5^4)$
$= 5^{4+4} = 5^8$
$(a^m \times a^n = a^{m+n})$

4. $5^2 + 5^{13} \div 5^9$ of $5^4 = 5^2 + 5^{13} \div (5^9 \times 5^4)$
$= 5^2 + 5^{13} \div (5^{9+4})$
$= 5^2 + 5^{13} \div 5^{13}$
$= 25 + 1 = 26$

5. $\sqrt{1296} = \sqrt{2^4 \times 3^4}$
$= 2^{4/2} \times 3^{4/2}$
$= 2^2 \times 3^2 = 36$

6. $\sqrt{17.64} = \sqrt{(1764/100)}$
$= \sqrt{(2^2 \times 3^2 \times 7^2)/10^2} = (2 \times 3 \times 7)/10$
$= 42/10 = 4.2$

7. $\sqrt[3]{5.832} = \sqrt[3]{(5832/1000)}$
$= \sqrt[3]{(2^3 \times 3^6)/10^3}$
$= (2^{3/3} \times 3^{6/3})/10^{3/3}$
$= (2 \times 3^2)/10$
$= 18/10$
$= 1.8$

8. Given that the area of a square shaped tile (the square of the side) = 1.44 sq. ft.

∴ The length of the side of the tile $= \sqrt{1.44}$
$= \sqrt{(144/100)} = \sqrt{\left(\frac{12^2}{10^2}\right)} = 12/10 = 1.2$ ft

9. $1^3 = 1;\ 2^3 = 8;\ 3^3 = 27;\ 4^3 = 64;\ 5^3 = 125;\ 6^3 = 216;\ 7^3 = 343;\ 8^3 = 512;\ 9^3 = 729;\ 10^3 = 1000$

∴ The possible digits in the unit's place of a perfect cube are 0, 1, 2, 3, 4, 5, 6, 7, 8 or 9.

10. Even

11. 4

12. 12

13. (a) 2197 (b) −2197

14. 5

15. (a) base = 2; exponent = 4

(b) base = −2; exponent = 4

$\Rightarrow x - \frac{2x}{5} - \frac{x}{3} = 20 \Rightarrow \frac{15x - 6x - 5x}{15} = 20$

$\frac{4x}{15} = 20 \Rightarrow 4x = 20 \times 15$

$x = \frac{20 \times 15}{4}$

$\Rightarrow x = 5 \times 15$

$\Rightarrow x = 75$

∴ The number of chocolates with Rani = 75

CONCEPT APPLICATION

1. Given that,

$A = 2x^3 - 3x^2 - 4x + 5$

$2B = 2(2x^2 - x^3 + x + 1) = 4x^2 - 2x^3 + 2x + 2$

$C = x^2 + x + 2$

$A + 2B - C = (2x^3 - 3x^2 - 4x + 5) + (4x^2 - 2x^3 + 2x + 2) - (x^2 + x + 2)$
$= -3x + 5$

The degree of A + 2B − C is 1.
Hence, the correct option is (b).

2. $3x^2 - [7x - \{5x^2 - (2x - 3)(4x - 2) - 5\} - 2]$
$= 3x^2 - [7x - \{5x^2 - (8x^2 - 4x - 12x + 6) - 5\} - 2]$
$= 3x^2 - [7x - \{5x^2 - (8x^2 - 16x + 6) - 5\} - 2]$
$= 3x^2 - [7x - \{5x^2 - (8x^2 - 16x + 6) - 5\} - 2]$
$= 3x^2 - [7x - \{5x^2 - 8x^2 + 16x - 6 - 5\} - 2]$
$= 3x^2 - [7x - \{5x^2 - 8x^2 + 16x - 6 - 5\} - 2]$
$= 3x^2 - [7x - \{-3x^2 + 16x - 11\} - 2]$
$= 3x^2 - [7x - \{-3x^2 + 16x - 11\} - 2]$
$= 3x^2 - [7x + 3x^2 - 16x + 11 - 2]$
$= 3x^2 - [3x^2 - 9x + 9]$
$= 3x^2 - 3x^2 + 9x - 9$
$= 9x - 9$
Hence, the correct option is (a).

3. Let x, y and z be the number of ₹1 coins, ₹2 coins and ₹5 coins, respectively.

Given, $y = 2x$
$z = 3y = 3(2x) = 6x$
$1(x) + 2(y) + 5(z) = ₹700$
$1x + 2(2x) + 5(6x) = ₹700$
$x + 4x + 30x = ₹700$
$35x = ₹700$
$x = 20$
$y = 2 \times 20 = 40$
$z = 6 \times 20 = 120$

The total number of coins $= x + y + z = 20 + 40 + 120 = 180$

Hence, the correct option is (c).

4. Given, AB = $(2x + 3y + 10)$ cm, BC = $(2x + 3y - 5)$ m, CD = $(4x + 3y + 6)$ cm and DA = $(2x - 3y + 7)$ cm

We know that, in a rectangle the opposite sides are equal.

AB = CD
$2x + 3y + 10 = 4x + 3y + 6$
$4x - 2x = 10 - 6$
$2x = 4$
$x = 2$

BC = DA
$2x + 3y - 5 = 2x - 3y + 7$
$3y + 3y = 7 + 5$
$6y = 12$

5. Let the number of flowers with Satya be x.

The number of flowers with Rukku $= \frac{3}{4}x$

Total number of flowers $= x + \frac{3x}{4} = 35$

$\frac{7x}{4} = 35 \Rightarrow 7x = 35 \times 4$

$7x = 140 \Rightarrow x = \frac{140}{7} \Rightarrow x = 20$

The number of flowers with Satya = 20

25. (a) $\sqrt[3]{2^9 \times 3^{12}} = 2^{9/3} \times 3^{12/3} = 2^3 \times 3^4 \rightarrow$ (s)

(b) $\sqrt[2]{2^{12} \times 3^8} = 2^{12/2} \times 3^{8/2} = 2^6 \times 3^4 \rightarrow$ (p)

(c) $\sqrt[3]{2^{12} \times 3^9} = 2^{12/3} \times 3^{9/3} = 2^4 \times 3^3 \rightarrow$ (q)

(d) $\sqrt{2^8 \times 3^{12}} = 2^{8/2} \times 3^{12/2} = 2^4 \times 3^6 \rightarrow$ (r)

Therefore, the correct match is:

(a) $\rightarrow$ (s), (b) $\rightarrow$ (p), (c) $\rightarrow$ (q), (d) $\rightarrow$ (r)

Short Answer Type Questions

26. (a) $(72)^{36}$ $\therefore$ Base = 72; Exponent = 36

(b) $(-8)^4$ $\therefore$ Base = −8; Exponent = 4

(c) 8^4 $\therefore$ Base = 8; Exponent = 4

27. (a) $360 = 2 \times 180$
$= 2 \times 2 \times 90$
$= 2 \times 2 \times 2 \times 45$
$= 2 \times 2 \times 2 \times 3 \times 15$
$= 2^3 \times 3^2 \times 5^1$

(b) $3675 = 3 \times 1225$
$= 3 \times 5 \times 245 = 3 \times 5 \times 5 \times 49$
$= 3 \times 5 \times 5 \times 7 \times 7 = 3^1 \times 5^2 \times 7^2$

28. $[3^3 + 4^3 + 5^3]^2 = [27 + 64 + 125]^2$
$= [216]^2 = [2^3 \times 3^3]^2$
$= [2^3 \times 3^3][2^3 \times 3^3]$
$= 2^{3+3} \times 3^{3+3} = 2^6 \times 3^6$

29. $21600 = (216)(100)$
$= (2^3 \times 3^3)(2^2 \times 5^2) = 2^{3+2} \times 3^3 \times 5^2$
$= 2^5 \times 3^3 \times 5^2$

$21600 = 2^5 \times 3^3 \times 5^2$
$= (2^4 \times 3^2 \times 5^2)(2 \times 3)$
$= (2^4 \times 3^2 \times 5^2)(6)$

The required number = 6

30. $13125 = 3^1 \times 5^4 \times 7^1 = [3^2 \times 5^5 \times 7^2] \div [3 \times 5 \times 7]$
$= [3^2 \times 5^5 \times 7^2] \div 105$

The required number = 105

31. $2^6 \times 2^3 + 2^{19} \div 2^{13} - 2^{11} \div 2^2$
$= 2^6 \times 2^3 + 2^{19-13} - 2^{11-2} = 2^6 \times 2^3 + 2^6 - 2^9$
$= 2^{6+3} + 2^6 - 2^9 = 2^9 + 2^6 - 2^9 = 2^6$

32. $\{7^2 \times 7^3\} \div 7^8 \times 7^2 + 4^2 - 3^2$
$= \{7^{2+3}\} \div 7^8 \times 7^2 + 4^2 - 3^2$
$= 7^5 \div 7^8 \times 7^2 + 4^2 - 3^2$
$= 7^{-3} \times 7^2 + 16 - 9 = 7^{-1} + 7 = \frac{1}{7} + 7 = 7\frac{1}{7}$

25. (a) $(-5)^3 = (-5)(-5)(-5) = -125$

(b) $(-2)^6 = (-2)(-2)(-2)(-2)(-2)(-2) = 64$

(c) $\left(\frac{3}{11}\right)^3 = \left(\frac{3}{11}\right)\left(\frac{3}{11}\right)\left(\frac{3}{11}\right) = \frac{27}{1331}$

(d) $\left(\frac{2}{3}\right)^1 \left(\frac{2}{3}\right)^2 \left(\frac{2}{3}\right)^3 = \left(\frac{2}{3}\right)\left(\frac{2}{3}\right)\left(\frac{2}{3}\right)\left(\frac{2}{3}\right)\left(\frac{2}{3}\right)\left(\frac{2}{3}\right) = \frac{64}{729}$

26. The exponent is the smallest composite number which is 4 and the base is the smallest odd prime number which is 3.

The required expression is $3^4 = 81$.

27. (a) We have $a^m \times a^n = a^{m+n}$

$(3/11)^5 \times (3/11)^6 \times (3/11)^{13} = (3/11)^{5+6+13}$
$= (3/11)^{24}$

(b) We have $a^m \div a^n = a^{m-n}$

$[(10)^{14} \times (5)^{17} \times (2)^{20}] \div [(10)^{13} \times (5)^{15} \times (2)^{17}]$
$= (10)^{14-13} \times (5)^{17-15} \times (2)^{20-17}$
$= (10)^1 \times (5)^2 \times (2)^3 = (5 \times 2) \times (5)^2 \times (2)^3$
$= (5)^{1+2} \times (2)^{1+3} = (5)^3 \times (2)^4$

22. (a) $\frac{3x}{5} + \frac{7x}{5} = 2 \Rightarrow \frac{3x + 7x}{5} = 2$

$\Rightarrow \frac{10x}{5} = 2 \Rightarrow 2x = 2$

$x = 1$

Hence, the correct option is (c).

23. (a) $2x - 7 = 15$
$2x = 22$
$x = 11$ (q)

(b) $2x - 15 = 9$
$2x = 24$
$x = 12$ (p)

(c) $2x + 5 = 23$
$2x = 23 - 5$
$2x = 18$

(d) $2x + 4 = 20$
$2x = 20 - 4$
$2x = 16$
$x = 8$ (s)

Therefore, the correct match is:

(a) $\rightarrow$ (q); (b) $\rightarrow$ (p); (c) $\rightarrow$ (r); (d) $\rightarrow$ (s)

26. $2x - 5 = 7 \Rightarrow 2x = 7 + 5$

$2x = 12 \Rightarrow x = \frac{12}{2}$

$x = 6$

27. $12 + x = 18 - x$

$x + x = 18 - 12$

$2x = 6$

$x = 3$

29. $7x + 2 = 8x + 2 \Rightarrow x = 0$.

$\therefore$ The number values is 1.

Hence, the correct option is (b)

31. Let the son's age be x years.

Father's age = $4x$ years

Short Answer Type Questions

33. (i) Coefficient of x in $4xy^2$ is $4y^2$, so the given statement is false.

(ii) The number of terms in the expression $4xy$ is 1, so the given statement is false.

(iii) $x^2y^3 - xy$ is a binominal is true.

(iv) $3x^2 - 2x + \frac{2}{3}$ is a polynomial, so the given statement is false.

34. (i) Like terms: $(4x^4, -9x^4)$, $(-7x^3, 12x^3, 4x^3)$ $(8x^2, 12x^2)$

(ii) Like terms: $(5xy, -3xy)$, $(-3x^2y, 15x^2y)$, $(-2x^2y^2, 5x^2y^2)$

35. (i) $x^{\frac{1}{2}} + y^{\frac{1}{2}} + z^{\frac{1}{2}}$ is not a polynomial since the exponents of the variables are fractions.

(ii) $x^2 + y^2$ is a polynomial.

(iii) $\sqrt{x} + 3$ is not a polynomial, since the variable $\left(\sqrt{x} = x^{\frac{1}{2}}\right)$ has fractional exponent.

(iv) $\sqrt{5} + x^5$ is a polynomial.

(v) 2016 is a polynomial of degree zero. It is a constant polynomial.

36. (i) $3x^5 - 7x^2 + 8x - 2x^8 + 10$ consists of 5 terms and the highest degree term is $-2x^8$. The degree of the polynomial is 8.

(ii) $2x^9 - 3x^2 - 14x^3 - 15x^4$ consists of 4 terms of those the highest degree term is $2x^9$. The degree of the polynomial is 9.

37. (i) In $17x^2y$, the numerical coefficient is 17.

(ii) In $12xy^3$, the numerical coefficient is 12.

(iii) In $\frac{3}{5}x$, the numerical coefficient is $\frac{3}{5}$.

(iv) In $\frac{-3}{2}x^2$, the numerical coefficient is $\frac{-3}{2}$.

38. $x = 3$, $y = 1$

(i) $3x - 2y = 3 \times 3 - 2 \times 1 = 9 - 2 = 7$

HINTS AND EXPLANATION

(ii) $\frac{22}{3}x^2 - \frac{7}{2}y^2 = \frac{22}{3} \times (3)^2 - \frac{7}{2}(1)^2$

$= \frac{22}{3} \times 9 - \frac{7}{2} \times 1 = 66 - \frac{7}{2}$

$= 66 - 3.5 = 62.5$

39. $x = 2,\ y = 3$

(i) $\frac{2x + 3y}{4x - 3y} = \frac{2 \times 2 + 3 \times 3}{4 \times 2 - 3 \times 3} = \frac{4 + 9}{8 - 9} = \frac{13}{-1} = -13$

(ii) $\frac{2x^2 - 7x + 2y}{2y^2 - 7y + 2x} = \frac{2(2)^2 - 7(2) + 2(3)}{2(3)^2 - 7(3) + 2(2)}$

$= \frac{2 \times 4 - 14 + 6}{2 \times 9 - 21 + 4} = \frac{8 - 8}{18 - 17} = \frac{0}{1} = 0$

40. $A + B - C = (2x + 3xy + 7x^2) + (3x - 2xy - 5x^2) - (2xy - 6x^2 - 3x)$

$= 2x + 3xy + 7x^2 + 3x - 2xy - 5x^2 - 2xy + 6x^2 + 3x$

$= (2x + 3x + 3x) + (3xy - 2xy - 2xy) + (7x^2 - 5x^2 + 6x^2)$

$= 8x + (3xy - 4xy) + (13x^2 - 5x^2)$

$= 8x - 1xy + 8x^2$

41. $(12x)\left(5x - \frac{3}{2}\right) = (12x)(5x) - (12x)\left(\frac{3}{2}\right)$

$= 60x^2 - 6x \times 3 = 60x^2 - 18x$

42. $(2x + 3)(3x - 2) = 2x(3x) - 2x(2) + 3(3x) - 3(2)$

$= 6x^2 - 4x + 9x - 6$

$= 6x^2 + 5x - 6$

43. Let $f(x)$ should be added to $2xy - 3x^2 + 6$, so that the sum is $4x^2 - 7xy + 15$.

$f(x) = 4x^2 - 7xy + 15 - (2xy - 3x^2 + 6)$

$= 4x^2 - 7xy + 15 - 2xy + 3x^2 - 6$

$= (4x^2 + 3x^2) + (-7xy - 2xy) + (15 - 6)$

$= 7x^2 - 9xy + 9$

44. Let $f(x)$ should be subtracted from $\frac{3}{2}x - \frac{7}{2}$, so that the difference is $\frac{7x}{2} - \frac{3}{2}$.

$f(x) = \frac{3x}{2} - \frac{7}{2} - \left(\frac{7x}{2} - \frac{3}{2}\right)$

$= \frac{3x}{2} - \frac{7}{2} - \frac{7x}{2} + \frac{3}{2} \Rightarrow \frac{-4x}{2} + \left(\frac{-4}{2}\right)$

$f(x) = -2x - 2$

45. $\frac{8x^2 - 12x^3 + 6x}{2x} = \frac{8x^2}{2x} - \frac{12x^3}{2x} + \frac{6x}{2x}$

$= 4x - 6x^2 + 3$

46. $3x - [4x + \{2x - 6(x - 2 - x)\}]$

$= 3x - [4x + \{2x - 6(x - 2 + x)\}]$

$= 3x - [4x + \{2x - 6x + 12 - 6x\}]$

$= 3x - [4x - 10x + 12]$

$= 3x - [-6x + 12]$

$= 3x + 6x - 12$

$= 9x - 12$

47. $\frac{15}{2}x - \frac{4}{3}[6x^2 - 9x(x - 3 - 2x)]$

$= \frac{15}{2}x - \frac{4}{3}[6x^2 - 9x(x - 3 + 2x)]$

$= \frac{15}{2}x - \frac{4}{3}[6x^2 - 9x(3x - 3)]$

$= \frac{15}{2}x - \frac{4}{3}[6x^2 - 27x^2 + 27x]$

$= \frac{15}{2}x - \frac{4}{3}(-21x^2) - \frac{4}{3}27x$

$= \frac{15}{2}x + 28x^2 - 36x = 28x^2 + \frac{15}{2}x - 36x$

$= 28x^2 + \left(\frac{15}{2} - 36\right)x = 28x^2 + \left(\frac{15 - 72}{2}\right)x$

$= 28x^2 - \frac{15}{2}x$

48. $3x + 7 = 18x \Rightarrow 7 = 18x - 3x$

$7 = 15x \Rightarrow x = \frac{7}{15}$

49. $-\frac{x}{4} + 6x = \frac{5}{4} \Rightarrow \frac{5}{4} = 6x - \frac{x}{4}$

$\frac{5}{4} = \frac{24x - x}{4} \Rightarrow \frac{5}{4} = \frac{23x}{4} \Rightarrow 23x = 5$

$x = \frac{5}{23}$

ASSESSMENT TEST

1. (a) $480 = 2 \times 240$

$= 2 \times 2 \times 120$

$= 2 \times 2 \times 2 \times 60$

$= 2 \times 2 \times 2 \times 2 \times 30$

$= 2 \times 2 \times 2 \times 2 \times 2 \times 15$

$= 2 \times 2 \times 2 \times 2 \times 2 \times 3 \times 5$

$= 2^5 \times 3 \times 5$

(b) $729 = 3 \times 243$

$= 3 \times 3 \times 81$

$= 3 \times 3 \times 3 \times 27$

$= 3 \times 3 \times 3 \times 3 \times 9$

$= 3 \times 3 \times 3 \times 3 \times 3 \times 3$

$= 3^6$

2. (a) $5^3 \times 5^5 = 5^{3+5} = 5^8$

$(a^m \times a^n = a^{m+n})$

(b) $(-2)^{12} \div (-2)^7 = (-2)^{12-7} = (-2)^5$

$(a^m \div a^n = a^{m-n})$

(c) $(2/3)^{35} \times (2/3)^{31}$

$= (2/3)^{35+31} = (2/3)^{66}$

(d) $(5/7)^{65} \div (5/7)^{32} = (5/7)^{65-32}$

$= (5/7)^{33}$

$(a^m \div a^n = a^{m-n})$

3. $(15^2 + 20^2)^2 = (225 + 400)^2$

$= (625)^2 = (5^4)^2 = (5^4)(5^4)$

$= 5^{4+4} = 5^8$

$(a^m \times a^n = a^{m+n})$

4. $5^2 + 5^{13} \div 5^9$ of $5^4 = 5^2 + 5^{13} \div (5^9 \times 5^4)$

$= 5^2 + 5^{13} \div (5^{9+4})$

$= 5^2 + 5^{13} \div 5^{13}$

$= 25 + 1 = 26$

5. $\sqrt{1296} = \sqrt{2^4 \times 3^4}$

$= 2^{4/2} \times 3^{4/2}$

$= 2^2 \times 3^2 = 36$

6. $\sqrt{17.64} = \sqrt{(1764/100)}$

$= \sqrt{(2^2 \times 3^2 \times 7^2)/10^2} = (2 \times 3 \times 7)/10$

$= 42/10 = 4.2$

7. $\sqrt[3]{5.832} = \sqrt[3]{(5832/1000)}$

$= \sqrt[3]{(2^3 \times 3^6)/10^3}$

$= (2^{3/3} \times 3^{6/3})/10^{3/3}$

$= (2 \times 3^2)/10$

$= 18/10$

$= 1.8$

8. Given that the area of a square shaped tile (the square of the side) = 1.44 sq. ft.

∴ The length of the side of the tile $= \sqrt{1.44}$

$= \sqrt{(144/100)} = \sqrt{\left(\frac{12^2}{10^2}\right)} = 12/10 = 1.2$ ft

9. $1^3 = 1;\ 2^3 = 8,\ 3^3 = 27;\ 4^3 = 64$

$5^3 = 125;\ 6^3 = 216;\ 7^3 = 343$

$8^3 = 512;\ 9^3 = 729;\ 10^3 = 1000$

∴ The possible digits in the units place of a perfect cube are 0, 1, 2, 3, 4, 5, 6, 7, 8 or 9.

10. Even

11. 4

12. 12

13. (a) 2197 (b) −2197

14. 5

15. (a) base = 2; exponent = 4

(b) base = −2; exponent = 4

Chapter 8

Ratio and Proportion

Geometry

REMEMBER

Before beginning this chapter, you should be able to:

- Recall division of numbers
- Compare numbers
- Recall units of different measures

- Know the names of different geometrical figures
- Identify lines and line segments, angles, triangles, rectangles, squares and circles

KEY IDEAS

After completing this chapter, you should be able to:

- Understand terms of a ratio
- Define properties of a ratio
- Understand simplest form of a ratio
- Describe proportion

- Understand basic concepts: Plane, lines and angles
- Learn about triangles: Types of triangles, properties of triangles, congruence of triangles and construction of triangles
- Learn about circles: Chord, secant, tangent, segment and sector
- Understand symmetry: Line symmetry

INTRODUCTION

Look around yourself and you will find numerous objects with various shapes. For example, when we look at the Sun, it is round in shape, but when we look at notebooks, it is square in shape. We have learnt that Mathematics involves numbers, symbols and algebraic expression. Interestingly, study of Maths is not only about numbers but also shapes. In this chapter, we will learn Geometry which deals with study of various shapes.

BASIC CONCEPTS

The term 'geometry' comes form the combination of two Greek words '*Geo*' (Earth) and '*Metria*' (Measure) meaning measurement of the Earth. Geometry is the study of properties of lines, angles, polygons and circles. We shall begin with some basic concepts.

Info Box!
A polygon is an enclosed figure made up of straight lines!

TABLE 8.1 Classification of polygons on the basis of number of sides

Number of Sides	Name of the Polygon
3	Triangle
4	Quadrilateral
5	Pentagon
6	Hexagon
7	Heptagon
8	Octagon
9	Nonagon
10	Decagon

Plane

A plane is a surface which extends indefinitely in all directions. For example, the surface of a table is a part of a plane. A black board is a part of a plane.

Line

A line is a set of infinite points. It has no end points and it is infinite in length. The figure given shows a line ℓ that extends to infinity on either side. If A and B are any two points on ℓ, we also denote the line ℓ as $\overleftrightarrow{AB}$, read as line AB.

Line Segment

A line segment is a part of a line. The line segment has two end points and it has a finite length.

In the above figure, AB is a line segment of ℓ consisting of the points A, B and all the points of ℓ lie between A and B. The line segment AB is also denoted as $\overline{AB}$. Here, A and B are the end points of $\overline{AB}$.

Ray

A ray has one end point and it extends infinitely on the other side.

Chapter 5

Product of means = 18 × 10 = 180

Product of extremes = Product of means

Product of extremes = 12 × 15 = 180

∴ 12, 18, 10, 15 are in proportion.

Find the value of x, if 2, 16, 5 and x are in proportion.

SOLUTION

Given that 2, 16, 5, x are in proportion

Product of extremes = Product of means

$2x = 16 \times 5$

$$x = \frac{16 \times 5}{2} = 8 \times 5 \Rightarrow x = 40$$

EXAMPLE 5.6

In a milk solution, water and milk are in the ratio of 2 : 15. If the quantity of pure milk is 6 L, then find the quantity of water in the solution.

SOLUTION

Let the quantity of water be x L.

$2 : 15 : : x : 6 \Rightarrow 2 \times 6 = 15 \times x \Rightarrow 12 = 15x$

$$\therefore x = \frac{12}{15} = \frac{4}{5} = 0.8 \text{ L} = 800 \text{ mL}$$

∴ The quantity of water in the solution = 800 mL.

Info Box!
The Golden Ratio is a unique number approximately equal to 1.618. Famous building, Parthenon in Greece has the Golden Ratio in it.

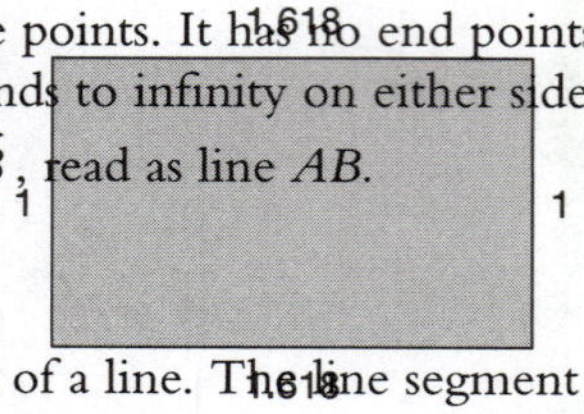

FIGURE 5.1 Golden rectangle with side lengths in Golden Ratio

Direct and Inverse Proportions

When a decrease or increase in a quantity directly results in corresponding decrease or increase in second quantity, then the two quantities are in direct proportion.

$y = 2$

Side AB $= 2x + 3y + 10 = 2(2) + 3(2) + 10$

$= 4 + 6 + 10 = 20$ cm

Side BC $= 2x + 3y - 5 = 2(2) + 3(2) - 5$

$= 4 + 6 - 5 = 5$ cm

Therefore, the perimeter of the rectangle

$= 2(AB + BC) = 2(20 + 5) = 50$ cm

Hence, the correct option is (c).

5. Let the amount with Mohan be 'x'.

The amount received by Vijay $= (1/3)x$

The amount received by Suresh

$= (2/5)$th $\times$ $(2/3)$rd x

The amount received by Venkat

$= (1/6)$th $\times$ $(3/5)$th $\times$ $(2/3)$rd x

The amount left with Mohan

$= (5/6)$th $\times$ $(3/5)$th $\times$ $(2/3)$rd x

₹3000 $= (5/6)$th $\times$ $(3/5)$th $\times$ $(2/3)$rd x

₹3000 $= 1/3\ x$

$x =$ ₹9000

The amount received by Suresh

$= (2/5)$th $\times$ $(2/3)$rd $\times 9000$

$=$ ₹2400

The amount received by Venkat

$=(1/6)$th $\times$ $(3/5)$th $\times$ $(2/3)$rd $\times 9000$

$=$ ₹600

The sum of amounts received by Suresh and Venkat $=$ ₹2400 $+$ ₹600 $=$ ₹3000

Hence, the correct option is (a).

ASSESSMENT TEST

1. (i) $2018x^{2019}$ is a monomial.

(ii) $x + 2019$ is a binomial.

(iii) $2017x$ is a monomial.

(iv) $\sqrt{3}\,x + \sqrt{5} + y$ is a trinomial.

2. (i) $2017x^7 + 2018x^6 + 2019x^5$

The highest exponent of the variable x is 7.

$\therefore$ Degree of the given polynomial is 7.

(ii) $x^2y - x^3y + xy^3 - x^2y^3$

Since it is a polynomial of two variables, the degree of the term is the sum of the exponents of the variables.

$\therefore$ The highest degree term is $-x^2y^3$.

$\therefore$ The degree of the polynomial is $2 + 3 = 5$

(iii) 2018 is a constant polynomial. Hence, its degree is zero.

3. (i) 5 times of x is $5x$.

3 times of y is $3y$.

If 5 times of x is added to 3 times of y, then the expression is $5x + 3y$.

(ii) One and half times $x = 1\frac{1}{2}x = \frac{3}{2}x$

Three and half times of $y = 3\frac{1}{2}y = \frac{7}{2}y$

One and half times of x subtracted from three and half times of y is $\frac{7}{2}y - \frac{3}{2}x$.

4. $x = 5,\ y = -2$

(i) $\dfrac{8x - 2y + 5}{2x + 4y - 10} = \dfrac{8\times 5 - 2\times(-2) + 5}{2\times 5 + 4(-2) - 10}$

$= \dfrac{40 + 4 + 5}{10 - 8 + 12}$

$= \dfrac{49}{14} = \dfrac{7}{2}$

(ii) $\dfrac{5x - 6y - 7}{3x + 6y + 12} = \dfrac{5\times 5 - 6(-2) - 7}{3\times 5 + 6(-2) + 12}$

$= \dfrac{25 + 12 - 7}{15 - 12 + 12}$

$= \dfrac{30}{5} = 2$

HINTS AND EXPLANATION

Chapter 5 Ratio and Proportion

REMEMBER

Before beginning this chapter, you should be able to:

- Recall division of numbers
- Compare numbers
- Recall units of different measures

KEY IDEAS

After completing this chapter, you should be able to:

- Understand terms of a ratio
- Define properties of a ratio
- Understand simplest form of a ratio
- Describe proportion

5. Let $f(x)$ be added to $7x + 5 - 8x^2$ to get $15x + 9x^2 - 5$.

$\therefore f(x) = 15x + 9x^2 - 5 - (7x + 5 - 8x^2)$

$= 15x + 9x^2 - 5 - 7x - 5 + 8x^2$

$= (9x^2 + 8x^2) + (15x - 7x) + (-5 - 5)$

$f(x) = 17x^2 + 8x - 10$

$\therefore 17x^2 + 8x - 10$ should be added to $7x + 5 - 8x^2$ to get $15x + 9x^2 - 5$.

6. Let $f(x)$ be subtracted from $2x^2 - 3x + 14$ to get $5x^2 + 7x - 5$.

$(2x^2 - 3x + 14) - (5x^2 + 7x - 5) = f(x)$

$2x^2 - 3x + 14 - 5x^2 - 7x + 5 = f(x)$

$(2x^2 - 5x^2) + (-3x - 7x) + (14 + 5) = f(x)$

$-3x^2 - 10x + 19 = f(x)$

$\therefore 19 - 10x - 3x^2$ should be subtracted from $2x^2 - 3x + 14$, so that the difference is $5x^2 + 7x - 5$.

7. $8x - 2\left[2x - 3\left(4x + 5 - \overline{2 - x}\right)\right]$

$= 8x - 2[2x - 3(4x + 5 - 2 + x)]$

$= 8x - 2[2x - 3(5x + 3)]$

$= 8x - 2[2x - 15x - 9]$

$= 8x - 2[-13x - 9]$

$= 8x + 26x + 18$

$= 34x + 18$

8. $2x - 15 = 3x - 20$

$-15 + 20 = 3x - 2x$

$5 = x$

$\therefore x = 5$

9. $\frac{2x}{3} - \frac{x}{2} + 2 = x$

$\frac{2x}{3} - \frac{x}{2} - x = -2$

$\frac{4x - 3x - 6x}{6} = -2$

$\frac{4x - 9x}{6} = -2$

$\frac{-5x}{6} = -2$

$x = \frac{2 \times 6}{5}$

$x = \frac{12}{5}$

10. Let the number be x.

The predecessor $= x - 1$

The successor $= x + 1$

Given that:

$x - 1 + x + 1 = 116$

$2x = 116$

$x = \frac{116}{2}$

$x = 58$

$\therefore$ The number is 58.

11. Let the father's age be x years.

Daughter's age $= \frac{x}{3}$ years.

Given that:

$x + \frac{x}{3} = 56 \Rightarrow \frac{3x + x}{3} = 56$

$\frac{4x}{3} = 56 \Rightarrow 4x = 56 \times 3$

$x = \frac{56 \times 3}{4} \Rightarrow x = 14 \times 3$

$x = 42$

$\therefore$ The age of the daughter $= \frac{1}{3} \times 42$ years

$= 14$ years

12. (i) $6 + 5 = 11$

(ii) $6 - 5 = 1$

(iii) $18/10 = 9/5$

(iv) $15/12 = 5/4$

Info Box!

The Golden Ratio is a unique number approximately equal to 1.618. Famous building, Parthenon in Greece has the Golden Ratio in it.

13. $4 \times 1 \times 1 \times 1 \times 2 \times 3 = 24$

14. The algebraic expression is $xy - (x + 30z/100)$

15. Total money = ₹50

Money spent on buying cookies $= 8p$

Change = ₹$(50 - 8p)$

(ii) Product of means $= 18 \times 10 = 180$

Product of extremes = Product of means

Product of extremes $= 12 \times 15 = 180$

$\therefore$ 12, 18, 10, 15 are in proportion.

EXAMPLE 5.5

Find the value of x, if 2, 16, 5 and x are in proportion.

SOLUTION

Given that 2, 16, 5, x are in proportion

Product of extremes = Product of means

$2x = 16 \times 5$

$x = \frac{16 \times 5}{2} = 8 \times 5 \Rightarrow x = 40$

EXAMPLE 5.6

In a milk solution, water and milk are in the ratio of 2 : 15. If the quantity of pure milk is 6 L, then find the quantity of water in the solution.

SOLUTION

Let the quantity of water be x L.

$2 : 15 :: x : 6 \Rightarrow 2 \times 6 = 15 \times x \Rightarrow 12 = 15x$

$\therefore x = \frac{12}{15} = \frac{4}{5} = 0.8$ L = 800 mL

$\therefore$ The quantity of water in the solution = 800 mL.

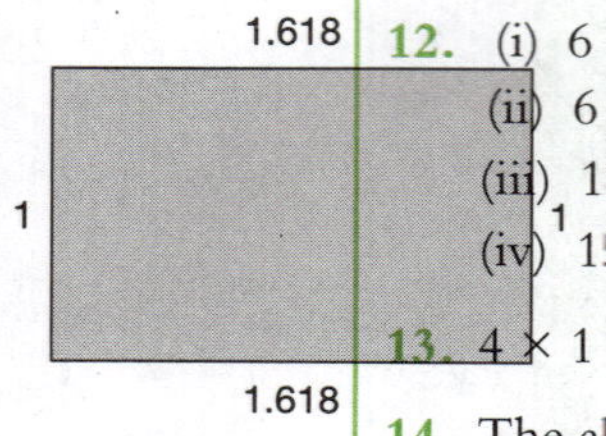

FIGURE 5.1 Golden rectangle with side lengths in Golden Ratio

Direct and Inverse Proportions

When a decrease or increase in a quantity directly results in corresponding decrease or increase in second quantity, then the two quantities are in direct proportion.

For example: A car at a speed of 10 km/h in 2 h travels 20 km. If the car moves at a speed of 20 km/h, it will cover 40 km in 2 h. Hence,

10 : 20 : : 20 : 40

When an increase in a quantity results in corresponding decrease in second quantity or *vice versa*, then the two quantities are in inverse proportion.

For example: A group of 12 workers take 12 days to construct a 4-km long highway. When two such groups work together, they complete the highway in 6 days. Hence, ratio of workers is inverse of ratio of time taken for construction.

Let ℓ_1 and ℓ_2 be a pair of lines and h be a transversal.

As shown in the figure, totally eight angles are formed.

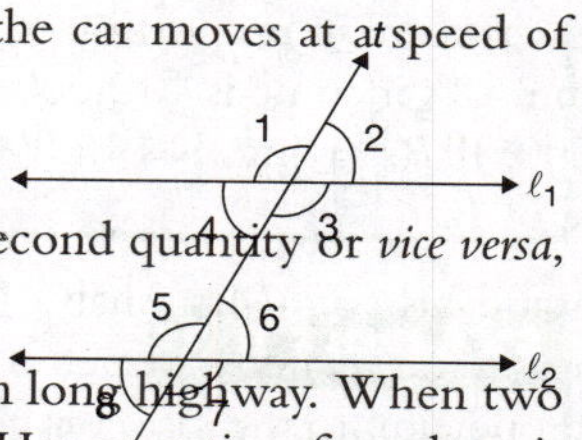

1. ∠1, ∠2, ∠7 and ∠8 are exterior angles and ∠3, ∠4, ∠5 and ∠6 are interior angles.
2. (∠1 and ∠5), (∠2 and ∠6), (∠3 and ∠7) and (∠4 and ∠8) are pairs of corresponding angles.
3. (∠1 and ∠3), (∠2 and ∠4), (∠5 and ∠7) and (∠6 and ∠8) are pairs of vertically opposite angles.
4. (∠4 and ∠6), and (∠3 and ∠5) are pairs of alternate interior angles.
5. (∠1 and ∠7) and (∠2 and ∠8) are pairs of alternate exterior angles.

If ℓ_1 and ℓ_2 are parallel, then

1. Corresponding angles are equal, i.e., ∠1 = ∠5, ∠2 = ∠6, ∠3 = ∠7 and ∠4 = ∠8.
2. Alternative interior angles are equal, i.e., ∠4 = ∠6 and ∠3 = ∠5.
3. Alternative exterior angles are equal, i.e., ∠1 = ∠7 and ∠2 = ∠8.
4. Exterior angles on the same side of the transversal are supplementary, i.e., ∠1 + ∠8 = 180° and ∠2 + ∠7 = 180°.
5. Interior angles on the same side of the transversal are supplementary, i.e., ∠4 + ∠5 = 180° and ∠3 + ∠6 = 180°.

EXAMPLE 8.1

∠*A* and ∠*B* are two complementary angles. If ∠*A* is 20° more than ∠*B*, then find the angles of ∠*A* and ∠*B*.

SOLUTION

Given that: $\angle A + \angle B = 90°$

$\angle B + 20° + \angle B = 90°$

$2\angle B = 70°$

$\angle B = 35°$

$\therefore \angle A = 90° - 35°$

$\angle A = 55°$

EXAMPLE 8.2

∠*P* and ∠*Q* are two supplementary angles. If ∠*P* is three times of ∠*Q*, then find the measurement of the angles *P* and *Q*.

SOLUTION

Given, $\angle P + \angle Q = 180°$

$3\angle Q + \angle Q = 180°$

$4\angle Q = 180°$

$\angle Q = 45°$

38. A and B's savings are in proportion to the ratio of their incomes. A's income is ₹12,000 and his savings is ₹4000. If B's savings is ₹12,000, then find the income of B.

39. Mr Kalyan and his wife Mrs Ahalya use different two-wheelers. The quantity of petrol they use in litres is in proportion to the ratio of the number of kilometres they travel in a month. Mr Kalyan uses 24 L of petrol and he travels a distance of 1200 km. If Mrs Ahalya travels 800 km, then find the number of litres of petrol that she uses in a month.

40. At a given point of time, the heights of trees are in proportion to the lengths of the shadows of the trees. A tree of height 25.6 m casts a shadow of 32 m. If the shadow of another tree at that point of time is 48 m, then find the height of that tree.

41. In the construction of a building, the volume of the walls is in proportion to the cost of construction. If a wall of volume 24 m^3 costs ₹18,600, then find the cost of construction of a wall of volume 36 m^3.

CONCEPT APPLICATION

1. P and Q's expenditures are in proportion to the ratio of their incomes. P's income is ₹32000 and his expenditure is ₹24000. If Q's expenditure is ₹36000, then find the income of Q.
   (a) ₹42000 (b) ₹39000
   (c) ₹48000 (d) ₹45000

2. If $x + 1$, $x - 3$, $x + 6$ and x are in proportion, then x = ______.
   (a) 9 (b) 12
   (c) 7 (d) 4

3. If we distribute 57 chocolates to three friends A, B and C in the ratio respectively, then find the number of chocolates received by C.
   (a) 19 (b) 27
   (c) 24 (d) 15

4. If 3 kg 500 g : 7 kg :: 27 kg : m kg, then m = ______.
   (a) 36 (b) 360
   (c) 540 (d) 54

5. In an exam, the marks secured by Manish and Nagesh are in the ratio 5 : 4. If Manish secured 12 marks more than Nagesh, then how many marks did Nagesh secure in that exam?
   (a) 108 (b) 48
   (c) 60 (d) 16

ASSESSMENT TEST

1. Find the ratio of the following.
   (i) 36 g, 54 g (ii) 24 L, 20 L 800 mL

2. The angles of a triangle are 40°, 60° and 80°. Find the ratio of the angles in the same order of the triangle.

3. Divide ₹3600 in the ratio 7 : 5.

4. The ratio of the ages of A and B is 3 : 8. If B's age is 24 years, then find the age of A.

5. In a basket, the number of blue, red and green balls are in the ratio 4 : 7 : 9. If there are a total of 960 balls, then find the number of green balls.

6. Check the following sets of numbers, whether they are in proportion.
   (i) 2, 3, 6, 9 (ii) $\frac{2}{3}, \frac{3}{4}, \frac{5}{6}, \frac{3}{5}$

7. Find the value of x in each of the following.
   (i) 2 : 5 : : x : 20 (ii) x : 10 : : 15 : 30

8. In a class, there are 70 students. If the ratio of the total number of students to that of girls is 5 : 2, then find the number of girls in the class.

9. The amount with A is ₹250 and his age is 25 years. Amount with B is ₹400. If the ratio of the amounts of A and B are in proportion to the ratio of their ages, then find the age of B.

10. In a proportion the product of extremes is 144. If one of the means is 9, then find the other.

11. Can the following measures be compared using the concept of ratio?

PRACTICE QUESTIONS

$\angle P = 3\angle Q$
$= 3 \times 45°$
$\angle P = 135°$

EXAMPLE 8.3

In the given figure, $\ell \parallel m$, $a = 40°$, then find all the other angles as mentioned in the figure.

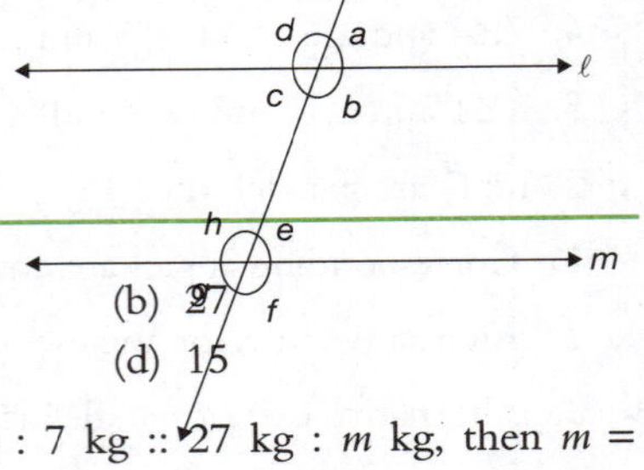

SOLUTION

Given that: $a = 40°$ and $\ell \parallel m$.

$b = 180° - 40° = 140°$ (since a, b are linear pair)

$b = d = 140°$ (vertically opposite angles)

$a = c = 40°$ (vertically opposite angles)

$a = e = 40°$ (corresponding angles)

$b = f = 140°$ (corresponding angles)

$h = f = 140°$ (vertically opposite angles)

$e = g = 40°$ (vertically opposite angles)

TRIANGLES

A three-sided simple closed figure is a triangle. In the given figure, ABC is a triangle. It has three sides AB, BC and CA. A, B and C are the three vertices of the triangle. $\angle CAB$, $\angle ABC$ and $\angle BCA$ are its three angles. Triangle ABC is denoted as ΔABC.

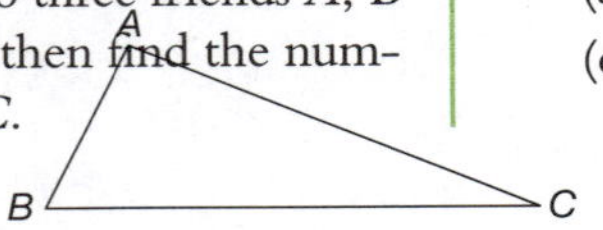

Info Box!
The relationship between triangles and their angles and sides is known as Trigonometry!

Types of Triangles

Based on their sides, triangles can be classified as follows:

1. **Scalene triangle:** A triangle in which no two sides are equal is a **scalene triangle**. In the given triangle, $AB \neq BC$, $BC \neq CA$ and $CA \neq AB$. Hence, it is a scalene triangle.

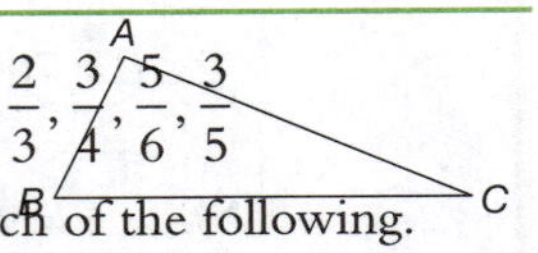

2. **Isosceles triangle:** A triangle in which any two sides are equal is an **isosceles triangle**. In the triangle given, $PQ = PR$. Hence, PQR is an isosceles triangle.

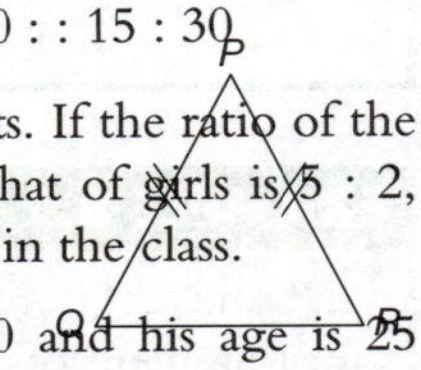

3. **Equilateral triangle:** A triangle in which all the three sides are equal is an **equilateral triangle**. In ΔXYZ, $XY = YZ = ZX$.
$\therefore$ XYZ is an equilateral triangle.

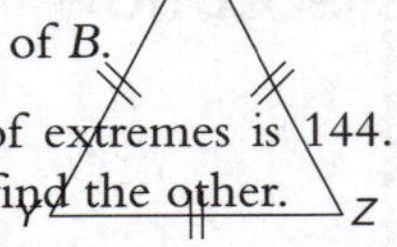

Based on the angles, triangles can be classified as follows:

1. **Acute-angled triangle:** A triangle in which all of the angles is acute is an **acute-angled triangle**.

For example: At a speed of 10 km/h in 2 h, a car travels 20 km. If the car moves at a speed of 20 km/h, it will cover 40 km in 2 h. Hence, 10 : 20 : : 20 : : 40

When an increase in a quantity results in corresponding decrease in second quantity or *vice versa*, then the two quantities are in inverse proportion.

For example: A group of 12 workers take 12 days to construct a 4-km long highway. When two such groups work together, they complete the highway in 6 days. Hence, ratio of workers is inverse of ratio of time taken for construction.

In the above figure, AP is a ray which has only one end point A. The ray AP is denoted as $\overrightarrow{AP}$. $\overrightarrow{AQ}$ is different from $\overrightarrow{AP}$. If A lies between P and Q, $\overrightarrow{AP}$ and $\overrightarrow{AQ}$ are said to be opposite rays.

Coplanar Lines

Two or more lines lying in a same plane are called coplanar lines.

Intersecting Lines

Two lines which meet at a point are called intersecting lines.

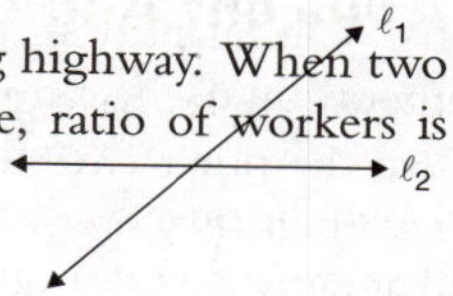

In the given figure, ℓ_1 and ℓ_2 are two intersecting lines.

Angle

Two rays which meet at a point are said to form an angle at their meeting point.

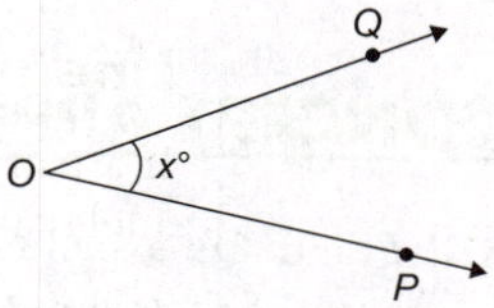

In the given figure, $\overrightarrow{OQ}$ and $\overrightarrow{OP}$ are two rays which have O as their meeting point and an angle with certain measurement is formed. The point O is called the **vertex** of the angle and $\overrightarrow{OQ}$ and $\overrightarrow{OP}$ are called the **sides** or **arms** of the angle. We denote the angle as $\angle QOP$ or $\angle POQ$ (or sometimes simply as $\angle O$). We see that $\angle QOP = \angle POQ$ (These are the two ways of representing the same angle). A common unit of measurement of angles is the **degree**. This unit is denoted by a small circle placed above and to the right of the number. For example, we write $\angle QOP = 34°$ and read it as 34 degrees.

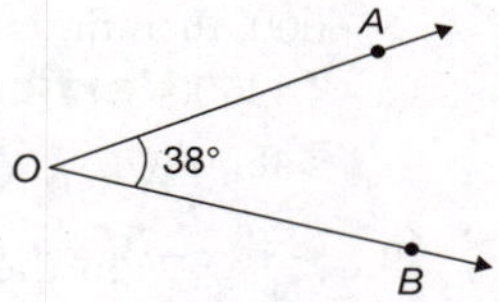

Let the measurement of an angle be $x°$.

1. If $0° < x < 90°$, it is called an **acute angle**.

Example: In the given figure, $\angle AOB$ is acute.

2. If $x = 90°$, it is called a **right angle**.

In the given figure, $\angle AOC$ is a right angle.

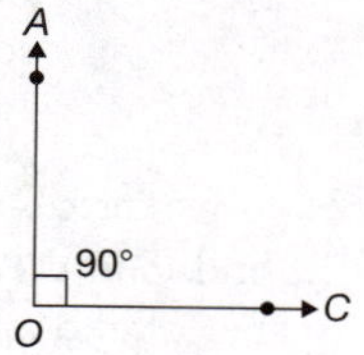

3. If $90° < x < 180°$, it is called an **obtuse angle**. For example, in the given figure, $\angle AOD$ is an obtuse angle.

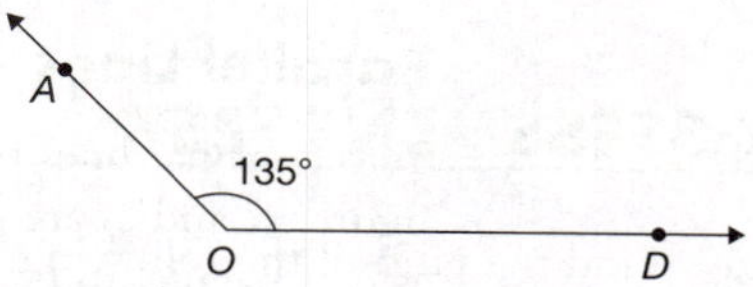

4. If $x = 180°$, it is the **angle of a straight line** or a **straight angle**. In the figure given, $\angle AOE = 180°$, $\overleftrightarrow{AE}$ is a straight line and O is a point on the line AE.

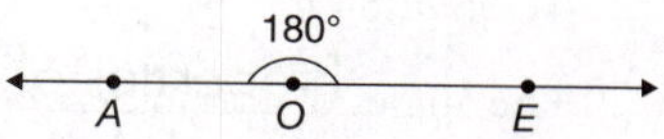

5. If $180° < x < 360°$, it is called **reflex angle**.

Example: 200°, 270° and 300°

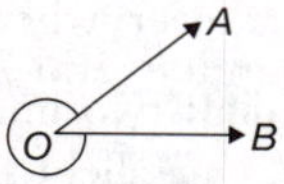

Perpendicular Lines

Two intersecting lines making an angle of 90° with each other are called perpendicular lines.

In the given figure, ℓ_1 and ℓ_2 are perpendicular lines. We write $\ell_1 \perp \ell_2$ and read this as ℓ_1 is perpendicular to ℓ_2.

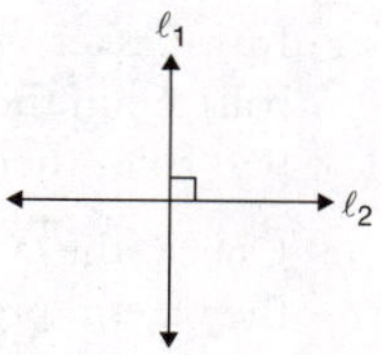

Complementary Angles

When the sum of two angles is 90°, the two angles are called complementary angles.

Example: If $x + y = 90°$, then $x°$ and $y°$ are called complementary angles.

PRACTICE QUESTIONS

38. *A* and *B*'s savings are in proportion to the ratio of their incomes. *A*'s income is ₹12,000 and his savings is ₹4000. If *B*'s savings is ₹12,000, then find the income of *B*.

39. Mr Kalyan and his wife Mrs Ahalya use different two-wheelers. The quantity of petrol they use in litres is in proportion to the ratio of the number of kilometres they travel in a month. Mr Kalyan uses 24 L of petrol and he travels a distance of 1200 km. If Mrs Ahalya travels 800 km, then find the number of litres of petrol that she uses in a month.

40. At a given point of time, the heights of trees are in proportion to the lengths of the shadows of the trees. A tree of height 23.6 m casts a shadow of 32 m. If the shadow of another tree at that point of time is 48 m, then find the height of that tree.

41. In the construction of a building, the volume of the walls is in proportion to the cost of construction. If a wall of volume 24 m^3 costs ₹18,600, then find the cost of construction of a wall of volume 36 m^3.

CONCEPT APPLICATION

1. *P* and *Q*'s expenditures are in proportion to the ratio of their incomes. *P*'s income is ₹32000 and his expenditure is ₹24000. If *Q*'s expenditure is ₹36000, then find the income of *Q*.
(a) ₹42000 (b) ₹39000
(c) ₹48000 (d) ₹45000

2. If $x + 1$, $x - 3$, $x + 6$ and x are in proportion, then x = ______.
(a) 9 (b) 12
(c) 7 (d) 4

3. If we distribute 57 chocolates to three friends *A*, *B* and *C* in the ratio respectively, then find the number of chocolates received by *C*.
(a) 19 (b) 27
(c) 24 (d) 15

4. If 3 kg 500 g : 7 kg :: 27 kg : *m* kg, then *m* = ______.
(a) 36 (b) 360
(c) 540 (d) 54

5. In an exam the marks secured by Manish and Nagesh are in the ratio 5 : 4. If Manish secured 12 marks more than Nagesh, then how many marks did Nagesh secure in that exam?
(a) 108 (b) 48
(c) 60 (d) 16

ASSESSMENT TEST

1. Find the ratio of the following.
(i) 36 g, 54 g (ii) 24 L, 20 L 800 mL

2. The angles of a triangle are 40°, 60° and 80°. Find the ratio of the angles in the same order of the triangle.

3. Divide ₹3600 in the ratio 7 : 5.

4. The ratio of the ages of *A* and *B* is 5 : 8. If *B*'s age is 24 years, then find the age of *A*.

5. In a basket, the number of blue, red and green balls are in the ratio 4 : 7 : 9. If there are a total of 960 balls, then find the number of green balls.

6. Check the following sets of numbers, whether they are in proportion.
(i) 2, 3, 6, 9 (ii) $\frac{2}{3}, \frac{3}{4}, \frac{5}{6}, \frac{3}{5}$

7. Find the value of *x* in each of the following.
(i) 2 : 5 : : *x* : 20 (ii) *x* : 10 : : 15 : 30

8. In a class, there are 70 students. If the ratio of the total number of students to that of girls is 5 : 2, then find the number of girls in the class.

9. The amount with *A* is ₹250 and his age is 25 years. Amount with *B* is ₹400. If the ratio of the amounts of *A* and *B* are in proportion to the ratio of their ages, then find the age of *B*.

10. In a proportion the product of extremes is 144. If one of the means is 9, then find the other.

11. Can the following measures be compared using the concept of ratio?

Supplementary Angles

When the sum of two angles is 180°, the two angles are called supplementary angles.

Example: If $a + b = 180°$, then $a°$ and $b°$ are called supplementary angles.

Adjacent Angles

If two angles have a common vertex and a common ray, and the other two sides lie on either side of the common ray, then they are said to be adjacent angles. In the given diagram, ∠AOD and ∠DOC are adjacent angles. ∠DOC and ∠COB are also adjacent angles.

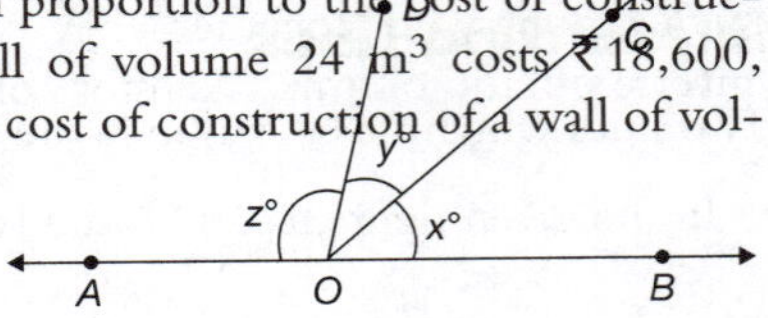

Linear Pair

If a pair of angles are adjacent and the non-common rays are opposite to each other, then the angles are said to form a linear pair.

Example: If O is a point between A and B and P is a point that does not lie on AB, then ∠AOP and ∠POB form a linear pair. The angles of a linear pair are supplementary.

Vertically Opposite Angles

When two lines intersect each other, four angles are formed. In the given figure, $\overleftrightarrow{AB}$ and $\overleftrightarrow{PQ}$ intersect at O. ∠AOP and ∠BOQ are vertically opposite angles. Similarly, ∠POB and ∠QOA are vertically opposite angles. Vertically opposite angles are equal.

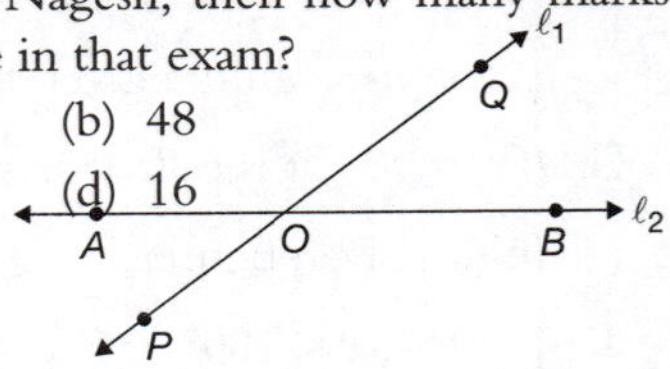

Concurrent Lines

Two or more lines in a plane passing through a same point are called concurrent lines.

Parallel Lines

Two coplanar lines that do not meet are called parallel lines. In the given figure, ℓ_1 and ℓ_2 are parallel lines. Symbolically, we write $\ell_1 \parallel \ell_2$ and read as ℓ_1 is parallel to ℓ_2.

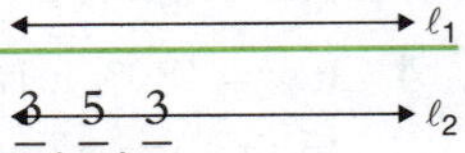

Properties of Parallel Lines

(i) For two given parallel lines, the perpendicular distance between the lines is the same everywhere.

(ii) If two lines lie in the same plane and are perpendicular to the same line, then they are parallel to each other.

(iii) If two lines are parallel to the same line, then they are parallel to each other.

(iv) One and only one parallel line can be drawn to a given line through a given point which is not on the given line.

Transversal

A straight line intersecting a pair of lines in two distinct points is a transversal for the two given lines.

2. With O as centre and a suitable radius draw an arc which cuts the line AB at X and Y respectively.
3. With X and Y as centres and more than half of XY as radius draw two arcs to meet each other at C. Join OC to get the ray OC. Now the angle BOC or angle AOC is 90°.

EXAMPLE 8.4

In the given figure, C is a point on the line segment BD. Find the measurements of $\angle ACB$ and $\angle ABC$.

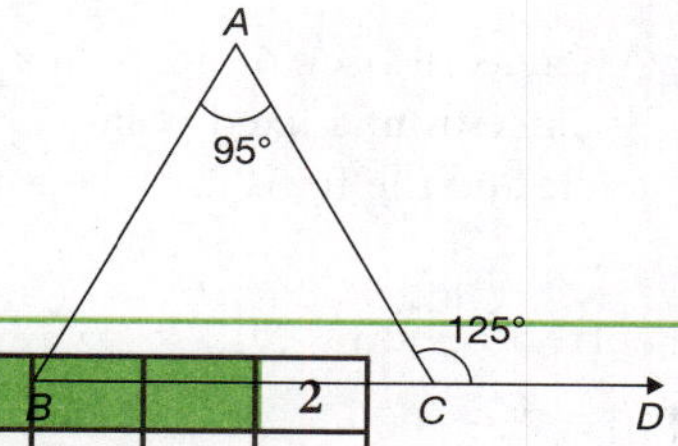

SOLUTION

$(\angle ACB, \angle ACD)$ is a linear pair.

$\Rightarrow \angle ACB + 125° = 180°$

$\angle ACB = 180° - 125° = 55°$

$\angle ABC + \angle CAB = \angle ACD$ (Exterior angle)

$\angle ABC + 95° = 125°$

$\angle ABC = 125° - 95° = 30°$

EXAMPLE 8.5

In the given figure, PTQ, PMR, SMT and QRS are straight lines. Find the angle of $\angle RMS$.

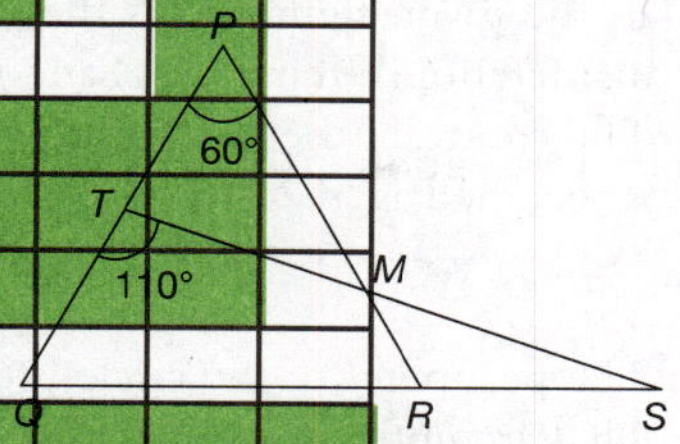

SOLUTION

Since PQ is a straight line and $\angle QTM = 110°$.

$\angle TPM + \angle PMT = \angle QTM$

$60° + \angle PMT = 110°$

$\Rightarrow \angle PMT = 110° - 60° = 50°$

$\Rightarrow \angle PMT = \angle RMS$ (vertically opposite angles)

$\Rightarrow \angle RMS = 50°$

EXAMPLE 8.6

In the figure, ABD, BCD are two triangles. BD is the bisector of $\angle ABC$ and $\angle ADC$. $\overline{AB} \parallel \overline{CD}$ and $\overline{AD} \parallel \overline{BC}$. If $\angle BCD = 50°$, then find the angle of $\angle BAD$.

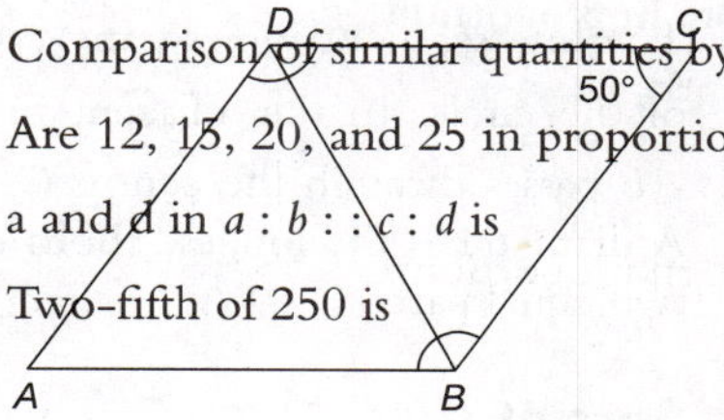

SOLUTION

$\angle BCD = 50°$ and $\overline{BC} \parallel \overline{AD}$.

$\angle CDA + \angle BCD = 180°$ (co-interior angles)

$\Rightarrow \angle CDA + 50° = 180°$

$\angle CDA = 180° - 50°$

$\angle CDA = 130°$

Similarly, $\angle ABC = 130°$ $(\because \overline{AB} \parallel \overline{CD})$

Since BD is the bisector of $\angle ADC$ and $\angle ABC$,

PRACTICE QUESTIONS

(i) The length (in cm) of the soft drink tin in the freezer and temperature inside the freezer in °C.

(ii) Average weight (in kg) of boys in a class and average weight (in kg) of girls in that class.

12. Find the ratio of the following:
    (i) 12 g and 120 g
    (ii) 360 L and 504 L
13. Ram and Sham are told by their mother to divide 68 chocolates in the ratio 6 : 11. How many chocolates do each one of them gets?
14. Are the following in proportion?
    (i) 3.2 : 4 and 8 : 10
    (ii) 1 : 2 and 2 : 1
15. Find the value of the term a in the following proportion.
    6 : 18 : : a : 54

CROSSWORD

Across

3. The equality of ratios
6. b and c in $a : b : : c : d$
9. b in $a : b$
10. The ratios 4 : 6 and 6 : 9 are
11. $a : b$ is in its lowest terms, the HCF of a and b is

Down

1. Does ratio have units?
2. a in $a : b$
4. Comparison of similar quantities by division
5. Are 12, 15, 20, and 25 in proportion?
7. a and d in $a : b : : c : d$ is
8. Two-fifth of 250 is

TEST YOUR CONCEPTS

Very Short Answer Type Questions

2. $8 : 12 = 4 \times 2 : 4 \times 3 = 2 : 3$

3. $15 : 12 = 3 \times 5 : 3 \times 4 = 5 : 4$

4. The required ratio is $3 \times 2 : 2 \times 3 = 6 : 6 = 1 : 1$

5. $3^2 : 3^0 = 9 : 1$

7. $\frac{2}{3} : \frac{4}{9}$

$= \frac{2}{3} \times 9 : \frac{4}{9} \times 9$

$= 6 : 4 = 3 : 2$

Hence, the correct option is (d).

9. 75 paise : ₹10 = $75 : 1000 = 25 \times 3 : 25 \times 40$

$= 3 : 40$

Hence, the correct option is (b).

10. 10 m : 1 km = 10 m : 1000 m

$10 \times 1 : 10 \times 100 = 1 : 100$

Hence, the correct option is (c).

11. (a) $\frac{1}{2} : \frac{2}{5} = 5 : 6 \rightarrow$ (r)

(b) $\frac{3}{4} : \frac{5}{2} = 3 : 10 \rightarrow$ (q)

(c) $\frac{2}{3} : \frac{3}{5} = 10 : 9 \rightarrow$ (s)

(d) $\frac{4}{3} : \frac{1}{5} = 20 : 3 \rightarrow$ (p)

Therefore, the correct match is:

(a) → (r), (b) → (q), (c) → (s), (d) → (p)

12. $ad = bc$

13. 1, 2, 3, x are in proportion.

$1(x) = 2(3)$

$\Rightarrow x = 6$

14. p, q, r, s are in proportion.

$p : q :: r : s$

$\frac{p}{q} = \frac{r}{s}$

15. 3, x, 6, 12 are in proportion.

$\frac{3}{x} = \frac{6}{12} \Rightarrow \frac{3}{x} = \frac{3}{6}$

$\Rightarrow x = 6.$

16. $x : 5 :: 4 : 20$

$\Rightarrow \frac{x}{5} = \frac{4}{20}$

$\frac{x}{5} = \frac{1}{5}$

$\Rightarrow x = 1$

17. (a) 2, 5, 7, 10

$2 \times 10 = 20$

$5 \times 7 = 35$

$2 \times 10 \neq 5 \times 7$

(b) $4 : 3 :: 8 : 6$

$\Rightarrow \frac{4}{3} = \frac{8}{6}$ (true)

(c) a, b, c, d are in proportion.

$\frac{a}{b} = \frac{c}{d} \Rightarrow bc = ad$

(d) $\frac{b}{c}$ need not be equal to $\frac{d}{a}$

Hence, the correct option is (b).

18. $x : 12 :: 12 : 18$

Product of extremes = Product of means

$\Rightarrow 18 \times x = 12 \times 12$

$\Rightarrow x = \frac{12}{18} \times 12 = \frac{12 \times 2}{3}$

$x = 8$

Hence, the correct option is (b).

19. $\frac{1}{2} \; \frac{1}{3} \; \frac{1}{4}$

$\frac{1}{2} \times x = \frac{1}{3} \times \frac{1}{4}$

$\angle ABC = \angle ABD + \angle CBD \quad (\because \angle ABD = \angle CBD)$

$2\angle ABD = 130° \Rightarrow \angle ABD = \angle CBD = \frac{130}{2} = 65°$

$\angle ADB + \angle BDC = 130°$ and $\angle ADB = \angle BDC = \frac{130}{2} = 65°$

In ΔABD, $\angle ABD + \angle ADB + \angle BAD = 180°$

$130° + \angle BAD = 180°$

$\angle BAD = 180° - 130° = 50°$

CIRCLES

A circle is a set of all points in a plane which are at a fixed distance from a fixed point. The fixed point is the centre of the circle and the fixed distance is the radius of the circle.

Info Box!

For a given area, a circle has the shortest perimeter among all shapes.

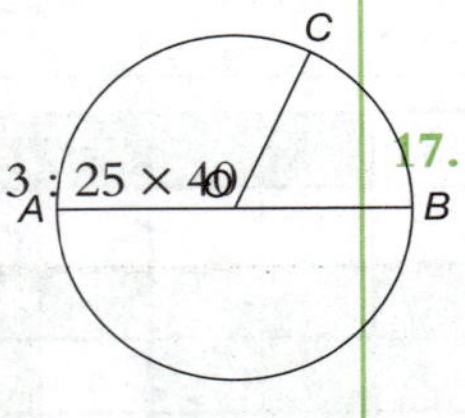

In the given figure, O is the centre of the circle and OC is the radius of the circle. AB is the diameter of the circle. OA and OB are also the radii of the circle. The diameter is twice the radius. The centre of the circle is generally denoted by 'O', the diameter is represented as 'd' and radius is specified as 'r'.

The perimeter of the circle is called the circumference of the circle. The circumference of the circle is π times the diameter. In the above circle with centre O, here, A, B and C are three points in the plane in which the circle lies. We see that $OA < r$, $OB = r$ and $OC > r$. The points O and A are inside the circle. The point B is located on the circle and C is a point outside the circle. The set of all points P in the plane of the circle for which $OP < r$ is called the **interior of the circle** and the set of points Q for which $OQ > r$ is called the **exterior of the circle**. B is a point on the circumference of the circle, $OB = r$. A is a point in the interior of the circle, $OA < r$. As C is a point in the exterior of the circle, $OC > r$.

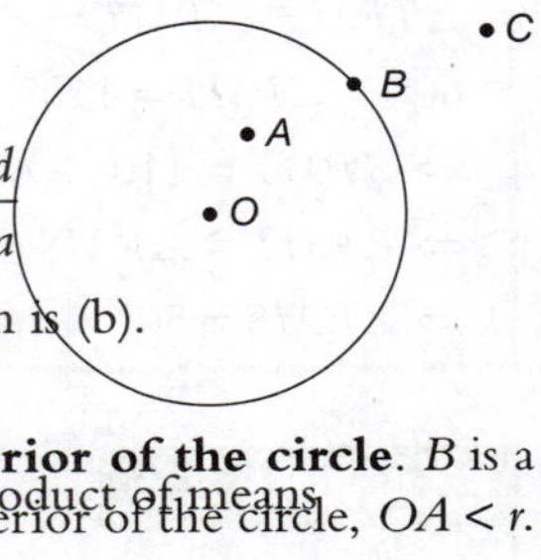

Chord

The line segment joining any two points on a circle is called a chord of the circle. In the adjacent figure, both $\overline{PQ}$ and $\overline{AB}$ are chords. AB passes through the centre O. Hence, it is a diameter of the circle. A diameter is the longest chord of the circle. It divides the circle into two equal parts.

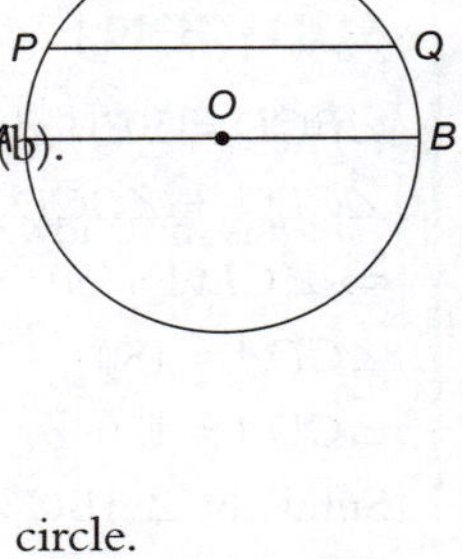

Secant

A line which intersects a circle in two distinct points is called secant of the circle.

HINTS AND EXPLANATION

In such a triangle, the square of the longest side is less than the sum of the squares of other two sides. In the above triangle, each of the angles A, B and C is less than 90°. Hence, ABC is an acute-angled triangle.

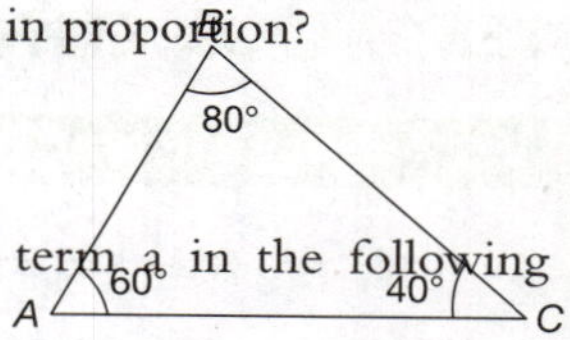

2. **Right-angled triangle:** A triangle which has a right angle is a **right-angled triangle**. In such a triangle, the square of the longest side and the hypotenuse is equal to the sum of the squares of other two sides. In the above triangle, $\angle ABC = 90°$. Hence, ABC is a right-angled triangle. In right triangle ABC, if $\overline{AC}$ is the longest side, then $AC^2 = AB^2 + BC^2$.

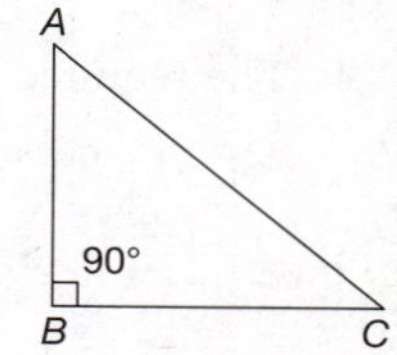

3. **Obtuse-angled triangle:** A triangle in which one angle is greater than 90° is an **obtuse-angled triangle**. In such a triangle, the square of the longest side is greater than the sum of the squares of the other two sides. In the given triangle, $\angle ABC > 90°$. Hence, ABC is an obtuse-angled triangle. In an obtuse-angled triangle ABC, if $\overline{AC}$ is the longest side, then $AC^2 > AB^2 + BC^2$.

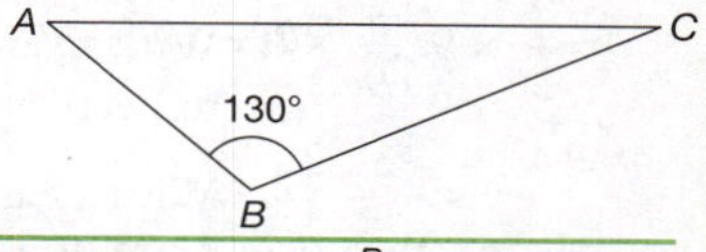

Isosceles Right-angled Triangle

A triangle in which two sides are equal and one angle is 90° is an isosceles right-angled triangle.

In the triangle PQR, PQ = QR and $\angle PQR = 90°$.

$\therefore$ PQR is an isosceles right triangle.

In such a triangle, the ratio of sides PQ, QR and RP is $1 : 1 : \sqrt{2}$.

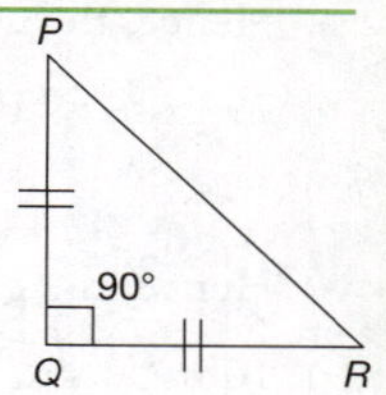

NOTES

1. A scalene triangle can be acute, right or obtuse angled.
2. An isosceles triangle can be acute, right or obtuse angled.
3. An equilateral triangle has to be acute. It cannot contain a right angle or an obtuse angle.

Given below are the statements of some of the properties of triangles:

1. The sum of the three angles of a triangle is 180°.
2. The exterior angle of a triangle is equal to the sum of the interior angles opposite to it.
3. The sum of any two sides of a triangle is greater than the third side. In ΔPQR, $PQ + QR > PR$, $QR + RP > PQ$ and $RP + PQ > QR$.
4. The difference between any two sides is less than the third side. In ΔPQR, $PQ - QR < PR$, $QR - RP < PQ$ and $RP - PQ < QR$
5. Angles opposite to equal sides are equal and vice versa. If $\angle P = \angle Q$, then $QR = PR$. If $QR = PR$, then $\angle P = \angle Q$.
6. If the angles are in increasing or decreasing order, the sides opposite to them also will be in this same order. If $\angle P > \angle Q$, then $QR > PR > PQ$.

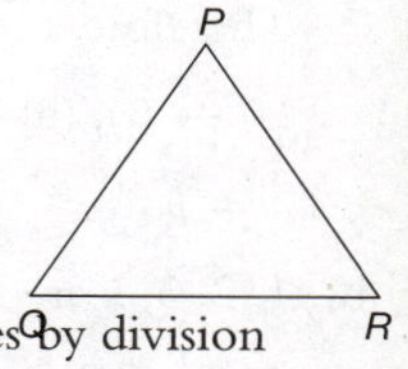

Constructions

We shall now look at the steps of constructing angles and bisector.

Congruent Angles (or) Equal Angles

Given: An angle PQR

(i) The length (in cm) of the soft drink can and the freezer and temperature inside that freezer in °C

(ii) Average weight (in kg) of boys in a class and average weight (in kg) of girls in that class.

12. Find the ratio of the following:
(i) 12 kg and 120 g
(ii) 360 L and 504 L

13. Ram and Shams are told by their mother to divide 68 chocolates in the ratio 6 : ... How many chocolates do each one of them get?

14. Are the following ratio in proportion?
(i) 5 : 2 and 8 : 10
(ii) 1 : 2 and 2 : 1

15. Find the value of the term a in the following proportion:
$6 : 18 : : a : 54$

CROSSWORD

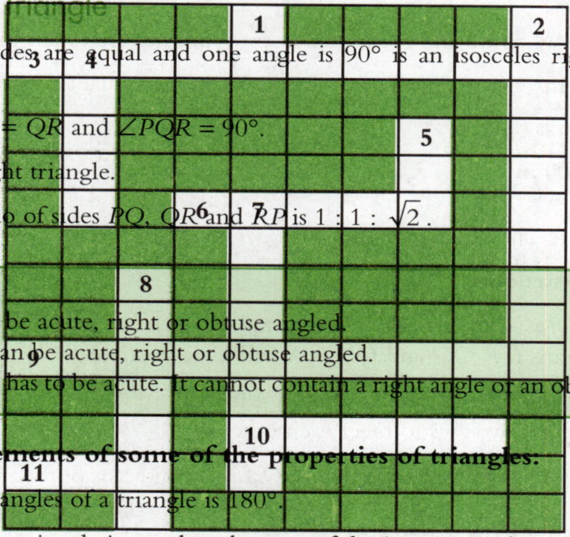

Across

3. The equality of ratios
6. b and c in $a : b : : c : d$
9. b in $a : b$
10. The ratios 4 : 6 and 6 : 9 are
11. $a : b$ is same as ...

Down

1. Does ratio have units?
2. a in $a : b$
4. Comparison of similar quantities by division
5. Are 12, 15, 20, and 25 in proportion?
7. a and d in $a : b : : c : d$ is
8. Two-fifth of 250 is

TEST YOUR CONCEPTS

Very Short Answer Type Questions

2. $8 : 12 = 4 \times 2 : 4 \times 3 = 2 : 3$

3. $15 : 12 = 3 \times 5 : 3 \times 4 = 5 : 4$

4. The required ratio is $3 \times 2 : 2 \times 3 = 6 : 6 = 1 : 1$

5. $3^2 : 3^0 = 9 : 1$

7. $\frac{2}{3} : \frac{4}{9}$

$= \frac{2}{3} \times 9 : \frac{4}{9} \times 9$

$= 6 : 4 = 3 : 2$

Hence, the correct option is (d).

9. 75 paise : ₹10 = 75 : 1000 = $25 \times 3 : 25 \times 40$

= 3 : 40

Hence, the correct option is (b).

10. 10 m : 1 km = 10 m : 1000 m

$10 \times 1 : 10 \times 100 = 1 : 100$

Hence, the correct option is (c).

11. (a) $\frac{1}{2} : \frac{2}{5} = 5 : 6 \rightarrow$ (r)

(b) $\frac{3}{4} : \frac{5}{2} = 3 : 10 \rightarrow$ (q)

(c) $\frac{2}{3} : \frac{3}{5} = 10 : 9 \rightarrow$ (s)

(d) $\frac{4}{3} : \frac{1}{5} = 20 : 3 \rightarrow$ (p)

Therefore, the correct match is:

(a) → (r), (b) → (q), (c) → (s), (d) → (p)

12. $ad = bc$

13. 1, 2, 3, x are in proportion.

$1(x) = 2(3)$

$\Rightarrow x = 6$

14. p, q, r, s are in proportion.

$p : q :: r : s$

$\frac{p}{q} = \frac{r}{s}$

15. 3, x, 6, 12 are in proportion.

$\frac{3}{x} = \frac{6}{12} \Rightarrow \frac{3}{x} = \frac{3}{6}$

$\Rightarrow x = 6.$

16. $x : 5 :: 4 : 20$

$\Rightarrow \frac{x}{5} = \frac{4}{20}$

$\frac{x}{5} = \frac{1}{5}$

$\Rightarrow x = 1$

17. (a) 2, 5, 7, 10

$2 \times 10 = 20$

$5 \times 7 = 35$

$2 \times 10 \neq 5 \times 7$

(b) $4 : 3 :: 8 : 6$

$\Rightarrow \frac{4}{3} = \frac{8}{6}$ (true)

(c) a, b, c, d are in proportion.

$\Rightarrow \frac{a}{b} = \frac{c}{d} \Rightarrow bc = ad$

$\frac{b}{c}$ need not be equal to $\frac{d}{a}$

Hence, the correct option is (b).

18. $x : 12 :: 12 : 18$

Product of extremes = Product of means

$\Rightarrow 18 \times x = 12 \times 12$

$\Rightarrow x = \frac{12}{18} \times 12 = \frac{12 \times 2}{3}$

$x = 8$

Hence, the correct option is (b).

19. $\frac{1}{2} : \frac{1}{3} :: \frac{1}{4} : x$

$\frac{1}{2} \times x = \frac{1}{3} \times \frac{1}{4}$

HINTS AND EXPLANATION

To construct: Angle AOB equal to PQR.

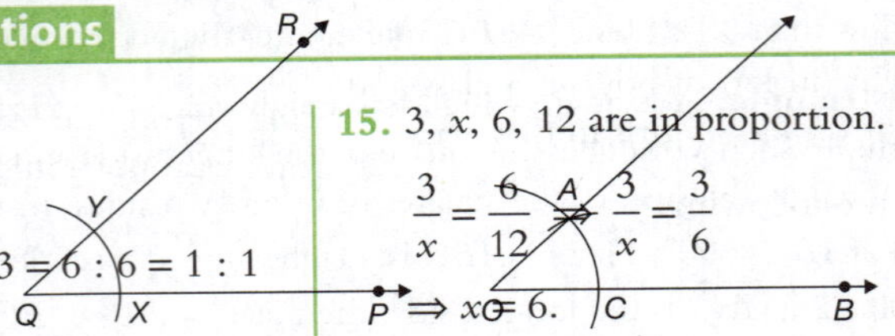

Steps of construction:

1. Draw a ray OB.
2. With Q as centre and a suitable radius draw an arc which cuts rays QP and QR at X and Y, respectively.
3. With O as centre and the same radius as in step (2) draw an arc which cuts ray OB at the point C.
4. With C as centre and XY as radius draw another arc to cut the arc in step (2) at A.
5. Join OA to get the ray OA. Now angle AOB is equal to angle PQR.

Bisector of an Angle

Given: An angle MON

To construct: The bisector of the angle MON

Steps of construction:

1. With O as centre and a suitable radius draw an arc which cuts rays OM and ON at X and Y, respectively.
2. With X and Y as centres and more than half of XY as radius draw two arcs to meet each other at A.
3. Join OA to get the ray OA. Now OA is the bisector of the angle MON.

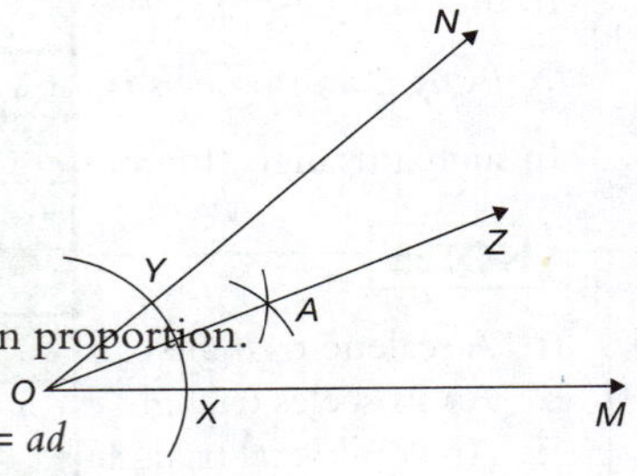

Construction of an Angle 60°

Steps of construction:

1. Draw a ray OA.
2. With O as centre and a suitable radius draw an arc which cuts the ray OA at X.
3. With X as centre and the same radius as in step (2), draw an arc to cut the arc in step (2) at B.
4. Join OB to get the ray OB. Now the angle BOA is 60°.

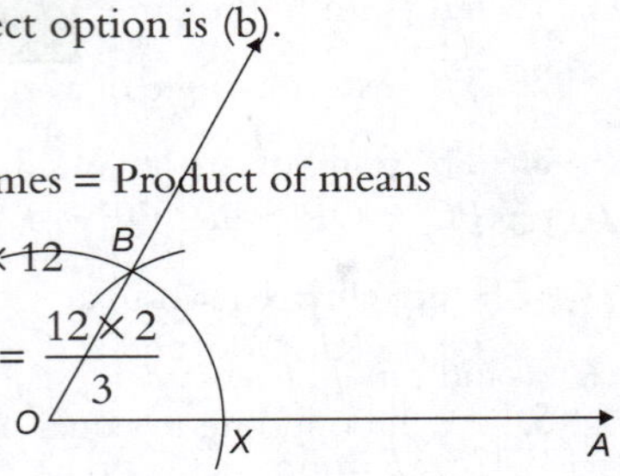

Construction of an Angle 90°

Steps of construction:

1. Draw a line AB. Mark a point O on AB.

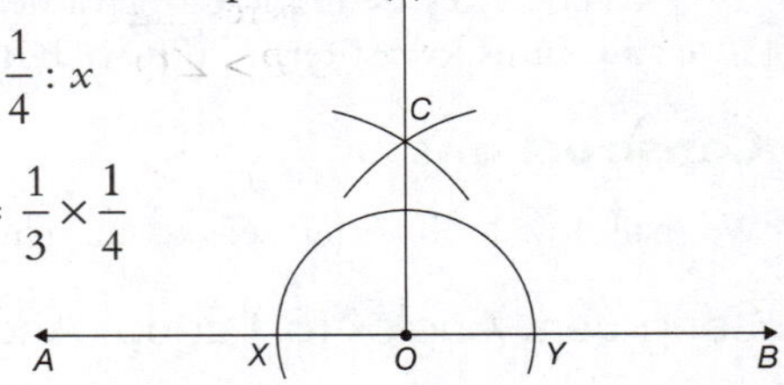

$x = \frac{1}{3} \times \frac{1}{4} \times 2$

$x = \frac{1}{6}$

Hence, the correct option is (b).

20. $1 : 4 = 9 : x$

$\frac{1}{4} = \frac{9}{x}$

$x = 9 \times 4$

$x = 36$ sq. units

Hence, the correct option is (b).

21. $12 : 5 = 48 : x$

$\frac{12}{5} = \frac{48}{x}$

$x = \frac{48}{12} \times 5$

$x = 4 \times 5$

$x = 20$ cm

Hence, the correct option is (b).

22. (a) $x : 5 :: 2 : 3$

$\frac{x}{5} = \frac{2}{3}$

$\Rightarrow x = \frac{10}{3} \rightarrow$ (r)

(b) $2 : x :: 4 : 3$

$\Rightarrow \frac{2}{x} = \frac{4}{3}$

$\Rightarrow x = 2 \times \frac{3}{4} = \frac{6}{4} = \frac{3}{2} \rightarrow$ (s)

(c) $2 : 5 :: x : 3$

$\Rightarrow \frac{2}{5} = \frac{x}{3}$

$\Rightarrow x = \frac{2}{5} \times 3 = \frac{6}{5} \rightarrow$ (p)

(d) $2 : 5 :: 3 : x$

$\frac{2}{5} = \frac{3}{x}$

$\Rightarrow x = 3 \times \frac{5}{2}$

$x = \frac{15}{2} \rightarrow$ (q)

Therefore, the correct match is:

(a) → (r), (b) → (s), (c) → (p), (d) → (q)

Short Answer Type Questions

23. (i) 360 mL, 500 mL

$360 : 500 = 36 : 50$

$= 2 \times 18 : 2 \times 25 = 18 : 25$

(ii) 4 h 20 min : 6 h

$= (4 \times 60 + 20) : 6 \times 60 = 260 : 360$

$= 26 : 36 = 13 : 18$

24. (i) $4\frac{1}{5} : 2\frac{3}{4}$

$= \frac{21}{5} : \frac{11}{4} = 84 : 55$

(ii) $2\frac{3}{8} : 3\frac{5}{6} = \frac{19}{8} : \frac{23}{6}$

LCM of 8 and 6 is 24.

$= \frac{19}{8} \times 24 : \frac{23}{6} \times 24 = 57 : 92$

25. (i) $\frac{1}{6} : \frac{3}{8}$

LCM of 6 and 8 is 24.

$\frac{1}{6} \times 24 : \frac{3}{8} \times 24$

$= 4 : 9 = \frac{1}{6} < \frac{3}{8}$

$\therefore$ 3 : 8 is greater.

(ii) $\frac{9}{16} : \frac{5}{12}$

LCM of 16, 12 is 48.

$\frac{9}{16} \times 48 : \frac{5}{12} \times 48 = 27 : 20$

$\frac{9}{16} > \frac{5}{12}$

$\therefore$ 9 : 16 is greater.

26. 68 : 85

$= 17 \times 4 : 17 \times 5 = 4 : 5$

27. 2 kg Sweet : Sugar : Milk : Others = 4 : 9 : 3

Weight of sugar in 2 kg of sweet

$= \frac{4}{4+9+3} \times 2 = \frac{4}{16} \times 2 = \frac{1}{2}$ kg = 500 g

28. Earnings of Arunachalam = ₹48800

Expenditure = ₹24000

(i) Ratio of earnings to expenditure

48800 : 24000

= 488 : 240

$= 8 \times 61 : 8 \times 30$

= 61 : 30

(ii) Savings = Income − Expenditure

= ₹48800 – ₹24000 = ₹24800

Expenditure : Savings

= 24000 : 24800

= 240 : 248 = 30 : 31

29. $\left(\frac{4}{2+3+4} - \frac{2}{2+3+4}\right)$ of total weight = 250 gm

$\left(\frac{4}{9} - \frac{2}{9}\right)$ of total weight = 250

$\left(\frac{2}{9}\right)$ of total weight = 250

Total weight $= \frac{250 \times 9}{2} = 1125$ gm

30. The ratio of weights of tomato, brinjal and cauliflower

$= \frac{1}{3} : \frac{2}{5} : \frac{3}{4} = 20 : 24 : 45$

Weight of cauliflower $= \frac{45}{20 + 24 + 45} \times 178$

$= \frac{45}{89} \times 178 = 45 \times 2 = 90$ kg.

31. Ratio of the numbers

$= \frac{3}{1} : \frac{4}{7} : \frac{2}{5} = 105 : 20 : 14$

The required numbers are

$\frac{105}{105+20+14} \times 278, \frac{20}{105+20+14} \times 278,$

$\frac{14}{105+20+14} \times 278$

The answer is 210, 40, 28.

32. Total number of students = 720

Number of girls = 720 − 300 = 420

Ratio of the number of girls to that of boys

$= 420 : 300 = 7 \times 60 : 5 \times 60 = 7 : 5$

33. (i) 2, 3, 2016, 2019

$2 \times 2019 = 4038$

$3 \times 2016 = 6048$

$2 \times 2019 \neq 3 \times 2016$

Hence, 2, 3, 2016 and 2019 are not in proportion.

(ii) 12, 15, 32, 40

$12 \times 40 = 480$

$15 \times 32 = 480$

$12 \times 40 = 15 \times 32$

Hence, 12, 15, 32 and 40 are in proportion.

34. (i) 17 : 68 : : 7 : x

$\Rightarrow \frac{17}{68} = \frac{7}{x}$

$\therefore \; x = 28$

(ii) 14 : 42 : : x : 27

$\frac{14}{42} = \frac{x}{27}$

$\frac{1}{3} = \frac{x}{27}$

$\therefore x = 9$

35. (i) 40, 18, 36, 20

$40 \times 20 = 800$

$18 \times 36 \neq 800$

$40 \times 18 = 720$

$36 \times 20 = 720$

40 : 36 : : 20 : 18

∴ 40, 36, 20, 18 are in proportion.

∴ Product of extremes = 720

(ii) $\frac{1}{4}, \frac{2}{3}, \frac{1}{3}, \frac{1}{8}$

$\frac{1}{4} \times \frac{1}{8} = \frac{1}{32}$

$\frac{2}{3} \times \frac{1}{3} = \frac{2}{9} \neq \frac{1}{32}$

$\frac{1}{4} \times \frac{1}{3} = \frac{1}{12}$

$\frac{2}{3} \times \frac{1}{8} = \frac{1}{12}$

$\therefore \frac{1}{4} : \frac{2}{3} : : \frac{1}{8} : \frac{1}{3}$

∴ Product of extremes $= \frac{1}{4} \times \frac{1}{3} = \frac{1}{12}$.

36. Given that: 1 person eats 3 mangoes.

The ratio of the number of person to mangoes is 1 : 3.

Now, 1 : 3 :: 8 : 24

∴ The number of persons and that of mangoes are in proportion.

37. 50 : 40 : : 150 : x

$\frac{50}{40} = \frac{150}{x} \Rightarrow \frac{5}{4} = \frac{150}{x}$

$x = 150 \times \frac{4}{5} \Rightarrow x = 120$

∴ Saurav got 120 marks.

38. Incomes of A and B are ₹12000 and ₹x, respectively.

Savings of A and B are ₹4000, ₹12000.

∴ 12000 : x = 4000 : 12000

$\frac{12000}{x} = \frac{4000}{12000} \Rightarrow \frac{12000}{x} = \frac{1}{3}$

$\Rightarrow x =$ ₹36000

∴ Income of B is ₹36000.

39. The quantity of petrol used by Kalyan and his wife Ahalya are 24 L and x L, respectively.

Distances traveled by them are 1200 km and 800 km, respectively.

⇒ 24 : x : : 1200 : 800

$\frac{24}{x} = \frac{1200}{800} \Rightarrow \frac{24}{x} = \frac{3}{2}; x = 24 \times \frac{2}{3} \Rightarrow x = 16$

∴ Petrol used by Mrs Ahalya is 16 L.

40. Given, 32 : 48 : : 25.6 : x

$\frac{32}{48} = \frac{25.6}{x} \Rightarrow \frac{2}{3} = \frac{25.6}{x}$

$x = 25.6 \times \frac{3}{2} = 38.4$ m

41. Given, 24 : 36 : : 18600 : x

$\frac{24}{36} = \frac{18600}{x} \Rightarrow x = \frac{18600}{24} \times 36$

$x = 18,600 \times \frac{3}{2} \Rightarrow x = 9300 \times 3 \Rightarrow x =$ ₹27900

CONCEPT APPLICATION

1. P and Q's expenditures are in proportion to the ratio of their savings.

⇒ P's expenditure : P's income = Q's expenditure : Q's income

⇒ ₹24000 : ₹32000 = ₹36000 : Q's income

⇒ 32000 × 36000 = 24000 × Q's income

⇒ Q's income $= \frac{32000 \times 36000}{24000} =$ ₹48000

Hence, the correct option is (c).

2. Given that $x + 1, x - 3, x + 6$ and x are in proportion.

$\Rightarrow (x - 3)(x + 6) = (x + 1)x$

$\Rightarrow x^2 + 6x - 3x - 18 = x^2 + x$

$\Rightarrow 6x - 3x - x = 18$

$\Rightarrow 2x = 18$

$\Rightarrow x = \frac{18}{2}$

$\Rightarrow x = 9$

Hence, the correct option is (a).

3. LCM of 3, 2 and 4 = 12

The ratio of number of chocolates distributed to A, B and C

$= \frac{1}{3} : \frac{1}{2} : \frac{3}{4} = \frac{1}{3} \times 12 : \frac{1}{2} \times 12 : \frac{3}{4} \times 1$

$= 4 : 6 : 9$

The number of chocolates received by

$C = \frac{9}{(4+6+9)} \times 57 = \frac{9}{19} \times 57 = 27$

Hence, the correct option is (b).

4. Given, 3 kg 500 g : 7 kg :: 27 kg : m kg

3 kg 500 g = 3000 g + 500 g = 3500 g; 7 kg = 7000 g; 27 kg = 27000 g; m kg = 1000 m g

$\Rightarrow$ 3500 : 7000 :: 27000 : 1000 m

$\Rightarrow 7000 \times 27000 = 3500 \times 1000$ m

$\Rightarrow m = \frac{7000 \times 27000}{3500 \times 1000}$

$\Rightarrow m = 54$

Hence, the correct option is (d).

5. Let the marks secured by Manish and Nagesh be $5x$ and $4x$, respectively.

$5x = 4x + 12$

$5x - 4x = 12 \Rightarrow x = 12$

Therefore, the marks secured by Nagesh = $4x = 4 \times 12 = 48$.

Hence, the correct option is (b).

ASSESSMENT TEST

1. (i) 36 : 54

= 2 : 3

(ii) 24 L, 20 L 800 mL

24000 : (20000 + 800)

= 24000 : 20800

= 240 : 208

= 15 : 13

2. 40° : 60° : 80°

= 4 : 6 : 8

= 2 : 3 : 4

3. $\frac{7}{7+5} \times 3600, \frac{7}{7+5} \times 3600$

$= \frac{7}{12} \times 3600, \frac{5}{12} \times 3600$

$= 7 \times 300, 5 \times 300 =$ ₹2100, ₹1500

4. Ratio of the ages of A and B is 3 : 8

Let the age of A be x.

3 : 8 :: x : 24

$8x = 24 \times 3$

$x = 9$

Age of A = 9 years

5. The ratio of the number of blue balls, red balls and green balls

= 4 : 7 : 9

The total number of balls is 960.

Number of green balls $= \frac{9}{4+7+9} \times 960$

$= \frac{9}{20} \times 960 = 9 \times 48 = 432$

6. (i) 2, 3, 6, 9

$2 \times 9 = 18$

$3 \times 6 = 18$

Product of extremes = Product of means

Hence, 2, 3, 6 and 9 are in proportion.

(ii) $\frac{2}{3}, \frac{3}{4}, \frac{5}{6}, \frac{3}{5}$

Product of extremes $= \frac{2}{3} \times \frac{3}{5} = \frac{2}{5}$

Product of extremes $= \frac{3}{4} \times \frac{5}{6} = \frac{5}{8}$

$\frac{2}{5} \neq \frac{5}{8}$

Hence, the set of numbers are not in proportion.

7. (i) 2 : 5 : : x : 20

$\Rightarrow \frac{2}{5} = \frac{x}{20} \Rightarrow x = \frac{2}{5} \times 20 = 8$

(b) $x : 10 :: 15 : 30$

$$\frac{x}{10} = \frac{15}{30}$$

$$\frac{x}{10} = \frac{1}{2} \Rightarrow x = 5$$

8. Total students in the class = 70

Let x be the number of girls in the class.

$70 : x = 5 : 2$

$$\frac{70}{x} = \frac{5}{2} \Rightarrow 70 \times \frac{2}{5} = x$$

$x = 28$

∴ Number of girls in the class = 28

9. Let the age of B be x.

$25 : x = 250 : 400$

$$\frac{25}{x} = \frac{250}{400} = \frac{5}{8}$$

$$x = 25 \times \frac{8}{5} = 40$$

∴ The age of B is 40 years.

10. Product of extremes = Product of means

$144 = 9 \times x$

$$x = \frac{144}{9} = 16$$

11. (i) No (ii) Yes

12. (i) 12/120 = 1 : 10
(ii) 360/504 = 5 : 7

13. Ram gets 24 chocolates and Sham gets 44 chocolates.

14. (i) Yes (ii) No

15. $a \times 18 = 54 \times 6$

$a = 54 \times 6/18$

$a = 18$

Chapter 6

Percentages and their Applications

REMEMBER

Before beginning this chapter, you should be able to:

- Recall equivalent fractions
- Compare fractions and decimals

KEY IDEAS

After completing this chapter, you should be able to:

- Express percentage as fraction and fraction as percentage
- Compare percentages
- Understand SP, CP, profit, loss, discount
- Understand simple interest

INTRODUCTION

Mathematics is a language of numbers and symbols. One of the most important symbols that we use on a daily basis is % (per cent). When we receive our report card, we see the percentage obtained. For example, if a student obtains 90%, it means that he overall scored 90 parts from 100. In this chapter, we shall learn the concept of percentage and solve the problems based on it.

PERCENTAGES

The term 'per cent' means 'for every hundred'.

A fraction, in which the denominator is 100, is a percentage. The denominator, i.e., 100 is denoted by a special symbol %, which is read as per cent.

> **Info Box!**
>
> The term 'per cent' is derived from the Latin term *per centum* which means per hundred.

Examples: $10/100 = 10\%$

$25/100 = 25\%$

$x/100 = x\%$

Since any ratio is a fraction, each ratio can also be expressed as a percentage.

Example: A ratio of 1/2 can be converted to a percentage figure as $\frac{1}{2} = \frac{1(50)}{2(50)} = \frac{50}{100} = 50\%$

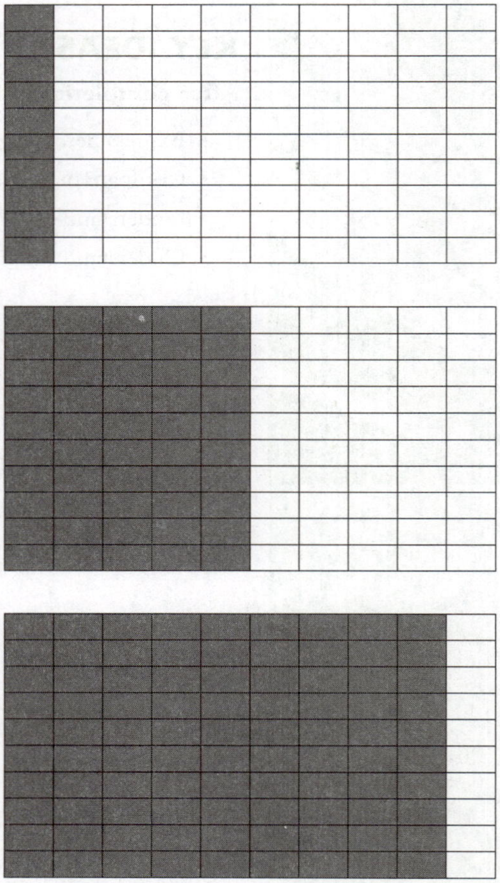

FIGURE 6.1 Representation of 10%, 50%, 90%

Expressing $x\%$ as a Fraction

Any percentage can be expressed as a decimal fraction by dividing the percentage figure by 100. As $x\% = x$ out of $100 = x/100$. So, 75% = 75 out of 100 = 75/100 = 3/4 or 0.75.

Expressing the Fraction a/b as a Decimal and as a Percentage

Any fraction can be expressed as a decimal and any decimal fraction can be converted into percentage by multiplying it by 100.

1/2 = 0.5 = 50%

1/4 = 0.25 = 25%

1/5 = 0.2 = 20%

1/3 = 0.33… = 33.33…%

EXAMPLE 6.1

Express 20% as a fraction.

SOLUTION

20% = 20/100 = 1/5

∴ 20% as a fraction is 1/5.

EXAMPLE 6.2

Express 35% as a decimal.

SOLUTION

35% = 35/100 = 0.35

EXAMPLE 6.3

Express 1/2 as per cent.

SOLUTION

1/2 = (1/2) × 100% = 50%

EXAMPLE 6.4

Find 40% of 60.

SOLUTION

40% of 60 = (40/100)60 = 24

Percentage, a Relative Value

When you obtain 16 marks out of 20 marks in your maths unit test, this would be an absolute value. Let us say that you got 80% in the maths unit test, it is understood that you got 80 marks out of 100 marks. However, if the maximum marks for the unit test is 50, then the marks you got is 80% of 50 or (80/100)50 = 40.

Hence, the actual score depends upon the maximum marks of the unit test and varies with the maximum marks. For example, if the maximum score is 60, 80% of 60 = 48. If the maximum marks are 70, 80% of 70 = 56. As the maximum marks vary, your marks may also vary. Hence, percentage is seen as a relative or comparative value. If the maximum marks are 100, your score is 80.

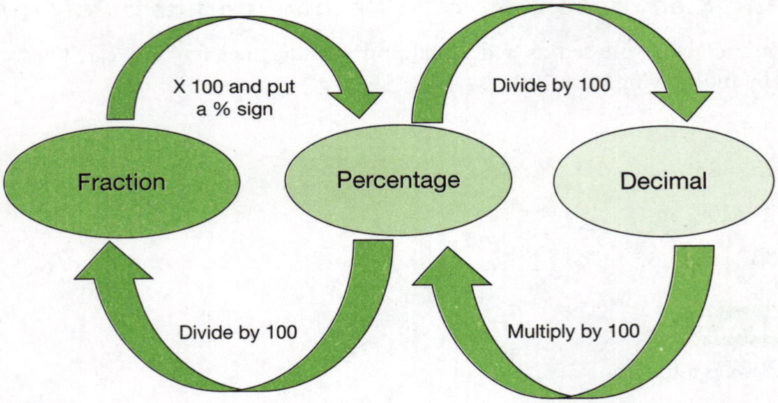

FIGURE 6.2 Conversions between decimal, fraction and percentage

EXAMPLE 6.5

Represent the following decimals as percentages.

(I) 2.30 **(II)** 0.85

SOLUTION

(I) $2.30 = 2.30 \times 100 \times \frac{1}{100}$

$= 2.30 \times 100\% = 230\%$

(II) $0.85 = 0.85 \times 100 \times \frac{1}{100}$

$= 0.85 \times 100\% = 85\%$

EXAMPLE 6.6

Represent the following percentages as fractions.

(I) 125% **(II)** 2.5%

SOLUTION

(I) $125\% = 125 \times \frac{1}{100}$

$= 5 \times \frac{1}{4} = \frac{5}{4}$

(II) $2.5\% = 2.5 \times \frac{1}{100}$

$= \frac{25}{1000} = \frac{1}{40}$

EXAMPLE 6.7

Represent the following fractions as percentages.

(I) $\frac{3}{5}$ **(II)** $\frac{5}{3}$

SOLUTION

(I) $\frac{3}{5} = \frac{3}{5} \times 100 \times \frac{1}{100}$

$= \frac{3}{5} \times 100\% = 3 \times 20\%$

$= 60\%$

(II) $\frac{5}{3} = \frac{5}{3} \times 100 \times \frac{1}{100}$

$= \frac{5}{3} \times 100\% = \frac{500}{3}\%$

$= 166\frac{2}{3}\%$

EXAMPLE 6.8

Banti has 50 chocolates with him, he ate 60% of those in a week. Find the number of chocolates left with him.

SOLUTION

Total number of chocolates = 50

Number of chocolates eaten = 60% of 50

Number of chocolates left = 40% of 50

$= 40 \times \frac{1}{100} \times 50 = 40 \times \frac{1}{2}$

$= 20$

EXAMPLE 6.9

Chanti distributed $\frac{3}{4}$th of his birthday cake to his friends. Find the percentage of the cake distributed to his friends.

SOLUTION

Fraction of the cake distributed = $\frac{3}{4}$

$\frac{3}{4} = \frac{3 \times 25}{4 \times 25} = \frac{75}{100}$

$= 75 \times \frac{1}{100} = 75\%$

PROFIT, LOSS AND DISCOUNT

The concept of percentage finds numerous applications in commercial Mathematics. When we go shopping, we frequently come across terms like sale, discount, price, etc. Let us understand the basic terms related to profit, loss and discount.

Profit and Loss

When a person buys an article for a certain price and then sells it for a different price, he makes a profit or incurs a loss.

Cost Price

The price at which an article is purchased is called its cost price (CP).

Selling Price

The price at which an article is sold is called its selling price (SP).

Profit and Loss

If the selling price of an article is greater than its cost price, we say that there is a profit (or) gain (p) and if it is less, we say that there is a loss (ℓ).

If $p < 0$, then there is a loss. If SP = CP, then there is no profit and no loss. Profit or loss is generally expressed as a percentage of the cost price.

Discount

Nowadays we know that the competition is very high in any business. So, in order to cope up with this competition and also to boost the sale of goods, shopkeepers offer rebate to customers. The rebate offered is called discount. Discount is always calculated on the market price (MP) of the article.

1. Discount = MP – SP
2. Discount Percentage $= \dfrac{\text{Discount}}{\text{MP}} \times 100\%$

Overheads

All the expenditure incurred on transportation, repairs, etc., (if any) are categorized as overheads. These overheads are always included in the cost price of the article.

EXAMPLE 6.10

The cost price of an article is ₹450. It is sold for ₹495. Find the profit percentage.

SOLUTION

CP = ₹450; SP = ₹495

SP > CP and SP – CP = profit

Profit = ₹(495 – 450) = ₹45

$$\text{Profit percentage} = \frac{\text{Profit}}{\text{CP}} \times 100\%$$

$$= \frac{45}{450} \times 100\% = 10\%$$

EXAMPLE 6.11

A book is sold at a profit of 20%. If its cost price is ₹20, then find its selling price.

SOLUTION

CP of the book = ₹20

Profit percentage = 20%

Profit = 20% of ₹20

$= 20 \times \frac{1}{100} \times ₹20 = ₹4$

Selling price = CP + Profit

= ₹(20 + 4) = ₹24

EXAMPLE 6.12

A shopkeeper sold an article for ₹280. If its cost price is ₹300, then find his loss percentage.

SOLUTION

CP of the article = ₹300

SP of the article = ₹280

SP < CP and loss = CP – SP = ₹(300 – 280) = ₹20

$\text{Loss percentage} = \frac{\text{Loss}}{\text{CP}} \times 100\%$

$= \frac{20}{300} \times 100\% = 6\frac{2}{3}\%$

EXAMPLE 6.13

The cost price of an article is ₹500. The article is marked as ₹700. If the shopkeeper sold it at a discount of 30%, then find the profit or loss percentage.

SOLUTION

The cost price of the article = ₹500

The marked price of the article = ₹700

$\text{Discount} = 30\% \text{ of } 700 = \frac{30}{100} \times 700 = ₹210$

Selling price = Marked price – Discount = ₹(700 – 210)

SP = ₹490

∴ SP < CP and loss = CP – SP

Loss = ₹(500 – 490) = ₹10

$\text{Loss percentage} = \frac{\text{Loss}}{\text{CP}} \times 100\%$

$= \frac{10}{500} \times 100\% = 2\%$

SIMPLE INTEREST

Interest is the money paid by a borrower to the lender which is received by the lender for a specific time period until repayment is done.

Example: If person A borrows ₹100 from person B, for a period of one year on the condition that he would repay ₹110 at the end of a year, the additional money of ₹10 is the interest. A is the borrower and B is the lender and ₹100 is the principal.

The definitions for specific terms which are used frequently are given below:

Principal or Sum

The money borrowed from an agency or an individual for a certain period of time is called the principal or sum.

Amount

The principal together with the interest is called the amount, i.e., Amount (A) = Principal (P) + Interest (I).

Rate of Interest

The interest on principal per annum is called the rate of interest per annum.

Simple Interest

If the principal remains the same for the entire loan period, then the interest paid is called simple interest.

Formula for the Computation of Simple Interest

Let P be the principal in rupees, R be the rate of interest and T denotes the number of years. Then, Simple Interest (SI) = PTR/100.

Also, Amount (A) = Principal (P) + Simple Interest (SI) $= P + \frac{PTR}{100} = P\left(1 + \frac{RT}{100}\right)$

EXAMPLE 6.14

Principal = ₹25000. Amount after 2 years is ₹30000. Find the rate of interest per annum.

SOLUTION

Interest = Amount − Principal

= ₹(30000 − 25000) = ₹5000

Rate of interest $= \frac{5000}{25000} \times 100\% = 20\%$

EXAMPLE 6.15

How much simple interest is to be paid on a loan of ₹20000 at 18% per annum for a period of 3 years?

SOLUTION

P = ₹20000, R = 18%, T = 3 years

$$SI = \frac{PTR}{100}$$

$$SI = \frac{20000 \times 3 \times 18}{100} = 600 \times 18 = ₹10800$$

∴ Interest to be paid at the end of 3 years = ₹10800

EXAMPLE 6.16

The simple interest on a sum of ₹12000 is ₹1440. Find the amount after 5 years.

SOLUTION

Interest for one year = ₹1440

Interest for five years = ₹(1440 × 5) = ₹7200

∴ Amount = Principal + Interest

Amount after five years = ₹12000 + ₹7200 = ₹19200

EXAMPLE 6.17

Mr Abhishek paid ₹360 as an interest for 8 months at 18% p.a. Find the principal value of the loan taken by him.

SOLUTION

Let the principal be P.

R = 18% p.a.

$$T = 8 \text{ months} = \frac{8}{12} \text{ years} = \frac{2}{3} \text{ years}$$

$$SI = \frac{PTR}{100}$$

$$360 = P \times \frac{2}{3} \times \frac{18}{100}$$

$$P = \frac{360 \times 3 \times 100}{2 \times 18} = 10 \times 300 = ₹3000$$

TEST YOUR CONCEPTS

Very Short Answer Type Questions

Direction for questions from 1 to 5: Fill in the blanks.

1. 5% of 500 = ______.
2. 75% of 1 = ______.
3. $\frac{1}{5}$ of x is ______ % of x.
4. 0.25 of x is equal to ______ % of x.
5. 60% is equal to ______.

Direction for questions from 6 to 10: Select the correct alternative from the given choices.

6. Which of the following is equal to 40% of x?
   (a) $4x$ (b) $0.04x$
   (c) $\frac{2}{5}x$ (d) None of these
7. Equivalent fraction to 110% is ______.
   (a) $\frac{12}{5}$ (b) $\frac{6}{5}$
   (c) $\frac{11}{10}$ (d) $\frac{8}{15}$
8. 100% of x is equal to ______.
   (a) $100x$ (b) $0.1x$
   (c) $0.01x$ (d) x
9. 15% of 50 is equal to ______.
   (a) 50% of 30 (b) 100% of 30
   (c) 7.5% of 25 (d) 100% of 7.5
10. 10% of 20% of 100 is equal to ______.
   (a) 30% of 100 (b) 2% of 100
   (c) 15% of 100 (d) 200% of 100

Direction for question 11: Match Column A with Column B.

11.

Column A			Column B
(a) 45%	( )	(p)	$\frac{3}{2}$
(b) 75%	( )	(q)	$\frac{9}{20}$
(c) 125%	( )	(r)	$\frac{3}{4}$
(d) 150%	( )	(s)	$\frac{5}{4}$

Direction for questions from 12 to 16: Fill in the blanks.

12. If SP > CP, then the difference between the selling price and the cost price is ______.
13. If the selling price is less than the cost price, then there is a ______ in this transaction.
14. If the cost price of an article is ₹55 and the selling price is ₹44, then the loss in this transaction is ______ and the loss % is ______.
15. If the cost price is equal to the selling price, then there is ______.
16. If the profit on selling an article is ₹50 and the cost price of the article is ₹500, then the profit percentage is ______.

Direction for questions from 17 to 21: Select the correct alternative from the given choices.

17. Which of the following is true?
   (a) 10% profit on cost price of ₹450 is ₹50.
   (b) If loss % on the cost price of ₹400 is 25%, then the selling price is ₹300.
   (c) Selling price – Loss = Cost price
   (d) Profit – Cost price = Selling price
18. The percentage of loss is calculated on the ______.
   (a) Selling price (d) Cost price
   (c) Marked price (b) None of these
19. Discount = ______.
   (a) Cost price + Selling price
   (b) Selling price – Marked price
   (c) Marked price – Cost price
   (d) Marked price – Selling price
20. The cost price of a car is ₹6,00,000. The car is sold for ₹5,40,000. Which of the following is true about this transaction?
   (a) 10% loss (b) 10% profit
   (c) 6% profit (d) 6% loss
21. If an article is sold for ₹150 at a loss of ₹50, then which of the following is true?
   (a) 20% loss (b) 10% loss
   (c) 25% loss (d) 50% loss

PRACTICE QUESTIONS

Direction for question 22: Match Column A with Column B.

22.

	Column A			Column B
(a)	CP = ₹200, SP = ₹210	( )	(p)	5% profit
(b)	SP = ₹500, CP = ₹400	( )	(q)	10% profit
(c)	CP = ₹700, SP = ₹770	( )	(r)	20% profit
(d)	CP = ₹800, SP = ₹960	( )	(s)	25% profit

Direction for questions 23 to 27: Fill in the blanks.

23. Amount = ______ + Interest.

24. The money taken as loan is called ______.

25. The additional money to be paid for using others money is called ______.

26. The money paid to the money lender which includes the interest and the principal is called _____.

27. The simple interest on ₹1000 at 10% p.a. for 10 years is ______.

Direction for questions 28 to 32: Select the correct alternative from the given choices.

28. If $I = \frac{PTR}{100}$ then T = ______.

(a) $\frac{PT}{100}$ (b) $\frac{100IR}{P}$

(c) $\frac{PR}{100I}$ (d) $\frac{100I}{PR}$

29. Interest on ₹500 at 12% p.a. for 1 year is ______.

(a) 50 (b) 60

(c) 70 (d) 80

30. Interest on a certain sum is ₹456 and the amount is ₹2988. The principal is ₹______.

(a) 2532

(b) 2522

(c) 3444

(d) 2352

31. A sum of ₹4700 is doubled in 6 years under simple interest at a certain rate of interest. The interest is ₹ ______.

(a) 2350

(b) 4700

(c) 9400

(d) Cannot be determined

32. The simple interest on ₹550 at the rate of 5% p.a. for 2 years is ______.

(a) ₹55 (b) ₹27.50

(c) ₹125 (d) ₹12.50

Direction for question 33: Match Column A with Column B.

33.

	Column A (in ₹)			Column B (in ₹)
(a)	P = 256, I = 23	( )	(p)	A = 289
(b)	P = 265, I = 34	( )	(q)	A = 279
(c)	P = 258, I = 31	( )	(r)	A = 269
(d)	P = 257, I = 12	( )	(s)	A = 299

Short Answer Type Questions

34. Find the values of 72% of 250 and 37.5% of 800.

35. Find the value 62% of 19 + 38% of 19.

36. Convert $\frac{12}{25}$ and $4\frac{2}{3}$ into percentages.

37. Express (i) 0.05 (ii) 5.0 into percentages.

38. If 10% of a number x is 25, then find the value of 20% of x.

39. If $\frac{3}{5}$ of a number 'R' is equal to 30, then find 40% of R.

40. If 20% of x + 40% of $\frac{x}{2}$ + 20% of $3x = 100$, then find the value of x.

41. The area of a square sheet is 250 sq. cm. If one-fourth of the sheet is painted red, then half of the sheet is painted green and the remaining is painted white. Find the percentage of the area painted in white.

42. In a tray, there are 240 eggs. Raju sold 24 eggs from it and he used 12 eggs for himself. Find the percentage of remaining eggs in the tray.

43. Saritha added 0.5 litre of water to 2 litres of pure milk. Find the percentage of pure milk in the solution.

44. CP = ₹990 and Loss = ₹220. Find the selling price and the percentage of loss.

45. CP = ₹800, MP = ₹1000 and SP = ₹900. Find the percentage of (i) discount and (ii) profit.

46. The percentage of profit made on selling an article is 12%. If the cost price of the article is ₹1200, then find the profit.

47. The loss incurred on selling an article for ₹720 is ₹360. Find the loss percentage.

48. Mr Surya and Mr Karthi got 15% and 25% profits respectively in their business. If their investments are ₹20 crores and ₹12 crores then who got more profit in rupees?

49. A fruit seller purchased 20 kg of grapes for ₹400. If he sells the grapes at a rate of ₹50 per kg, then find his profit percentage.

50. Mr Akhil sold his bike for ₹42000. Its cost price was ₹60000. Find his loss and the loss percentage.

51. Mr Tarak purchased two horses for ₹7,50,000. He sold one horse for ₹4,00,000 and the other for ₹5,00,000. Find his profit and the profit percentage on selling both the horses.

52. P = ₹6000, A = ₹6660 and the time period is 1 year. Find the interest and the rate of interest per annum.

53. A = ₹7920, I = ₹720 and, T = 2 years. Find the principal and rate of interest.

54. P = 12000, Rate = 12% p.a., T = 12 months. Find the interest and the amount.

55. Rate = 15% p.a., P = ₹70000, A = ₹1,01,500. Find the time period.

56. In how many years, a certain sum becomes triple itself at 12% p.a.?

57. (a) A certain sum becomes double in 3 years, find the rate of interest.
(b) Find the simple interest on ₹8900 for $2\frac{1}{2}$ years at the rate of 18% p.a.

58. The population of a city increases every year 8% over its previous year. If the population of the city at the beginning of the year 2015 was 15,00,000. What would be the population of the city at the beginning of the year 2016?

59. Mr Crazyarala took a loan of ₹10,000 at the rate of 12% p.a. simple interest and lent this money to his neighbour at 18% simple interest for 2 years. If he cleared the loan in two years, then find his profit in this transaction.

CONCEPT APPLICATION

1. In a toy shop there are 500 balls of which 125 are blue, 150 are red and the remaining are yellow. What percentage of the balls in the shop are yellow?
(a) 25% (b) 30%
(c) 45% (d) 40%

3. An article is sold at a discount of 25%. Find the marked price of the article if its selling price is ₹1200.
(a) ₹1600 (b) ₹900
(c) ₹1425 (d) ₹1500

3. If CP : SP : MP = 2 : 3 : 4, then which of the following is true?
(A) Profit percentage = 50%
(B) Discount percentage = 25%
(a) Only (A)
(b) Only (B)
(c) Neither (A) nor (B)
(d) Both (A) and (B)

4. If a sum doubles in four years at the rate of R% per annum simple interest, then 3R = ______.
(a) 30 (b) 45
(c) 75 (d) 90

5. If 45% of x is 90, then x% of x ______.
(a) 2000 (b) 400
(c) 180 (d) 360

PRACTICE QUESTIONS

ASSESSMENT TEST

1. Simplify:

   (i) 30% of 340 (ii) $8\frac{1}{3}$% of 270

2. (i) Express 70% as a decimal.

   (ii) Express 240% as a fraction.

   (iii) Express $8\frac{1}{5}$ as a percentage.

3. Find the equivalent percentage of 200 gm over 20 kg.

4. A circle is inscribed in a square. The area of the circle is 154 sq. m and the area of the square is 196 sq. cm. Find the percentage of the area unoccupied by the circle in the square.

5. Find the profit or loss percentage in the following cases.

   (i) Cost price = ₹500, marked price = ₹700 and discount = ₹250.

   (ii) Selling price = ₹1200 and profit = ₹200.

6. On selling of 12 dozens of bananas for ₹360, a fruit seller got ₹120 profit. Find the cost price of banana per dozen.

7. A dealer sold two cell phones, he got 20% profit on one and 20% loss on the other. If the cost price of each cell phone is ₹20000, then find the profit or loss percentage.

8. The simple interest on a certain sum P is I and the amount is A. The rate of interest is R. Write the equations for P, R, T and A. $I = \frac{PTR}{100}$.

9. A sum of ₹12660 lent on simple interest at the rate of 15% p.a. for 5 years. Find the amount at the end of 5 years.

10. Mr Bhardwaj took a loan of ₹36000 from a money lender at 24% p.a., he cleared the loan in 9 months. Find the interest paid by Mr Bhardwaj to the money lender.

11. Anish spends ₹3000 from his pocket money of ₹5000 and saves the rest. What is the percentage of the money that he has saved?

12. In a class of 50 students, 26% are non-vegetarians. Calculate the number of non-vegetarian students.

13. In a class of 20 students, 5 are boys and remaining are girls. Find the percentage of girls.

14. How much interest will be paid at rate of 6% per annum on a borrowing of ₹800 for 2 years?

15. How much will be the amount to be paid after 2 years on a borrowing of ₹4000 at an interest of 10% per annum?

CROSSWORD

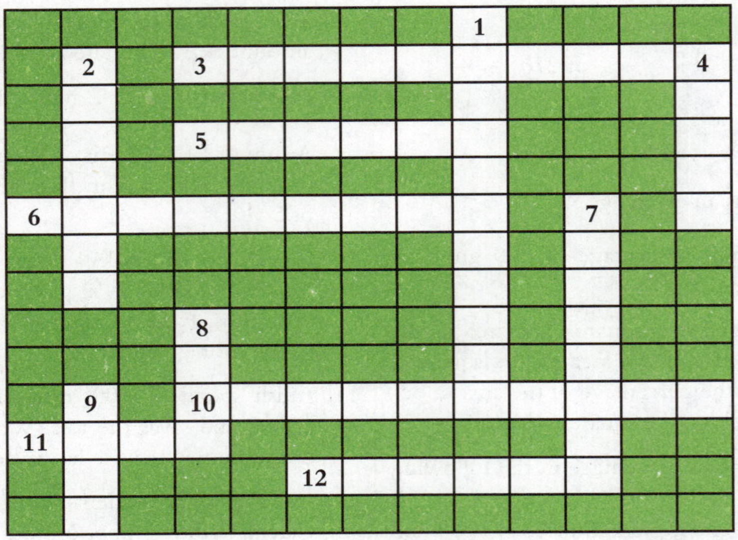

Across

3. A fraction with denominator hundred
5. The selling price is more than its cost price
6. Interest is subtracted from amount
10. Money spent in a business
11. Money is borrowed from the bank
12. The total money returned

Down

1. The total loan amount is paid in equal values in equal time periods
2. 100% of 100
4. 18% of 50 and 50% of 18
7. The additional money given to the lender by the borrower
8. Profit
9. The cost price is more than its selling price

TEST YOUR CONCEPTS

Very Short Answer Type Questions

1. 25
2. 3/4
3. 20
4. 25
5. 3/5
6. (c)
7. (c)
8. (d)
9. (d)
10. (b)
11. (a) → (q), (b) → (r), (c) → (s), (d) → (p)
12. Profit
13. Loss
14. ₹11; 20%
15. No profit and no loss
16. 10%
17. (b)
18. (b)
19. (d)
20. (a)
21. (c)
22. (a) → (p), (b) → (s), (c) → (q), (d) → (r)
23. Principal
24. Principal
25. Interest
26. Amount
27. ₹1000
28. (d)
29. (b)
30. (a)
31. (b)
32. (a)
33. (a) → (q), (b) → (s), (c) → (p), (d) → (r)

Short Answer Type Questions

34. (i) 180 (ii) 300
35. 19
36. (i) 48% (ii) $466\frac{2}{3}\%$
37. (i) 5% (ii) 500%
38. 50
39. 20
40. 100
41. 25%
42. 85%
43. 80%
44. ₹770; $22\frac{2}{9}\%$
45. (i) 10% (ii) 12.5%
46. ₹144
47. $33\frac{1}{3}\%$
48. Both of them got equal profit.
49. 150%
50. ₹18000; 30%
51. ₹1,50,000, 20%
52. ₹660; 11%
53. ₹7200; 5%
54. ₹1440; ₹13440
55. 3 years
56. $16\frac{2}{3}$ years
57. (a) $33\frac{1}{3}\%$ (b) ₹4005
58. ₹16,20,600
59. ₹1200

ANSWER KEYS

CONCEPT APPLICATION

1. (c)
2. (a)
3. (d)
4. (c)
5. (b)

ASSESSMENT TEST

1. (i) 102 (ii) 22.5
2. (i) 0.7 (ii) 12/5 (iii) 820%
3. 1%
4. $21\frac{3}{7}\%$
5. (i) 10% loss (ii) 20% profit
6. ₹20
7. No loss, no gain
9. ₹22155
10. ₹6480
11. 40%
12. 13
13. 75
14. ₹96
15. ₹4800

CROSSWORD

Across

3. Percentage
5. Profit
6. Principal
10. Investment
11. Loan
12. Amount

Down

1. Installment
2. Hundred
4. Equal
7. Interest
8. Gain
9. Loss

TEST YOUR CONCEPTS

Very Short Answer Type Questions

1. 5% of 500 = $\frac{5}{100} \times 500 = 5 \times 5 = 25$

2. 75% of 1 = $\frac{75}{100} \times 1 = \frac{3}{4}$

3. $\frac{1}{5}$ of $x = \frac{x}{5} \times 100\% = 20\%$ of x

4. 0.25 of $x = 0.25 \times 100\%$ of $x = 25\%$ of x

5. $60\% = \frac{60}{100} = \frac{6}{10} = \frac{3}{5}$

6. 40% of $x = \frac{40}{100} \times x = \frac{2}{5}x$

   Hence, the correct option is (c).

7. $110\% = \frac{110}{100} = \frac{11}{10}$

   Hence, the correct option is (c).

8. 100% of $x = \frac{100}{100} \times x = x$

   Hence, the correct option is (d).

9. 15% of 50 = $15 \times \frac{1}{100} \times 50 = 15 \times \frac{1}{2} = 7.5$

   $= 7.5 \times 100\%$

   = 100% of 7.5

   Hence, the correct option is (d).

10. 10% of 20% of 100 = $\frac{10}{100} \times \frac{20}{100} \times 100$

    $= \frac{200}{100} = 2$

    $= 2 \times \frac{1}{100} \times 100$

    = 2% of 100

    Hence, the correct option is (b).

11. (a) $45\% = \frac{45}{100} = \frac{9}{20} \rightarrow$ (q)

    (b) $75\% = \frac{75}{100} = \frac{3}{4} \rightarrow$ (r)

    (c) $125\% = \frac{125}{100} = \frac{5}{4} \rightarrow$ (s)

    (d) $150\% = \frac{150}{100} = \frac{3}{2} \rightarrow$ (p)

    Therefore, the correct match is:

    (a) → (q), (b) → (r), (c) → (s), (d) → (p)

12. SP – CP = Profit

13. Loss

14. Loss = ₹(55 – 44) = ₹11

    Loss % = $\frac{11}{55} \times 100\% = \frac{1}{5} \times 100\% = 20\%$

15. No profit and no loss.

16. Profit = ₹50; CP = ₹500

    Profit percentage = $\frac{50}{500} \times 100\% = \frac{50}{5}\% = 10\%$

17. (a) 10% on ₹450 is ₹45.

    (b) 25% on ₹400 = $\frac{25}{100} \times$ ₹400 = ₹100

    ∴ Selling price = ₹(400 – 100) = ₹300

    Hence, the correct option is (b).

20. Loss = ₹(6,00,000 – 5,40,000)

    = ₹60000

    ⇒ 60000 is 10% of 6 lakhs.

    Hence, the correct option is (a).

21. SP = ₹150, Loss = ₹50

    CP = ₹(150 + 50) = ₹200

    Loss % = $\frac{50}{200} \times 100\% = 25\%$

    Hence, the correct option is (c).

22. (a) Profit % = $\frac{10}{200} \times 100\% = 5\% \rightarrow$ (p)

    (b) Profit % = $\frac{100}{400} \times 100\% = 25\% \rightarrow$ (s)

    (c) Profit % = $\frac{70}{700} \times 100\% = 10\% \rightarrow$ (q)

    (d) Profit % = $\frac{160}{800} \times 100\% = 20\% \rightarrow$ (r)

    Therefore, the correct match is:

    (a) → (p), (b) → (s), (c) → (q), (d) → (r)

23. Principal

24. Principal

25. Interest

26. Amount

27. $I = \frac{PTR}{100} = \frac{1000 \times 10 \times 10}{100} = ₹1000$

28. $T = \frac{100I}{PR}$

Hence, the correct option is (d).

29. $I = \frac{PTR}{100} = \frac{500 \times 1 \times 12}{100} = 60$

Hence, the correct option is (b).

30. $P = A - I$

$= ₹(2988 - 456) = ₹2532$

Hence, the correct option is (a).

31. $A = P + I$ and $A = 2P$

$I = P$

$\therefore I = ₹4700$

Hence, the correct option is (b).

32. $I = \frac{PTR}{100}$

$I = \frac{550 \times 2 \times 5}{100}$

$= ₹55$

Hence, the correct option is (a).

33. $A = P + I$

(a) 256 + 23 = 279

(b) 265 + 34 = 299

(c) 258 + 31 = 289

(d) 257 + 12 = 269

Therefore, the correct match is:

(a) → (q), (b) → (s), (c) → (p), (d) → (r)

Short Answer Type Questions

34. (i) 72% of 250

$= 72 \times \frac{1}{100} \times 250$

$= 72 \times \frac{1}{2} \times 5 = 36 \times 5$

$= 180$

(ii) 37.5% 800

$= 37.5 \times \frac{1}{100} \times 800 = 37.5 \times 8 = 300$

35. 62% of 19 + 38% of 19

$= 100\%$ of $19 = \frac{100}{100} \times 19 = 19$

36. (i) $\frac{12}{25}$

$= \frac{12}{25} \times 100 \times \frac{1}{100} = \frac{12}{25} \times 100\%$

$= 12 \times 4\% = 48\%$

(ii) $4\frac{2}{3} = \frac{4 \times 3 + 2}{3} = \frac{14}{3}$

$\Rightarrow \frac{14}{3} = \frac{14}{3} \times 100 \times \frac{1}{100}$

$= \frac{14}{3} \times 100\% = \frac{1400}{3}\% = 466\frac{2}{3}\%$

37. (i) $0.05 = 0.05 \times 100 \times \frac{1}{100} = 0.05 \times 100\% = 5\%$

(ii) $5.0 = 5.0 \times 100 \times \frac{1}{100} = 500\%$

38. 10% of a number x is 25.

$2 \times 10\%$ of the number x is 2×25.

20% of the number x is 50.

39. $\frac{3}{5} \times R = 30$

$R = 30 \times \frac{5}{3}$

$R = 50$

40% of $R = \frac{40}{100} \times 50$

$= 20$

40. 20% of x + 40% of $\frac{x}{2}$ + 20% of $3x$

$= 100$

20% of x + 20% of x + 60% of $x = 100$

(20% + 20% + 60%) of $x = 100$

100% of $x = 100$

$\Rightarrow x = 100$

41. Area of the square painted in white

$= 250 - \frac{1}{4} \times 250 - \frac{1}{2} \times 250$

$= \left(1 - \frac{1}{4} - \frac{1}{2}\right)(250) = \left(1 - \frac{3}{4}\right)(250) = \frac{1}{4}(250)$

$\therefore$ The percentage of the area painted in white $= \frac{1}{4}(100\%)$, i.e., 25%.

42. $\Rightarrow$ 24 is 10% of 240.

$\Rightarrow$ 12 is 5% of 240.

Hence, (100 – 15)% = 85% of eggs are remaining in the tray.

43. The quantity of milk in the solution = 2 litres

Total quantity of the solution

= 2 + 0.5 = 2.5 litres

Percentage of milk in the solution

$= \frac{2}{2.5} \times 100\% = \frac{20}{25} \times 100\% = 80\%$

44. CP = ₹990, Loss = ₹220

SP = CP – Loss = ₹(990 – 220) = ₹770

$\text{Loss \%} = \frac{\text{Loss}}{\text{CP}} \times 100\%$

$= \frac{220}{990} \times 100\% = \frac{2}{9} \times 100\%$

$= \frac{200}{9}\% = 22\frac{2}{9}\%$

45. CP = ₹850, MP = ₹1000, SP = ₹900

Discount = MP – SP = ₹(1000 – 900)

= ₹100

(i) $\text{Discount \%} = \frac{\text{Discount}}{\text{Marked price}} \times 100\%$

$= \frac{100}{1000} \times 100\% = 10\%$

(ii) Profit = SP – CP = ₹(900 – 800) = ₹100

$\text{Profit \%} = \frac{\text{Profit}}{\text{CP}} \times 100\%$

$= \frac{100}{800} \times 100\% = 12.5\%$

46. CP = ₹1200, Profit = 12% CP

Profit = 12% of ₹1200

$= \frac{12}{100} \times ₹1200 = ₹144$

47. SP = ₹720, Loss = ₹360

CP = SP + Loss = ₹720 + ₹360

= ₹1080

$\therefore$ Loss percentage $= \frac{\text{Loss}}{\text{CP}} \times 100\%$

$= \frac{360}{1080} \times 100\% = \frac{1}{3} \times 100\%$

$= 33\frac{1}{3}\%$

48. Mr Surya:

Investment = ₹20 crores

Profit = 15% of 20 crores

$= \frac{15}{100} \times 20$

= ₹3 crores

Mr Karthi:

Investment = ₹12 crores

Profit per cent = 25%

Profit = 25% of 12 crores

$= \frac{25}{100} \times 12 = ₹3$ crores

$\therefore$ Both of them got equal profits.

49. The cost of 20 kg grapes = ₹400

The cost of 1 kg grapes $= ₹\frac{400}{20} = ₹20$

The selling price of 1 kg of grapes = ₹50

Profit = SP – CP = ₹(50 – 20)

= ₹30

$\text{Profit \%} = \frac{\text{Profit}}{\text{CP}} \times 100\%$

$= \frac{30}{20} \times 100\% = 3 \times 50\% = 150\%$

50. SP = ₹42000

CP = ₹60000

Loss = CP – SP

= ₹(60000 – 42000)

= ₹18000

$\text{Loss \%} = \frac{\text{Loss}}{\text{CP}} \times 100\%$

$= \frac{18000}{60000} \times 100\% = \frac{180}{6}\% = 30\%$

51. CP = ₹7,50,000

Total selling price = 4 lakhs + 5 lakhs

= ₹9 lakhs

Profit = SP – CP

= ₹(9,00,000 – 7,50,000) = ₹1,50,000

Profit % = $\frac{\text{Profit}}{\text{CP}} \times 100\%$

$= \frac{1,50,000}{7,50,000} \times 100\% = \frac{15}{75} \times 100\% = 20\%$

52. P = ₹6000, A = ₹6660, T = 1 year

I = A – P

I = 6660 – 6000

= ₹660

Rate of interest = $\frac{100I}{PT}\%$

$= \frac{100 \times 660}{1 \times 6000 \times}\% = 11\%$

53. A = ₹7920, I = ₹720, T = 2 years

P = A – I = ₹(7920 – 720) = ₹7200

P = ₹7200

Rate of interest = $\frac{1 \times 100}{P \times T}\%$

$= \frac{720 \times 100}{7200 \times 2}\% = 5\%$ pa

54. P = ₹12000, Rate = 12% p.a.

T = 12 months, = 1 year

$I = \frac{PTR}{100} = \frac{1200 \times 1 \times 2}{100} =$ ₹1,440

A = P + I = ₹(12,000 + 1440) = ₹13440

55. Rate = 15% p.a., P = ₹70000

A = 1,01,500

I = A – P = ₹(1,01,500 – 70000) = ₹31500

$I = \frac{PTR}{100}$

$T = \frac{100I}{PR}$

$T = \frac{100 \times 31500}{70000 \times 15} = 3$ years

56. Rate = 12% pa

T = ?

A = 3P

I = A – P = 3P – P = 2P

$T = \frac{100I}{PR}$

$T = \frac{100 \times 2P}{P \times 12} = \frac{100}{6} = \frac{50}{3} = 16\frac{2}{3}$ years

57. (a) A = 2P

I = A – P

= 2P – P = P

T = 3 years

$R = \frac{100I}{PT} = \frac{100 \times P}{P \times 3} = \frac{100}{3} = 33\frac{1}{3}\%$

∴ Rate of interest is $33\frac{1}{3}\%$ p.a.

(b) $T = 2\frac{1}{2}$ years $= \frac{5}{2}$ years

P = ₹8900

R = 18% pa

$I = \frac{PTR}{100}$

$= = \frac{8900}{100} \times \frac{5}{2} \times 18$

= 89 × 5 × 9 = ₹4005

58. The population at the beginning of 2015 is 15,00,000.

The population at the beginning of 2016

$= \frac{8}{100} \times 15,00,000 + 15,00,000$

= 1,20,000 + 15,00,000

= 16,20,000

59. P = ₹10000

Rate = 12% pa

T = 2 years

$I_1 = \frac{PTR}{100}$

$= \frac{10000 \times 2 \times 12}{100} =$ ₹2400

Amount lent

P = ₹10000, Rate = 18% p.a.

T = 2 years

$I_2 = \frac{PTR}{100} = \frac{10000 \times 2 \times 18}{100} =$ ₹3600

Profit = $I_2 - I_1$ = ₹(3600 – 2400) = ₹1200

CONCEPT APPLICATION

1. The number of yellow balls in the shop = 500 – 125 – 150 = 500 – 275 = 225

The percentage of yellow balls in the shop

$$= \frac{225}{500} \times 100 = 45\%.$$

Hence, the correct option is (c).

2. Given, discount = 25% of MP

SP = ₹1,200

⇒ MP – discount Discount = 1200

⇒ MP – 25% of MP = 1200

⇒ 75% of MP = 1200

$$\Rightarrow MP = 1200 \times \frac{100}{75} = 1600$$

Therefore, marked price of the article = ₹1,600.

Hence, the correct option is (a).

3. Given, CP : SP : MP = 2 : 3 : 4

Let the CP, SP and MP be ₹200, ₹300 and ₹400, respectively.

Then, profit = SP – CP = ₹300 – ₹200 = ₹100

$$\text{Profit percentage} = \frac{\text{Profit}}{\text{CP}} \times 100$$

$$= \frac{100}{200} \times 100 = 50\%$$

Discount = MP – SP = ₹400 – ₹300 = ₹100

$$\text{Discount percentage} = \frac{\text{Discount}}{\text{CP}} \times 100$$

$$= \frac{100}{400} \times 100 = 25\%$$

Hence, both (a) and (b) are true.

Hence, the correct option is (d).

4. Let the sum be P = ₹100.

As given, P = ₹100, A = ₹200, T = 4 years.

Then, SI = A – P = ₹200 – ₹100 = ₹100

$$\text{We have SI} = \frac{PTR}{100}$$

$$\Rightarrow 100 = \frac{100 \times 4 \times R}{100} \Rightarrow R = \frac{100}{4} = 25 \Rightarrow 3R = 75$$

Hence, the correct option is (c).

5. Given 45% of x = 90

$$\Rightarrow \frac{45}{100} \times x = 90$$

$$\Rightarrow x = 90 \times \frac{100}{45} = 200$$

Therefore, x% of x = 200% of 200

$$= \frac{200}{100} \times 200 = 400.$$

Hence, the correct option is (b).

ASSESSMENT TEST

1. (i) 30% of 340

$$\frac{30}{100} \times 340 = 3 \times 34 = 102$$

(iii) $8\frac{1}{3}$% of 270

$$= \frac{25}{3} \times \frac{1}{100} \times 270$$

$$= 22.5$$

2. (i) $70\% = 70 \times \frac{1}{100} = \frac{7}{10} = 0.7$

(ii) $240\% = 240 \times \frac{1}{100} = \frac{24}{10} = \frac{12}{5}$

(iii) $8\frac{1}{5} = \left(8\frac{1}{5}\right) \times 100 \times \frac{1}{100}$

$$= \left(8\frac{1}{5}\right) \times 100\% = \left(\frac{41}{5}\right) \times 100\% = 820\%$$

3. $$\frac{200 \text{ gm}}{20 \text{ kg}} = \frac{200 \text{ g}}{20 \times 1000 \text{ g}} \times 100\%$$

$$= \frac{200}{20 \times 1000} \times 100\% = 1\%$$

4. Area unoccupied by the circle in the square

= Area of the square – Area of the circle

= 196 – 154 = 42 sq. cm

Percentage of area unoccupied in the square

$= \frac{42}{196} \times 100\% = \frac{6}{7} \times 25\%$

$= \frac{150}{7}\% = 21\frac{3}{7}\%$

5. (i) Cost price (CP) = ₹500

Marked price (MP) = ₹700

Discount = ₹250

SP = MP – discount

= ₹(700 – 250) = 450

Here, SP < CP, there is a loss.

Loss = CP – SP = ₹(500 – 450) = ₹50

$\text{Loss } \% = \frac{\text{Loss}}{\text{CP}} \times 100\%$

$= \frac{50}{500} \times 100\% = 10\%$

(ii) SP = ₹1200

Profit = ₹200

CP = SP – Profit = ₹(1200 – 200) = ₹1000

$\text{Profit } \% = \frac{\text{Profit}}{\text{CP}} \times 100\%$

$= \frac{200}{1000} \times 100\% = 20\%$

6. CP of 12 dozen banana

= SP – Profit = ₹(360 – 120) = ₹240

CP of 1 dozen banana = ₹ $\frac{240}{12}$ = ₹20

7. **Case I:**

20% profit on ₹20000

$= \frac{20}{100} \times$ ₹20000 = ₹4000

Case II:

20% loss on ₹20000

$\frac{20}{100} \times$ ₹20000 = ₹4000

∴ Loss and gain are equal. Hence, there is no loss or no gain for the shopkeeper.

8. $I = \frac{PTR}{100}$

A = P + I

$P = \frac{100I}{TR}$

$R = \frac{100I}{PT}$

$T = \frac{100I}{PR}$

$A = P + I = P + \frac{PTR}{100} = P(1 + \frac{TR}{100})$

9. P = ₹12660

Rate = 15% p.a.

T = 5 years

$I = \frac{PTR}{100} = \frac{12660 \times 5 \times 15}{100} = 9495$

A = P + I

= 12660 + 9495 = ₹22155

10. P = 36000

R = 24% pa

T = 9 months = $\frac{9}{12}$ years

$I = \frac{PTR}{100} = \frac{36000}{100} \times \frac{9}{12} \times 24 = 360 \times \frac{3}{4} \times 24$

$= 360 \times 3 \times 6 = 6480$

∴ Interest paid by Mr Bhardwaj to the money lender = ₹6480

11. Total money = ₹5000

Amount spent = ₹3000

Amount saved = ₹2000

Percentage of money saved

= (Amount saved/total amount) × 100%

= (2000/5000) × 100

= 40%

12. Number of non-vegetarians in class = 26% of 50

= 13

HINTS AND EXPLANATION

13. Number of boys = 5

Number of girls = 15

Total no. of students = 20

Percentage of girls = $\left(\frac{15}{20}\right) \times 100$

$= 75\%$

14. Interest to be paid = $800 \times \frac{6}{100} \times 2$

$= 96$

15. Interest to be paid = $4000 \times \frac{10}{100} \times 2$

Amount to be paid = 4000 + 800

= ₹4800

Chapter 7

Algebra

REMEMBER

Before beginning this chapter, you should be able to:

- Know numbers and symbols
- Write expressions in numbers and symbols

KEY IDEAS

After completing this chapter, you should be able to:

- Learn terms of an expression
- Define polynomial and types of polynomials
- Understand addition and subtraction of polynomials
- Understand multiplication and division of a polynomials with a monomial
- Describe linear equation, simple equation, properties of equations
- Solve equation in one variable

INTRODUCTION

An algebraic expression is a mathematical phrase that has various components like numbers, letters and some symbols. In this chapter, we will learn what these components are called in an expression and how are they used.

ALGEBRAIC EXPRESSIONS

In this chapter, we shall look at various algebraic concepts and their definitions such as constant, variable, terms, like terms, algebraic expression, application of four fundamental operations, i.e., addition, subtraction, multiplication and division. Apart from this, we shall also discuss the methods of solving simple equations.

Info Box!

The word 'algebra' is dervied from the Arabic word ' al-jabr'.

Constant

A number having a fixed numerical value is called a constant.

Examples: 2, 3, 7, –8, 1.4, $\frac{2}{3}$, etc.

Variable

A number which can take various numerical values is known as a variable.

Examples: x, y, z, etc.

A number which is a power of another variable where the power is not zero is also a variable.

Examples: x^3, y^2, z^4, etc.

A number which is the product of a constant and a variable is also a variable.

Examples: $5x^4$, $8x^3$, $-8x$, etc.

A combination of two or more variables separated by a '+' sign or a '–' sign is also a variable.

Examples: $x^2 - y^4 + z^6$, $x^3 + y^3 + z^2$, etc.

Algebraic Expression

A combination of constants and variables connected by '+' or '–' or '×' or '÷' signs is known as an algebraic expression.

Examples: $8x^2 + 5$, $4x^3 + 2xy - 8xy^2 + 6$, etc.

Terms

Several parts of an algebraic expression, separated by '+' or '–' signs are called the terms of the expression.

Example: In the expression, $8x - 14y + 9$, we say that $8x$, $-14y$ and 9 are terms.

Coefficient of a Term

Consider the term $9x^4$. In this case, 9 is called the numerical coefficient of x^4 and x^4 is said to be the literal coefficient of 9.

In case of $6xy$, the numerical coefficient is 6 and the literal coefficient is xy.

Like Terms

The terms having the same literal coefficients are called like terms.

Examples: (i) $2x^4$, $-6x^4$ and $9x^4$ are like terms.

(ii) $18x^2y^3$, $-15x^2y^3$ and $17x^2y^3$ are like terms.

Unlike Terms

The terms having different literal coefficients are called unlike terms.

Example: $-13x^2$, $17x^3$, $14x^4$ are unlike terms.

Polynomial

An algebraic expression in which the variables involved have only non-negative integer powers is called a polynomial.

Example: $3y + 4x^2 - 7$, $2x^3 + 4y^2 - 8x + 9$, etc.

The expression $5x^4 - 7x^3 + 9x^2 - 3x^{5/2}$ is not a polynomial since it has powers of x which are negative and fractions.

A polynomial that contains only one variable is known as a polynomial in that variable.

Example: $8x + 15$ is a polynomial in the variable x and $2y^2 + 2y^3$ is a polynomial in the variable y.

A polynomial that contains two variables, say x and y is known as a polynomial in two variables.

Example: $x^3y^2 - 2x^4y^3 + 5xy$ is a polynomial in x and y variables.

Degree of a Polynomial in One Variable

The highest exponent of the variable in a polynomial of one variable is called the degree of the polynomial.

Examples: (a) $x^4 - 5x^2 - x + 7$ is a polynomial of degree 4.

(b) $7x^9 - 3x^6 + 7x^3 - x^2 - 5$ is a polynomial of degree 9.

Types of polynomials with respect to the number of terms:

1. **Monomial:** An expression containing only one term is called a monomial.

   Examples: $3x$, $5x^2y$, $6xyz$, etc.

2. **Binomial:** An expression containing two terms is called a binomial.

   Examples: $2x - 3y$, $5x^2y^2 - 7$, $xy - 3y$

3. **Trinomial:** An expression containing three terms is called a trinomial.

   Examples: $2x - 3y + 4z$, $3xy^2 - xy + 5$.

TABLE 7.1 Common algebraic terms

Term	Notation
Variable	x
Variable term	$7x$
Constant	4
Constant term	45
Algebraic expression	$7x - 45$
Algebraic statement	$7x - 45 = 4$

Value of an Expression

In Mathematics, we come across many situations where we need to find out the value of an expression. The value of an expression purely depends upon the values of the variables that form the expression.

Example: When $x = 6$, the value of the expression $3x - 2$ is $3 \times 6 - 2 = 16$.

And the value of $8x + y$, when $x = 1$ and $y = -2$ is $8(1) - 2 = 8 - 2 = 6$.

EXAMPLE 7.1

Find the number of terms in the following expressions.

(I) $3x^2y$ **(II)** $4x^3 - y^3$ **(III)** $5x^5 + y - 2$

SOLUTION

(I) $3x^2y$ has <u>one</u> term.

(II) $4x^3 - y^3$ has <u>two</u> terms.

(III) $5x^5 + y - 2$ has <u>three</u> terms.

EXAMPLE 7.2

Name the following algebraic expressions with respect to the number of terms.

(I) $2x^2y - 7x + 6$ **(II)** $3xy - 5$ **(III)** $-8x$

SOLUTION

(I) $2x^2y - 7x + 6$ has three terms, hence it is a trinomial.

(II) $3xy - 5$ has two terms, hence it is a binomial.

(III) $-8x$ has one term, hence it is a monomial.

EXAMPLE 7.3

Write the following expressions in the exponential form.

(I) $2 \times 5 \times 7 \times x \times x \times x \times y \times y$

(II) $3 \times 3 \times 3 \times 11 \times x \times x \times x \times x \times y \times y \times y$

(III) $2 \times 3 \times 5 \times x \times y \times x \times y \times x \times y \times y$

SOLUTION

(I) $2 \times 5 \times 7 \times x \times x \times x \times y \times y = 2\ (5)\ (7)\ x^3y^2$

(II) $3 \times 3 \times 3 \times 11 \times x \times x \times x \times x \times y \times y \times y = 3^3 \times 11 \times x^4 \times y^3$

(III) $2 \times 3 \times 5 \times x \times y \times x \times y \times x \times y \times y = 2\ (3)\ (5)\ x^3y^4$

OPERATIONS ON POLYNOMIALS

Let us understand the various operations, such as addition, subtraction, multiplication and division, which are performed on polynomials.

Addition of Polynomials

The sum of two or more polynomials can be obtained by arranging the terms and then adding the numerical coefficients of like terms.

EXAMPLE 7.4

Let $A = 3x^2 - 7xy + 6$ and $B = 7xy - 5x^2 + 15$.

Find:

(I) $A + B$ **(II)** $2A + B$

SOLUTION

(I) $A + B = (3x^2 - 7xy + 6) + (7xy - 5x^2 + 15)$

$= (3x^2 - 5x^2) + (-7xy + 7xy) + (6 + 15)$

$= -2x^2 + 0 + 21$

$= -2x^2 + 21$

(II) $2A + B = 2(3x^2 - 7xy + 6) + (7xy - 5x^2 + 15)$

$= 6x^2 - 14xy + 12 + 7xy - 5x^2 + 15$

$= 6x^2 - 5x^2 - 14xy + 7xy + 12 + 15$

$= 1x^2 - 7xy + 27$

Subtraction of Polynomials

The difference of two polynomials can be obtained by arranging the terms and subtracting the numerical coefficients of the like terms.

EXAMPLE 7.5

Let $A = 3x^2 - 7xy + 6$ and $B = 7xy - 5x^2 + 15$.

Find:

(I) $A - B$ **(II)** $3A - 2B$

SOLUTION

(I) $A - B = (3x^2 - 7xy + 6) - (7xy - 5x^2 + 15)$

$= 3x^2 - 7xy + 6 -7xy + 5x^2 - 15)$

$= (3x^2 + 5x^2) + (-7xy -7xy) + (6 - 15)$

$= 8x^2 -14xy -9$

(II) $3A - 2B = 3(3x^2 - 7xy + 6) - 2(7xy - 5x^2 + 15)$

$= 9x^2 - 21xy + 18 - 14xy + 10x^2 - 30$

$= 19x^2 - 35xy - 12$

EXAMPLE 7.6

Simplify: $8m - [3m - \{2m + 3 - 2(4m - 4)\}]$

SOLUTION

$8m - [3m - \{2m + 3 - 2(4m - 4)\}]$

$= 8m - [3m - \{(2 - 8)m + (3 + 8\}]$

$= 8m - [3m - \{-6m + 11\}]$

$= 8m - [3m + 6m - 11]$

$= 8m - [9m - 11]$

$= 8m - 9m + 11 = 11 - m$

Multiplication of a Polynomial with a Monomial

The result of multiplication of a polynomial is obtained by multiplying each term of the polynomial by the monomial and then taking the algebraic sum of these products.

EXAMPLE 7.7

Multiply $(2x^2 - 4x + 6y)$ by $2xy$.

SOLUTION

$(2x^2 - 4x + 6y)\ (2xy)$

$= (2x^2)\ (2xy) - 4x(2xy) + 6y\ (2xy)$

$= 4x^3y - 8x^2y + 12xy^2$

EXAMPLE 7.8

Simplify: $5(2x - 3) - x(3 - 2x) + 2x^2$

SOLUTION

$5(2x - 3) - x(3 - 2x) + 2x^2$

$= 10x - 15 - 3x + 2x^2 + 2x^2$

$= 10x - 3x + 2x^2 + 2x^2 - 15$

$= 7x + 4x^2 - 15$

$= 4x^2 + 7x - 15$

EXAMPLE 7.9

Find the product of polynomial $(x + 2)$ and $(2x + 3)$.

SOLUTION

$(x + 2)\ (2x + 3)$
$= x(2x + 3) + 2(2x + 3)$
$= 2x^2 + 3x + 4x + 6$
$= 2x^2 + 7x + 6$

Thus, the sum or product of two or more polynomials is also a polynomial.

Division of a Polynomial by a Monomial

To divide a polynomial by a monomial, we need to divide each term of the polynomial by the monomial.

EXAMPLE 7.10

Divide $16x^3 + 12x^2 + 8x$ by $4x$.

SOLUTION

$$\frac{16x^3 + 12x^2 + 8x}{4x} = \frac{16x^3}{4x} + \frac{12x^2}{4x} + \frac{8x}{4x} = 4x^2 + 3x + 2$$

EQUATIONS

We shall understand the various terms and concepts related to equations as given below.

Algebraic Expressions

Expressions of the form $4x$, $(x + 5)$, $(4x + y)$ are algebraic expressions. x and 5 are the terms of $(x + 5)$ and $4x$ and y are the terms of $4x + y$. Algebraic expressions are made up of numbers, symbols and basic arithmetic operations.

Mathematical Sentence

Two expressions joined by the equality sign (=) or an inequality sign ($<, >, \leq, \geq$) are mathematical sentences.

Examples: $2 + 5 = 7$, $8 - 3 = 6$, $7x - 8 = 4$, $2 + 3 > 4$, $6 - 2 < 2$ are some mathematical sentences. Those which have the equality sign are equations and those which have an inequality sign are inequations.

Mathematical Statement

A mathematical sentence that can be verified as either true or false is a mathematical statement.

Example: $15 + 8 = 12 + 11$. This is a true statement. $14 - 3 \geq 17$. This is a false statement.

All sentences involving only numerical expressions can be verified as either true or false. Hence, they are statements.

Open Sentences

Sentences which are true for some values of the variable and false for the other values of the variable are called open sentences. When a certain value is substituted for the variable, the sentence becomes a statement, regardless of whether it is true or false.

For example: $2x - 3 = 7$. This is an open sentence. When we substitute 5 for x, we get a true statement. When we substitute any other value, we get a false statement.

Equation

An open sentence containing the equality sign is an equation. In other words, an equation is a sentence in which there is an equality sign between two algebraic expressions.

Examples: $2x - 5 = 8$, $3y + 4 = 2$, $x^2 - 7x + 12 = 0$ are equations. Here, x and y are unknown quantities and 2, 5, 8, 3, etc., are known quantities.

Linear Equation

An equation, in which the highest index of the unknowns present is one, is a linear equation. $2x + 3 = 4$, $3x + 4y = 8$ are some linear equations.

Simple Equation

A linear equation which has only one unknown is a simple equation. $8x - 3 = 5$ and $4x + 4 = 3x - 6$ are examples of simple equations. The part of an equation which is to the left side of the equality sign is known as the left hand side, it is abbreviated as LHS. The part of an equation which is to the right side of the equality sign is known as the right hand side, abbreviated as RHS. The process of finding the value of an unknown in an equation is called solving the equation. The value/values of the unknown found after solving an equation is/are called the solution(s) or the root(s) of the equation. Before we learn how to solve an equation, let us review the basic properties of equality.

Solving an Equation in One Variable

The following steps are involved in solving an equation.

Step 1: Always ensure that the unknown quantities are on the LHS and the known quantities or constants are on the RHS.

Step 2: Add all the terms containing the unknowns on the LHS and all the known values on the RHS so that each side of the equation contains only one term. On the LHS, the number with which the unknown is multiplied is called the coefficient.

Step 3: Divide both sides of the equation by the coefficient of the unknown.

Properties of Equality

1. **Addition Property:** If equal numbers are added to both sides of equality, the equality remains the same. If $x = y$, then $x + z = y + z$.

2. **Subtraction Property:** If equal numbers are subtracted from both sides of equality, the equality remains the same. If $x = y$, then $x - z = y - z$.

3. **Multiplication property:** If both sides of equality are multiplied by the same number, the equality remains the same. If $x = y$, then $(x)(z) = (y)(z)$.

4. **Division Property:** If both sides of equality are divided by a non-zero number, the equality remains the same. If $x = y$, then, $x/z = y/z$ where $z \neq 0$.

EXAMPLE 7.11

Solve for x: $5x - 6 = 9$

SOLUTION

$5x - 6 = 9$

$\Rightarrow 5x = 9 + 6$

$\Rightarrow x = \frac{15}{5}$

$\Rightarrow x = 3$

EXAMPLE 7.12

Solve for x: $\frac{3x}{2} + \frac{x}{3} = x + \frac{x}{6} + 6$

SOLUTION

$\frac{3x}{2} + \frac{x}{3} = x + \frac{x}{6} + 6$

$\frac{3x}{2} + \frac{x}{3} - x - \frac{x}{6} = 6$

$\frac{3 \times 3x + 2 \times x - 6 \times x - 1 \times x}{6} = 6$

$\frac{9x + 2x - 6x - 1x}{6} = 6$

$11x - 7x = 6 \times 6$

$4x = 36$

$x = 9$

EXAMPLE 7.13

The sum of two consecutive odd numbers is 164. Find the numbers.

SOLUTION

Let the two consecutive odd numbers be x and $x + 2$.

Given that: $(x) + (x + 2) = 164$

$2x + 2 = 164$

$2(x + 1) = 164$

$x + 1 = \frac{164}{2}$

$x + 1 = 82$

$x = 82 - 1$

$\Rightarrow x = 81$

$\therefore$ The two consecutive odd numbers are 81 and 83.

EXAMPLE 7.14

The present age of a person is $\frac{1}{3}$ of the present age of his father. If the sum of their ages is 60 years, then find the age of the son.

SOLUTION

Let the present age of father be x years.

$\therefore$ The present age of the son = $\frac{x}{3}$ years.

Given that: $x + \frac{x}{3} = 60$

$$\frac{x}{1} + \frac{x}{3} = 60 \Rightarrow \frac{3 \times x + 1 \times x}{3} = 60$$

$$\frac{3x + x}{3} = 60 \Rightarrow \frac{4x}{3} = 60$$

$$4x = 60 \times 3 \Rightarrow 4x = 180$$

$$x = \frac{180}{4}$$

$$x = 45$$

$\therefore$ The age of son = $\frac{1}{3} \times 45 = 15$ years.

TEST YOUR CONCEPTS

Very Short Answer Type Questions

Direction for questions from 1 to 5: Fill in the blanks.

1. A quantity which has no fixed value is called a/an _______.

2. A quantity which has a fixed numerical value is called a/an _______.

3. A combination of constants and variables connected by one or more fundamental operating signs is a/an _______.

4. The exponents of the variables of a polynomial must be _______ integers.

5. The terms having same literal coefficients are called _______.

Direction for questions from 6 to 10: Select the correct alternative from the given choices.

6. Which of the following is a polynomial?

(a) $3x - \frac{2}{x}$ (b) $x^2 - \sqrt{3}$

(c) $\sqrt{x} + 5$ (d) $x + x^{3/2}$

7. The degree of the polynomial $8x^7 - 7x^6 + 6x^5 - 15x^3$ is _______.

(a) 8 (b) 7

(c) 15 (d) 3

8. Which of the following is a trinomial?

(a) xyz (b) $x^2 - xy$

(c) x^3 (d) None of these

9. The numerical coefficient of $2x^5y^3$ is _______.

(a) 5 (b) 3

(c) 8 (d) 2

10. The number of second degree terms in the expression $2x^3 - 3x^2y + 5x^2 - 6xy^2 + 8x^2y - 4x^2y^2$ is _______.

(a) 3 (b) 2

(c) 1 (d) 4

Direction for question 11: Match Column A with Column B.

11.

Column A (Polynomial)			Column B (Degree of the polynomial)
(a)	$9x^3 + 7x^2 + 6x + 5$	( )	(p) 2
(b)	$\frac{3}{5}x^2 - 7x^4 - 2$	( )	(q) 3
(c)	$8x^5 - 9x^6 + 4$	( )	(r) 4
(d)	$5x^2 - 8x + 3$	( )	(s) 5
			(t) 6

Direction for questions from 11 to 16: Fill in the blanks.

12. $3x^2y + 7x^2y =$ _______.

13. $\frac{5}{2}x^2 - \frac{3}{2}x^2 =$ _______.

14. $2017xy - 2xy =$ _______.

15. $\frac{3}{4}(4x - 8) =$ _______.

16. $\frac{2xy - 6x}{2x} =$ _______.

Direction for questions from 17 to 22: Select the correct alternative from the given choices.

17. $\frac{2}{3}x + 3x + \frac{1}{3}x =$ _______.

(a) $4x$ (b) $\frac{5}{3}x$

(c) $\frac{3}{2}(x)$ (d) $\frac{5}{2}x$

18. $2x - 2\left(x - \frac{1}{2}\right) =$ _______.

(a) x (b) $2x$ (c) 2 (d) 1

19. $2x(3 - 2x) =$ _______.

(a) $6x - 4x^2$ (b) $6x - 2x^2$

(c) $3 - 4x$ (d) $3 - 4x^2$

PRACTICE QUESTIONS

20. $\frac{4x^2 - 8x + 10}{2} =$ ________.

(a) $2x^2 - 4x + 5$ (b) $2x^2 - 8x + 10$
(c) $2x^2 - 4x + 10$ (d) $2x^2 - 8x + 5$

21. $3x\left(\frac{2}{3}x - \frac{1}{3x}\right) =$ ________.

(a) $2x^2 - 3$ (b) $2x^2 - 1$
(c) $2x - 1$ (d) $2x^2 - 2$

Direction for question 22: Match Column A with Column B.

22.

	Column A			Column B
(a)	$\frac{3x}{2}(2x - 3)$	( )	(p)	$3x^2 - \frac{9x}{2}$
(b)	$\frac{2x}{3}(3x - 2)$	( )	(q)	$\frac{9x^2}{2} - 3x$
(c)	$\frac{3x}{2}(3x - 2)$	( )	(r)	$2x^2 - \frac{4x}{3}$
(d)	$\frac{2x}{3}(2x - 3)$	( )	(s)	$\frac{4x^2}{3} - 2x$

Direction for questions from 23 to 27: Fill in the blanks.

23. If $x + 5 = 8$, then $x =$ ________.

24. If $\frac{1}{2}x + \frac{3}{4} = 1$, then $x =$ ________.

25. If $\frac{3x}{5} + \frac{7x}{5} = 2$, then $x =$ ________.

26. If $2x - 5 = 7$, then $x =$ ________.

27. If $12 + x = 18 - x$, then $x =$ ________.

Direction for questions from 28 to 31: Select the correct alternative from the given choices.

28. The highest power of the variable in a linear equation is ________.

(a) 0 (b) 1
(c) 2 (d) Can be of any value

29. The number of value(s) of x, which satisfy $7x + 2 = 8x + 2$ is ________.

(a) 0 (b) 1 (c) 2 (d) 3

30. The sum of two consecutive natural numbers is 45. Which of the following represents the above statement?

(a) $(x + 1) + (x + 2) = 45$
(b) $(x) + (x + 1) = 45$
(c) $(x - 1) + x = 45$
(d) All the above

31. The age of a man is 4 times his son's age and the sum of their ages is 60 years. Which of the following represents the above statement?

(a) $x + 60 = 4x$ (b) $4x - x = 60$
(c) $x + 4x = 60$ (d) $4x + 60 = x$

Direction for question 32: Match Column A with Column B.

32.

	Column A			Column B
(a)	$2x - 7 = 15$	( )	(p)	12
(b)	$2x - 15 = 9$	( )	(q)	11
(c)	$2x + 5 = 23$	( )	(r)	9
(d)	$2x + 4 = 20$	( )	(s)	8

Short Answer Type Questions

33. State whether the following statements are true or false.

(i) The coefficient of x in the expression $4xy^2$ is 4.
(ii) The number of terms in the expression $4xy$ is 3.
(iii) $x^2y^3 - xy$ is a binomial.
(iv) $3x^2 - 2x + 2/3$ is not a polynomial.

34. List out the like terms in the following expressions.

(i) $4x^4, -7x^3, 8x^2, 12x^3, -9x^4, -5x, 4x^3, 12x^2$
(ii) $5xy, -3x^2y, 2xy^3, -2x^2y^2, 5x^2y, -3xy, 5x^2y^2$

35. Which of the following algebraic expressions are polynomials?

(i) $x^{1/2} + y^{1/2} + z^{1/2}$ (ii) $x^2 + y^2$
(iii) $\sqrt{x} + 3$ (iv) $\sqrt{5} + x^5$ (v) 2016

36. Write the degree of the following polynomials.

(i) $3x^5 - 7x^2 + 8x - 2x^8 + 10$
(ii) $2x^9 - 3x^2 - 14x^3 - 15x^4$

37. Write the numerical coefficients of the following.

(i) $17x^2y$ (ii) $12xy^3$
(iii) $\frac{3}{5}x$ (iv) $\frac{-3}{2}x^2$

PRACTICE QUESTIONS

38. If $x = 3$ and $y = 1$, then find the values of

(i) $3x - 2y$ (ii) $\frac{22}{3}x^2 - \frac{7}{2}y^2$

39. If $x = 2$ and $y = 3$, then find the values of

(i) $\frac{2x + 3y}{4x - 3y}$ (ii) $\frac{2x^2 - 7x + 2y}{2y^2 - 7y + 2x}$

40. $A = 2x + 3xy + 7x^2$, $B = 3x - 2xy - 5x^2$ and $C = 2xy - 6x^2 - 3x$. Find the value of $A + B - C$.

41. Find the product of $(12x)$ and $(5x - \frac{3}{2})$.

42. Find the product of $(2x + 3)$ and $(3x - 2)$.

43. What should be added to $2xy - 3x^2 + 6$ so that the sum is $4x^2 - 7xy + 15$?

44. What should be subtracted from $\frac{3}{2}x - \frac{7}{2}$ so that the difference is $\frac{7x}{2} - \frac{3}{2}$?

45. Simplify: $\frac{8x^2 - 12x^3 + 6x}{2x}$

46. Simplify: $3x - [4x + \{2x - 6(x - \overline{2 - x})\}]$

47. Simplify: $\frac{15}{2} \times - \frac{4}{3}[6x^2 - 9x(x - \overline{3 - 2x})]$

48. Solve for x: $3x + 7 = 18x$

49. Solve for x: $\frac{x}{4} = 6x - \frac{5}{4}$

50. Solve for x: $\frac{2x}{3} + 4 = \frac{8}{3}(2x - 6)$

51. Write the following statements in symbolic form.

(i) A number is doubled and added to 6, the result is equal to 14.

(ii) The sum of a number and three fifth of the number is equal to 24.

(iii) Twenty years ago, the age of a man was half of his present age.

52. The sum of three consecutive natural numbers is 90. Find the greatest number.

53. The length of a rectangle is 5 cm more than its breadth. If the perimeter of the rectangle is 42 cm, then find the length of the rectangle.

54. The cost of a pizza is $2\frac{1}{2}$ times the cost of a burger. If the sum of the costs of one burger and one pizza is ₹105, then find the cost of the burger.

55. Chintu's pocket money is ₹120. He saves one-third of his expenditure. Find his savings.

56. Rani has some chocolates with her. If she gives $\frac{2}{5}$ of the chocolates to her brother and $\frac{1}{3}$ of total chocolates to her sister, then she is left with 20 chocolates. Find the number of chocolates that Rani had initially.

57. Rukku has $\frac{3}{4}$ of the number of flowers that Satya has. The number of flowers with Rukku and Satya is 35, then find the number of flowers with Satya.

CONCEPT APPLICATION

1. If $A = 2x^3 - 3x^2 - 4x + 5$, $B = 2x^2 - x^3 + x + 1$ and $C = x^2 + x + 2$, then find the degree of $A + 2B - C$.

(a) 0 (b) 1 (c) 2 (d) 3

2. Simplify: $3x^2 - [7x - \{5x^2 - (2x - 3)(4x - 2) - 5\} - 2]$

(a) $9x - 9$ (b) $8x - 9$

(c) $7x - 9$ (d) $6x - 9$

3. A bag consists of ₹1, ₹2 and ₹5 coins. The number of ₹2 coins is equal to twice the number of ₹1 coins. The number of ₹5 is equal to thrice the number of ₹2 coins. If the total amount in the bag is ₹700, then find the total number of coins in the bag.

(a) 150 (b) 160

(c) 180 (d) 200

4. Let ABCD be a rectangle of four sides AB = $(2x + 3y + 10)$ cm, BC = $(2x + 3y - 5)$ cm, CD = $(4x + 3y + 6)$ cm and DA = $(2x - 3y + 7)$ cm. Find the perimeter of the rectangle.

(a) 30 cm (b) 40 cm

(c) 50 cm (d) 60 cm

5. Mohan has some amount, he gave (1/3)rd of the amount to Vijay, (2/5)th of the remaining amount gave to Suresh and (1/6)th of the remaining amount to Venkat. Finally, Mohan left with ₹3000. What is the sum of amounts received by Suresh and Venkat?

(a) ₹3000 (b) ₹5000

(c) ₹7000 (d) ₹8000

ASSESSMENT TEST

1. Name the following algebraic expressions based on the number of terms.
   (i) $2018x^{2019}$ (ii) $x + 2019$
   (iii) $2017x$ (iv) $\sqrt{3}x + \sqrt{5} + y$
2. Write the degree of the following polynomials.
   (i) $2017x^7 + 2018x^6 + 2019x^5$
   (ii) $x^2y - x^3y + xy^3 - x^2y^3$
   (iii) 2018
3. Write the expressions for the following statements.
   (i) 5 times of x is added to 3 times of y.
   (ii) One and half times of x is subtracted from 3 and half times of y.
4. If $x = 5$ and $y = -2$, then find the value of
   (i) $\dfrac{8x - 2y + 5}{2x + 4y + 12}$ (ii) $\dfrac{5x - 6y - 7}{3x + 6y + 12}$
5. What should be added to $7x + 5 - 8x^2$, so that the sum is $15x + 9x^2 - 5$?
6. What should be subtracted from $2x^2 - 3x + 14$, so that the difference is $5x^2 + 7x - 5$?
7. Simplify: $8x - 2[2x - 3(4x + 5 - \overline{2 - x})]$
8. Solve for x: $2x - 15 = 3x - 20$
9. Solve for x: $\dfrac{2x}{3} - \dfrac{x}{2} + 2 = x$
10. The sum of the predecessor and the successor of a number is 116. Find the number.
11. The sum of the ages of a man and his daughter is 56 years. If the daughter's age is $\frac{1}{3}$ of his father's age, then find the age of the daughter.
12. If $x = 6$ and $y = 5$, then find the values of the following:
    (i) $x + y$ (ii) $x - y$
    (iii) $3x/2y$ (iv) $3y/2x$
13. If $x = 1$, $y = 2$ and $z = 3$, find the value of $4x^2yz$.
14. Write an algebraic expression that describes the sum of x and 30% of z subtracted from the product of x and y.
15. Ajay buys 8 cookies costing ₹p each. If he gives the shopkeeper ₹50, how much change he gets back?

CROSSWORD

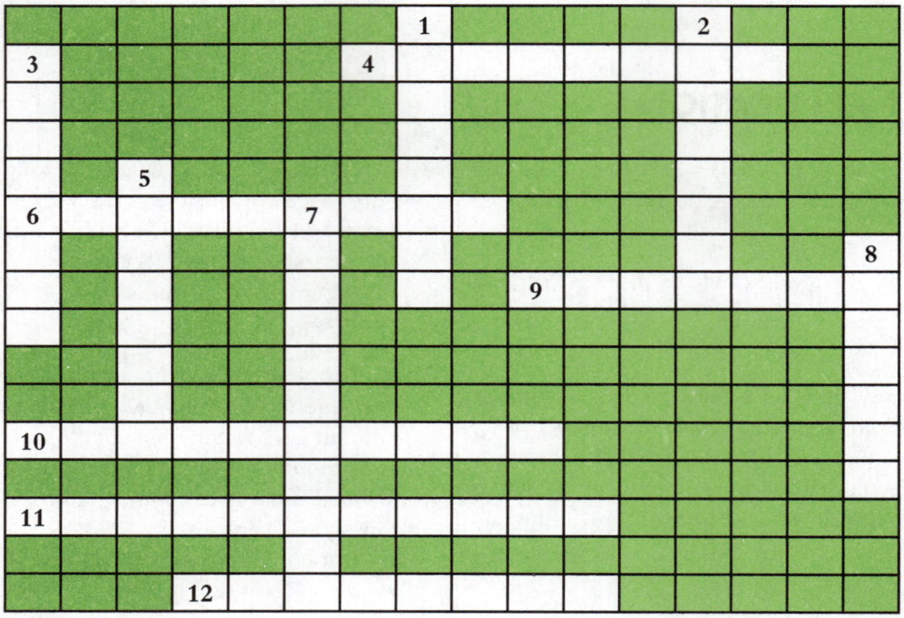

Across

4. There are no terms in the polynomial except the term x
6. The expansion of the square of $(x + y)$
9. The branch of mathematics which involves the use of letters, symbols and numbers
10. It is an algebraic expression in two terms whose degrees are 3 and 4 respectively
11. $x + x + x = 3x$, 3 is
12. If $x + 5 = 17$, then $x = 12$

Down

1. It is not a variable
2. This one is also called a literal
3. Two algebraic expressions are connected by the symbol =
5. $a + b$
7. An algebraic expression which has two or more than two terms is
8. $a \times b = c$; a and b are

TEST YOUR CONCEPTS

Very Short Answer Type Questions

1. variable
2. constant
3. algebraic expression
4. non-negative integers
5. like terms
6. (b)
7. (b)
8. (d)
9. (d)
10. (c)
11. (a) → (q), (b) → (r), (c) → (t), (d) → (p)
12. $10x^2y$
13. x^2
14. $2015xy$
15. $3x - 6$
16. $y - 3$
17. (a)
18. (d)
19. (a)
20. (a)
21. (b)
22. (a) → (p), (b) → (r), (c) → (q), (d) → (s)
23. 3
24. $\frac{1}{2}$
25. 1
26. 6
27. 3
28. (b)
29. (b)
30. (d)
31. (c)
32. (a) → (q), (b) → (p), (c) → (r), (d) → (s)

Short Answer Type Questions

33. (i) False (ii) False
    (iii) True (iv) False
34. (i) $4x^4, -9x^4; -7x^3, 12x^3, 4x^3; 8x^2, 12x^2;$
    (ii) $5xy, -3xy; -3x^2y, 5x^2y; -x^2y^2, 5x^2y^2;$
35. (ii), (iv), (v) are polynomials
36. (i) 8 (ii) 9
37. (i) 17 (ii) 12 (iii) $\frac{3}{5}$ (iv) $\frac{-3}{2}$
38. (i) 7 (ii) 62.5
39. (i) −13 (ii) 0
40. $8x - xy + 8x^2$
41. $60x^2 - 18x$
42. $6x^2 + 5x - 6$
43. $7x^2 - 9xy + 9$
44. $-2x - 2$
45. $4x - 6x^2 + 3$
46. $9x - 12$
47. $28x^2 - \frac{57}{2}x$
48. $\frac{7}{15}$
49. $\frac{5}{23}$
50. $\frac{30}{7}$
51. (i) $2x + 6 = 14$ (ii) $x + \frac{3x}{5} = 24$
    (iii) $x - 20 = \frac{x}{2}$
52. 31
53. 13 cm
54. ₹30
55. ₹30
56. 75
57. 20

ANSWER KEYS

CONCEPT APPLICATION

1. (b)
2. (a)
3. (c)
4. (c)
5. (a)

ASSESSMENT TEST

1. (i) Monomial (ii) Binomial
   (iii) Monomial (iv) Trinomial
2. (i) 7 (ii) 5 (iii) 0
3. (i) $5x + 3y$ (ii) $\frac{7}{2}y - \frac{3}{2}x$
4. (i) $\frac{7}{2}$ (ii) 2
5. $17x^2 + 8x - 10$
6. $19 - 10x - 3x^2$
7. $34x + 18$
8. 5
9. $\frac{12}{5}$
10. 58
11. 14 years
12. (i) 11 (ii) 1
    (iii) 9/5 (iv) 5/4
13. 24
14. $xy - (x + 30z/100)$
15. ₹$(50 - 8p)$

CROSSWORD

Across

4. Monomial
6. Trinomial
9. Algebra
10. Polynomial
11. Coefficient
12. Solution

Down

1. Constant
2. Variable
3. Equation
5. Binomial
7. Multinomial
8. Factors

TEST YOUR CONCEPTS

Very Short Answer Type Questions

6. $x^2 - \sqrt{3}$

   Hence, the correct option is (b).

7. The degree of the polynomial is the highest exponent of a variable of $8x^7 - 7x^6 + 6x^5 - 15x^3$, i.e., 7.

   Hence, the correct option is (b).

8. None of the given expressions are trinomials.

   Hence, the correct option is (d).

9. The numerical coefficient of $2x^5y^3$ is 2.

   Hence, the correct option is (d).

10. Only $5x^2$ is the second degree term.

    Hence, the correct option is (c).

11. (a) $9x^3 + 7x^2 + 6x + 5$: degree $= 3 \rightarrow$ (q)

    (b) $\frac{3}{5}x^2 - 7x^4 - 2$: degree $= 4 \rightarrow$ (r)

    (c) $8x^5 - 9x^6 + 4$: degree $= 6 \rightarrow$ (t)

    (d) $5x^2 - 8x + 3$: degree $= 2 \rightarrow$ (p)

12. $3x^2y + 7x^2y = (3 + 7)\, x^2y = 10x^2y$

13. $\frac{5}{2}x^2 - \frac{3}{2}x^2 = \left(\frac{5}{2} - \frac{3}{2}\right)x^2$

    $= \left(\frac{5-3}{2}\right)x^2 = \frac{2}{2}x^2 = x^2$

14. $2017xy - 2xy = (2017 - 2)xy = 2015xy$

15. $\frac{3}{4}(4x - 8) = \frac{3}{4} \times 4x - \frac{3}{4} \times 8 = 3x - 6$

16. $\frac{2xy - 6x}{2x} = \frac{2xy}{2x} - \frac{6x}{2x} = y - 3$

17. $\frac{2}{3}x + 3x + \frac{1}{3}x = \frac{2}{3}x + \frac{1}{3}x + 3x$

    $= \frac{2x + x}{3} + 3x = \frac{3x}{3} + 3x = x + 3x = 4x$

    Hence, the correct option is (a).

18. $2x - 2\left(x - \frac{1}{2}\right) = 2x - 2x + 2 \times \frac{1}{2}$

    $= 0 + 1 = 1$

    Hence, the correct option is (d).

19. $2x\,(3 - 2x)$

    $= 2x(3) - 2x(2x)$

    $= 6x - 4x^2$

    Hence, the correct option is (a).

20. $\frac{4x^2 - 8x + 10}{2} = \frac{4x^2}{2} - \frac{8x}{2} + \frac{10}{2}$

    $= 2x^2 - 4x + 5$

    Hence, the correct option is (a).

21. $3x\left(\frac{2}{3}x - \frac{1}{3x}\right) = 3x \times \frac{2}{3}x - 3x \times \frac{1}{3x}$

    $= 2x^2 - 1$

    Hence, the correct option is (b).

22. (a) $\frac{3x}{2}(2x - 3) = \frac{3x}{2} \times 2x - \frac{3x}{2} \times 3$

    $= 3x^2 - \frac{9x}{2}$ (p)

    (b) $\frac{2x}{3}(3x - 2) = \frac{2x}{3} \times 3x - \frac{2x}{3} \times 2$

    $= 2x^2 - \frac{4x}{3}$ (r)

    (c) $\frac{3x}{2}(3x - 2) = \frac{3x}{2} \times 3x - \frac{3x}{2} \times 2$

    $= \frac{9x^2}{2} - 3x$ (q)

    (d) $\frac{2x}{3}(2x - 3) = \frac{2x}{3} \times 2x - \frac{2x}{3} \times 3$

    $= \frac{4x^2}{3} - 2x$ (s)

    Therefore, the correct match is:

    (a) → (p), (b) → (r), (c) → (q), (d) → (s)

23. $x + 5 = 8 \Rightarrow x = 8 - 5 \Rightarrow x = 3$

24. $\frac{1}{2}x + \frac{3}{4} = 1$

    $\Rightarrow \frac{1}{2}x = 1 - \frac{3}{4}$

    $\frac{x}{2} = \frac{4-3}{4}$

    $\frac{x}{2} = \frac{1}{4} \Rightarrow x = \frac{1}{4} \times 2 = \frac{1}{2}$

25. $\frac{3x}{5} + \frac{7x}{5} = 2 \Rightarrow \frac{3x + 7x}{5} = 2$

$\Rightarrow \frac{10x}{5} = 2 \Rightarrow 2x = 2$

$x = 1$

26. $2x - 5 = 7 \Rightarrow 2x = 7 + 5$

$2x = 12 \Rightarrow x = \frac{12}{2}$

$x = 6$

27. $12 + x = 18 - x$

$x + x = 18 - 12$

$2x = 6$

$x = 3$

29. $7x + 2 = 8x + 2 \Rightarrow x = 0.$

$\therefore$ The number values is 1.

Hence, the correct option is (b)

31. Let the son's age be x years.

Father's age = $4x$ years

$\therefore x + 4x = 60$

Hence, the correct option is (c).

32. (a) $2x - 7 = 15$

$2x = 22$

$x = 11$ (q)

(b) $2x - 15 = 9$

$2x = 24$

$x = 12$ (p)

(c) $2x + 5 = 23$

$2x = 23 - 5$

$2x = 18$

$x = 9$ (r)

(d) $2x + 4 = 20$

$2x = 20 - 4$

$2x = 16$

$x = 8$ (s)

Therefore, the correct match is:

(a) $\rightarrow$ (q); (b) $\rightarrow$ (p); (c) $\rightarrow$ (r); (d) $\rightarrow$ (s)

Short Answer Type Questions

33. (i) Coefficient of x in $4xy^2$ is $4y^2$, so the given statement is false.

(ii) The number of terms in the expression $4xy$ is 1, so the given statement is false.

(iii) $x^2y^3 - xy$ is a binominal is true.

(iv) $3x^2 - 2x + \frac{2}{3}$ is a polynomial, so the given statement is false.

34. (i) Like terms: $(4x^4, -9x^4)$, $(-7x^3, 12x^3, 4x^3)$ $(8x^2, 12x^2)$

(ii) Like terms: $(5xy, -3xy)$, $(-3x^2y, 5x^2y)$, $(-2x^2y^2, 5x^2y^2)$

35. (i) $x^{\frac{1}{2}} + y^{\frac{1}{2}} + z^{\frac{1}{2}}$ is not a polynomial since the exponents of the variables are fractions.

(ii) $x^2 + y^2$ is a polynomial.

(iii) $\sqrt{x} + 3$ is not a polynomial, since the variable $\left(\sqrt{x} = x^{\frac{1}{2}}\right)$ has fractional exponent.

(iv) $\sqrt{5} + x^5$ is a polynomial.

(v) 2016 is a polynomial of degree zero. It is a constant polynomial.

36. (i) $3x^5 - 7x^2 + 8x - 2x^8 + 10$ consists of 5 terms and the highest degree term is $-2x^8$. The degree of the polynomial is 8.

(ii) $2x^9 - 3x^2 - 14x^3 - 15x^4$ consists of 4 terms of those the highest degree term is $2x^9$. The degree of the polynomial is 9.

37. (i) In $17x^2y$, the numerical coefficient is 17.

(ii) In $12xy^3$, the numerical coefficient is 12.

(iii) In $\frac{3}{5}x$, the numerical coefficient is $\frac{3}{5}$.

(iv) In $\frac{-3}{2}x^2$, the numerical coefficient is $\frac{-3}{2}$.

38. $x = 3, y = 1$

(i) $3x - 2y = 3 \times 3 - 2 \times 1 = 9 - 2 = 7$

HINTS AND EXPLANATION

(ii) $\dfrac{22}{3}x^2 - \dfrac{7}{2}y^2 = \dfrac{22}{3} \times (3)^2 - \dfrac{7}{2}(1)^2$

$= \dfrac{22}{3} \times 9 - \dfrac{7}{2} \times 1 = 66 - \dfrac{7}{2}$

$= 66 - 3.5 = 62.5$

39. $x = 2, y = 3$

(i) $\dfrac{2x+3y}{4x-3y} = \dfrac{2\times2+3\times3}{4\times2-3\times3}$

$= \dfrac{4+9}{8-9} = \dfrac{13}{-1} = -13$

(ii) $\dfrac{2x^2-7x+2y}{2y^2-7y+2x} = \dfrac{2(2)^2-7(2)+2(3)}{2(3)^2-7(3)+2(2)}$

$= \dfrac{2\times4-14+6}{2\times9-21+4} = \dfrac{8-8}{18-17} = \dfrac{0}{1} = 0$

40. $A + B - C = (2x + 3xy + 7x^2) + (3x - 2xy - 5x^2) - (2xy - 6x^2 - 3x)$

$= (2x + 3xy + 7x^2 + 3x - 2xy - 5x^2 - 2xy + 6x^2 + 3x)$

$= (2x + 3x + 3x) + (3xy - 2xy - 2xy) + (7x^2 - 5x^2 + 6x^2)$

$= 8x + (3xy - 4xy) + (13x^2 - 5x^2)$

$= 8x - 1xy + 8x^2$

41. $(12x)\left(5x - \dfrac{3}{2}\right) = (12x)(5x) - (12x)\left(\dfrac{3}{2}\right)$

$= 60x^2 - 6x \times 3 = 60x^2 - 18x$

42. $(2x + 3)(3x - 2)$

$= (2x)(3x) - (2x)(2) + 3(3x) - (3)(2)$

$= 6x^2 - 4x + 9x - 6$

$= 6x^2 + 5x - 6$

43. Let $f(x)$ should be added to $2xy - 3x^2 + 6$, so that the sum is $4x^2 - 7xy + 15$.

$f(x) = 4x^2 - 7xy + 15 - (2xy - 3x^2 + 6)$

$= 4x^2 - 7xy + 15 - 2xy + 3x^2 - 6$

$= (4x^2 + 3x^2) + (-7xy - 2xy) + (15 - 6)$

$= 7x^2 - 9xy + 9$

44. Let $f(x)$ should be subtracted from $\dfrac{3}{2}x - \dfrac{7}{2}$, so that the difference is $\dfrac{7x}{2} - \dfrac{3}{2}$.

$f(x) = \dfrac{3x}{2} - \dfrac{7}{2} - \left(\dfrac{7x}{2} - \dfrac{3}{2}\right)$

$= \dfrac{3x}{2} - \dfrac{7}{2} - \dfrac{7x}{2} + \dfrac{3}{2} \Rightarrow \dfrac{3x}{2} - \dfrac{7x}{2} - \dfrac{7}{2} + \dfrac{3}{2}$

$= \dfrac{3x-7x}{2} + \left(\dfrac{-7+3}{2}\right) \Rightarrow \dfrac{-4x}{2} + \left(\dfrac{-4}{2}\right)$

$f(x) = -2x - 2$

45. $\dfrac{8x^2 - 12x^3 + 6x}{2x} = \dfrac{8x^2}{2x} - \dfrac{12x^3}{2x} + \dfrac{6x}{2x}$

$= 4x - 6x^2 + 3$

46. $3x - \left[4x + \left\{2x - 6\left(x - \overline{2 - x}\right)\right\}\right]$

$= 3x - [4x + \{2x - 6(x - 2 + x)\}]$

$= 3x - [4x + \{2x - 6x + 12 - 6x\}]$

$= 3x - [4x - 10x + 12]$

$= 3x - [-6x + 12]$

$= 3x + 6x - 12$

$= 9x - 12$

47. $\dfrac{15}{2}x - \dfrac{4}{3}\left[6x^2 - 9x(x - \overline{3 - 2x})\right]$

$= \dfrac{15}{2}x - \dfrac{4}{3}[6x^2 - 9x(x - 3 + 2x)]$

$= \dfrac{15}{2}x - \dfrac{4}{3}[6x^2 - 9x(3x - 3)]$

$= \dfrac{15}{2}x - \dfrac{4}{3}[6x^2 - 27x^2 + 27x]$

$= \dfrac{15}{2}x + \dfrac{4}{3} \times 21x^2 - \dfrac{4}{3} \times 27x$

$= \dfrac{15}{2}x + 28x^2 - 36x = 28x^2 + \dfrac{15}{2}x - 36x$

$= 28x^2 + \left(\dfrac{15}{2} - 36\right)x = 28x^2 + \left(\dfrac{15-72}{2}\right)x$

$= 28x^2 - \dfrac{15}{2}x$

48. $3x + 7 = 18x \Rightarrow 7 = 18x - 3x$

$7 = 15x \Rightarrow x = \dfrac{7}{15}$

49. $\dfrac{x}{4} = 6x - \dfrac{5}{4} \Rightarrow \dfrac{5}{4} = 6x - \dfrac{x}{4}$

$\dfrac{5}{4} = \dfrac{24x - x}{4} \Rightarrow \dfrac{5}{4} = \dfrac{23x}{4} \Rightarrow 23x = 5$

$x = \dfrac{5}{23}$

50. $\frac{2x}{3} + 4 = \frac{8}{3}(2x - 6)$

$\frac{2x}{3} + 4 = \frac{16x}{3} - 16 \Rightarrow 4 + 16 = \frac{16x}{3} - \frac{2x}{3}$

$20 = \frac{16 - 2x}{3} \Rightarrow 20 = \frac{14x}{3}$

$20 \times 3 = 14x \Rightarrow 60 = 14x$

$\frac{60}{14} = x \Rightarrow \frac{30}{7} = x$

$\therefore x = \frac{30}{7}$

51. (i) A number is doubled and added to 6, the result is equal to 14.

Let the number be x.

Double the number = $2x$

It is added to 6.

$\Rightarrow 2x + 6$

The result is equal to 14.

$\Rightarrow 2x + 6 = 14$

(ii) Let the number be x.

$\frac{3}{5}$ of the number = $\frac{3x}{5}$

Given that $x + \frac{3x}{5} = 24$

(iii) Let the present age of the man be x years. 20 years ago the age of the man = $(x - 20)$ years

Given that $x - 20 = \frac{x}{2}$

52. Let the three consecutive natural numbers be $(x - 1)$, (x) and $(x + 1)$.

Given that:

$(x - 1) + (x) + (x + 1) = 90$

$x - 1 + x + x + 1 = 90$

$x = \frac{90}{3}$

$x = 30$

$\therefore$ The three numbers are $30 - 1 = 29$, 30 and $30 + 1 = 31$.

$\therefore$ The greatest number is 31.

53. Let the breadth of the rectangle be x cm.

Length of the rectangle = $(x + 5)$ cm

Perimeter of the rectangle = $2(\ell + b) = 42$ cm

$2(x + 5 + x) = 42 \Rightarrow 2x + 5 = \frac{42}{2}$

$2x + 5 = 21 \Rightarrow 2x = 21 - 5$

$x = \frac{16}{2} \Rightarrow x = 8$ cm

$\therefore$ Length of the rectangle = $x + 5 = 8 + 5 = 13$ cm

54. Let the cost of the burger be ₹x.

The cost of the pizza = $\left(2\frac{1}{2}\right)(x) = \frac{5}{2}x$

Given that:

$\frac{5x}{2} + x = 105 \Rightarrow \frac{5x + 2x}{2} = 105$

$\frac{7x}{2} = 105 \Rightarrow x = \frac{105 \times 2}{7}$

$x = 15 \times 2 \Rightarrow x = 30$

$\therefore$ The cost of the burger = ₹30.

55. Let the expenditure of Chintu be ₹x.

Savings of Chintu = $\frac{1}{3} \times x = \frac{x}{3}$

Chintu's pocket money = $x + \frac{x}{3}$

$x + \frac{x}{3} = 120 \Rightarrow \frac{3x + x}{2} = 120$

$\frac{4x}{3} = 120$

$4x = 120 \times 3$

$x = \frac{120 \times 3}{4}$

$x = 30 \times 3 \Rightarrow x = 90$

$\therefore$ Savings of Chintu $= \frac{1}{3}x = \frac{90}{3} = ₹30$

56. Let the number of chocolates with Rani be x.

Number of chocolates given to her brother = $\frac{2}{5}x$

Number of chocolates given to her sister = $\frac{1}{3}x$

Number of chocolates left with her = 20

$\Rightarrow x - \frac{2x}{5} - \frac{x}{3} = 20 \Rightarrow \frac{15x - 6x - 5x}{15} = 20$

$\frac{4x}{15} = 20 \Rightarrow 4x = 20 \times 15$

$x = \frac{20 \times 15}{4}$

$\Rightarrow x = 5 \times 15$

$\Rightarrow x = 75$

$\therefore$ The number of chocolates with Rani = 75

57. Let the number of flowers with Satya be x.

The number of flowers with Rukku = $\frac{3}{4}x$

Total number of flowers = $x + \frac{3x}{4} = 35$

$\frac{7x}{4} = 35 \Rightarrow 7x = 35 \times 4$

$7x = 140 \Rightarrow x = \frac{140}{7} \Rightarrow x = 20$

The number of flowers with Satya = 20

CONCEPT APPLICATION

1. Given that,

$A = 2x^3 - 3x^2 - 4x + 5$

$2B = 2(2x^2 - x^3 + x + 1) = 4x^2 - 2x^3 + 2x + 2$

$C = x^2 + x + 2$

$A + 2B - C = (2x^3 - 3x^2 - 4x + 5) + (4x^2 - 2x^3 + 2x + 2) - (x^2 + x + 2)$

$= -3x + 5$

The degree of A + 2B – C is 1.

Hence, the correct option is (b).

2. $3x^2 - [7x - \{5x^2 - (2x - 3)(4x - 2) - 5\} - 2]$

$= 3x^2 - [7x - \{5x^2 - (8x^2 - 4x - 12x + 6) - 5\} - 2]$

$= 3x^2 - [7x - \{5x^2 - (8x^2 - 16x + 6) - 5\} - 2]$

$= 3x^2 - [7x - \{5x^2 - (8x^2 - 16x + 6) - 5\} - 2]$

$= 3x^2 - [7x - \{5x^2 - 8x^2 + 16x - 6 - 5\} - 2]$

$= 3x^2 - [7x - \{5x^2 - 8x^2 + 16x - 6 - 5\} - 2]$

$= 3x^2 - [7x - \{-3x^2 + 16x - 11\} - 2]$

$= 3x^2 - [7x - \{-3x^2 + 16x - 11\} - 2]$

$= 3x^2 - [7x + 3x^2 - 16x + 11 - 2]$

$= 3x^2 - [3x^2 - 9x + 9]$

$= 3x^2 - 3x^2 + 9x - 9$

$= 9x - 9$

Hence, the correct option is (a).

3. Let x, y and z be the number of ₹1 coins, ₹2 coins and ₹5 coins, respectively.

Given, $y = 2x$

$z = 3y = 3(2x) = 6x$

$1(x) + 2(y) + 5(z) = ₹700$

$1x + 2(2x) + 5(6x) = ₹700$

$x + 4x + 30x = ₹700$

$35x = ₹700$

$x = 20$

$y = 2 \times 20 = 40$

$z = 6 \times 20 = 120$

The total number of coins = $x + y + z$

$= 20 + 40 + 120 = 180$

Hence, the correct option is (c).

4. Given, AB = $(2x + 3y + 10)$ cm, BC = $(2x + 3y - 5)$ m, CD = $(4x + 3y + 6)$ cm and DA = $(2x - 3y + 7)$ cm

We know that, in a rectangle the opposite sides are equal.

AB = CD

$2x + 3y + 10 = 4x + 3y + 6$

$4x - 2x = 10 - 6$

$2x = 4$

$x = 2$

BC = DA

$2x + 3y - 5 = 2x - 3y + 7$

$3y + 3y = 7 + 5$

$6y = 12$

$y = 2$

Side AB $= 2x + 3y + 10 = 2(2) + 3(2) + 10$

$= 4 + 6 + 10 = 20$ cm

Side BC $= 2x + 3y - 5 = 2(2) + 3(2) - 5$

$= 4 + 6 - 5 = 5$ cm

Therefore, the perimeter of the rectangle

$= 2(AB + BC) = 2(20 + 5) = 50$ cm

Hence, the correct option is (c).

5. Let the amount with Mohan be 'x'.

The amount received by Vijay $= (1/3)x$

The amount received by Suresh

$= (2/5)$th $\times$ $(2/3)$rd x

The amount received by Venkat

$= (1/6)$th $\times$ $(3/5)$th $\times$ $(2/3)$rd x

The amount left with Mohan

$= (5/6)$th $\times$ $(3/5)$th $\times$ $(2/3)$rd x

₹3000 $= (5/6)$th $\times$ $(3/5)$th $\times$ $(2/3)$rd x

₹3000 $= 1/3\ x$

$x =$ ₹9000

The amount received by Suresh

$= (2/5)$th $\times$ $(2/3)$rd $\times 9000$

$=$ ₹2400

The amount received by Venkat

$=(1/6)$th $\times$ $(3/5)$th $\times$ $(2/3)$rd $\times 9000$

$=$ ₹600

The sum of amounts received by Suresh and Venkat = ₹2400 + ₹600 = ₹3000

Hence, the correct option is (a).

ASSESSMENT TEST

1. (i) $2018x^{2019}$ is a monomial.

(ii) $x + 2019$ is a binomial.

(iii) $2017x$ is a monomial.

(iv) $\sqrt{3}\,x + \sqrt{5} + y$ is a trinomial.

2. (i) $2017x^7 + 2018x^6 + 2019x^5$

The highest exponent of the variable x is 7.

$\therefore$ Degree of the given polynomial is 7.

(ii) $x^2y - x^3y + xy^3 - x^2y^3$

Since it is a polynomial of two variables, the degree of the term is the sum of the exponents of the variables.

$\therefore$ The highest degree term is $-x^2y^3$.

$\therefore$ The degree of the polynomial is $2 + 3 = 5$

(iii) 2018 is a constant polynomial. Hence, its degree is zero.

3. (i) 5 times of x is $5x$.

3 times of y is $3y$.

If 5 times of x is added to 3 times of y, then the expression is $5x + 3y$.

(ii) One and half times $x = 1\frac{1}{2}x = \frac{3}{2}x$

Three and half times of $y = 3\frac{1}{2}y = \frac{7}{2}y$

One and half times of x subtracted from three and half times of y is $\frac{7}{2}y - \frac{3}{2}x$.

4. $x = 5,\ y = -2$

(i) $$\frac{8x - 2y + 5}{2x + 4y - 10} = \frac{8\times 5 - 2\times(-2) + 5}{2\times 5 + 4(-2) - 10}$$

$$= \frac{40 + 4 + 5}{10 - 8 + 12}$$

$$= \frac{49}{14} = \frac{7}{2}$$

(ii) $$\frac{5x - 6y - 7}{3x + 6y + 12} = \frac{5\times 5 - 6(-2) - 7}{3\times 5 + 6(-2) + 12}$$

$$= \frac{25 + 12 - 7}{15 - 12 + 12}$$

$$= \frac{30}{5} = 2$$

5. Let $f(x)$ be added to $7x + 5 - 8x^2$ to get $15x + 9x^2 - 5$.

$\therefore f(x) = 15x + 9x^2 - 5 - (7x + 5 - 8x^2)$

$= 15x + 9x^2 - 5 - 7x - 5 + 8x^2$

$= (9x^2 + 8x^2) + (15x - 7x) + (-5 -5)$

$f(x) = 17x^2 + 8x - 10$

$\therefore$ $17x^2 + 8x - 10$ should be added to $7x + 5 - 8x^2$ to get $15x + 9x^2 - 5$.

6. Let $f(x)$ be subtracted from $2x^2 - 3x + 14$ to get $5x^2 + 7x - 5$.

$(2x^2 - 3x + 14) - (5x^2 + 7x - 5) = f(x)$

$2x^2 - 3x + 14 - 5x^2 - 7x + 5 = f(x)$

$(2x^2 - 5x^2) + (-3x - 7x) + (14 + 5) = f(x)$

$-3x^2 - 10x + 19 = f(x)$

$\therefore$ $19 - 10x - 3x^2$ should be subtracted from $2x^2 - 3x + 14$, so that the difference is $5x^2 + 7x - 5$.

7. $8x - 2\left[2x - 3\left(4x + 5 - \overline{2 - x}\right)\right]$

$= 8x - 2[2x - 3(4x + 5 - 2 + x)]$

$= 8x - 2[2x - 3(5x + 3)]$

$= 8x - 2[2x - 15x - 9]$

$= 8x - 2[-13x - 9]$

$= 8x + 26x + 18$

$= 34x + 18$

8. $2x - 15 = 3x - 20$

$-15 + 20 = 3x - 2x$

$5 = x$

$\therefore x = 5$

9. $\frac{2x}{3} - \frac{x}{2} + 2 = x$

$\frac{2x}{3} - \frac{x}{2} - x = -2$

$\frac{4x - 3x - 6x}{6} = -2$

$\frac{4x - 9x}{6} = -2$

$\frac{-5x}{6} = -2$

$x = \frac{2 \times 6}{5}$

$x = \frac{12}{5}$

10. Let the number be x.

The predecessor $= x - 1$

The successor $= x + 1$

Given that:

$x - 1 + x + 1 = 116$

$2x = 116$

$x = \frac{116}{2}$

$x = 58$

$\therefore$ The number is 58.

11. Let the father's age be x years.

Daughter's age $= \frac{x}{3}$ years.

Given that:

$x + \frac{x}{3} = 56 \Rightarrow \frac{3x + x}{3} = 56$

$\frac{4x}{3} = 56 \Rightarrow 4x = 56 \times 3$

$x = \frac{56 \times 3}{4} \Rightarrow x = 14 \times 3$

$x = 42$

$\therefore$ The age of the daughter $= \frac{1}{3} \times 42$ years

$= 14$ years

12. (i) $6 + 5 = 11$
(ii) $6 - 5 = 1$
(iii) $18/10 = 9/5$
(iv) $15/12 = 5/4$

13. $4 \times 1 \times 1 \times 1 \times 2 \times 3 = 24$

14. The algebraic expression is $xy - (x + 30z/100)$

15. Total money = ₹50

Money spent on buying cookies $= 8p$

Change = ₹$(50 - 8p)$

HINTS AND EXPLANATION

Chapter

8

Geometry

REMEMBER

Before beginning this chapter, you should be able to:

- Know the names of different geometrical figures
- Identify lines and line segments, angles, triangles, rectangles, squares and circles

KEY IDEAS

After completing this chapter, you should be able to:

- Understand basic concepts: Plane, lines and angles
- Learn about triangles: Types of triangles, properties of triangles, congruence of triangles and construction of triangles
- Learn about circles: Chord, secant, tangent, segment and sector
- Understand symmetry: Line symmetry

INTRODUCTION

Look around yourself and you will find numerous objects with various shapes. For example, when we look at the Sun, it is round in shape, but when we look at notebooks, it is square in shape. We have learnt that Mathematics involves numbers, symbols and algebraic expression. Interestingly, study of Maths is not only about numbers but also shapes. In this chapter, we will learn Geometry which deals with study of various shapes.

BASIC CONCEPTS

The term 'geometry' comes form the combination of two Greek words '*Geo*' (Earth) and '*Metria*' (Measure) meaning measurement of the Earth. Geometry is the study of properties of lines, angles, polygons and circles. We shall begin with some basic concepts.

> ***Info Box!***
>
> A polygon is an enclosed figure made up of straight lines!

TABLE 8.1 Classification of polygons on the basis of number of sides

Number of Sides	Name of the Polygon
3	Triangle
4	Quadrilateral
5	Pentagon
6	Hexagon
7	Heptagon
8	Octagon
9	Nonagon
10	Decagon

Plane

A plane is a surface which extends indefinitely in all directions. For example, the surface of a table is a part of a plane. A black board is a part of a plane.

Line

A line is a set of infinite points. It has no end points and it is infinite in length. The figure given shows a line ℓ that extends to infinity on either side. If A and B are any two points on ℓ, we also denote the line ℓ as $\overleftrightarrow{AB}$, read as line AB.

Line Segment

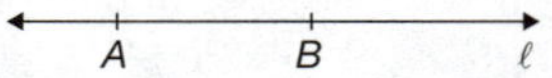

A line segment is a part of a line. The line segment has two end points and it has a finite length.

In the above figure, AB is a line segment, it is a part of line ℓ, consisting of the points A, B and all the points of ℓ lie between A and B. The line segment AB is also denoted as $\overline{AB}$. Here, A and B are the end points of $\overline{AB}$.

Ray

A ray has one end point and it extends infinitely on the other side.

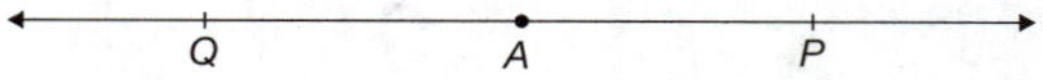

In the above figure, AP is a ray which has only one end point A. The ray AP is denoted as $\overrightarrow{AP}$. $\overrightarrow{AQ}$ is different from $\overrightarrow{AP}$. If A lies between P and Q, $\overrightarrow{AP}$ and $\overrightarrow{AQ}$ are said to be opposite rays.

Coplanar Lines

Two or more lines lying in a same plane are called coplanar lines.

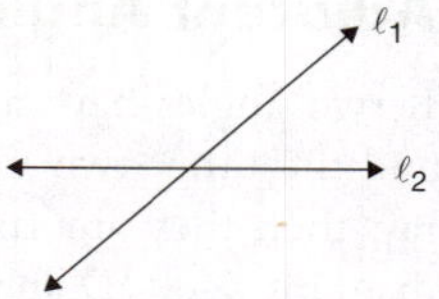

Intersecting Lines

Two lines which meet at a point are called intersecting lines.

In the given figure, ℓ_1 and ℓ_2 are two intersecting lines.

Angle

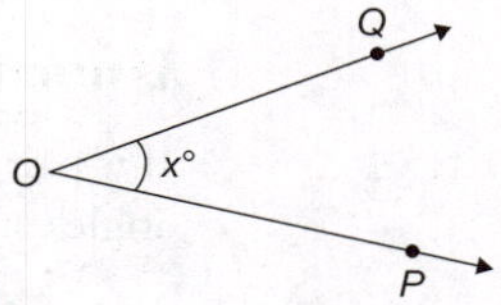

Two rays which meet at a point are said to form an angle at their meeting point.

In the given figure, $\overrightarrow{OQ}$ and $\overrightarrow{OP}$ are two rays which have O as their meeting point and an angle with certain measurement is formed. The point O is called the **vertex** of the angle and $\overrightarrow{OQ}$ and $\overrightarrow{OP}$ are called the **sides** or **arms** of the angle. We denote the angle as $\angle QOP$ or $\angle POQ$ (or sometimes simply as $\angle O$). We see that $\angle QOP = \angle POQ$ (These are the two ways of representing the same angle). A common unit of measurement of angles is the **degree**. This unit is denoted by a small circle placed above and to the right of the number. For example, we write $\angle QOP = 34°$ and read it as 34 degrees.

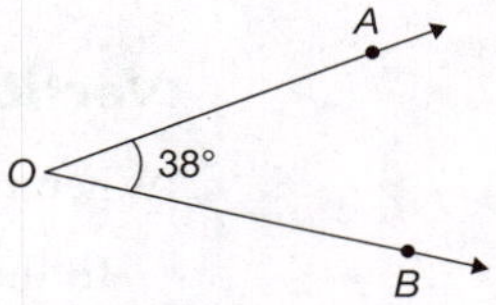

Let the measurement of an angle be $x°$.

1. If $0° < x < 90°$, it is called an **acute angle**.

   Example: In the given figure, $\angle AOB$ is acute.

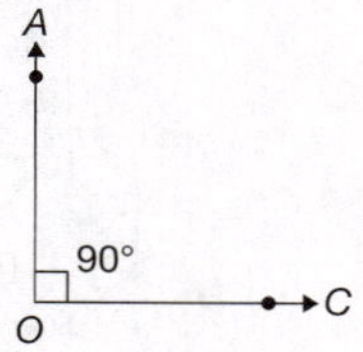

2. If $x = 90°$, it is called a **right angle.**

   In the given figure, $\angle AOC$ is a right angle.

3. If $90° < x < 180°$, it is called an **obtuse angle**. For example, in the given figure, $\angle AOD$ is an obtuse angle.

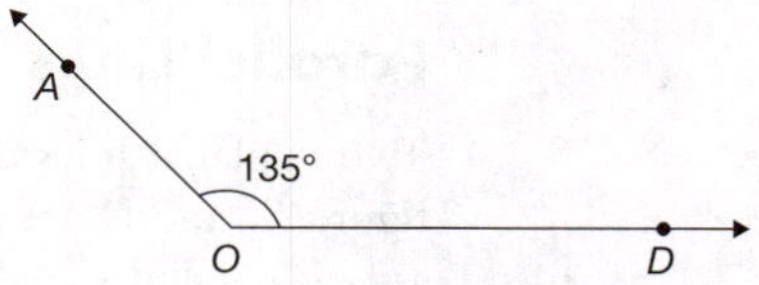

4. If $x = 180°$, it is the **angle of a straight line** or a **straight angle**. In the figure given, $\angle AOE = 180°$, $\overleftrightarrow{AE}$ is a straight line and O is a point on the line AE.

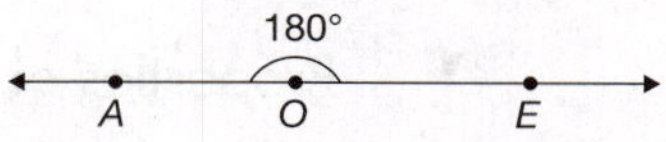

5. If $180° < x < 360°$, it is called **reflex angle.**

   Example: 200°, 270° and 300°

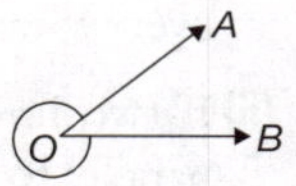

Perpendicular Lines

Two intersecting lines making an angle of 90° with each other are called perpendicular lines.

In the given figure, ℓ_1 and ℓ_2 are perpendicular lines. We write $\ell_1 \perp \ell_2$ and read this as ℓ_1 is perpendicular to ℓ_2.

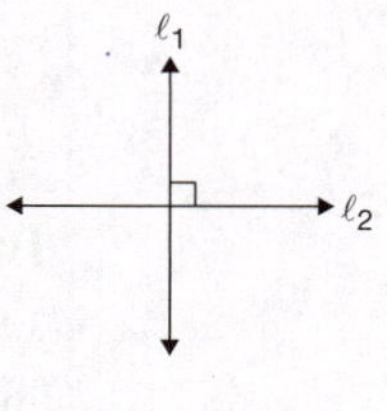

Complementary Angles

When the sum of two angles is 90°, the two angles are called complementary angles.

Example: If $x + y = 90°$, then $x°$ and $y°$ are called complementary angles.

Supplementary Angles

When the sum of two angles is 180°, the two angles are called supplementary angles.

Example: If $a + b = 180°$, then $a°$ and $b°$ are called supplementary angles.

Adjacent Angles

If two angles have a common vertex and a common ray and the other two sides lie on either side of the common ray, then they are said to be adjacent angles. In the given diagram, $\angle AOD$ and $\angle DOC$ are adjacent angles. $\angle DOC$ and $\angle COB$ are also adjacent angles.

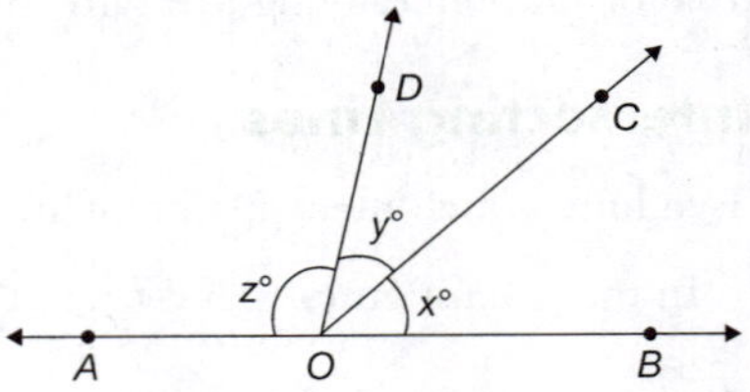

Linear Pair

If a pair of angles are adjacent and the non-common rays are opposite to each other, then the angles are said to form a linear pair.

Example: If O is a point between A and B and P is a point that does not lie on AB, then $\angle AOP$ and $\angle POB$ form a linear pair. The angles of a linear pair are supplementary.

Vertically Opposite Angles

When two lines intersect each other, four angles are formed.

In the given figure, $\overleftrightarrow{AB}$ and $\overleftrightarrow{PQ}$ intersect at O. $\angle AOP$ and $\angle BOQ$ are vertically opposite angles. Similarly, $\angle POB$ and $\angle QOA$ are vertically opposite angles. Vertically opposite angles are equal.

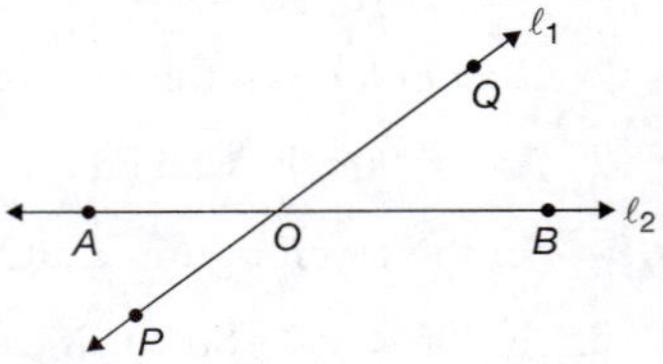

Concurrent Lines

Two or more lines in a plane passing through a same point are called concurrent lines.

Parallel Lines

Two coplanar lines that do not meet are called parallel lines. In the given figure, ℓ_1 and ℓ_2 are parallel lines. Symbolically, we write $\ell_1 \parallel \ell_2$ and read as ℓ_1 is parallel to ℓ_2.

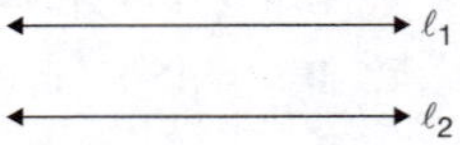

Properties of Parallel Lines

(i) For two given parallel lines, the perpendicular distance between the lines is the same everywhere.

(ii) If two lines lie in the same plane and are perpendicular to the same line, then they are parallel to each other.

(iii) If two lines are parallel to the same line, then they are parallel to each other.

(iv) One and only one parallel line can be drawn to a given line through a given point which is not on the given line.

Transversal

A straight line intersecting a pair of lines in two distinct points is a transversal for the two given lines.

Let ℓ_1 and ℓ_2 be a pair of lines and t be a transversal.

As shown in the figure, totally eight angles are formed.

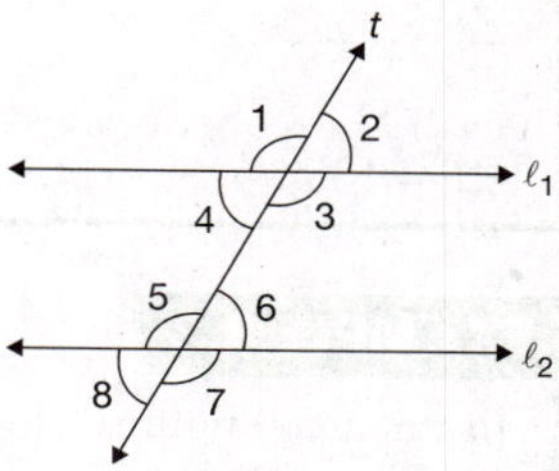

1. $\angle 1$, $\angle 2$, $\angle 7$ and $\angle 8$ are exterior angles and $\angle 3$, $\angle 4$, $\angle 5$ and $\angle 6$ are interior angles.
2. ($\angle 1$ and $\angle 5$), ($\angle 2$ and $\angle 6$), ($\angle 3$ and $\angle 7$) and ($\angle 4$ and $\angle 8$) are pairs of corresponding angles.
3. ($\angle 1$ and $\angle 3$), ($\angle 2$ and $\angle 4$), ($\angle 5$ and $\angle 7$) and ($\angle 6$ and $\angle 8$) are pairs of vertically opposite angles.
4. ($\angle 4$ and $\angle 6$), and ($\angle 3$ and $\angle 5$) are pairs of alternate interior angles.
5. ($\angle 1$ and $\angle 7$) and ($\angle 2$ and $\angle 8$) are pairs of alternate exterior angles.

If ℓ_1 and ℓ_2 are parallel, then

1. Corresponding angles are equal, i.e., $\angle 1 = \angle 5$, $\angle 2 = \angle 6$, $\angle 3 = \angle 7$ and $\angle 4 = \angle 8$.
2. Alternative interior angles are equal, i.e., $\angle 4 = \angle 6$ and $\angle 3 = \angle 5$.
3. Alternative exterior angles are equal, i.e., $\angle 1 = \angle 7$ and $\angle 2 = \angle 8$.
4. Exterior angles on the same side of the transversal are supplementary, i.e., $\angle 1 + \angle 8 = 180°$ and $\angle 2 + \angle 7 = 180°$.
5. Interior angles on the same side of the transversal are supplementary, i.e., $\angle 4 + \angle 5 = 180°$ and $\angle 3 + \angle 6 = 180°$.

EXAMPLE 8.1

$\angle A$ and $\angle B$ are two complementary angles. If $\angle A$ is 20° more than $\angle B$, then find the angles of $\angle A$ and $\angle B$.

SOLUTION

Given that: $\angle A + \angle B = 90°$

$\angle B + 20° + \angle B = 90°$

$2\angle B = 70°$

$\angle B = 35°$

$\therefore \angle A = 90° - 35°$

$\angle A = 55°$

EXAMPLE 8.2

$\angle P$ and $\angle Q$ are two supplementary angles. If $\angle P$ is three times of $\angle Q$, then find the measurement of the angles P and Q.

SOLUTION

Given, $\angle P + \angle Q = 180°$

$3\angle Q + \angle Q = 180°$

$4\angle Q = 180°$

$\angle Q = 45°$

$\angle P = 3\angle Q$

$= 3 \times 45°$

$\angle P = 135°$

EXAMPLE 8.3

In the given figure, $\ell \parallel m$, $a = 40°$, then find all the other angles as mentioned in the figure.

SOLUTION

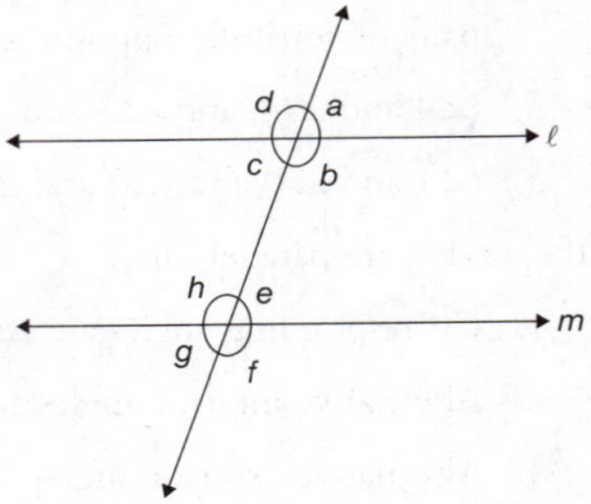

Given that: $a = 40°$ and $\ell \parallel m$

$b = 180° - 40° = 140°$ (since a, b are linear pair)

$b = d = 140°$ (vertically opposite angles)

$a = c = 40°$ (vertically opposite angles)

$a = e = 40°$ (corresponding angles)

$b = f = 140°$ (corresponding angles)

$h = f = 140°$ (vertically opposite angles)

$e = g = 40°$ (vertically opposite angles)

TRIANGLES

A three-sided simple closed figure is a triangle. In the given figure, ABC is a triangle. It has three sides AB, BC and CA. A, B and C are the three vertices of the triangle. $\angle CAB$, $\angle ABC$ and $\angle BCA$ are its three angles. Triangle ABC is denoted as ΔABC.

Info Box!

The relationship between triangles and their angles and sides is known as Trigonometry!

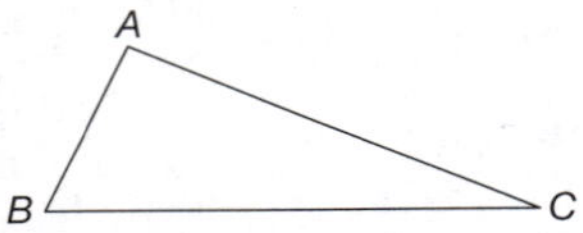

Types of Triangles

Based on their sides, triangles can be classified as follows:

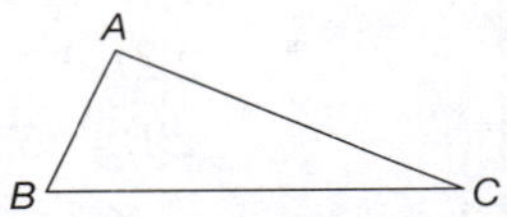

1. **Scalene triangle:** A triangle in which no two sides are equal is a **scalene triangle**. In the given triangle, $AB \neq BC$, $BC \neq CA$, and $CA \neq AB$. Hence, it is a scalene triangle.

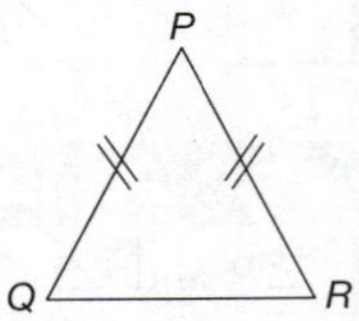

2. **Isosceles triangle:** A triangle in which any two sides are equal is an **isosceles triangle**. In the triangle given, $PQ = PR$. Hence, PQR is an isosceles triangle.

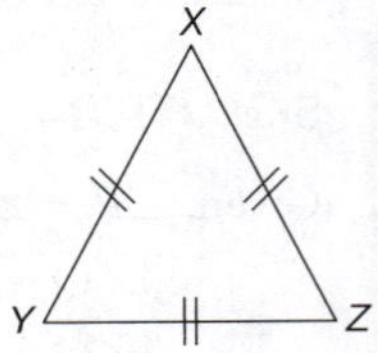

3. **Equilateral triangle:** A triangle in which all the three sides are equal is an **equilateral triangle**. In ΔXYZ, $XY = YZ = ZX$. $\therefore$ XYZ is an equilateral triangle.

Based on the angles, triangles can be classified as follows:

1. **Acute-angled triangle:** A triangle in which all the angles are acute is an **acute-angled triangle**.

In such a triangle, the square of the longest side is less than the sum of the squares of other two sides. In the above triangle, each of the angles *A*, *B* and *C* is less than 90°. Hence, *ABC* is an acute-angled triangle.

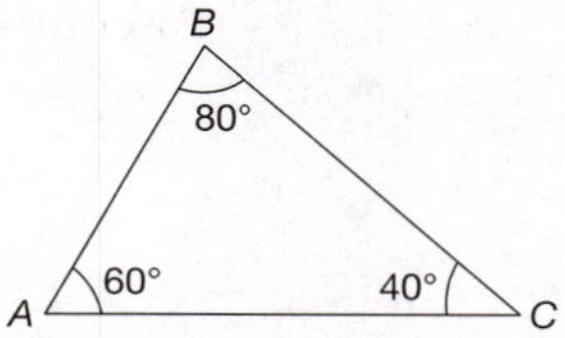

2. **Right-angled triangle:** A triangle which has a right angle is a **right-angled triangle**. In such a triangle, the square of the longest side and the hypotenuse is equal to the sum of the squares of other two sides. In the above triangle, $\angle ABC = 90°$. Hence, *ABC* is a right-angled triangle. In right triangle *ABC*, if $\overline{AC}$ is the longest side, then $AC^2 = AB^2 + BC^2$.

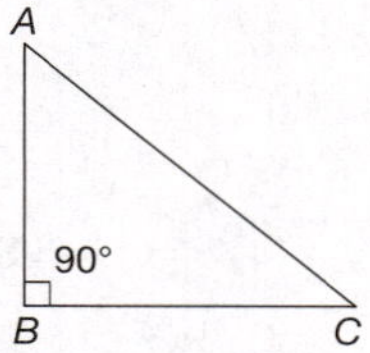

3. **Obtuse-angled triangle:** A triangle in which one angle is greater than 90° is an **obtuse-angled triangle**. In such a triangle, the square of the longest side is greater than the sum of the squares of the other two sides. In the given triangle, $\angle ABC > 90°$. Hence, *ABC* is an obtuse-angled triangle. In an obtuse-angled triangle *ABC*, if $\overline{AC}$ is the longest side, then $AC^2 > AB^2 + BC^2$.

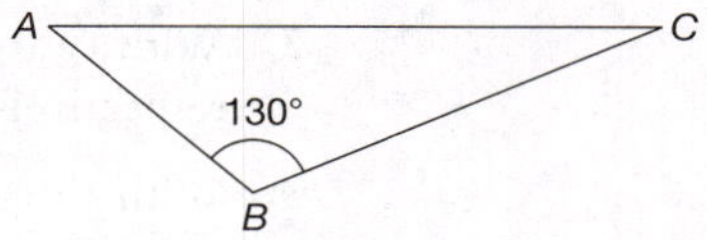

Isosceles Right-angled Triangle

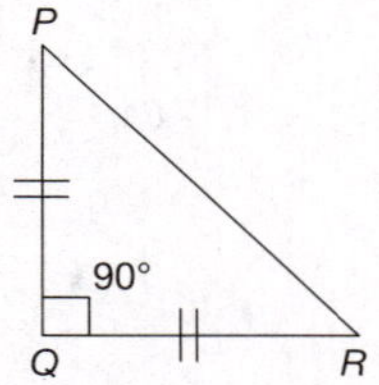

A triangle in which two sides are equal and one angle is 90° is an isosceles right-angled triangle.

In the triangle *PQR*, $PQ = QR$ and $\angle PQR = 90°$.

$\therefore$ *PQR* is an isosceles right triangle.

In such a triangle, the ratio of sides *PQ*, *QR* and *RP* is $1 : 1 : \sqrt{2}$.

NOTES

1. A scalene triangle can be acute, right or obtuse angled.
2. An isosceles triangle can be acute, right or obtuse angled.
3. An equilateral triangle has to be acute. It cannot contain a right angle or an obtuse angle.

Given below are the statements of some of the properties of triangles:

1. The sum of the three angles of a triangle is 180°.
2. The exterior angle of a triangle is equal to the sum of the interior angles opposite to it.
3. The sum of any two sides of a triangle is greater than the third side. In ΔPQR, $PQ + QR > PR$, $QR + RP > PQ$ and $RP + PQ > QR$.
4. Difference between any two sides is less than the third side. $PQ - QR < PR$, $QR - RP < PQ$ and $RP - PQ < QR$
5. Angles opposite to equal sides are equal and vice versa. If $\angle P = \angle Q$, then $QR = PR$. If $QR = PR$, then $\angle P = \angle Q$.
6. If the angles are in increasing or decreasing order, the sides opposite to them also will be in the same order. If $\angle P > \angle Q > \angle R$, then $QR > PR > PQ$.

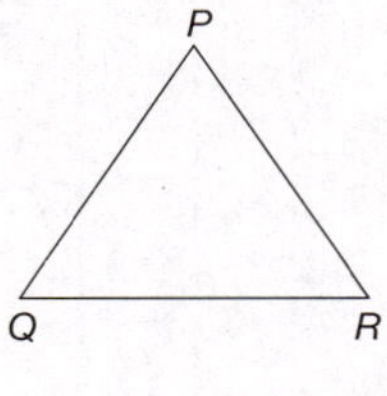

Constructions

We shall now look at the steps of constructing angles and bisector.

Congruent Angles (or) Equal Angles

Given: An angle *PQR*

To construct: Angle *AOB* equal to *PQR*.

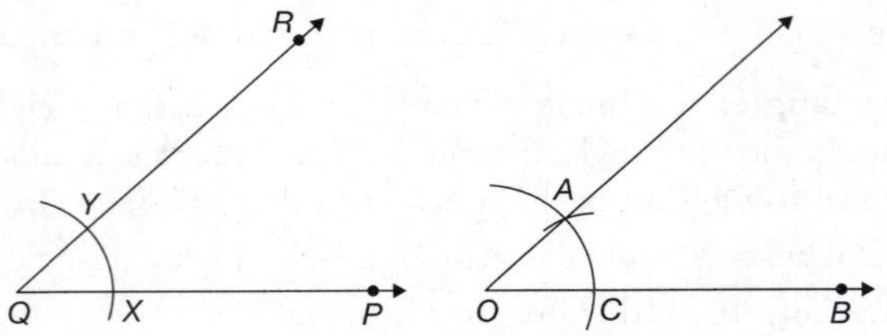

Steps of construction:

1. Draw a ray *OB*.
2. With *Q* as centre and a suitable radius draw an arc which cuts rays *QP* and *QR* at *X* and *Y*, respectively.
3. With *O* as centre and the same radius as in step (2) draw an arc which cuts ray *OB* at the point *C*.
4. With *C* as centre and *XY* as radius draw another arc to cut the arc in step (2) at *A*.
5. Join *OA* to get the ray *OA*. Now angle *AOB* is equal to angle *PQR*.

Bisector of an Angle

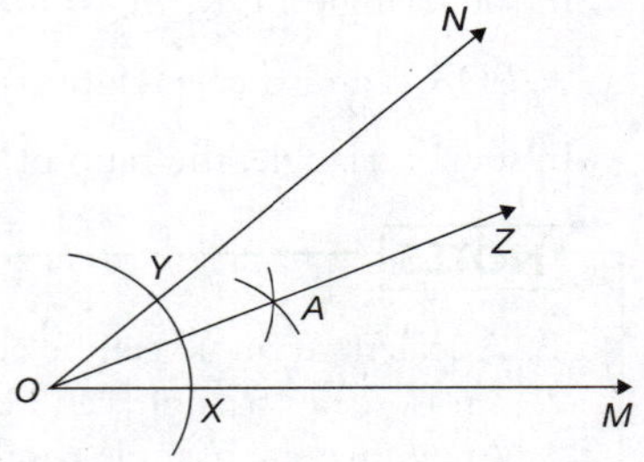

Given: An angle *MON*

To construct: The bisector of the angle *MON*

Steps of construction:

1. With *O* as centre and a suitable radius draw an arc which cuts rays *OM* and *ON* at *X* and *Y*, respectively.
2. With *X* and *Y* as centres and more than half of *XY* as radius draw two arcs to meet each other at *A*.
3. Join *OA* to get the ray *OA*. Now *OA* is the bisector of the angle *MON*.

Construction of an Angle 60°

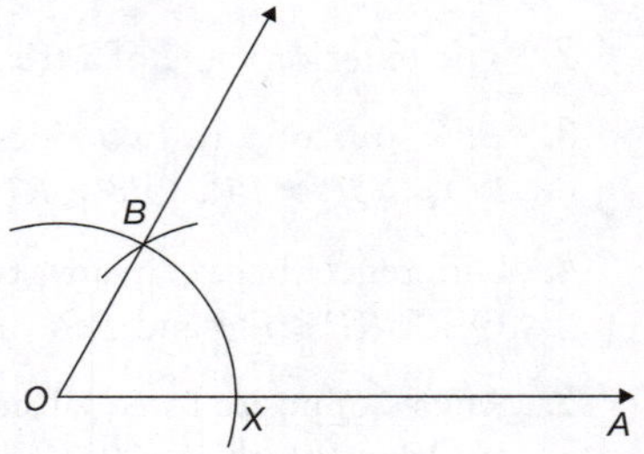

Steps of construction:

1. Draw a ray *OA*.
2. With *O* as centre and a suitable radius draw an arc which cuts the ray *OA* at *X*.
3. With *X* as centre and the same radius as in step (2), draw an arc to cut the arc in step (2) at *B*.
4. Join *OB* to get the ray *OB*. Now the angle *BOA* is 60°.

Construction of an Angle 90°

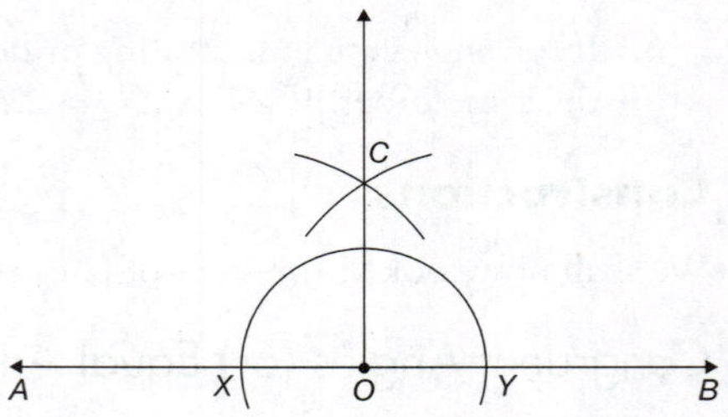

Steps of construction:

1. Draw a line AB. Mark a point *O* on *AB*.

2. With O as centre and a suitable radius draw an arc which cuts the line AB at X and Y respectively.

3. With X and Y as centres and more than half of XY as radius draw two arcs to meet each other at C. Join OC to get the ray OC. Now the angle BOC or angle AOC is 90°.

EXAMPLE 8.4

In the given figure, C is a point on the line segment BD. Find the measurements of $\angle ACB$ and $\angle ABC$.

SOLUTION

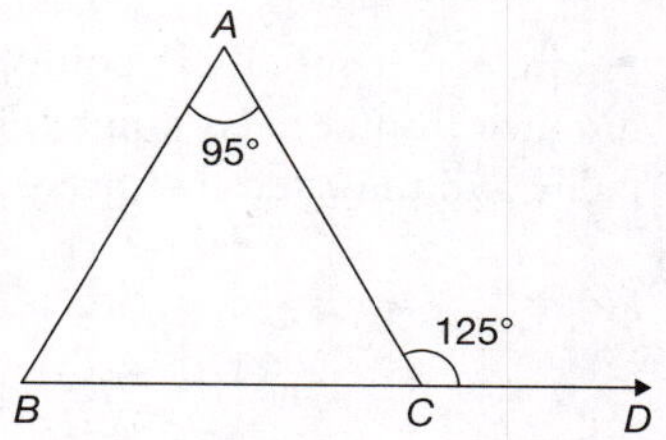

($\angle ACB$, $\angle ACD$) is a linear pair.

$\Rightarrow \angle ACB + 125° = 180°$

$\angle ACB = 180° - 125° = 55°$

$\angle ABC + \angle CAB = \angle ACD$ (Exterior angle)

$\angle ABC + 95° = 125°$

$\angle ABC = 125° - 95° = 30°$

EXAMPLE 8.5

In the given figure, PTQ, PMR, SMT and QRS are straight lines. Find the angle of $\angle RMS$.

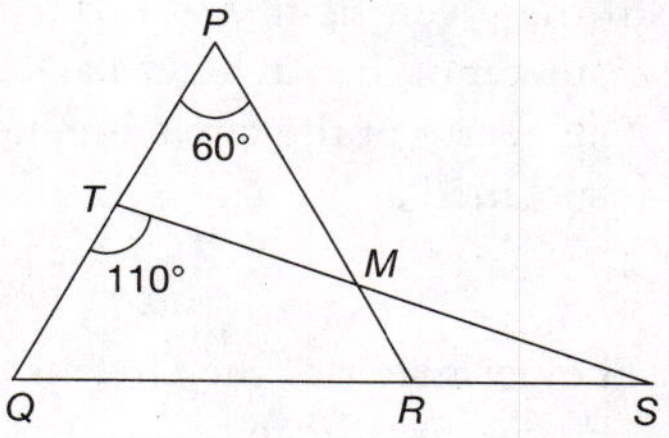

SOLUTION

Since PQ is a straight line and $\angle QTM = 110°$.

$\angle TPM + \angle PMT = \angle QTM$

$60° + \angle PMT = 110°$

$\Rightarrow \angle PMT = 110° - 60° = 50°$

$\Rightarrow \angle PMT = \angle RMS$ (vertically opposite angles)

$\Rightarrow \angle RMS = 50°$

EXAMPLE 8.6

In the figure, ABD, BCD are two triangles. BD is the bisector of $\angle ABC$ and $\angle ADC$. $\overline{AB} \parallel \overline{CD}$ and $\overline{AD} \parallel \overline{BC}$. If $\angle BCD = 50°$, then find the angle of $\angle BAD$.

SOLUTION

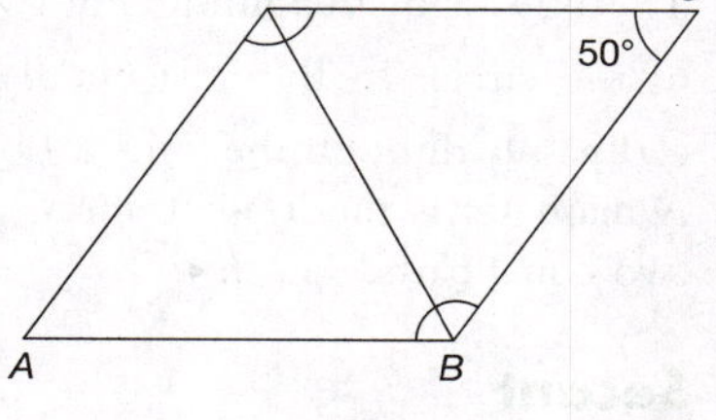

$\angle BCD = 50°$ and $\overline{BC} \parallel \overline{AD}$.

$\angle CDA + \angle BCD = 180°$ (co-interior angles)

$\Rightarrow \angle CDA + 50° = 180°$

$\angle CDA = 180° - 50°$

$\angle CDA = 130°$

Similarly, $\angle ABC = 130°$ ($\because \overline{AB} \parallel \overline{CD}$)

Since BD is the bisector of $\angle ADC$ and $\angle ABC$,

$\angle ABC = \angle ABD + \angle CBD \quad (\because \angle ABD = \angle CBD)$

$2\angle ABD = 130° \Rightarrow \angle ABD = \angle CBD = \dfrac{130}{2} = 65°$

$\angle ADB + \angle BDC = 130°$ and $\angle ADB = \angle BDC = \dfrac{130}{2} = 65°$

In $\Delta\ ABD$, $\angle ABD + \angle ADB + \angle BAD = 180°$

$130° + \angle BAD = 180°$

$\angle BAD = 180° - 130° = 50°$

CIRCLES

A circle is a set of all points in a plane which are at a fixed distance from a fixed point. The fixed point is the centre of the circle and the fixed distance is the radius of the circle.

Info Box!

For a given area, a circle has the shortest perimeter among all shapes.

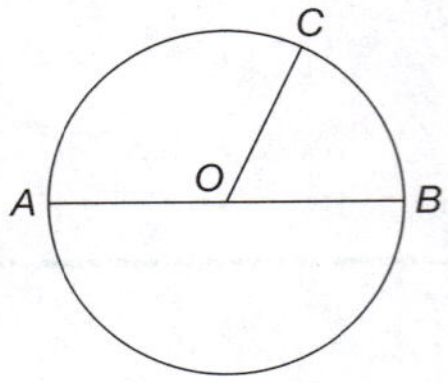

In the given figure, O is the centre of the circle and OC is the radius of the circle. AB is the diameter of the circle. OA and OB are also the radii of the circle. The diameter is twice the radius. The centre of the circle is generally denoted by 'O', the diameter is represented as 'd' and radius is specified as 'r'.

$$\therefore \qquad d = 2r$$

The perimeter of the circle is called the circumference of the circle. The circumference of the circle is π times the diameter. In the above circle with centre O, here, A, B and C are three points in the plane in which the circle lies. We see that $OA < r$, $OB = r$ and $OC > r$. The points O and A are inside the circle. The point B is located on the circle and C is a point outside the circle. The set of all points P in the plane of the circle for which $OP < r$ is called the **interior of the circle** and the set of points Q for which $OQ > r$ is called the **exterior of the circle**. B is a point on the circumference of the circle, $OB = r$. A is a point in the interior of the circle, $OA < r$. As C is a point in the exterior of the circle, $OC > r$.

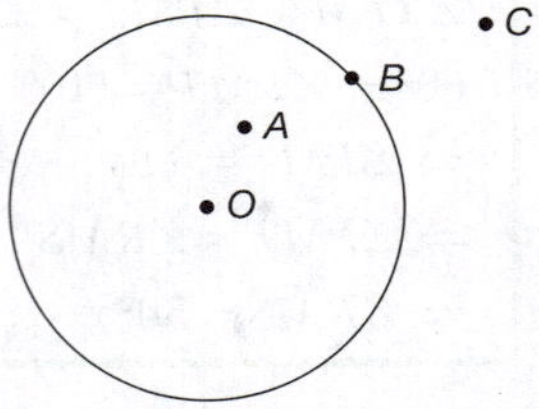

Chord

The line segment joining any two points on a circle is called a chord of the circle. In the adjacent figure, both $\overline{PQ}$ and $\overline{AB}$ are chords. AB passes through the centre O. Hence, it is a diameter of the circle. A diameter is the longest chord of the circle. It divides the circle into two equal parts.

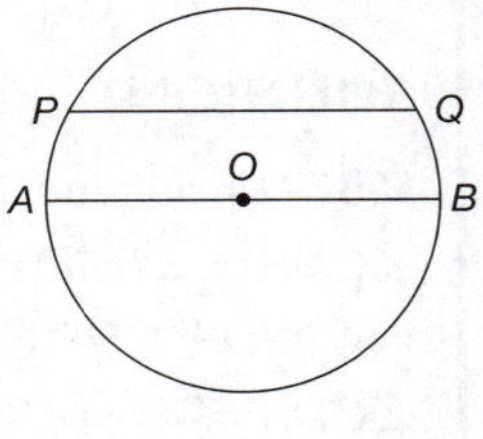

Secant

A line which intersects a circle in two distinct points is called secant of the circle.

Tangent

A line lying in the plane of the circle that meets the circle in exactly one point is called a tangent to the circle. The point at which it meets the circle is the point of tangency or point of contact.

Arc

A continuous piece of a circle is called an arc of the circle. The end points of a diameter of a circle divide the circle into two equal arcs. Each of these arcs is called semicircle. The region enclosed by a semicircle and the diameter together with the semicircle is called a semi-circular region. If the length of an arc is less than that of a semicircle, it is a **minor arc**. If the length is more, then it is a **major arc**.

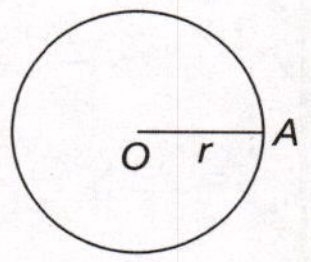

Circumference

The whole arc of the circle is called its circumference.

Circumference of a circle = $2\pi r$, where $\pi = \dfrac{22}{7}$ and r is the radius of the circle.

Angle Subtended by a Pair of Points

The angle subtended by two points A and B at the point P is the angle APB. The angle subtended by an arc or a chord is the angle subtended by the end points of the arc or chord.

Segment of a Circle

The part of a circular region bounded by an arc AB and the chord AB, including the arc and chord is called the segment of the circle. If the arc is minor, then the segment is also minor. If the arc is major, then the segment is also major.

Sector of a Circle

In a circle with centre O, the union of an arc AB and the bounding radii, OA and OB is called the sector AOB. If the arc is minor, then the sector is minor. If the arc is major, then the sector is major.

Quadrant

A sector of an angle 90° is called a quadrant.

EXAMPLE 8.7

Find the circumference of the circle whose radius is 7 cm.

SOLUTION

Circumference of the circle = $2\pi r$

$$= 2 \times \frac{22}{7} \times 7 = 44 \text{ cm}$$

EXAMPLE 8.8

The circumference of a circle is 22 cm. Find the diameter of the circle.

SOLUTION

Given that: $2\pi r = 22$ cm

$2 \times \frac{22}{7} \times r = 22$ cm

$r = 22 \times \frac{7}{2 \times 22} = \frac{7}{2}$

$\therefore$ Diameter of the circle $= 2r = 2 \times \frac{7}{2} = 7$ cm

SYMMETRY

Let us examine the following figure drawn on a rectangular piece of paper.

What do you infer? We can observe that when the figure is folded about the dotted line, the two parts on either side of the dotted lines coincide. This property of geometrical figure is called **line symmetry**.

Info Box!

Knowledge of geometry was used by the Greeks in making buildings!

Dumbell shape

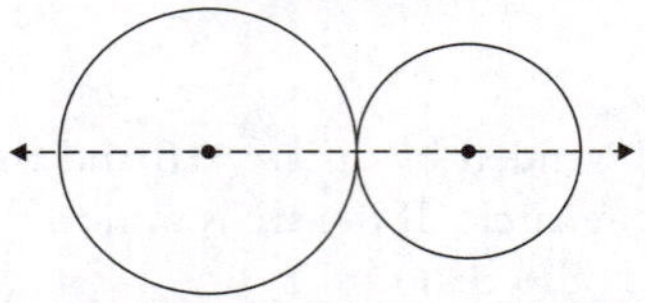

Two circles touching externally

Let us see one more example.

Trace a geometrical figure on a rectangular piece of paper as shown below.

Now fold the paper along the dotted line. You will find that the two parts of the figure on either sides of the line coincide. Thus the line divides the figure into two identical parts. In this case, we say that the figure is symmetrical about the dotted line or line symmetric. Also, the dotted line is called 'THE LINE OF SYMMETRY' or 'THE AXIS OF SYMMETRY'.

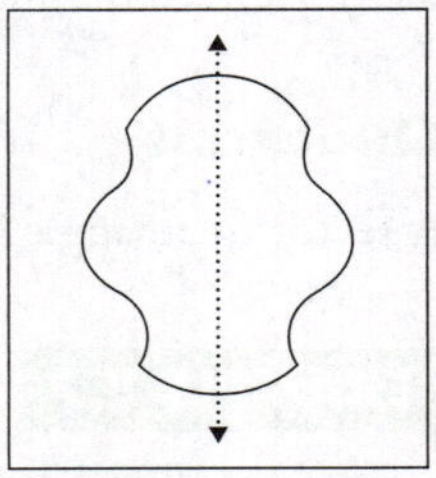

So, a geometrical figure is said to be **line symmetric or symmetrical about a line** if there exists at least one line in the figure such that the parts of the figure on either sides of the line coincide when it is folded about the line.

EXAMPLE 8.9

ABCD is a rhombus. Draw its lines of symmetry.

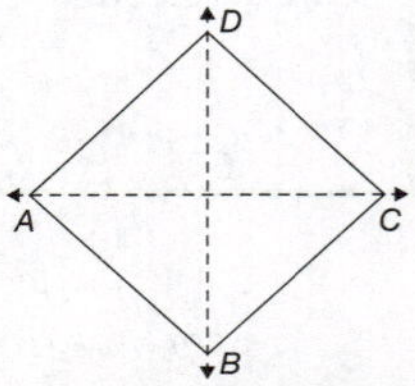

SOLUTION

The diagonals of a rhombus are the lines of symmetry of rhombus.

EXAMPLE 8.10

Draw a line of symmetry of an isosceles right triangle.

SOLUTION

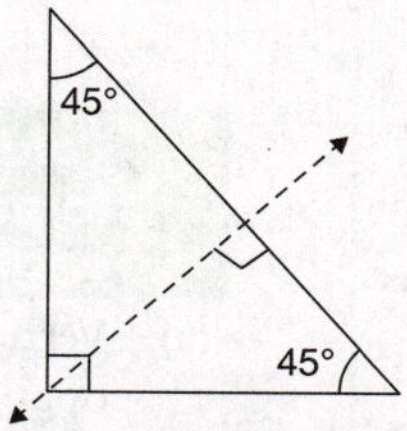

EXAMPLE 8.11

Draw all the lines of symmetry of a square.

SOLUTION

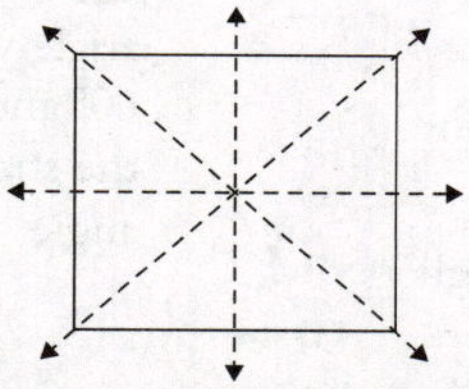

EXAMPLE 8.12

Draw the line(s) of symmetry for the first four words of English alphabet, if exist.

SOLUTION

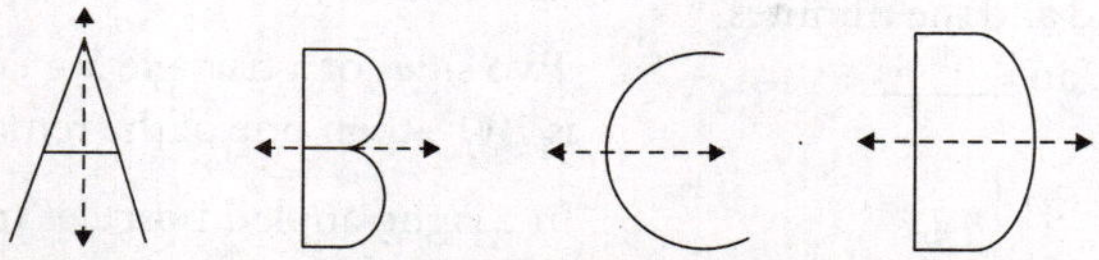

TEST YOUR CONCEPTS

Very Short Answer Type Questions

Direction for questions from 1 to 5: Fill in the blanks.

1. An angle which is 30° less than the right angle is ______.
2. An angle which is 50° less than the straight angle is ______.
3. An angle which is complementary to itself is ______.
4. A line which intersects two or more lines at distinct points is called ______.
5. If ℓ is a transversal of p and q, a pair of corresponding angles is equal, then the lines p and q are ______.

Direction for questions from 6 to 10: Select the correct alternative from the given choices.

6. Which of the following is a complementary angle to 36°?
   (a) 36° (b) 64°
   (c) 72° (d) 54°
7. Which of the following is a reflex angle?
   (a) 90° (b) 120°
   (c) 180° (d) 200°
8. The angle between the hours hand and the minutes hand of a clock at 6'O clock is a/an ______.
   (a) right angle
   (b) acute angle
   (c) straight angle
   (d) obtuse angle
9. Which of the following pairs of angles are supplementary?
   (a) (0, 180°)
   (b) (90°, 90°)
   (c) (120°, 60°)
   (d) All the above
10. Two lines $\overleftrightarrow{AB}$ and $\overleftrightarrow{CD}$ intersect at 'P'. The number of pairs of adjacent angles formed is ______.
   (a) 2 (b) 3
   (c) 4 (d) 6

Direction for question 11: Match Column A with Column B.

11.

Column A (a pair of angles)		Column B (Ratio of the angles)
(a) Vertically opposite angles	( )	(p) 2 : 1
(b) 120° and its supplement	( )	(q) 1 : 2
(c) 30° and its complement	( )	(r) 3 : 4
(d) A straight angle and a reflex angle which is 60° more than the straight angle	( )	(s) 1 : 1

Direction for questions from 12 to 16: Fill in the blanks.

12. If two of the angles of a triangle are 70° and 80°, then the third angle of the triangle is ______.
13. If two sides of a triangle are 7 cm and 10 cm, then the largest possible integer value of the third side is ______.
14. Two sides of a triangle are equal. If one of its angles is 100°, then one of the remaining angles is ______.
15. In a right-angled isosceles triangle, the measures of the angles are ______.
16. In a ΔABC, $\angle B = 65°$ and $\angle C = 80°$, then the longest side is ______.

Direction for questions from 17 to 21: Select the correct alternative from the given choices.

17. Which of the following is true?
   (A) A triangle can have utmost two right angles.
   (B) A triangle can have two obtuse angles.
   (C) A triangle can have three acute angles.
   (a) A, B and C (b) Only B and C
   (c) Only B (d) Only C

PRACTICE QUESTIONS

18. Which of the following is false?
    (A) The sum of any two sides of a triangle is equal to the third side.
    (B) The sum of the exterior angles of a triangle is equal to 360°.
    (a) A and B
    (b) Only A
    (c) Only B
    (d) None of these

19. Which of the following is an acute triangle?
    (a) Isosceles triangle
    (b) Equilateral triangle
    (c) Right triangle
    (d) None of the above

20. Which of the following is true?
    (A) Triangle is a polygon.
    (B) An isosceles triangle can be obtuse.
    (C) All scalene triangles are acute.
    (a) Only A
    (b) Only B and C
    (c) Only A and B
    (d) A, B and C

21. Which of the following is the length of the sides of a triangle?
    (a) 3 cm, 7 cm, 10 cm
    (b) 2 cm, 5 cm, 7 cm
    (c) 6 cm, 12 cm, 19 cm
    (d) 7 cm, 24 cm, 25 cm

Direction for question 22: Match Column A with Column B.

22.

Column A (Triangle)		Column B (Angles of triangle)
(a) Right triangle	( )	(p) 60°, 20°,100°
(b) Isosceles triangle	( )	(q) 60°, 60°, 60°
(c) Acute triangle	( )	(r) 60°, 30°, 90°
(d) Scalene triangle	( )	(s) 40°, 40°, 100°

Direction for questions from 23 to 32: Observe the given figure and fill in the blanks.

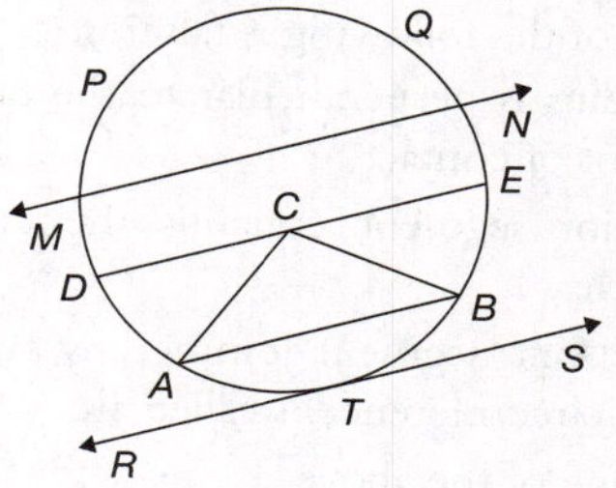

23. If 'C' is the centre of the circle and A is the point on the circle, then AC is called _______ of the circle.

24. If A, B are the points on the circle. The line segment AB is called ______ of the circle.

25. P, Q are the points on the circle. The part of the circle, PQ is called ______ of the circle.

26. The region bounded by the line segment AB and the part of the circle ATB is called _______ of the circle.

27. The line RS which touches the circle at T is called ______ to the circle.

28. The line intersecting the circle at M and N is called ______ of the circle.

29. $\overline{DE}$ is passing through the centre, DE is called ______ of the circle.

30. The arc DTE is called ______ of the circle.

31. The region bounded by the two radii CA and CB and the arc AB is called ______.

32. A sector of an angle 90° is called _____.

Direction for questions from 33 to 37: Select the correct alternative from given choices.

33. Which of the following is true?
    (a) Diameter passes through the centre of the circle.
    (b) The longest chord is the diameter.
    (c) The diameter is equal to 2 times the radius.
    (d) All the above

34. Which of the following is an angle of the major sector?

(a) 60° (b) 100°
(c) 200° (d) 400°

35. Which of the following is false?
(a) Radius is perpendicular to the tangent at the point of contact.
(b) Major segment contains the centre of the circle.
(c) The line segment joining any two points on the circumference is called arc.
(d) None of the above

36. Which of the following is the angle of a quadrant?
(a) 60° (b) 90°
(c) 180° (d) 360°

37. Which of the following can be the angle subtended by a minor arc at the centre?
(a) 100° (b) 220°
(c) 180° (d) 270°

Direction for questions from 38 to 42: Fill in the blanks.

38. An isosceles triangle has ______ line (s) of symmetry.

39. A semicircle has ______ line (s) of symmetry.

40. A quadrant of a circle has ______ lines of symmetry.

41. The letter *I* has ______ lines of symmetry.

42. A letter *X* has ______ lines of symmetry.

Direction for questions from 43 to 47: Select the correct alternative from the given choices.

43. Which of the following can have infinite lines of symmetry?
(A) Ellipse (B) Semicircle (C) Line segment
(a) A, B (b) A, C
(c) B, C (d) C

44. Which of the following letters of English alphabet has only two lines of symmetry?
(a) *Y* (b) *W*
(c) *H* (d) *E*

45. Which of the following has no line of symmetry?
(a) *P* (b) Q
(c) *R* (d) All of these

46. Which of the following have exactly 3 lines of symmetry?
(a) *M* (b) Equilateral triangle
(c) *N* (d) Line segment

47. Which of the following has no line of symmetry?

(a) 

(b) 

(c) 

(d) 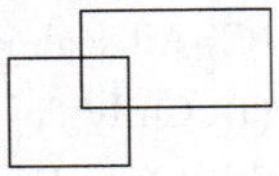

Direction for question 48: Match Column A with Column B.

48.

Column A			Column B
(a) Two lines of symmetry	( )	(p)	
(b) Three lines of symmetry	( )	(q)	
(c) Four lines of symmetry	( )	(r)	
(d) No line of symmetry	( )	(s)	

Short Answer Type Questions

49. Two supplementary angles are in the ratio 3 : 7. Find the difference between the angles.

50. Find the supplement of 50°36′ 52″.

51. In the figure, *t* intersects two parallel lines *p* and *q*. Find the angles of $4x - 15°$ and $3x - 15°$.

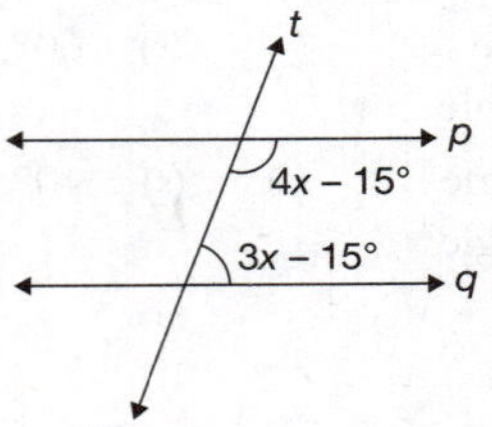

52. In the figure, $\ell \parallel m$ and $r \parallel t$. They intersect at P, Q, R and S as shown in the figure. Find the angles of $\angle SPQ$ and $\angle PSR$.

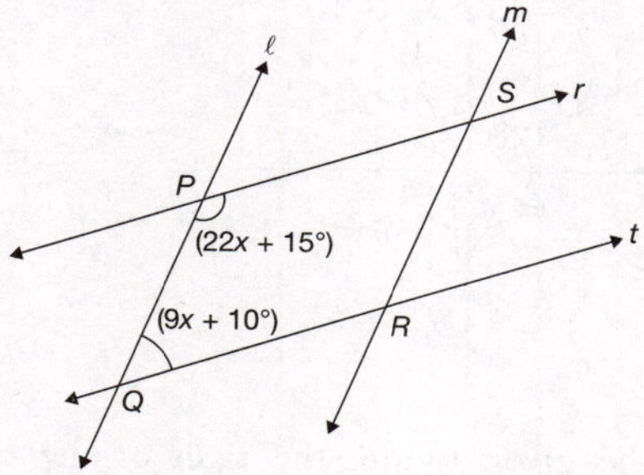

53. In a triangle ABC, if $\angle A = 70°$ and $AB = AC$, then find the measures of $\angle B$ and $\angle C$.

54. List out all the triangles formed in the figure.

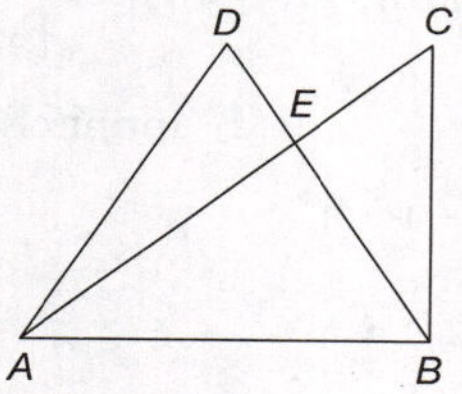

55. In the figure, $\overline{DC} \parallel \overline{AB}$. If $\angle ACB = 40°$ and $\angle CAD = 30°$, AC is the bisector of $\angle DAB$, then find the angle of $\angle ADC$.

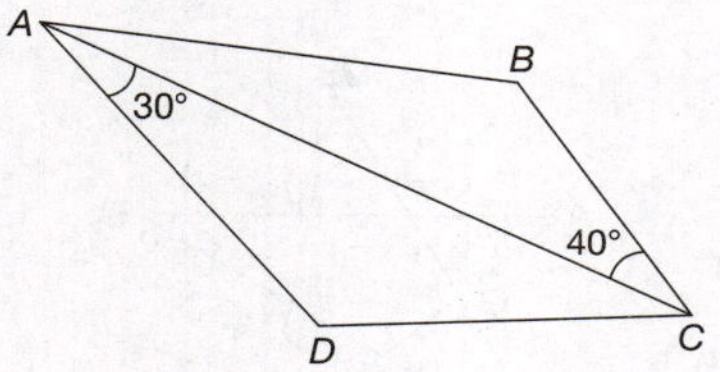

56. In the given figure, $AB = BC$, $\angle BAC = 70°$ and BC is produced to E, $AC = CD$ and $\angle ADE$ is the exterior angle of ΔADC. Find the angle of $\angle ADE$.

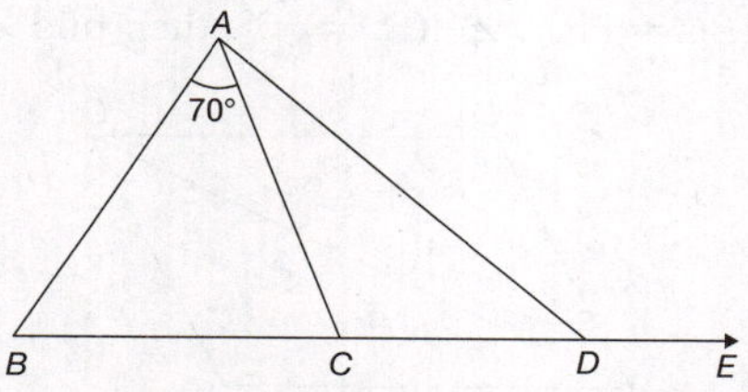

57. In the figure, PS and QT are two straight lines intersecting at the point R. $PR = RQ$. If $\angle PRQ = 98°$ and $\angle TSR = 40°$, then find the angles of $\angle T$ and $\angle Q$.

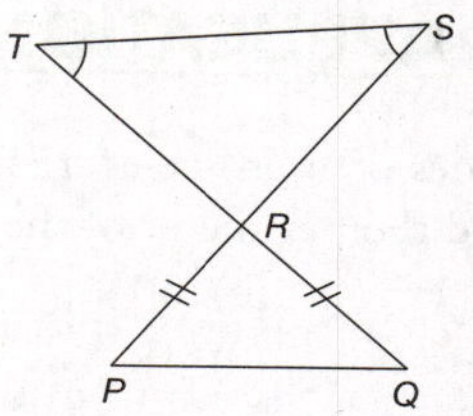

58. In the given figure, $\angle QPR = 50°$, $\angle QRS = 135°$ and $PQ = PR$ and $ST = SR$. Find the angle of $\angle S$.

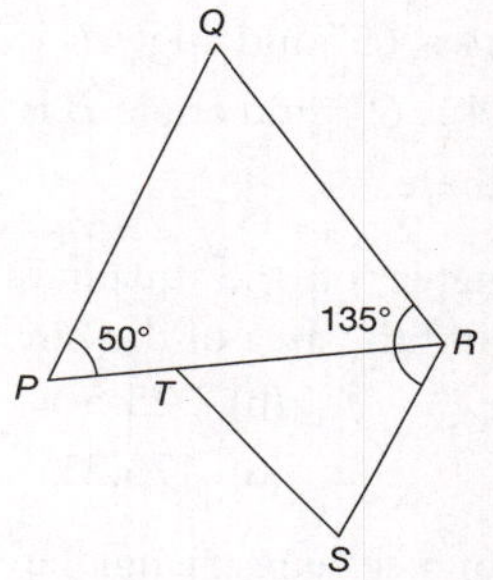

59. The radius of a circle is 10.5 cm. Find its circumference.

60. The circumference of a circle is 132 cm. Find the length of its diameter.

61. Draw a chord of length 6 cm in a circle of radius 4 cm and shade the major segment.

62. Make a sector of angle 90° in a circle of radius 3.5 cm.

63. The circumference of a circle is 220 cm. Find the perimeter of its quadrant.

64. Draw the line of symmetry for the following.

(a)

(b)
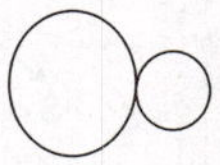

(c)
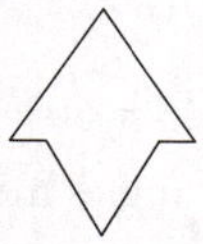

(d)
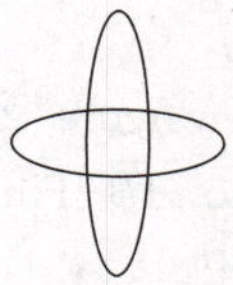

65. Construct an equilateral triangle of side 4 cm and draw all its lines of symmetry.

66. Draw an acute angle POQ and draw its line symmetry.

67. Write all the letters of English alphabet which has exactly two lines of symmetry and draw their lines of symmetry.

CONCEPT APPLICATION

1. The two sides of an isosceles triangle are 6 cm and 12 cm. Find the perimeter of the triangle (in cm).
   (a) 32 (b) 30
   (c) 24 (d) 18

2. Which of the following cannot be the measures of an isosceles triangle *ABC*?
   (a) Angle *A* is 50° and angle *B* is 80°
   (b) Angle *A* is 65° and angle *B* is 50°
   (c) Angle *A* is 60° and angle *B* is 70°
   (d) All of these

3. The perimeter of the quadrant of a circle is 37.5 cm. Find the area of the circle (in cm^2).
   (a) 346.5 (b) 325.5
   (c) 275.25 (d) 173.25

4. The sides of a scalene triangle are integers in cm. If the perimeter of the triangle is 15 cm, then how many such triangles exist?
   (a) One (b) Two
   (c) Three (d) Infinitely many

5. 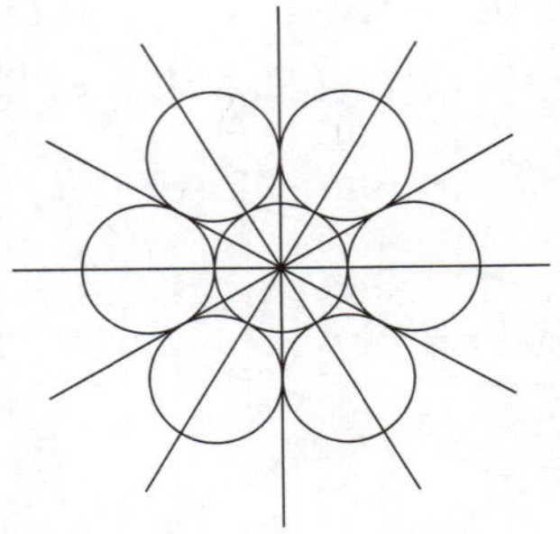

   In the given figure, the radii of the circles are equal. The middle circle is touching all the other circles and each of the other circles is touching exactly three circles as shown in the figure. What is the total number of lines of symmetry that can be drawn for the given figure?
   (a) 3 (b) 6
   (c) 12 (d) Infinitely many

ASSESSMENT TEST

1. In the figure $\overline{PA} \parallel \overline{QB}$. If *AT* and *BS* intersect at *C*, find $\angle ACS$.

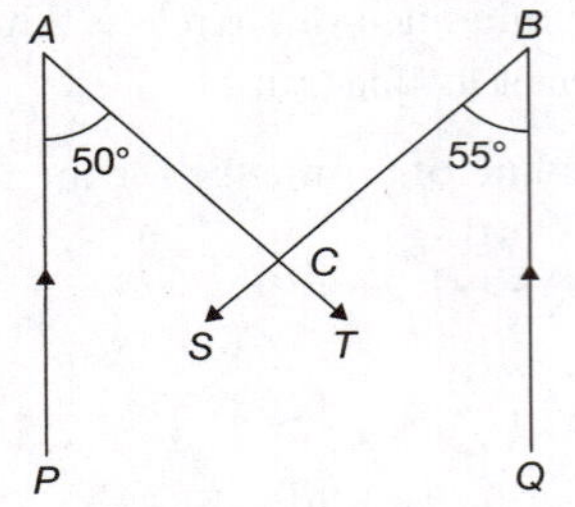

2. In the given figure, $\angle A = 40°$, $\angle 3 = 60°$ and $\overleftrightarrow{PQ}$ is parallel to $\overleftrightarrow{AB}$. Find the other angles mentioned in the figure.

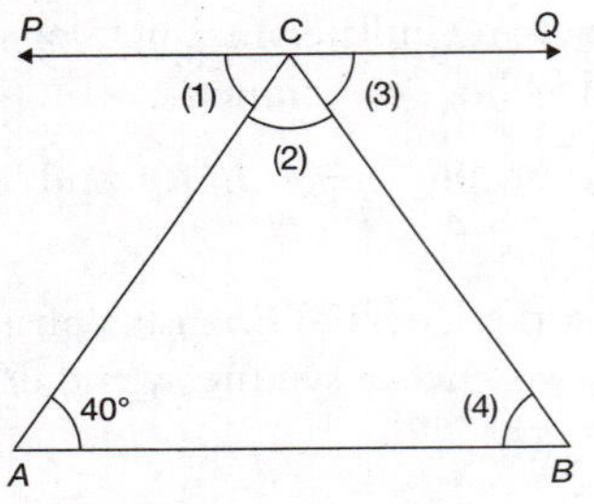

3. List out all the triangles formed in the figure.

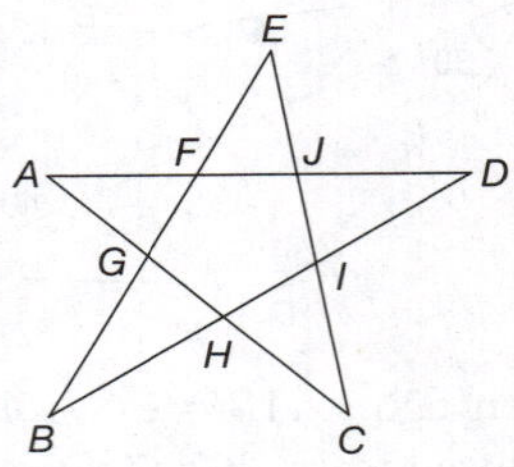

4. In the figure, $\overline{AB} \parallel \overline{CD}$ and $\overline{AD} \parallel \overline{BC}$. If $\angle ABC = 110°$, $\angle ACD = 30°$, then find $\angle ADC$.

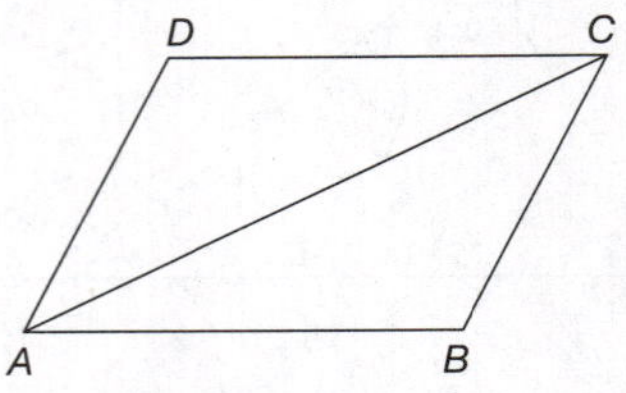

5. In the figure, *AB* = *AC* and *BC* is procured to *D*, if $\angle CDE = 20°$ and $\angle BAC = 80°$, then find the angle of $\angle CED$.

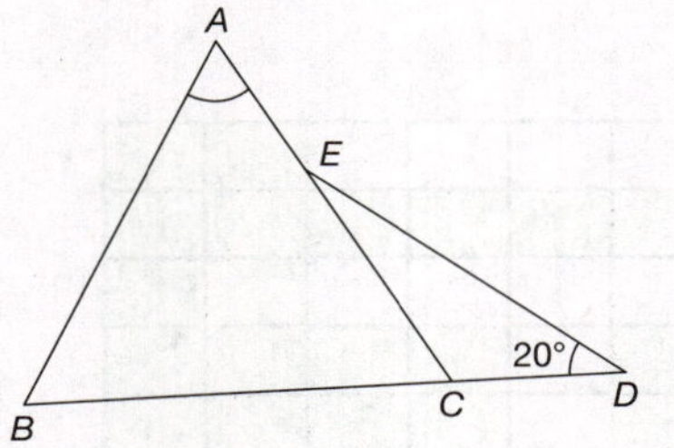

6. Find the perimeter of a semicircle of radius 7 cm.

7. Find the perimeter of the quadrant of a circle of radius 14 cm.

8. Find the diameter of a circle whose circumference is 39.6 cm.

Direction for questions 1 and 2: Draw the following and indicate their lines of symmetry.

9. Two congruent intersecting circles.

10. A square inscribed in a circles.

11. Complete the following figures to have the specified number line of symmetry and draw their lines of symmetry.

(a)

(4 lines of symmetry)

(b)

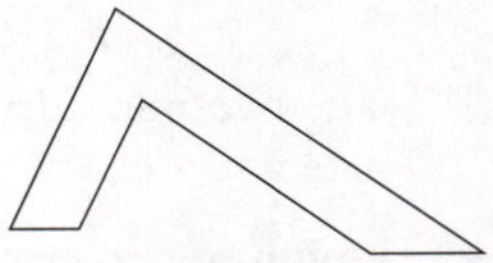

(1 line of symmetry)

12. Identify the shapes on the basis of description.
    (i) A three-sided polygon with all sides equal
    (ii) The longest side of a right-angled triangle.

13. Identify the following pairs of angles as complimentary and supplementary
    (i) 60° and 30°
    (ii) 45° and 135°
    (iii) 60° and 10°
    (iv) 80° and 10°

14. From the following figure, identify,
    (i) Pairs of intersecting lines
    (ii) Parallel lines
    (iii) Concurrent lines

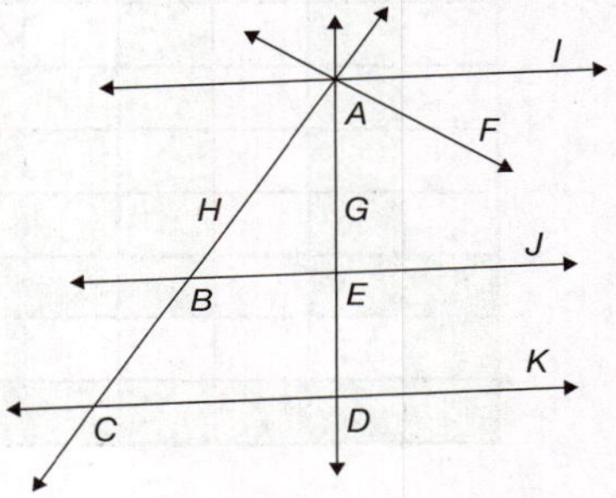

15. Identify the parallel and perpendicular lines:
    (i) Railways tracks
    (ii) Hands of a clock at 12:15
    (iii) Upright pole to the ground
    (iv) Two upright trees

CROSSWORD

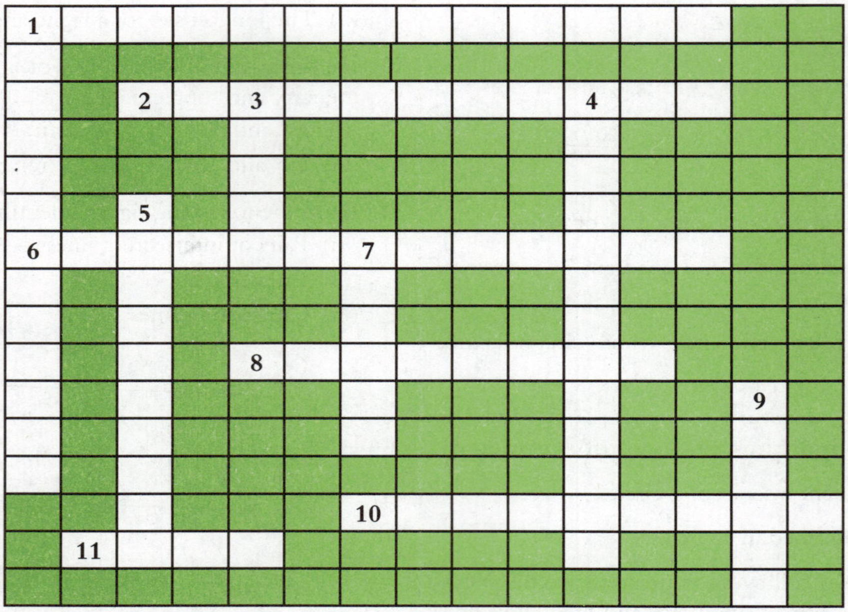

Across

1. Angle P is 30 degrees and angle Q is 60 degrees
2. The line intersecting two or more lines at different points is
6. Straight lines intersecting at right angles
8. Non-intersecting lines
10. The two interior non-adjacent angles which lie on either side of the transversal is
11. The rays which form the angle are

Down

1. The two non-adjacent angles which are not alternate is
3. Union of two rays
4. Sum of these angles is 180 degrees
5. Geometrical instrument
7. Unit for measuring angles
9. The common point of the arms of an angle

TEST YOUR CONCEPTS

Very Short Answer Type Questions

1. 60°
2. 130°
3. 45°
4. transversal
5. parallel
6. (d)
7. (d)
8. (c)
9. (d)
10. (c)
11. (a) → (s), (b) → (p), (c) → (q), (d) → (r)
12. 30°
13. 16 cm
14. 40°
15. 45°, 45°, 90°
16. *AB*
17. (d)
18. (b)
19. (b)
20. (c)
21. (d)
22. (a) → (r), (b) → (s), (c) → (q), (d) → (p)
23. radius
24. chord
25. arc
26. segment
27. tangent
28. secant
29. diameter
30. semicircle
31. sector
32. quadrant
33. (d)
34. (c)
35. (c)
36. (b)
37. (a)
38. one
39. one
40. one
41. two
42. two
43. (d)
44. (c)
45. (d)
46. (b)
47. (d)
48. (a) → (p), (b) → (q), (c) → (r), (d) → (s)

Short Answer Type Questions

49. 72°
50. $129^\circ\ 23^{1}\ 08^{11}$
51. 75°
52. 125°, 55°
53. 55°, 55°
54. ΔABD, ΔABC, ΔAED and ΔBEC
55. 120°
56. 145°
57. 42°, 41°
58. 40°
59. 66 cm
60. 42 cm
63. 125 cm

CONCEPT APPLICATION

1. (b)
2. (c)
3. (a)
4. (c)
5. (b)

ASSESSMENT TEST

1. 75°
2. $\angle 1 = 40°$, $\angle 2 = 80°$, $\angle 4 = 60°$
4. 110°
5. 30°
6. 36 cm
7. 50 cm
8. 12.6 cm

CROSSWORD

Across

1. Complementary
2. Transversal
6. Perpendicular
8. Parallel
10. Alternate
11. Arms

Down

1. Corresponding
3. Angle
4. Supplementary
5. Protractor
7. Degrees
9. Vertex

TEST YOUR CONCEPTS

Very Short Answer Type Questions

1. The required angle = 90° – 30° = 60°
2. The required angle = 180° – 50° =130°
3. 45° + 45° = 90°

   ∴ 45° is the complement of itself.

6. 90° – 36° = 54°

   Hence, the correct option is (d).

7. Reflex angle lies between 180° and 360°.

   Hence, the correct option is (d)

8. Option (c) follows.

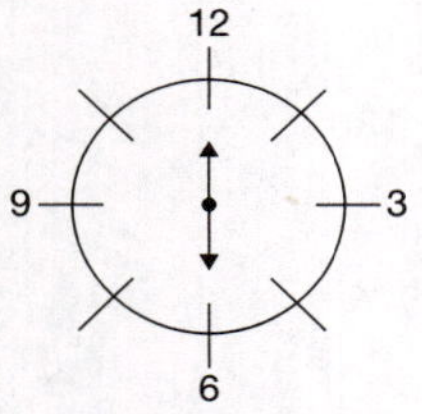

   The required angle is a straight angle.

   Hence, the correct option is (c).

9. If the sum of two angles is 180°, then the two angles are supplementary.

   Hence, the correct option is (d)

10. 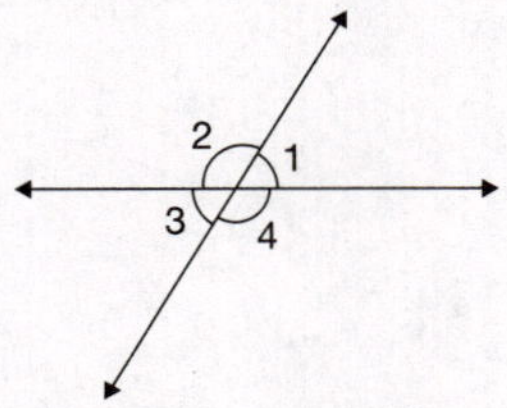

   (1, 2), (2, 3), (3, 4), (4, 1)

   Hence, the correct option is (c).

11. (a) Vertically opposite angles are equal. Hence, their ratio is 1 : 1.

   (b) The supplement of 120° is 60°. The required ratio 120° : 60° = 2 : 1.

   (c) The complement of 30° is 60°.

   ∴ The required ratio is 30° : 60° = 1 : 2.

   (d) Straight angle = 180°

   Reflex angle which is 60° more than the straight angle is 180° + 60° = 240°

   The required ratio is 180° : 240° = 3 : 4

   Therefore, the correct match is:

   (a) → (s), (b) → (p), (c) → (q), (d) → (r)

12. Sum of the angles of a triangle is equal to 180°.

   Sum of the given two angles
   = 70° +80° = 150°

   ∴ Third angle = 180° – 150° = 30°

13. $10 - 7 < x < 10 + 7$

   ∴ 16 cm is the measure of the third side.

14. 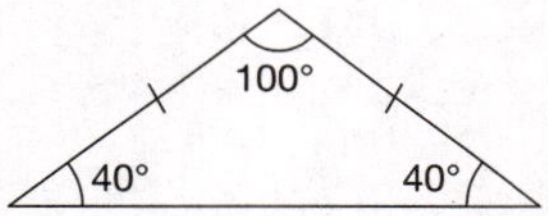

   One of the base angles is 40°.

15. In a right-angled isosceles triangle, the angles are 45°, 45° and 90°.

16. $\angle B = 65°$, $\angle C = 80°$

   $\Rightarrow \angle A = 35°$

   ⇒ The side opposite to 80° is the longest side that is AB.

19. Equilateral triangle is an acute angled triangle.

   Hence, the correct option is (b).

21. 7, 24, 25 can be the sides of the triangle.

   Hence, the correct option is (d).

42. X has two lines of symmetry. 

43. A line segment has infinite lines of symmetry.

   Hence, the correct option is (d).

44. 

   Hence, the correct option is (c).

45. P, Q and R have no lines of symmetry.

   Hence, the correct option is (d).

46. Equilateral triangle has 3 lines of symmetry.

   Hence, the correct option is (b).

48. (a) → (p), (b) → (q), (c) → (r), (d) → (s)

Short Answer Type Questions

49. Let the two supplementary angles be $3x$ and $7x$.

$3x + 7x = 180°$

$10x = 180°$

$x = 18°$

Difference between the angles $= 7x - 3x = 4x$

$= 4 \times 18° = 72°$

50. The supplement of $50° \, 36' \, 52'' = 180° - (50° \, 36' \, 52'')$

$= 179° \, 59'60'' - 50° \, 36'52''$

$= 129° \, 23'08''$

$\therefore$ The supplement of $50^0 \, 36' \, 52''$ is $129° \, 23' \, 08''$.

51.

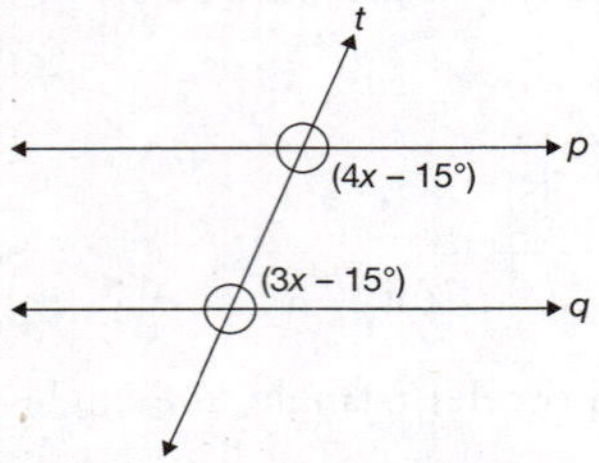

Given p, q are parallel lines and t is a transversal.

Given angles are co-interior angles.

$\Rightarrow 4x - 15° + 3x - 15° = 180°$

$\Rightarrow 7x - 30° = 180°$

$\Rightarrow 7x = 210°$

$x = 30°$

$\therefore 4x - 15° = 4 \times 30° - 15°$

$= 120° - 15°$

$= 105°$

$3x - 15° = 3x - 15°$

$= 3 \times 30° - 15$

$= 90 - 15°$

$= 75°$

52.

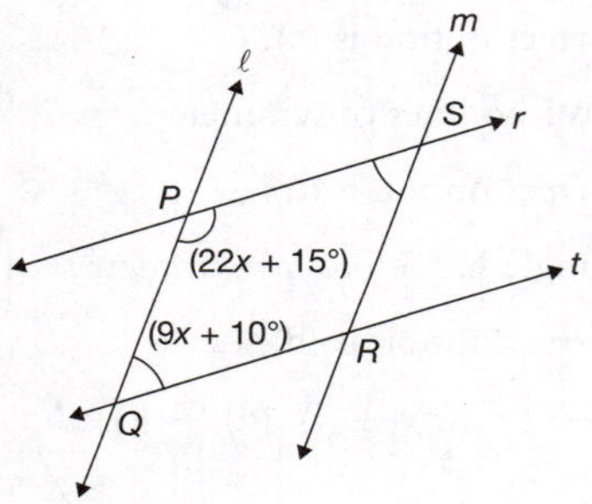

$\angle P + \angle Q = 180°$ (since they are co-interior angles and $r \parallel t$)

$\Rightarrow 22x + 15 + 9x + 10 = 180°$

$31x = 180° - 25°$

$31x = 155°$

$x = 5°$

$\therefore \angle P = 22x + 15°$

$= 22 \times 5° + 15°$

$= 110° + 15° = 125°$

Given $\ell \parallel m$,

$\angle P + \angle S = 180°$

$125° + \angle S = 180°$

$\angle S = 55°$

53. Given $\angle A = 70°$

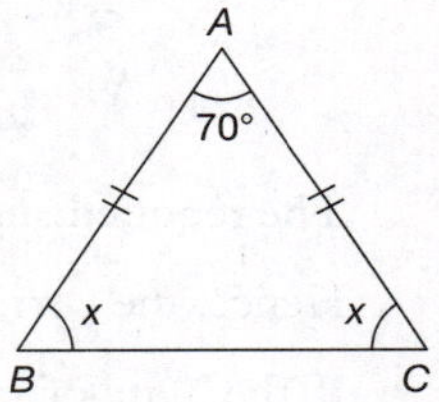

$AB = AC$

We know that:

$70° + 2x° = 180°$

$2x° = 180° - 70° = 110°$

$x° = \dfrac{110°}{2} = 55°$

$\Rightarrow \angle B = \angle C = 55°$

54.

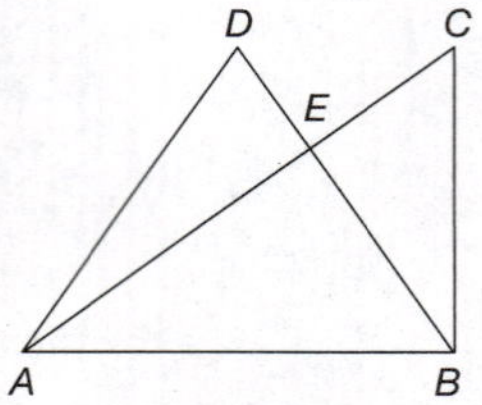

The following are the triangles formed in the figure.

ΔABD, ΔABC, ΔABE, ΔAED and ΔBEC.

55.

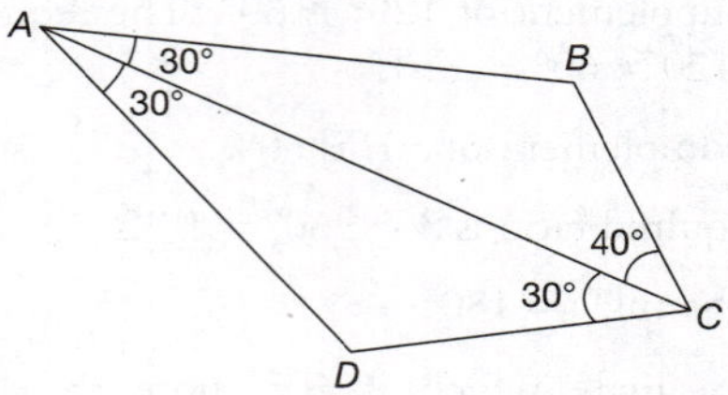

Given $\angle CAD = 30°$, $\angle ACB = 40°$.

As AC is the bisector of $\angle BAD$, $\angle CAD = \angle BAC = 30°$.

Given, $\overline{AB} \parallel \overline{DC}$.

$\therefore \angle ACD = \angle BAC = 30°$

In ΔADC, $\angle ADC = 180° - 30° - 30° = 120°$

56.

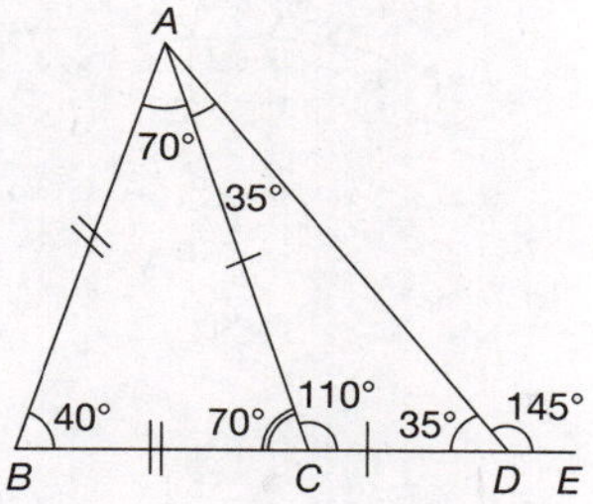

Since $AB = BC$, $\angle BAC = \angle ACB = 70°$

$\therefore \angle ABC = 180° - 70° - 70° = 40°$

$\Rightarrow \angle ACD = 180° - 70° = 110°$

$AC = CD$ (given)

$\Rightarrow \angle CAD = \angle ADC = \dfrac{180° - 110°}{2} = 35°$

$\therefore \angle ADE = 180° - 35° = 145°$

57.

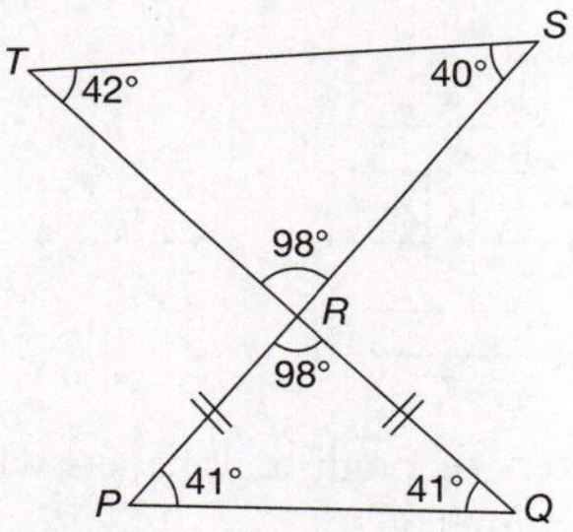

$\angle TRS = \angle PRQ = 98°$ (vertically opposite angles)

In ΔTRS,

$\angle RTS = 180° - 98° - 40°$

$= 180° - 138°$

$= 42°$

In ΔPRQ, $\angle RPQ = \angle RQP$ (since $PR = QR$)

$= \dfrac{180° - 98°}{2} = \dfrac{82°}{4} = 41°$

58. In the figure, PQR and TRS are triangles.

In ΔPQR, $PQ = PR$

$\Rightarrow \angle Q = \angle R$

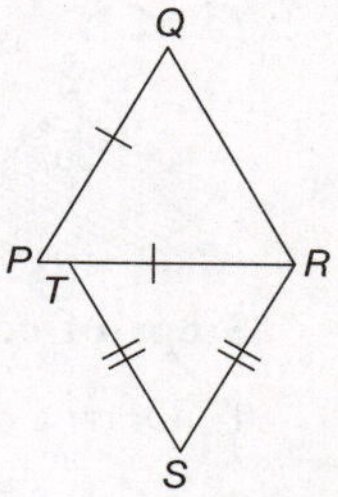

$\angle P + \angle Q + \angle R = 180°$

$50° + \angle R + \angle R = 180°$

$2\angle R = 130°$

$\angle R = 65°$

$\therefore \angle Q = \angle R = 65°$

In ΔTRS, $\angle TRS = 135° - 65°$

$\angle TRS = 70°$

In ΔTRS, $TS = SR$

$\Rightarrow \angle STR = \angle TRS = 70°$

$\Rightarrow \angle S = 180° - (70° + 70°)$

$\angle S = 40°$

59. Given $r = 10.5$ cm

Circumference $= 2\pi r$

$= 2 \times \dfrac{22}{7} \times 10.5$

$= 44 \times 1.5$

$= 66$ cm

60. Circumference $= 2\pi r = 132$ cm

$2 \times \dfrac{22}{7} \times r = 132$

$r = \dfrac{132 \times 7}{2 \times 22}$ $r = 21$ cm

Diameter $= 2r = 2(21) = 42$ cm

61.

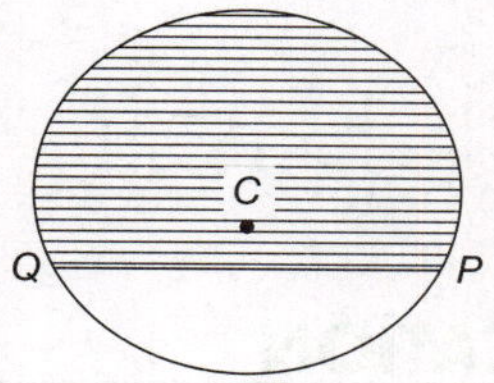

Steps of construction:

1. Draw a circle of radius 4 cm and mark the centre as C.
2. Mark a point P on the circle.
3. Draw an arc with P as centre and radius 6 cm to cut the circle at Q.
4. Join $\overline{PQ}$.
5. Shade the segment which contains the centre 'C'.

62.

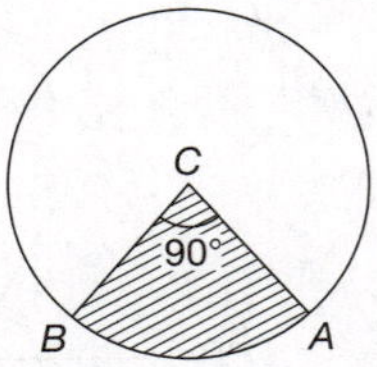

Steps of construction:

1. Draw a circle of radius 3.5 cm.
2. Mark the centre as C.
3. Mark a point A on the circle and join A to C.
4. Mark a point B on the circle such that $\angle ACB =$ 90° with the help of a protractor.
5. Join BC.
6. Shade the region bounded by the radii AC and BC, the arc AB.

63. Circumference of the circle $(2\pi r) = 220$ cm

$2 \times \frac{22}{7} \times r = 220$

$r = 35$ cm

The length of the arc of the quadrant

$= \frac{1}{4}$ of the circumference

$= \frac{1}{4} \times 220 = 55$ cm

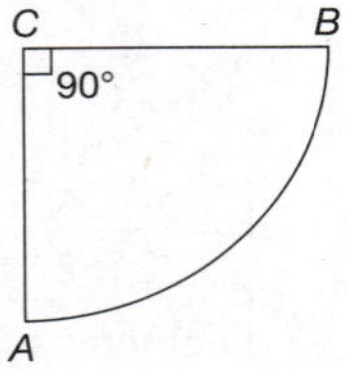

Perimeters of the quadrant

$= 2 \times$ Radius + Length of the arc

$= 2 \times 35 + 55$

$= 70 + 55 = 125$ cm

64.

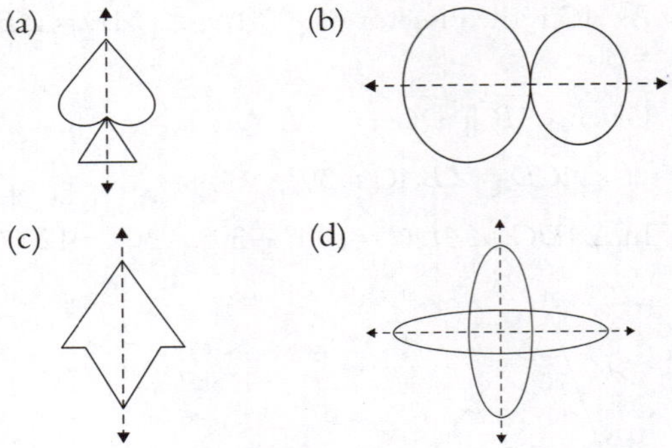

65.

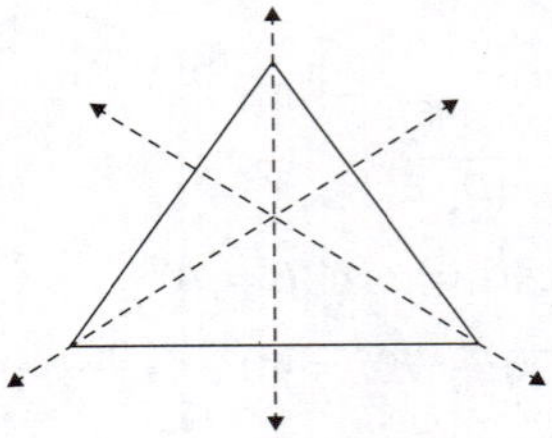

66.

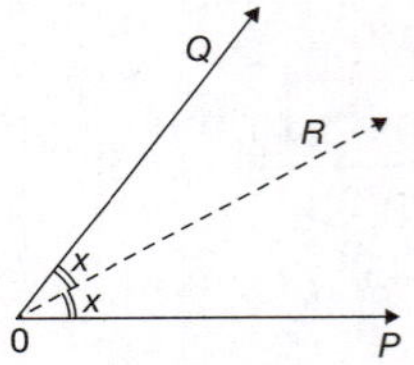

67.

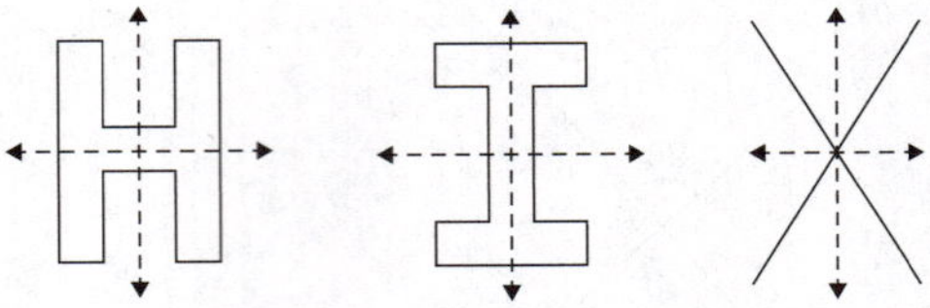

There are three letters of English alphabets which have two lines of symmetry.

CONCEPT APPLICATION

1. Given that the two sides of an isosceles triangle are 6 cm and 12 cm.

The third side can be of length 6 cm or 12 cm.

If the length of the third side is 6 cm, then triangle cannot be formed with the measurements 6 cm, 6 cm and 12 cm, since 6 cm + 6 cm is not greater than 12 cm.

If the length of the third side is 12 cm, then a triangle will be formed with the measurements 6 cm, 12 cm and 12 cm.

Moreover, it is an isosceles triangle.

Hence, the perimeter of the triangle is 6 cm + 12 cm + 12 cm = 30 cm.

Hence, the correct option is (b).

2. If any two angles of a triangle are equal, then the triangle is isosceles.

The sum of all the angles of a triangle is 180°.

Choice (a): Angle A is 50° and angle B is 80°.

Angle $C = 180° - 50° - 80° = 50°$. $\Rightarrow ABC$ is an isosceles triangle.

Choice (b): Angle A is 65° and angle B is 50°.

Angle $C = 180° - 65° - 50° = 65°$. $\Rightarrow ABC$ is an isosceles triangle.

Choice (c) Angle A is 60° and angle B is 70°.

Angle $C = 180° - 60° - 70° = 50° \Rightarrow ABC$ is not an isosceles triangle.

Hence, choice (c) follows.

Hence, the correct option is (c).

3. Given that the perimeter of the quadrant of a circle is 37.5 cm.

$\Rightarrow (2\pi r/4) + 2r = 37.5$

$\Rightarrow (11r/7) + 2r = 37.5$

$\Rightarrow (11/7 + 2)r = 37.5$

$\Rightarrow (25/7)r = 37.5$

$\Rightarrow r = 10.5$

The area of the circle (in cm^2) $= \pi r^2$.

$= (22/7)(10.5)2$

$= (22)(1.5)(10.5)$

$= (33)(10.5)$

$= 346.5$

Hence, the correct option is (a).

4. Given that the sides of the scalene triangle are integers in cm and the perimeter of the triangle is 15 cm.

We know that, no two sides are equal in a scalene triangle.

Also, in a triangle, the sum of any two sides is greater than the third side and the difference of any two sides is less than the third side.

As the perimeter of a scalene triangle is 15 cm, the measures of the sides can be (2 cm, 6 cm, 7 cm), (3 cm, 5 cm, 7 cm) and (4 cm, 5 cm, 6 cm).

Hence, choice (c) follows.

Hence, the correct option is (c).

5. The lines of symmetry are shown in the figure. The number of lines of symmetry is 6.

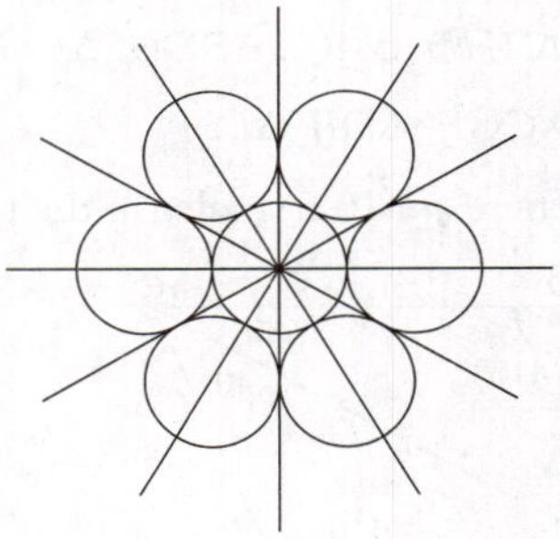

Hence, the correct option is (b).

ASSESSMENT TEST

1.

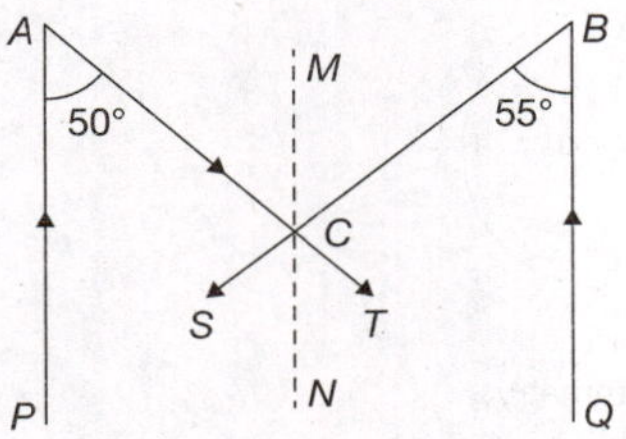

Given that $\overline{AP} \parallel \overline{BQ}$.

Draw $\overline{MN} \parallel \overline{AP} \parallel \overline{BQ}$.

$\angle PAC = \angle ACM$ (Alternate angles)

$\Rightarrow \angle ACM = 50°$

Similarly $\angle BCM = \angle CBQ = 55°$

$\Rightarrow \angle ACB = 50° + 55° = 105°$

$\Rightarrow \angle ACS = 180° - 105° = 75°$

($\angle ACB$ and $\angle ACS$ linear pair)

2. Given $\overleftrightarrow{PQ} \parallel \overline{AB}$.

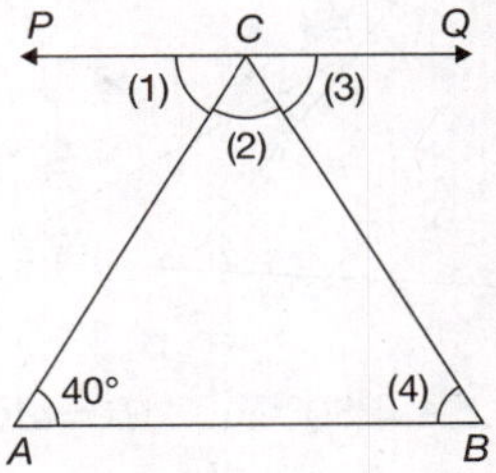

$\angle A = \angle(1)$ (alternate angles)

$\angle(1) = 40°$

$\angle(3) = \angle 4$ (alternate angles)

$\therefore \angle 4 = 60°$

$\angle(1) + \angle(2) + \angle(3) = 180°$ (straight angle)

$40° + \angle 2 + 60° = 180°$

$\angle 2 = 80°$

3.

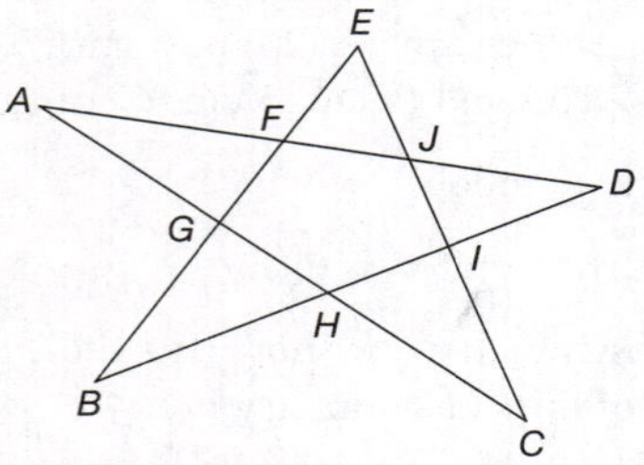

$\Delta AGF, \Delta AHD, \Delta ACJ, \Delta BGH, \Delta BFD, \Delta BEI$

$\Delta CHI, \Delta CGE, \Delta DIJ, \Delta EFJ$

Hence, there are 10 triangles in the figure.

4.

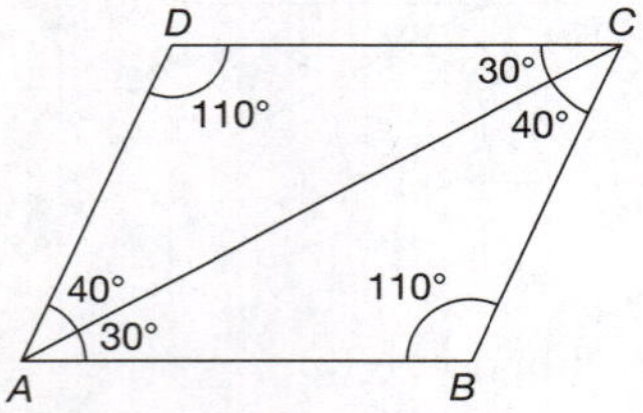

Given $\overline{AB} \parallel \overline{CD}$, $\angle ABC = 110°$ and $\angle ACD = 30°$

$\Rightarrow \angle CAB = 30°$ (Alternate angles)

$\therefore$ In ΔABC, $\angle BCA = 180° - 110° - 30° = 40°$

Since $\overline{AD} \parallel \overline{BC}$, $\angle DAC = \angle ACB = 40°$ (Alternate angles)

In ΔADC, $\angle ADC = 180° - 30° - 40° = 110°$.

5.

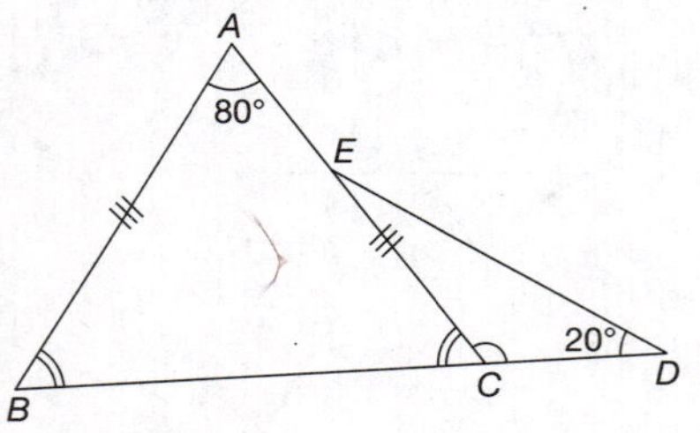

In ΔABC, $\angle A = 80°$ and $AB = AC \Rightarrow \angle B = \angle C$.

$$\therefore \angle B = \angle C = \frac{180° - 80°}{2} = 50°$$

$\Rightarrow \angle ACD = 180° - 50° = 130°$

In ΔECD,

$\angle CED = 180° - 130° - 20° = 30°$

6. Perimeter of semicircle $= \frac{1}{2} \times$ Circumference of the circle + Diameter

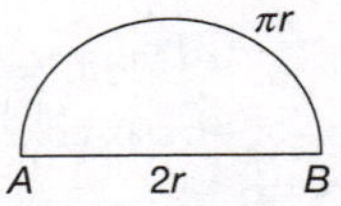

Given, $r = 7$ cm

$$\text{Perimeter} = \frac{1}{2} \times 2\pi r + 2r$$

$$= \frac{22}{7} \times 7 + 2 \times 7$$

$$= 22 + 14$$

$$= 36 \text{ cm}$$

7. Perimeter of a quadrant $= 2r + \frac{1}{4} \times 2\pi r$

Given, $r = 14$ cm

$$\text{Perimeter} = 2 \times 14 + \frac{1}{2} \times \frac{22}{7} \times 14$$

$$= 28 + 22$$

$$= 50 \text{ cm}$$

8. Given, the circumference of the circle = 39.6 cm

$2\pi r = 39.6$ cm

$$2 \times \frac{22}{7} \times r = 39.6$$

$$2r = 39.6 \times \frac{7}{22}$$

$2r = 1.8 \times 7$

$2r = 12.6$ cm

$\therefore$ Diameter of the circle = 12.6 cm

9.

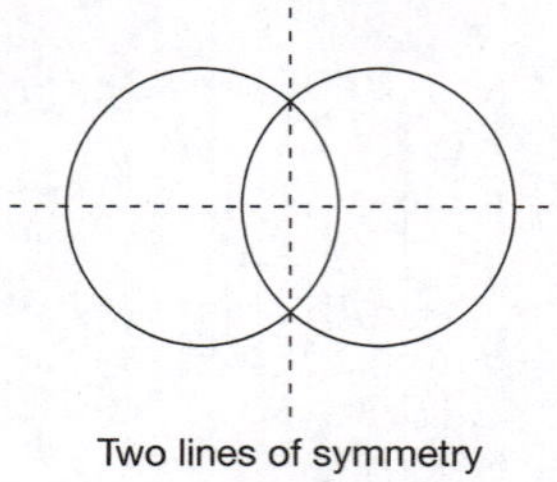

Two lines of symmetry

10.

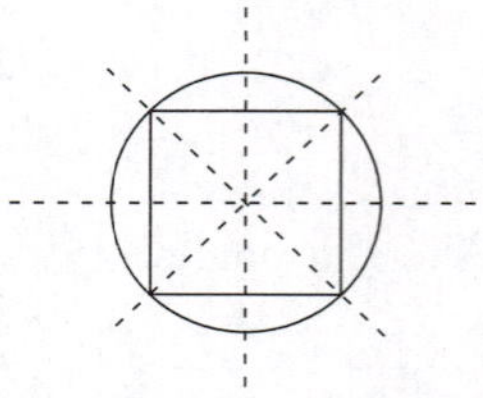

Four lines of symmetry

11. (a)

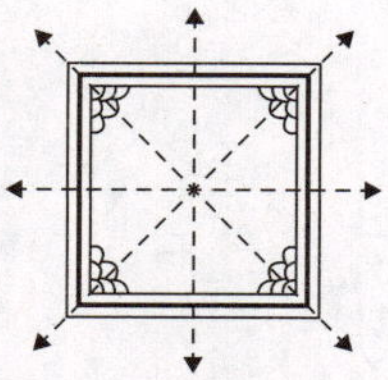

(4 lines of symmetry)

(b) The following is the one of the possible figures.

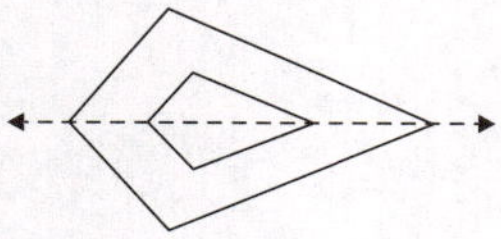

(1 line of symmetry)

12. (i) Equilateral triangle
(ii) Hypotenuse

13. (i) Complementary
(ii) Supplementary
(iii) neither
(iv) Complementary

14. (i) *F* and *G*, *F* and *H*, *F* and *I*, *G* and *I*, *H* and *I*, *J* and *H*, *J* and *G*, *J* and *F*, *K* and *G*, *K* and *H*
(ii) $J \parallel I$, $J \parallel K$, $I \parallel K$
(iii) *F*, *G*, *H* and *I*

15. (i) Parallel
(ii) Perpendicular
(iii) Perpendicular
(v) Parallel

Chapter

9

Mensuration

REMEMBER

Before beginning this chapter, you should be able to:

- Recall different units of lengths
- Understand the meaning of area and volume

KEY IDEAS

After completing this chapter, you should be able to:

- Determine areas of rectangles and squares
- Calculate surface areas and volumes of cubes and cuboids

INTRODUCTION

Mensuration is a branch of Mathematics that deals with the computation of geometric magnitudes, such as the length of a line segment, the area of a surface and the volume of a solid. In this chapter, we shall deal with the computation of areas and perimeters of plane figures (rectangle and square), surface areas and volumes of cube and cuboid.

PLANE FIGURES

A figure lying on a plane is called a plane figure. Triangles, rectangles and circles are some examples of plane figures. A plane figure is a closed figure if it has no free end. It is called a simple closed figure if it does not cross itself. A plane figure is made up of lines or curves or both. The part of the plane which is enclosed by a simple closed figure is called a plane region. The magnitude of a plane region is called its area.

> **Info Box!**
>
> A characteristic feature of quadrilateral is that the sum of all inetrior angles in 360°.

A line segment has one dimension such as length. Hence, its size is measured in terms of its length.

A planar region has two dimensions such as length and breadth. Hence, its size is measured in terms of its area.

The perimeter of a closed planar figure is the total length of the line segments enclosing the figure.

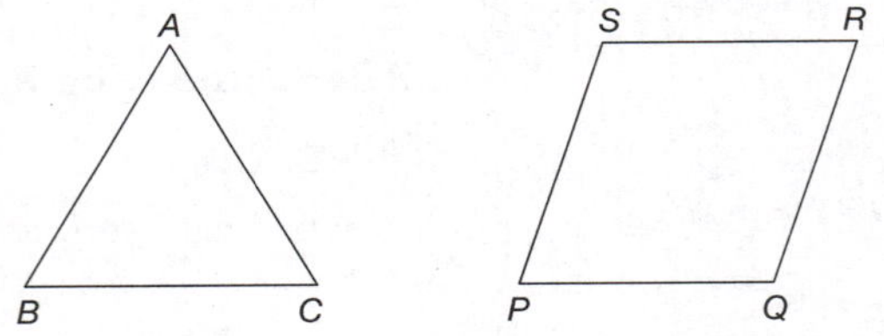

FIGURE 9.1 A Triangle and a quadrilateral

In the above figures, ABC is a triangle and $PQRS$ is a quadrilateral.

The perimeter of the $\Delta ABC = AB + BC + CA$.

The perimeter of the quadrilateral $PQRS = PQ + QR + RS + SP$.

Units of Measurement

The length of a line segment is measured in units such as centimetres, inches, metres, feet, etc.

Area is measured in units such as square centimetres, square inches, square meters, square feet, etc.

TABLE 9.1 Basic unit conversions

Length	Volume	Weight
1 km = 1000 m	1 kL = 1000 L	1 kg = 1000 g
1 m = 0.001 km	1 L = 0.001 L	1 g = 0.001 kg
1 m = 1000 mm	1 L = 1000 mL	1 g = 1000 mg
1 mm = 0.001 m	1 mL = 0.001 L	1 mg = 0.001 g

Area of a Rectangle

A rectangle is a closed figure having four sides, in which the opposite sides are equal and each angle measures 90°. In the above rectangle *ABCD*, $AB = 5$ cm and $BC = 4$ cm. Each of the small squares in the rectangle *ABCD* measures 1 cm by 1 cm and the area occupied by each small square is 1 sq. cm. There are 4 rows, each row consisting of 5 unit squares.

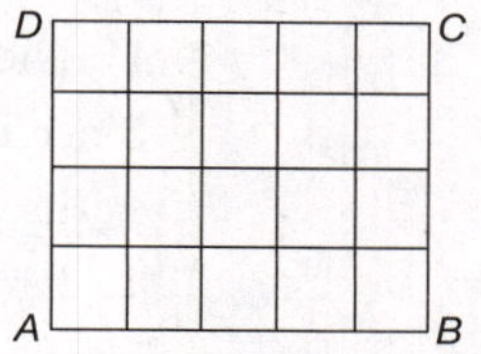

FIGURE 9.2 A rectangle

$\therefore$ The area occupied by the rectangle = (4) (5) = 20 sq. cm

The number of unit squares in the rectangle *ABCD* is equal to the product of the number of unit squares along the length and the number of unit squares along the breadth.

Thus, we see that the area of a rectangle = (Length) × (Breadth)

Perimeter of a rectangle = 2 (Length + Breadth)

Area of a Square

A square is a rectangle in which all the sides are equal.

Area of a rectangle = (Length) × (Breadth)

In a square, Length = Breadth (Side)

$\therefore$ Area of a square = $(\text{Side})^2$

Perimeter of a square = 4 (Side)

Info Box!

Al squares are rectangles but all rectangles are not sqaures!

NOTE

Area of a right isosceles triangle = $\dfrac{a^2}{2}$, where a is the length of each sides of the triangle which is equal.

EXAMPLE 9.1

The side of a square is 5 m and the perimeter a rectangle is equal to the perimeter of the square. If the length of the rectangle is 6 m, then find the ratio of the areas of the square and the rectangle.

SOLUTION

The side of a square = 5 m

The length of a rectangle = 6 m

Let the breadth of a rectangle be '*b*' m.

Since the perimeter of the rectangle is equal to the perimeter of the square,

$2(6 + b) = 4 \times 5$

$6 + b = 10$

$b = 4$ m

The ratio of the areas of the square and the rectangle = $5^2 : 6 \times 4 = 25 : 24$

EXAMPLE 9.2

A sign board indicating SCHOOL ZONE is in the form of an equilateral triangle with perimeter 120 cm. Find the length of the side of the equilateral triangle.

SOLUTION

Let the side of the board be 'a' cm.

Since the board is in the shape of an equilateral triangle,

Perimeter = $3a$

$\therefore\ 3a = 120$

$$a = \frac{120}{3} = 40 \text{ cm}$$

$\therefore$ The length of the side of the board = 40 cm

EXAMPLE 9.3

If the three sides of a triangle are the distinct prime factors of 525 (in cm), then find the perimeter of the triangle.

SOLUTION

The prime factors of 525 are 5, 3 and 7.

Perimeter of a triangle = 5 + 3 + 7 = 15 cm

SOLIDS

A plane figure may have one dimension or two dimensions. A circle is said to be unidimensional. Triangles and quadrilaterals have two dimensions. For two-dimensional figures, the dimensions are length, breadth, width or height. But many objects with a definite shape such as a brick, a matchbox, a pencil, a marble, a tank, an ice cream cone, etc., have a third dimension. These objects are known as solids.

Thus, a solid is a three-dimensional object. In general, any object that occupies space and has a definite shape is called a solid. Solids like cubes, cuboids, etc., have plane or flat surfaces.

Prism

Prism is a solid figure in which two identical and parallel polygons form the top and the bottom faces. The lateral faces are parallelograms.

Info Box!

A prism takes its name from the shape of its base.

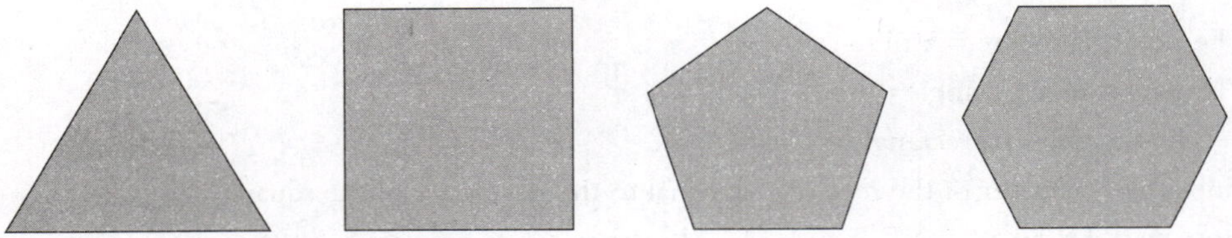

FIGURE 9.3 Various shapes of the base of prism (triangle, square, pentagon, hexagon)

The line joining the centres of the two parallel polygons is called the axis of the prism and the length of the axis is referred to as the height of the prism.

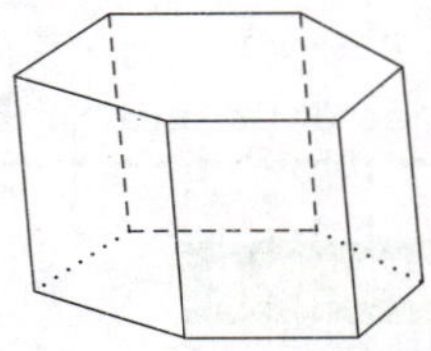

FIGURE 9.4 A Hexagonal prism

If the two parallel and identical polygons are regular, and if the axis is perpendicular to the base, then the prism is called a right prism. The lateral surfaces of a right prism are rectangles.

Consider two congruent and parallel triangular planes *ABC* and *PQR*. If we join the corresponding vertices of both the planes, i.e., *A* to *P*, *B* to *Q* and *C* to *R*, then the resultant solid formed is a triangular prism.

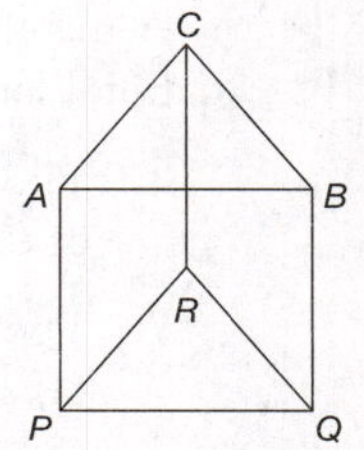

FIGURE 9.5 A triangular prism

> **NOTE**
>
> The following points remain true for all prisms:
> 1. The number of faces = The number of sides of the base + 2
> 2. The number of vertices = Number of sides of the base × 2
> 3. The number of edges of a prism = Number of sides of the base × 3

Pyramid

A pyramid is a solid figure obtained by joining the vertices of a polygon to a point in the space by straight lines. The base of the solid obtained is the polygon and the lateral faces are triangles. The fixed point in space where all the triangles (i.e., lateral faces) meet is called its vertex.

In the figure, the base *ABCD* is a quadrilateral. All the vertices of the base are joined to a fixed point *O* in space by straight lines. The resultant solid obtained is called a pyramid.

A straight line joining the vertex and the centre of the base is called the axis of the pyramid. If the axis is not perpendicular to the base, then it is an oblique pyramid.

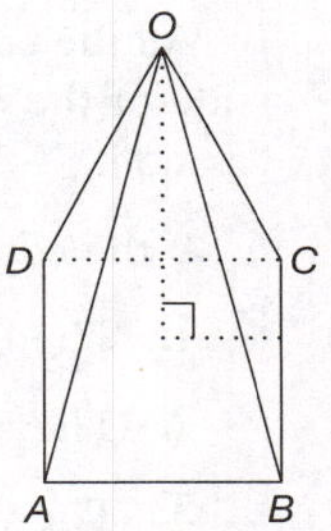

FIGURE 9.6 A geometrical pyramid

> **NOTE**
>
> The following points remain true for all pyramids:
> 1. The number of faces = The number of sides of the base + 1
> 2. The number of vertices = The number of sides of the base + 1
> 3. The number of edges = 2 (The number of sides of the base)

Cuboid

A cuboid is a solid bounded by six rectangular faces and the opposite faces are congruent. In the given figure, faces *ABFE* and *DCGH* are congruent. Similarly, faces *BCGF* and *ADHE* are congruent and faces *ABCD* and *EFGH* are congruent. Each face is a rectangle. The line segments like *AB*, *BC* and *BF* are called edges. A cuboid has 6 faces and 12 edges.

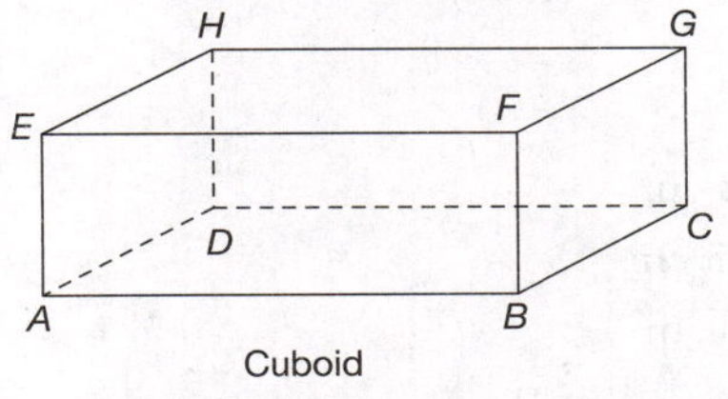

FIGURE 9.7 A Cuboid

A matchbox, a brick, a room, etc., are in the shape of a cuboid. The three dimensions of the cuboid, length (ℓ), breadth (b) and height (h) are generally denoted by $\ell \times b \times h$.

1. The lateral surface area(LSA) of a cuboid $= ph = 2(\ell + b)h$ sq. units, where p is the perimeter of the base.
2. The total surface area of a cuboid = LSA + 2(base area) $= 2(\ell + b)h + 2\ell b = 2(\ell b + bh + \ell h)$ sq. units.
3. The volume of a cuboid $= Ah = (\ell b)h = \ell bh$ cubic units, where A is the area of the base.

NOTE

If a box made of wood of thickness t has inner dimensions ℓ, b and h, then the outer length $= \ell + 2t$, the outer breadth $= b + 2t$ and the outer height $= h + 2t$.

Cube

In a cuboid, if all the dimensions, i.e., its length, breadth and height are equal, then the solid is called a cube.

All the edges of a cube are equal in length and each edge is called the side of the cube. Thus, the size of a cube is completely determined by its sides.

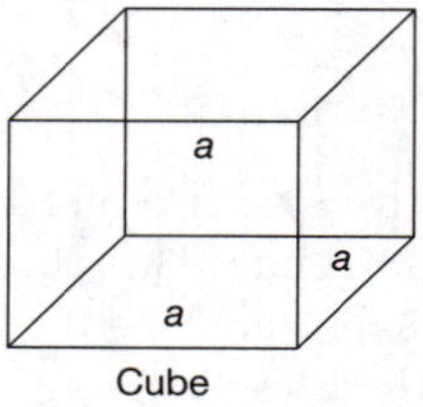

FIGURE 9.8 A cube

If the edge of cube is a unit, then:

1. The LSA of the cube $= 4a^2$ sq. units.
2. The total surface area of the cube = LSA + 2(area of base) $= 4a^2 + 2a^2 = 6a^2$ sq. units.
3. The volume of the cube $= a^3$ cubic units.

EXAMPLE 9.4

Write the number of vertices, edges and faces of a pentagonal prism?

SOLUTION

The number of vertices $= 2 \times 5 = 10$

Number of sides of the base = 5

The number of edges $= 3 \times 5 = 15$

The number of faces $= 5 + 2 = 7$

EXAMPLE 9.5

The dimensions of a gift box are 1.8 cm × 1.5 cm × 0.8 cm. Find how much gift paper is required to cover it? (Ignore the overlaps)

SOLUTION

Length of the gift box = 1.8 cm

Breadth of the gift box = 1.5 cm

Height of the gift box = 0.8 cm

The area of the gift paper to cover gift box = Total surface area of the box

$= 2(\ell b + bh + h\ell)$

$= 2(1.8 \times 1.5 + 1.5 \times 0.8 6 0.8 \times 1.8)$

$= 2(2.7 + 1.2 + 1.44)$

$= 2(5.34) = 10.68$ sq. cm

EXAMPLE 9.6

If the lateral surface area of a cube is 72 sq. cm, then find the total surface area of the cube.

SOLUTION

Let the edge of the cube be 'a' cm.

Lateral surface area of the cube $4a^2 = 72$

$a^2 = \frac{72}{4} = 18$

The total surface area of a cube $= 6a^2 = 6 \times 18 = 108$ sq. cm

EXAMPLE 9.7

The inner dimensions of a geometry box are 12 cm × 8 cm × 2 cm. How many erasers of length 4 cm, breadth 2 cm and height 1 cm can be placed in the geometry box?

SOLUTION

Number of erasers that can be placed into the geometry box

$$= \frac{\text{Volume of the geometry box}}{\text{Volume of each eraser}} = \frac{12 \times 8 \times 2}{4 \times 2 \times 1} = 3 \times 4 \times 2 = 24$$

TEST YOUR CONCEPTS

Very Short Answer Type Questions

Direction for questions from 1 to 5: Fill in the blanks.

1. If the length of a rectangle is equal to the breadth of the rectangle then the rectangle becomes a _______.

2. The side of an equilateral triangle is 672-cm long, then the perimeter of the triangle is _______.

3. The lengths of two sides of an isosceles triangle are 2016 cm and 2017 cm, then the maximum possible perimeter of a triangle is _______.

4. If the sum of the length and the breadth of a rectangle is 1009 cm, then the perimeter of the rectangle is _______.

5. A square of the perimeter is p units, then its area is _______ sq. units.

Direction for questions from 6 to 10: Select the correct alternative from the given choices.

6. If the angles of a triangle are in the ratio 1 : 1 : 1, then the ratio of their sides is _______.
   (a) 1 : 1 : 1 (b) 1 : 2 : 3
   (c) $1 : \sqrt{3} : 2$ (d) $1 : 1 : \sqrt{2}$

7. If the side of a square is doubled, then the area of the square _______.
   (a) remains same (b) becomes double
   (c) becomes triple (d) becomes 4 times

8. If the area of a square is 25 m^2, then the side of the square is _______ (m).
   (a) 125 (b) 625
   (c) $\frac{1}{25}$ (d) 5

9. The area and perimeter of a square are numerically equal, then the numerical value of the side of the square is _______.
   (a) 3 (b) 4
   (c) 5 (d) 6

10. The length and breadth of a rectangle are in the ratio 3 : 2. The perimeter of the rectangle is 10 cm, then its length is _______ (in cm).
    (a) 2 (b) 5
    (c) 3 (d) 4

Direction for question 11: Match the Column – A with the Column – B.

11. In the given figure, $ABCD$ is a rectangle and $ADEF$ is a square. The area of ΔADE is $\frac{49}{2}$ sq. cm and $CE = 2DE$.

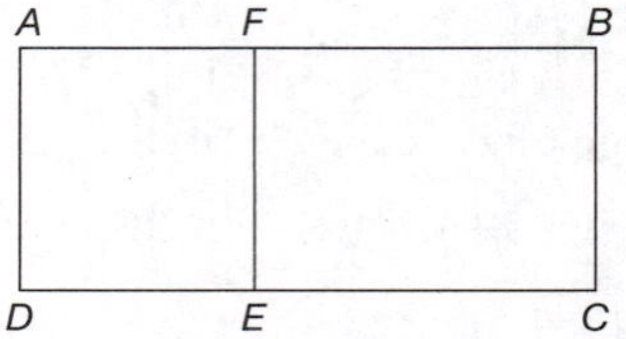

Using the above data, match Column A with Column B.

	Column A		Column B
(a)	The perimeter of a square $ADEF$ (in cm)	( )	(p) 56
(b)	The area of a square $ADEF$ (in sq. cm)	( )	(q) 28
(c)	The perimeter of a rectangle $ABCD$ (in cm)	( )	(s) 147
(d)	The area of a rectangle $ABCD$ is (in sq. cm)	( )	(r) 49

Direction for questions from 12 to 16: Fill in the blanks.

12. The total surface area of a cube of an edge 10 cm is _______.

13. The volume of a cuboidal box is 24 cm^3 and base area is 12 sq. cm, then the height of the box is _______.

14. The perimeter of a base of a cuboid is 16 cm and the height of the cuboid is 2 cm, then the lateral surface area of the cuboid is _______.

15. The sum of the lengths of all the edges of a cube is 60 cm, then the length of the edge of the cube is _______.

16. The edge of a cube is increased by 100%, then the lateral surface area of the cube is increased by _______%.

PRACTICE QUESTIONS

Direction for questions from 17 to 21: Select the correct alternative from the given choices.

17. The ratio of the lateral surface area and the total surface area of a cube is ________.
(a) 1 : 2 (b) 2 : 3
(c) 3 : 2 (d) 1 : 4

18. The lateral surface area of a matchbox which is 6 cm long, 2 cm wide and 1.5 cm thick is ________ sq. cm.
(a) 30 (b) 34
(c) 42 (d) 24

19. The total surface area of a cuboid which is 2.5 m long, 2 m wide and 1.4 m high is ________ sq. cm.
(a) 11.3 (b) 22.6
(c) 12.6 (d) 7

20. A cube is to be coloured in such a way that no two opposite faces have the same colour, then the minimum number of colours required is ________.
(a) 6 (2) 2
(c) 3 (d) 4

21. If the edge of a cube is doubled, then the volume of the cube is ________ that of the initial cube.
(a) 4 times (b) 8 times
(c) 12 times (d) 6 times

Direction for question 22: Match Column A with Column B.

22.

Column A		Column B
(a) Number of vertices of a triangular prism	( )	(p) 5
(b) Number of edges of a cube	( )	(q) 12
(c) Number of surfaces of a square pyramid	( )	(s) 8
(d) Number of vertices of a cuboid	( )	(r) 6

Short Answer Type Questions

23. Let *a*, *b* and *c* be the three sides of a triangle (in cm) such that $a + b = 2015$, $b + c = 2016$ and $c + a = 2017$, then find the perimeter of the triangle.

24. The area of a square field is 49 m. How many times Sunil has to run around the square field to cover 224 m?

25. A rectangular sheet is cut along its length into five equal squares as shown in the figure. The area of a square is 16 cm^2. Find the perimeter of the rectangle.

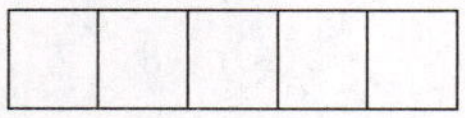

26. Four identical strips in the form of right isosceles triangles are removed from the four corners of a square sheet of side 8 cm. Find the area of the remaining sheet, if the length of each equal sides of the triangles is 4 cm.

27. In the given figure, *ABCD* is a rectangle. I, II and III are squares. Find the area of the shaded region.

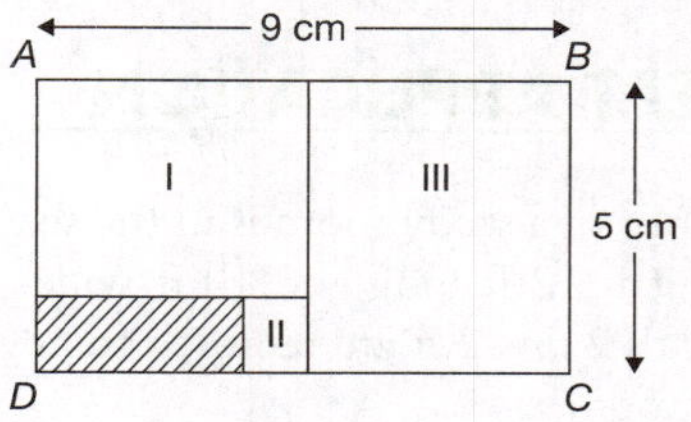

28. From a square sheet of side 8 cm, a piece of a paper width 2 cm is removed along the border. Then find the area of the removed piece of paper.

29. A hall in the shape of rectangle is 16 feet long and 12 feet wide. How many tiles with 2 feet × 1 feet are required to cover the floor of the hall?

30. Two persons *A* and *B* took a wire of equal length. '*A*' bent it in the form of a rectangle with perimeter 12 cm. *B* bent it in the form of a square, then find the area of the square formed.

31. If the area of a rectangle is 24 sq. cm and the length and breadth are integers in cm, then find the maximum possible perimeter of the rectangle.

32. The perimeter of a rectangle is 26 cm. The length and the breadth of the rectangle are integers. Find the number of possible pairs of length and breadth. Also find the maximum possible area of the rectangle.

33. Two sides of a triangle are 2016 cm and 2017 cm, then find the minimum possible perimeter of the triangle which is an integer in cm.

34. A Rubik's cube of edge 3 cm is formed with 27 identical cubes. Find the edge of each identical cube.

35.

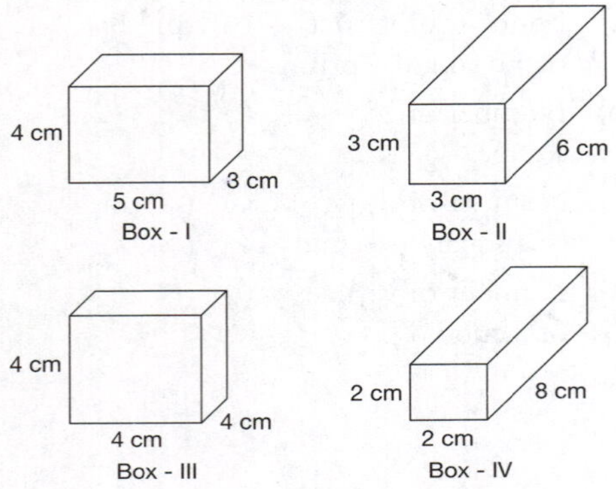

Tarun made 4 types of boxes as shown in the figure. Arrange them in the descending order of their volumes.

36. The dimensions of a room are 20 ft × 15 ft × 12 ft. Find the cost of painting the walls of the room at ₹20 per sq. ft.

37. Four identical square pieces of side 2 cm are removed from the four corners of a square sheet of side 6 cm. The remaining paper is folded to form a cuboidal box without lid. Find the outer surface area of the box.

38. The dimensions of a trench are 6 m × 3 m × 4.5 m. Find the cost incurred in digging it at ₹250 per cubic metre.

39. A cuboidal container which is 30-cm long, 20-cm wide and 15-cm high is full of water. The water is to be poured into cubical containers of each edge which is 10 cm. How many such containers are required?

CONCEPT APPLICATION

1. The floor of a study room is in the shape of a rectangle, it is 12 ft long and 10 ft wide. How many tiles with 2 ft × 2 ft are required to cover the floor of the room?
   (a) 120 (b) 60
   (c) 40 (d) 30

2. The perimeter of a rectangle is 30 cm. The length and breadth of the rectangle are integers in cm. Find the number of possible pairs of length and breadth in cm.
   (a) 1 (b) 6
   (c) 7 (d) 8

3. The inner dimensions of a rectangular box are 45 cm × 30 cm × 20 cm. How many match boxes of length 6 cm, breadth 3 cm and height 2 cm can be placed in the rectangular box?
   (a) 500 (b) 650
   (c) 750 (d) 1500

4. Four dice of edge each 1 cm are stacked so as to form a cuboid. Find the total surface area of the cuboid (in square centimetres).
   (a) 4 (b) 8
   (c) 9 (d) 18

5. Two sides of a triangle are 2018 cm and 2019 cm, then find the minimum possible perimeter of the triangle which is an integer in cm.
   (a) 4037 (b) 4038
   (c) 4039 (d) 8069

ASSESSMENT TEST

1. The length of each equal sides of an isosceles triangle is 13 cm and the perimeter of the triangle is 36 cm. Find the length of the unequal side of the triangle.
2. A rectangle of perimeter 276 cm is cut into five equal squares as shown below. Find the area of each squares.

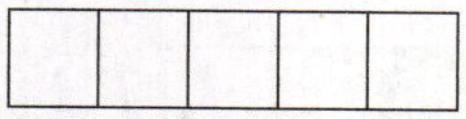

3. Two identical rectangles of dimensions 8 cm × 6 cm are overlapping as shown in the figure. The overlapped part is a square of side 2 cm. Find the area of the given figure.

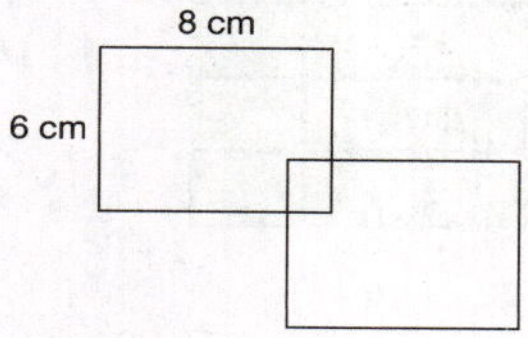

4. In the given figure, *ABCD* is a square of side 6 cm and *CDE* is an equilateral triangle. Find the perimeter of the figure.

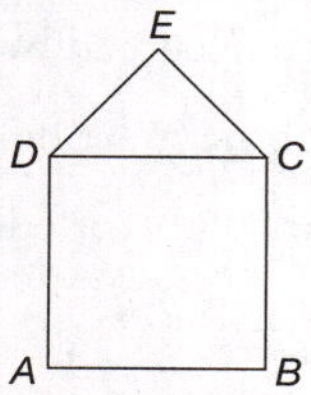

5. The edge of a cube is 3 cm. Find the total surface area and the volume of the cube.
6. Write the number of vertices, edges and faces of a pentagonal pyramid?
7. A container of dimensions 20 cm × 15 cm × 5 cm is full of water. If it is leaking at the rate of 25 millilitres per second, then how long will it take to empty the container?
8. Four identical cubes of edge 5 cm are placed side by side to form a cuboid of length 20 cm. Find the total surface area and volume of the cuboid.
9. There is a cubical box of edge 6 cm. Its top and bottom are covered with red colour canvas and the other four faces is covered with blue colour canvas. How much red colour and blue colour canvas cloth is required?
10. A car runs 20 times around a rectangular track which is 200-m long and 150-m wide. How much distance does the car cover?
11. Find the perimeter of an equilateral triangle with side 8 cm.
12. Border of a square-shaped frame which is 16-m long needs to be painted. If the cost of painting 1 m of border is ₹4, how much would it cost to paint the entire border of the frame?
13. A 10-m long hall has a floor area of 100 m^2. Find its perimeter.
14. The perimeter of a 40-cm wide rectangle is 160 cm. Find its area.
15. A cube-shaped oil tank which is 1.5-m long is full of oil. If 500 L of oil spills out from the tank, how much oil remains in it?

PRACTICE QUESTIONS

CROSSWORD

Across

4. A quadrilateral of equal angles

5. The region bounded by the sides of a plane figure

6. A rectangle with equal adjacent sides

8. Total length of the boundary of a plane figure

10. A solid with rectangular faces

11. These are twelve for a cube or cuboid

Down

1. Hundred centimetres

2. One-hundredth of a metre

4. Amount of space occupied by a solid

7. The edges of cuboid meet here

9. These are six for a cube or cuboid

10. A solid with square faces

TEST YOUR CONCEPTS

Very Short Answer Type Questions

1. square
2. 2016 cm
3. 6050 cm
4. 2018 cm
5. $\frac{p^2}{16}$
6. (a)
7. (d)
8. (d)
9. (b)
10. (c)
11. (a) → (q); (b) → (r); (c) → (p); (d) → (s)
12. 600 cm^2
13. 2 cm
14. 32 sq. cm
15. 5 cm
16. 300%
17. (b)
18. (d)
19. (b)
20. (b)
21. (b)
22. (a) → (r); (b) → (q); (c) → (p); (d) → (s)

Short Answer Type Questions

23. 3024 cm
24. 8
25. 48 cm
26. 32 sq. cm
27. 3 sq. cm
28. 48 sq. cm
29. 96
30. 9 cm^2
31. 50 cm
32. 6; 42 sq. cm
33. 4035 cm
34. 1 cm
35. III, I, II, IV
36. ₹16800
37. 20 sq. cm
38. ₹20250
39. 9

CONCEPT APPLICATION

1. (d)
2. (c)
3. (c)
4. (d)
5. (c)

ASSESSMENT TEST

1. 10 cm
2. 529 sq. cm
3. 92 sq. cm
4. 30 cm
5. 54 cm^2; 27 cm^3
6. 6, 10, 6
7. 60 seconds (or) 1 minute
8. 450 sq. cm, 500 cubic cm
9. 72 sq. cm, 144 sq. cm
10. 1400 m
11. 24 cm
12. ₹256
13. 40 m
14. 1600 cm^2
15. 2875 L

CROSSWORD

Across

3. Rectangle
5. Area
6. Square
8. Perimeter
10. Cuboid
11. Edges

Down

1. Metre
2. Centimetre
4. Volume
7. Vertices
9. Faces
10. Cube

ANSWER KEYS

TEST YOUR CONCEPTS

Very Short Answer Type Questions

2. The side of an equilateral triangle (a) = 672 cm

$\therefore$ Perimeter of the equilateral triangle

$= 3a = 3(672) = 2016$ cm

3. The two sides of an isosceles triangle are 2016 cm and 2017 cm.

Since the given triangle is an isosceles triangle. So, the third side is either 2016 cm or 2017 cm.

The maximum possible perimeter of the triangle = 2016 + 2017 + 2017 = 6050 cm

4. $\ell + b = 1009$ cm

Perimeter of the rectangle $= 2(\ell + b) = 2 \times 1009$

$= 2018$ cm

5. Let the side of a square be 'a'.

$4a = p$

$a = \frac{p}{4}$

Area of the square $= a^2 = \left(\frac{p}{4}\right)^2 = \frac{p^2}{16}$ sq. units.

6. Since the angles of a triangle are in the ratio 1 : 1 : 1, the triangle is an equilateral triangle.

$\therefore$ The ratio of the sides = 1 : 1 : 1

Hence, the correct option is (a).

7. Let the side of a square be a.

Since the side of a square is doubled.

$\Rightarrow$ New side $= 2a$

Area of the square $= (2a)^2 = 4a^2$.

$\therefore$ Area of the square becomes 4 times.

Hence, the correct option is (d).

8. Let the side of a square be a.

Area of square $a^2 = 25$

$a = \sqrt{25} = 5$ m

Hence, the correct option is (d).

9. Let the side of the square be a.

Since area and perimeter of a square are numerically equal,

$a^2 = 4a$

$\therefore a = 4$

Hence, the correct option is (b).

10. Given $\ell : b = 3 : 2$

Let $\ell = 3x$, $b = 2x$

Perimeter of the rectangle $= 2(3x + 2x) = 10x$

$\therefore 10x = 10$

$x = 1$

$\therefore$ Length $= 3x = 3 \times 1 = 3$ cm

Hence, the correct option is (c).

11. Let $AD = DE = a$

Area of a right isosceles triangle = 49/2 sq. cm

$\therefore$ Area of square $ADEF$, $a^2 = 49$

$\Rightarrow a = \sqrt{49}$

$\Rightarrow a = 7$ cm

$\Rightarrow AD = DE = EF = AF = BC = 7$ cm

$FB = CE = 2DE = 14$ cm

$AB = CD = 7 + 14 = 21$ cm

(a) Perimeter of the square $ADEF = 4(7) = 28 \rightarrow$ (q)

(b) Area of the square $ADEF = 49 \rightarrow$ (r)

(c) Perimeter of the rectangle $ABCD = 2(7 + 21) = 2(28) = 56 \rightarrow$ (p)

(d) Area of the rectangle ABCD = (7)(21)

$= 147\text{ cm}^2 \rightarrow$ (s)

Therefore, the correct match is:

(a) $\rightarrow$ (q); (b) $\rightarrow$ (r); (c) $\rightarrow$ (p); (d) $\rightarrow$ (s)

12. The edge of a cube $a = 10$ cm

Total surface area of the cube $= 6a^2 = 6(10)^2$

$= 600\text{ cm}^2$

13. The volume of the cuboidal box = 24 cu. cm

Base area of the cuboidal box = 12 sq. cm

Height of the cuboidal box $= \dfrac{\text{Volume}}{\text{Base area}}$

$= \dfrac{24}{12} = 2$ cm

14. The perimeter of the base of the cuboid = 16 cm

Height of the cuboid = 2 cm

Lateral surface area of the cuboid

= Perimeter of the base × Height

$= 16 \times 2 = 32$ sq. cm

15. Let the edge of the cube be a cm.

Number of edges of the cube = 12

Sum of the lengths of all the edges of the cube = 60 cm

$\therefore 12a = 60$

$a = \dfrac{60}{12} = 5$

∴ Edge of the cube = 5 cm

16. Let the edge of the cube be a units.

Lateral surface area of the cube = $4a^2$ sq. units.

If edge of the cube is increased by 100%, then new edge = $2a$.

The lateral surface area of the new cube

$= 4(2a)^2 = 16a^2$ sq. units

Increase in area $= 16a^2 - 4a^2 = 12a^2$

% increase in area $= \dfrac{12a^2 \times 100\%}{4a^2} = 300\%$

17. Let the edge of the cube be 'a'.

Lateral surface area : Total surface area

$= 4a^2 : 6a^2 = 2 : 3$

Hence, the correct option is (b).

18. Lateral surface area of the match box $= 2(\ell + b)h$

$= 2(6 + 2)(1.5) = 2(8)(1.5) = 24$ sq. cm

Hence, the correct option is (d).

19. Total surface area of the cuboid $= 2(\ell b + bh + h\ell)$

$= 2(2.5 \times 2 + 2 \times 1.4 + 1.4 \times 2.5)$

$= 2(5 + 2.8 + 3.5) = 2(11.3)$

$= 22.6$ sq. cm

Hence, the correct option is (b).

20. Number of faces of the cube = 6

∴ Minimum number of colours required = 2

Hence, the correct option is (b).

21. Let the edge of the cube be a.

Volume of the cube $= a^3$

If edge of the cube is doubled, then new edge = $2a$.

New volume $= (2a)^3 = 8a^3$

∴ Volume of the cube is 8 times that of the initial cube.

Hence, the correct option is (b).

Short Answer Type Questions

23. Given,

$a + b = 2015$

$b + c = 2016$

$c + a = 2017$

$2(a + b + c) = 6048$

$a + b + c = 3024$ cm

∴ Perimeter of the triangle = 3024 cm

24. Let side of the square field be a.

$a^2 = 49$

$a = \sqrt{49} = 7$ m

Distance covered by Sunil in one round = Perimeter of a square $= 4 \times 7 = 28$ cm

Number of rounds

$= \dfrac{\text{Total distance}}{\text{Distance covered in one round}} = \dfrac{224}{28} = 8$

25. The area of the square = 16 cm^2

$\therefore a^2 = 16$

$a = 4$ cm

Length of the rectangle = 4(5) = 20 cm

Breadth of the rectangle = 4 cm

Perimeter of the rectangle = 2(20 + 4)

= 2(24) = 48 cm

26. Side of the square sheet = 8 cm

Area of the square = 8^2 = 64 sq. cm

Side of the isosceles triangle, (a) = 4 cm

Area of the isosceles triangle = $\frac{1}{2}a^2$

$= \frac{1}{2} \times 4 \times 4$

= 8 sq. cm

Area of the remaining paper

= Area of the square − 4 × Area of the isosceles triangle

= 64 − 4(8) = 64 − 32

= 32 sq. cm

27. Length of the rectangle $ABCD$ = 9 cm

Breadth of the rectangle = 5 cm

Side of the square III = 5 cm

Side of the square I = 9 − 5 = 4 cm

Side of the square II = 5 − 4 = 1 cm

Length of the shaded region = 4 − 1 = 3 cm

Breadth of the shaded region = 1 cm

Area of the shaded region = 3 × 1 = 3 sq. cm

28. Side of an outer square sheet = 8 cm

Area of an outer square = 8^2 = 64 sq. cm

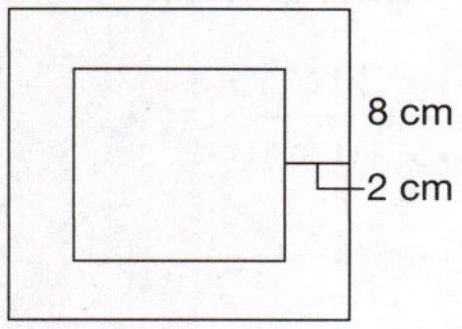

Width of a removed piece of paper = 2 cm

Side of the inner square = 8 − 2(2) = 8 − 4 = 4 cm

Area of the inner square = 4^2 = 16 sq. cm

Area of the removed paper = Area of the outer square − Area of the inner square

= 64 − 16 = 48 sq. cm

29. Length of the rectangular hall = 16 ft

Breadth of the rectangular hall = 12 ft

Length of the tile = 2 ft

Breadth of the tile = 1 ft

Number of tiles required to cover the floor of the hall = $\frac{\text{Area of the rectangle}}{\text{Area of the tile}} = \frac{16 \times 12}{2 \times 1} = 96$

30. Let the side of the square be a.

Since A and B took an equal length of the wire.

∴ Perimeter of the square = Perimeter of the rectangle

$4a = 12$

$a = 3$ cm

Area of the square = $a^2 = 3^2 = 9$ cm^2

31. Let ℓ and b be the length and breadth of the rectangle respectively (in cm).

Area of the rectangle = ℓb = 24 sq. cm

The possible values of (ℓ, b) = (24, 1), (12, 2), (8, 3), (6, 4)

∴ The maximum possible perimeter of the rectangle, $2(\ell + b) = 2(24 + 1)$ cm = 50 cm.

32. Let the length and breadth of a rectangle be 'l' and 'b' respectively.

Perimeter of a rectangle = $2(\ell + b)$

∴ $2(\ell + b) = 26$

$\ell + b = 13$

The possible pairs are (12, 1), (11, 2), (10, 3), (9, 4), (8, 5) and (7, 6).

Number of possible pairs = 6

The maximum possible area of a rectangle

= 6 × 7 = 42 sq. cm

33. The two sides of a triangle are 2016 cm and 2017 cm. We know that the sum of any two sides of a triangle is greater than the third side.

Let the third side of the triangle be a cm.

$2016 + 2017 > a$

$4033 > a$ (1)

The difference of any two sides of the triangle is less than the third side.

$$2017 - 2016 < a$$

$$1 < a \quad (2)$$

From (1) and (2), we get:

To get the minimum perimeter (in integral measure) of a triangle, a should be minimum, i.e., $a = 2$.

$\therefore$ The minimum possible perimeter of the triangle

$= 2016 + 2017 + 2$

$= 4035$ cm

34. Edge of the Rubik's cube = 3 cm

Volume of Rubik's cube = 3^3 cu. cm = 27 cu. cm

Let the edge of each identical cube be 'a' cm.

Number of identical cubes = 27

Volume of each identical cube = a^3

$$= \frac{\text{Volume of Rubik's cube}}{\text{Number of identical cubes}} = \frac{27}{27} = 1$$

$a^3 = 1^3 \Rightarrow a = 1$

$\therefore$ Edge of each identical cube = 1 cm

35. Volume of the box I = $\ell \times b \times h$

$= 5 \times 3 \times 4 = 60$ cu. cm

Volume of the box II = $6 \times 3 \times 3$

$= 54$ cu. cm

Volume of the box III = $4 \times 4 \times 4$

$= 64$ cu. cm

Volume of the box IV = $8 \times 2 \times 2$

$= 32$ cu. cm

Descending order of their volumes: III, I, II, IV.

36. Length of a room = 20 ft

Breadth of a room = 15 ft

Height of a room = 12 ft

Area of the 4 walls of the room = Lateral surface area of the room = $2(\ell + b)h$

$= 2(20 + 15)12$

$= 24(35) = 840$ sq. ft

The cost of painting the walls of the room at ₹20 per sq. ft

$= 840 \times$ ₹20 = ₹16800

37. Side of a square paper = 6 cm

Side of each square piece = 2 cm

Total surface area of a box = Area of the sheet – 4(Area of each piece)

$= 6 \times 6 - 4\ (2 \times 2)$

$= 36 - 16 = 20$ sq. cm

38. Length of the trench = 6 m

Breadth of the trench = 3 m

Depth of the trench = 4.5 cm

The volume of the trench = $6 \times 3 \times 4.5 = 81$ cu. m

The cost incurred in digging it at ₹250 per cu m

$= 81 \times$ ₹250 = ₹20250

39. Length of the cuboidal container = 30 cm

Breadth of the cuboidal container = 20 cm

Height of the cuboidal container = 15 cm

Edge of the cubical container = 10 cm

The required number of cubical containers

$$= \frac{\text{Volume of the cuboidal container}}{\text{Volume of each cubical container}}$$

$$= \frac{30 \times 20 \times 15}{10 \times 10 \times 10} = 9$$

CONCEPT APPLICATION

1. Number of tiles required to cover the floor the room $= \dfrac{12 \times 10}{2 \times 2} = 30$

Hence, the correct option is (d).

2. Given, $2\ (l + b) = 30$ cm

$(l + b) = 15$ cm

The possible pairs are (14, 1), (13, 2), (12, 3), (11, 4), (10, 5), (9, 6), (8, 7).

Hence, the correct option is (c).

3. Number of match boxes that can be placed in the rectangular box

$$= \frac{45 \times 30 \times 20}{6 \times 3 \times 2}$$

$= 750$

Hence, the correct option is (c).

4. The dimensions of a cuboid are 4 cm × 1 cm × 1 cm.

The total surface area of a cuboid

$= 2\,(lb + bh + hl)$ sq. cm

The total surface area of a cuboid formed

$= 2\,(4 \times 1 + 1 \times 1 + 1 \times 4)$

$= 2 \times 9 = 18$ sq. cm

Hence, the correct option is (d).

5. The given sides are 2018 cm and 2019 cm.

The sum of the sides is 4037 cm and the difference between the sides is 1 cm.

The length of the third side must lie between 1 cm and 4037 cm.

The smallest integer after 1 is 2, therefore the length of the third side is 2 cm.

The minimum possible perimeter of the triangle

$= 2 + 2018 + 2019 = 4039$ cm.

Hence, the correct option is (c).

ASSESSMENT TEST

1. Let the unequal side of an isosceles triangle be a cm.

Equal sides of an isosceles triangle = 13 cm

Perimeter of an isosceles triangle $= a + 13 + 13 = 36$

$\Rightarrow a = 36 - 26$

$\Rightarrow a = 10$ cm

2.

Let the side of the square be a cm.

Length of the rectangle $= 5a$ cm

Breadth of the rectangle $= a$ cm

Perimeter of the rectangle $= 2(5a + a) = 12a$.

$\therefore\ 12a = 276$

$$a = \frac{276}{12} = 23 \text{ cm}$$

The area of the square $= a^2 = 23^2 = 529$ sq. cm

3. Area of the given figure

$= 2$(Area of the rectangle) − Area of the square

$= 2(8 \times 6) - 2^2 = 96 - 4$

$= 92$ sq. cm

4. Side of the square $ABCD = 6$ cm

Side of the equilateral triangle $CDE = 6$ cm

Perimeter of the given figure

$= AB + BC + CE + DE + AD$

$= 6 + 6 + 6 + 6 + 6 = 30$ cm

5. Given, the edge of the cube, $a = 3$ cm

Total surface area $= 6\,a^2 = 6(3)^2 = 54$ cm^2

Volume $= a^3 = (3)^3 = 27$ cm^3

6. Given $n = 5$. The number of vertices $= 5 + 1 = 6$

The number of edges $= 2 \times 5 = 10$

The number of faces $= 5 + 1 = 6$

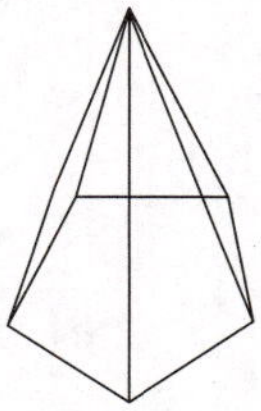

7. Length of the container = 20 cm

Breadth of the container = 15 cm

Height of the container = 5 cm

Volume of the container = 20 × 15 × 5

= 1500 cu. cm

= 1500 millilitres (Q1 cu. cm = 1 millilitre)

Time taken to empty the container $= \frac{1500}{25}$

= 60 seconds (or) 1 minute

8. Edge of each cube = 5 cm

Since four identical cubes are placed side by side to form a cuboid.

Length of the cuboid = 20 cm

Breadth of the cuboid = 5 cm

Height of the cuboid = 5 cm

Total surface area of the cuboid

= 2(20 × 5 + 5 × 5 + 5 × 20)

= 2(100 + 25 + 100) = 2(225) = 450 sq. cm

Volume of the cuboid = 20 × 5 × 5 = 500 cu cm

9. Edge of the cubical thermocol box (a) = 6 cm

The area of red colour canvas required

$= 2a^2 = 2(6)^2$

= 2 × 36 = 72 sq. cm

The area of blue colour canvas cloth required

$= 4a^2 = 4(6)^2$

= 4(36) = 144 sq. cm

10. Perimeter of the rectangle = 2(length and breadth)

2(200 + 150) = 2(350) = 700

Since the car revolves around it 20 times, distance covered by it = 2 × 700

= 1400 m

11. Perimeter = 8 + 8 + 8

= 24 cm

12. Perimeter of the frame = 4 × 16 = 64 m

Painting cost for 1 m = ₹4

Painting cost for 64 m = ₹4 × 64 = ₹256

13. Area of hall = $l \times b$

$100 = 10 \times b$

$b = 100/10$

$b = 10$ m

Perimeter = 2(10 + 10)

= 40 m

14. Perimeter = $2(l + b)$

$160 = 2(l + 40)$

$l = 40$ cm

Area = $l \times b$

Area = 1600 cm^2

15. Length of the tank = 150 cm

Volume of the tank = 150 × 150 × 150

= 3,375,000 cc = 3375 L

Water remaining in the tank = 3375 – 500

= 2875 L

Chapter

10 Statistics

REMEMBER

Before beginning this chapter, you should be able to:

- Understand the data in a tabular form
- Understand pictures

KEY IDEAS

After completing this chapter, you should be able to:

- Present data in charts, graphs, etc.
- Understand statistical graphs: Bar graphs and pie graphs

INTRODUCTION

The word '**statistics**' is derived from the Latin word '*status*' or the Italian word '*stata*' or the Greek word '*Statistik*' which means **political state**. Political states had to collect information about their citizens to facilitate governance and to plan for development. Then in due course of time, statistics evolved as a branch of Mathematics which deals with the collection, classification and analysis of numerical data.

In this chapter, we shall learn about statistical graphs and their measures of central tendency.

DATA

The word data means information which is contained in the form of numerical figures or a set of given facts.

Example: The percentage of marks scored by 10 pupils of a class in a test is given as

72, 84, 82, 96, 94, 98, 99, 67, 92 and 93

The set of these figures is the data related to the marks scored by 10 pupils in a class test.

Info Box!

Tally marks is a fast method recording information about numbers in groups of five. Each of the first four numbers are presented by one vertical line and a diagonal line across them represents the fifth number.

NOTE

1. The data obtained from direct observation is called raw data. The marks obtained by 10 students in a monthly test is an example of raw data or ungrouped data.
2. The difference between the highest and the lowest values of the data is called 'range'. *Example:* The range of the data of the first 25 natural numbers is 25 − 1 = 24.

TABLE 10.1 Tally chart

<table>
<tr><th>Number</th><th>Tallies</th></tr>
<tr><td>One</td><td>|</td></tr>
<tr><td>Two</td><td>| |</td></tr>
<tr><td>Three</td><td>| | |</td></tr>
<tr><td>Four</td><td>| | | |</td></tr>
</table>

Some Basic Definitions

Before getting into the details of tabular representation of data, let us review some basic definitions.

1. **Observation:** Each numerical figure in a data is called an observation.
2. **Frequency:** The number of times a particular observation occurs is called its frequency.

Tabulation or Presentation of Data

A systematic arrangement of data in a tabular form is called tabulation or presentation of the data. This grouping results in a table called the frequency table which indicates the number of scores within each group. Many conclusions about the characteristics of the data, the behaviour of variables, etc., can be drawn from this table.

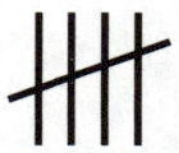

FIGURE 10.1 Tally number 5

The quantitative data that is to be analysed statistically can be represented as individual series or discrete series.

1. **Individual series:** Any raw data which is collected wholly forms an individual series.

   Examples: (a) The weight of 8 students: 35, 40, 36, 42, 32, 30, 50 and 46 (in kg)

   (b) The marks scored by 12 students in a test in Mathematics is as follows.

   45, 72, 76, 57, 49, 64, 75, 88, 92, 90, 60 and 55

2. **Discrete series:** A discrete series is formulated from raw data by taking the frequency of the observations into consideration.

Types of Data

When the data is collected directly from the source and is original, it is called primary data. For example, surveys, experimental observations, etc.

The secondary data means the information that has already been collected by any other person and is readily available for future study. For example, data collected from a book, internet, etc.

EXAMPLE 10.1

Given below is the data showing the number of children in a family, in a locality of 15 families. 1, 3, 5, 4, 3, 2, 1, 1, 3, 2, 2, 1, 4, 2 and 1. Draw the frequency table to represent the data.

SOLUTION

Arranging the data in ascending order we have: 1, 1, 1, 1, 1, 2, 2, 2, 2, 3, 3, 3, 4, 4, 5. To count, we can use tally marks. We record tally marks in bunches of five, the fifth one crossing the other diagonally, i.e., ~~IIII~~.

Thus, we may prepare a frequency table as shown below:

Number of Children	Tally Marks	Number of Families (Frequency)
1	~~IIII~~	5
2	IIII	4
3	III	3
4	II	2
5	I	1

Statistical Graphs

The information provided by a numerical frequency distribution is easily understood when represented by diagrams or graphs. The diagrams act as visual aids and they create a lasting impression in the viewer's mind. This enables the investigator to make quick conclusions about the distribution.

There are different types of graphs or diagrams to represent statistical data. Some of them are

1. Bar graph
2. Pie chart
3. Line graph

Bar Graph

The important features of bar graphs are given below.

(i) Bar graphs are used to represent unclassified frequency distributions.

(ii) The frequency of a value of a variable is represented by a bar (rectangle) whose length (i.e., height) is equal (or proportional) to the frequency.

(iii) The breadth of the bar is arbitrary and the breadth of all the bars is equal.

(iv) Uniform spaces should be left between any two consecutive bars.

(v) All the bars should rest on the same line called base line.

Info Box!

Histograms are similar to bar graphs, but a histogram groups numbers into ranges.

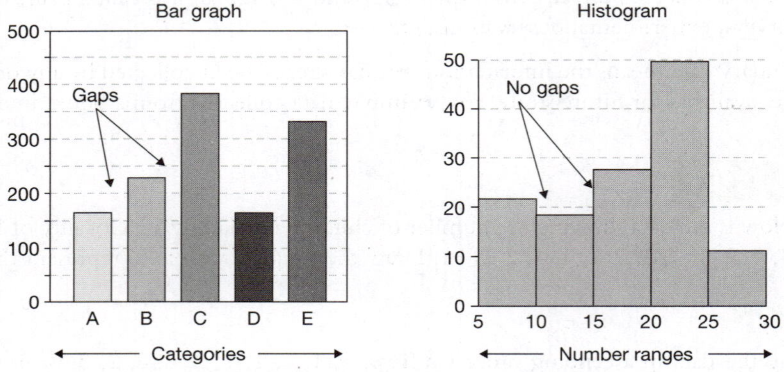

FIGURE 10.2 Bar graph vs Histogram

EXAMPLE 10.2

The number of different flavours of ice creams sold by a shop keeper during a particular day is given below.

Ice creams	Vanilla	Chocolate	Butterscotch	Strawberry
Number of ice creams	25	17	14	22

Draw a bar graph to represent the given data.

SOLUTION

To draw a bar graph, take ice cream flavours along the *X*-axis and the number of ice creams along the *Y*-axis.

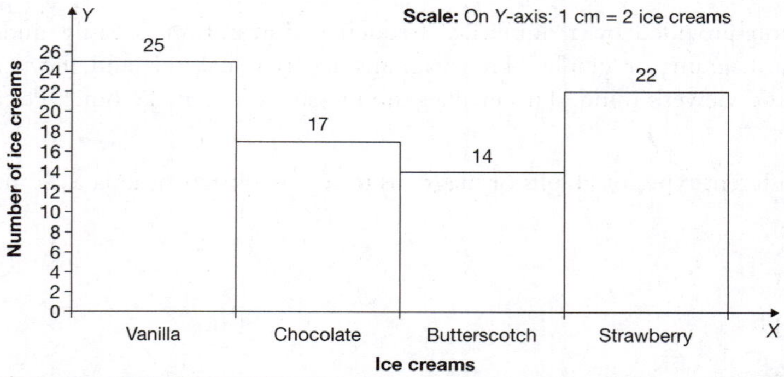

EXAMPLE 10.3

The graph given below shows the number of enrolments of nursery children over a period of 6 years.

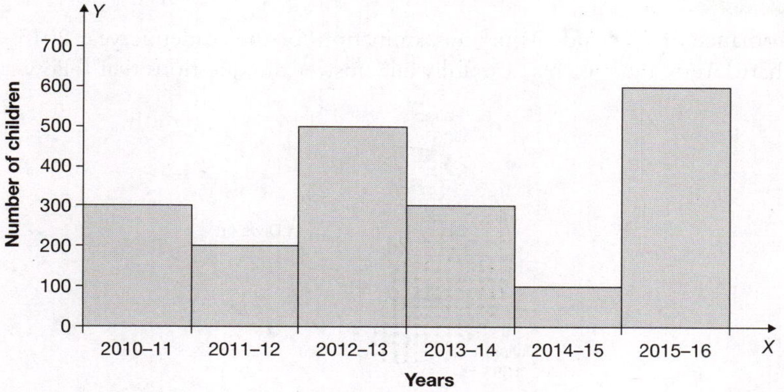

Study the graph carefully and answer the following questions.

(I) In which year was the enrolment of children highest?

(II) In which two years was the enrolment of children equal?

(III) What was the increase in the number of children between 2013-14 and 2015-16?

SOLUTION

(I) In the year 2015-16.

(II) In the years 2010-11 and 2013-14.

(III) The increase in the number of children between 2013-14 and 2015-16 = 600 − 300 = 300.

Pie Graph or Pie Chart

Statistical data can also be presented in the form of a pie graph. In the pie graph, a circle is divided into various sectors, in proportion to the various component parts of the total.

The adjoining figure shows the result of 7th class students.

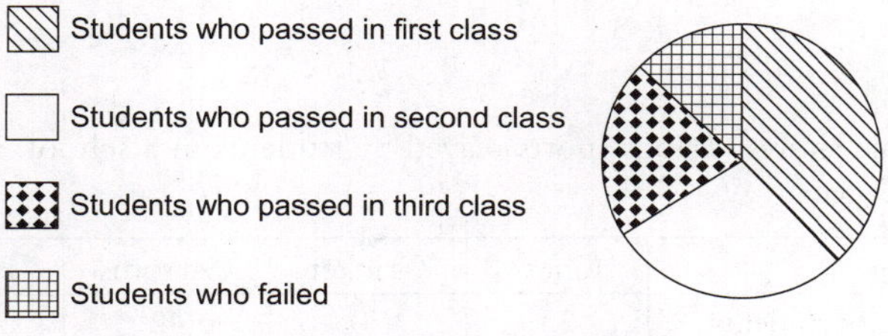

FIGURE 10.3 A pie chart

Steps for the Construction of a Pie Diagram

Step 1: Take the total value of all the items equal to 360°.

Step 2: Convert each component of the data into degrees using the following formula.

$$\text{Degree of any component} = \frac{\text{Component value}}{\text{Total value}} \times 360°$$

Info Box!

Pi could be written up to hundred decimal places as 3.1415926535897 93238462643383279502884197169399375105820974944592307816406286208998628034825342117 0679

Step 3: Draw a circle with an appropriate radius.
Step 4: Mark the angles at the centre of the circle and draw the sectors.

EXAMPLE 10.4

The performance of 720 students in an examination for the academic year 2015–16 is shown in a pie chart. Study the pie chart carefully and answer the questions that follow.

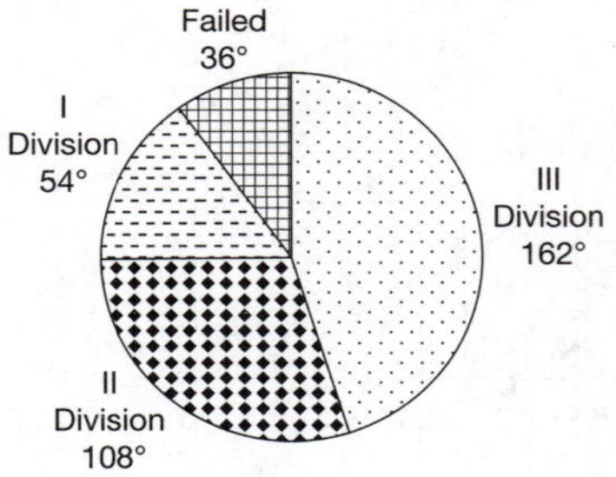

(I) Find the number of students who passed in the first division.
(II) Find the ratio of the number of students who passed to that of failed.
(III) Find the percentage of the number of students who failed in the examination.

SOLUTION

(I) The angle at the centre = 360°

Angle of sector representing the first division = 54°

Total number of students = 720

The number of students who passed in the first division $= \dfrac{54° \times 720}{360°} = 54 \times 2 = 108$

(II) Angle of sector representing the students who passed in the exam = 324°

Angle of sector representing failed students = 36°

The ratio of the number of students who passed to that of failed = 324 : 36 = 9 : 1

(III) The percentage of students who failed in the examination $= \dfrac{36 \times 100\%}{360} = 10\%$

EXAMPLE 10.5

The following table shows various sports played by students in a school. Draw a pie chart to represent the given data.

Sports	Chess	Cricket	Carroms	Football
Number of students	35	70	42	63

SOLUTION

Pie chart for the given data can be drawn using the following steps.

(1) Draw a circle with suitable radius.

(2) Mark the angles at the centre of the circle and draw the sectors.

Sports	Number of Students	Angle of Sector
Chess	35	$\frac{35}{210} \times 360° = 60°$
Cricket	70	$\frac{70}{210} \times 360° = 120°$
Carroms	42	$\frac{42}{210} \times 360° = 72°$
Football	63	$\frac{63}{210} \times 360° = 108°$

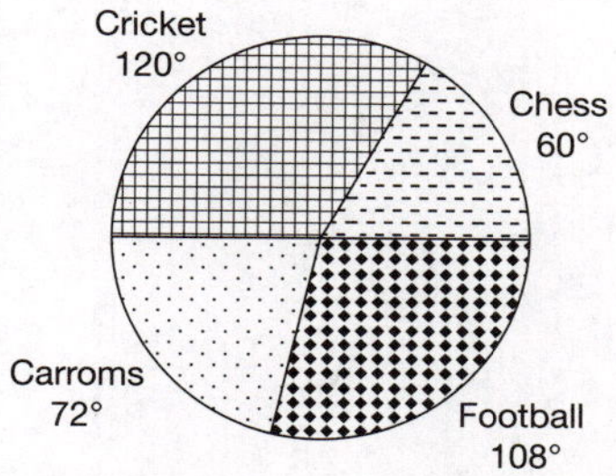

Line Graph

When a table related to two variables x and y is given, take every x value and the corresponding y value as different points. By plotting the obtained points on a graph paper and joining these points by means of lines, the graph obtained is called a line graph.

EXAMPLE 10.6

The number of runs given by a bowler in a one-day match in 10 overs is given below. Draw the line graph for the given data.

Overs	1	2	3	4	5	6	7	8	9	10
Number of runs	2	8	5	10	4	7	20	12	7	11

SOLUTION

To draw a line graph, mark overs along the X-axis and the number of runs along the Y-axis.

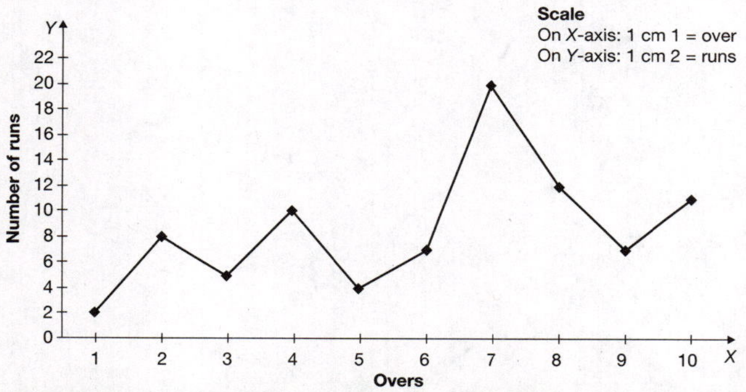

Some Important Terms Related to Data Collection and Record

1. **Average:** A number representing the central value of a collection of data is called the average. For example: 60 is the average mark in the Mathematics test in a class. It means that 60 lies somewhere between the maximum and minimum marks obtained by the students.
2. **Mean:** It is the central calculated value of a group of numbers. It is calculated by dividing sum of all the observations by number of observations. For example, if marks obtained by a class of four students in Mathematics test are: 70, 80, 90 and 100, then mean would be $(70 + 80 + 90 + 100)/4$
3. **Median:** It is the central value of a group of data that has been arranged in ascending or descending order.
4. **Mode:** It is that number in a group of data which occurs most frequently.

TEST YOUR CONCEPTS

Very Short Answer Type Questions

Direction for questions from 1 to 5: Fill in the blanks.

1. In a bar graph, if a bar of height 4 cm represents 28 units, then the height of a bar representing 350 units is _______.
2. In a pie chart, the sum of the angles of all its components is _______.
3. In a pie chart, the central angle of the component 120, when the total value is 360 is _______.
4. In a bar graph, a bar of length 3.2 cm represents 96 units, then the number of units represented by a bar graph of length 2.1 cm is _______.
5. In a pie chart, if the central angle of a component is 108° and its value is 24, then the total value of all the components of the data is _______.

Direction for questions from 6 to 10: Select the correct alternative from given choices.

The bar graph shows the number of students using different modes of transport to commute from residence to school.

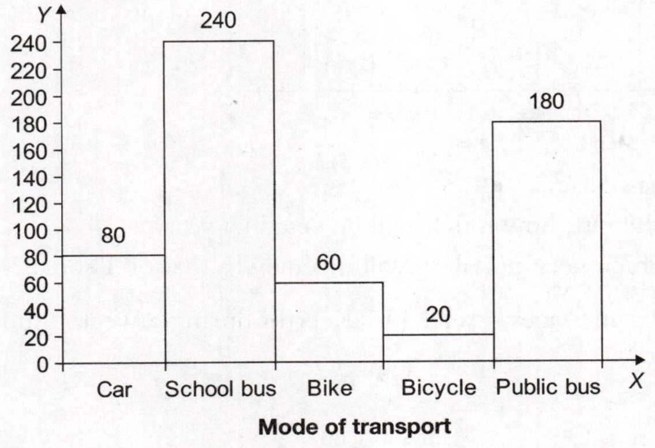

From the bar graph, answer the following questions:

6. What is the total number of pupils who travel by school bus and by bike?
   (a) 200 (b) 320
   (c) 300 (d) 100
7. How many more pupils travel by public bus than by car?
   (a) 100 (b) 120
   (c) 160 (d) 220
8. The number of pupils who travel by bike is 3 times than that of the number of pupils who travel by _______.
   (a) Bicycle (b) Public bus
   (c) Car (d) School bus
9. If 6 girls travel to school by bicycle, then how many boys travel by bicycle?
   (a) 20 (b) 16
   (c) 14 (d) 6
10. The ratio of the number of pupils who travel by school bus and who travel by public bus is _______.
    (a) 3 : 4 (b) 1 : 1
    (c) 4 : 3 (d) 1 : 2

Direction for question 11: Match Column A with Column B.

11. For a given data, Rithik drew a bar graph and Krithik drew a pie chart. By reading both diagrams, they understood that 3 cm is equivalent to 36°. Column A consists of the lengths of four bars out of six of the bar graph. Column B consists of sector angles which represent the components of the pie chart.

Column A		Column B
(a) 4 cm	( )	(p) 36°
(b) 6.5 cm	( )	(q) 102°
(c) 7 cm	( )	(r) 12°
(d) 8.5 cm	( )	(s) 84°
		(t) 78°
		(u) 48°

Short Answer Type Questions

12. A bar graph is drawn to the scale of 1 cm = k units. The length of the bar representing 260 units is 5.2 cm. Find the value of k.
13. In a pie chart, a component is represented as a sector with sector angle 108°, then find the percentage of the value of the component totally.

PRACTICE QUESTIONS

14. The given pie chart shows the amount of money spent by a school on various sports in the year 2015.

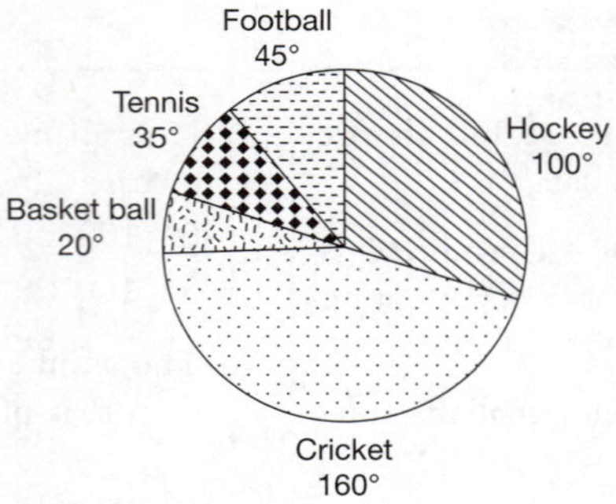

Study the pie chart carefully and answer the following questions.

(i) If the amount spent on football was ₹9000, then how much more money was spent on hockey than on football?

(ii) If the amount spent on football was ₹9000, then what was the total amount spent on all sports?

15. The bar graph given below shows the monthly salaries of four men. Study the graph carefully and answer the questions that follow.

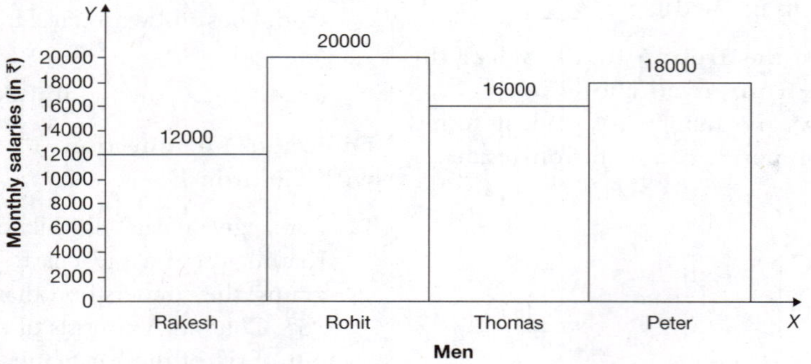

(i) What is the difference between Rohit's and Peter's salaries?

(ii) If Rakesh spends ₹10000 of his salary and saves the rest, how much will he save in a year?

(iii) If Thomas's salary is increased by ₹2000, then which persons' salary will be equal to that of Thomas?

16. The line graph given below shows the number of text messages received by Keerthi during a week. Study the graph carefully and answer the questions that follow.

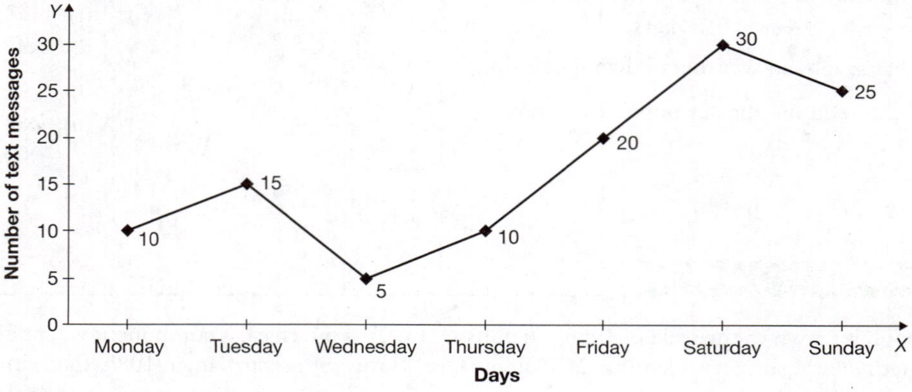

(i) On which day did Keerthi receive the lowest number of text messages?
(ii) On which day did Keerthi receive exactly 20 text messages?
(iii) Find the total number of text messages received by Keerthi in the week.

17. The following table shows the marks scored by a student in an annual examination in various subjects. Draw a bar graph to represent the given data.

Subject	Telugu	Hindi	English	Maths	Science	Social Studies
Marks	80	74	82	94	90	88

18. The following table shows the household expenditure of a family on different items. Draw a pie chart to represent the given data.

Item	Rent	Food	Clothing	Education	Others
Expenditure	25%	30%	10%	15%	20%

19. The following table shows the number of toys sold by a mart during a week. Draw a line graph to represent the given data.

Week	Mon	Tue	Wed	Thurs	Fri	Sat	Sun
Number of Toys	21	10	17	24	10	16	20

20. The line graph shows the attendance of 35 students over a week.

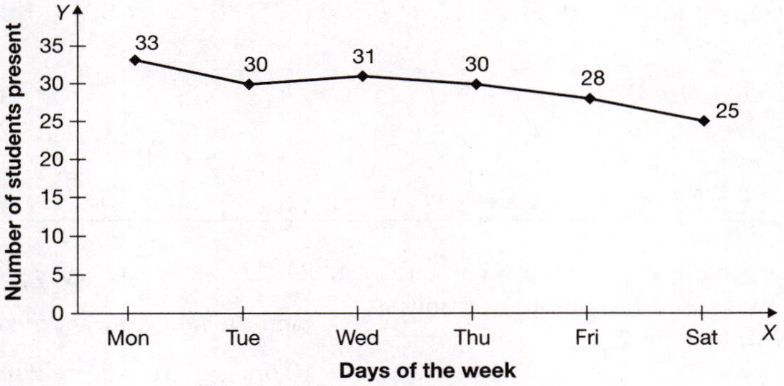

(i) On which day of the week was more number of students present?
(ii) If 18 boys were present on Thursday, then how many girls were present on the same day?

CONCEPT APPLICATION

1. The following table shows various sports played by students in a school.

Sport	Football	Volleyball	Badminton	Chess
Number of students	68	34	56	42

If we represent these values in the form of a bar graph, then the height of the bar corresponding to football is 13.6 cm. Find the difference between the heights of the bars corresponding to volley ball and badminton.

(a) 4.4 cm (b) 6.8 cm (c) 8.8 cm (d) 7.7 cm

2. The following table shows participation in various recreational activities by students of a class during the summer holidays.

Recreational activity	Swimming	Painting	Cycling	Dancing
Number of students	27	9	15	21

If we represent these values in the form of a pie chart, then find the central angle of the sector representing dancing.

(a) 114° (b) 90° (c) 105° (d) 98°

3. The following table shows the number of marks secured by the students of a class in a 50 marks exam.

Score	Number of students
Less than or equal to 10 marks	2
More than 10 marks and less than or equal to 20 marks	5
More than 20 marks and less than or equal to 30 marks	9
More than 30 marks and less than or equal to 40 marks	14
More than 40 marks and less than or equal to 50 marks	10

How many students secured less than or equal to 30 marks in that exam?

(a) 9 (b) 14 (c) 23 (d) 16

4. The ages of 10 teachers in a school are as follows:

22, 33, 45, 52, 36, 27, 28, 57, 39 and 25 years.

Find the difference between the ages of the eldest and the youngest teacher.

(a) 33 years (b) 35 years (c) 57 years (d) 22 years

5. Among the following numbers, 11, 18, 17, 25, 16, 15, 11, 18, 19, 22, 7, 8, 16, 15, 18, 19, which number has the highest frequency?

(a) 11 (b) 18 (c) 15 (d) 19

ASSESSMENT TEST

1. In a bar graph, the length of a bar is 5.5 cm and it represents 450 units. Find the number of units represented by a bar of length 2.2 cm.
2. In a pie chart, if the central angle of a component is 72° and its value is 48, then find the central angle of a component of value 108.
3. The following table shows the number of students in different classes of a high school. Draw a bar graph to represent the given data.

Classes	VI	VII	VIII	IX	X
Number of students	37	42	35	50	48

4. The following table shows the percentage of people having different blood groups. Draw a pie chart to represent the given data.

Blood group	A	B	AB	O
Percentage of people	20	45	20	15

5. The marks obtained by 7 students in Science test are given below:

24, 22, 30, 28, 32, 26, 34

Find the range, mean. median and mode.

6. 10 oranges are collected from a tree with following weights (in g).

22, 15, 20, 18, 16, 28, 20

Find the mode of the data given above.

7. Find median of the temperature in °C) recorded in Manali over a week as given below:

3, 4, 5, 3, 7, 8, 4

8. The mean of 5 observations is 16. Find the sum of these observations.
9. In class test, Priya obtained following scores in five subjects:

80, 90, 85, 70, 100

Find the range and minimum marks obtained.

10. Calculate data of 6 observations with mean as 10.

PRACTICE QUESTIONS

CROSSWORD

Across

2. Information in numerical form
5. 360° times the ratio of component value and the sum of values of all components
6. Circle is divided like these to represent a data
8. Angle of all sectors together
10. In bar graph the value of the data is proportional to this
11. Circular graph
12. In this graph, data is converted into rectangles

Down

1. Data can be represented in pictures.
3. In pie chart, the value of component is proportional to this
4. These are the parts of a kind of a graph
7. Data represented as a line
9. In bar graph all bars are equal in this

TEST YOUR CONCEPTS

Very Short Answer Type Questions

1. 50 cm
2. 360°
3. 120°
4. 63
5. 80
6. (c)
7. (a)
8. (a)
9. (c)
10. (c)
11. (a) → (u); (b) → (t); (c) → (s); (d) → (q)

Short Answer Type Questions

12. 50
13. 30%
14. (i) ₹11000 (ii) ₹72000
15. (i) ₹2000 (ii) ₹24000 (iii) Peter
16. (i) Wednesday (ii) Friday (iii) 115
20. (i) Monday (ii) 12

CONCEPT APPLICATION

1. (a)
2. (c)
3. (d)
4. (b)
5. (b)

ASSESSMENT TEST

1. 180
2. 162°

CROSSWORD

Across

2. Data
5. Sector angle
6. Sectors
8. Three sixty
10. Height
11. Pie chart
12. Bar graph

Down

1. Pictograph
3. Angle
4. Bars
7. Line graph
9. Width

TEST YOUR CONCEPTS

Very Short Answer Type Questions

1. The height of a bar representing 28 units is 4 cm.

The height of the bar representing 350 units

$= \frac{350 \times 4}{28} = 50$ cm

3. The sum of the angles of all components = 360°

Total value = 360

The central angle of the component 120

$= \frac{120 \times 360°}{360} = 120°$

4. The length of a bar representing 96 units is 3.2 cm.

The number of units represented by a bar graph of length 2.1 cm $= \frac{2.1 \times 96}{3.2} = 63$ units

5. The central angle of the component 24 = 108°

The sum of the angles of all components = 360°

The total value of all the components

$= \frac{24 \times 360°}{108°} = 80$

6. The number of pupils who travel by school bus and by bike = 240 + 60 = 300.

Hence, the correct option is (c).

7. The number of pupils who travel by public bus = 180

The number of pupils who travel by car = 80

∴ The required difference = 180 – 80 = 100

Hence, the correct option is (a).

8. The number of pupils who travel by bike = 60

The number of pupils who travel by bicycle = 20

The number of pupils who travel by bike is 3 times that of the number of pupils who travel by bicycle.

Hence, the correct option is (a).

9. The number of girls travelling to school by bicycle = 6.

The number of boys who travel to school by bicycle = 20 – 6 = 14

Hence, the correct option is (c).

10. The number of pupils who travel by school bus = 240

The number of pupils who travel by public bus = 180

The ratio of pupils who travel by school bus and who travel by public bus = 240 : 180 = 4 : 3

Hence, the correct option is (c).

11. Given, the lengths of the bar 3 cm equivalent to sector angle of 36°.

(a) The sector angle of a circle, if the length of the bar 4 cm $= \frac{4 \times 36°}{3} = 48° \rightarrow$ (u)

(b) The sector angle of a circle, if the length of the bar 6.5 cm $= \frac{6.5 \times 36°}{3} = 78° \rightarrow$ (t)

(c) The sector angle of a circle, if the length of the bar 7 cm $= \frac{7 \times 36°}{3} = 84° \rightarrow$ (s)

(d) The sector angle of a circle, if the length of the bar 8.5 cm $= \frac{8.5 \times 36°}{3} = 102° \rightarrow$ (q)

Therefore, the correct match is as follows:

(a) → (u); (b) → (t); (c) → (s); (d) → (q)

Short Answer Type Questions

12. The length of the bar representing 260 units is 5.2 cm.

The number of units represented by a bar of length 1 cm $= \frac{260}{5.2} = 50$ units

$\therefore k = 50$

13. The central angle of the component = 108°

The sum of the angles of all components = 360°

The percentage of the component value

$= \frac{108° \times 100\%}{360°} = 30\%$

14. (a) The amount spent on football = ₹9000

The central angle of the component football = 45°

The central angle of the component hockey = 100°

Amount spent on hockey = $\frac{100° \times 9000}{45°}$

= ₹20000

∴ The required difference ₹20000 – ₹9000 = ₹11000

(b) The amount spent on football = ₹9000

Central angle of the component football = 45°

Total amount spent on all sports = $\frac{360° \times 9000}{45°}$

= ₹72000

15. (a) Rohit's salary = ₹20000

Peter's salary = ₹18000

The difference between Rohit's and Peter's salary

= ₹20000 – ₹18000 = ₹2000

(b) Rakesh's monthly salary = ₹12000

Month's expenditure = ₹10000

Monthly saving = ₹12000 – ₹10000 = ₹2000

Savings of Rakesh in a year = 12 × 2000 = ₹24000

(c) Thomas's initial salary = ₹16000

After increasing ₹2000, the salary of Thomas

= 16000 + 2000 = ₹18000

Peter's salary = ₹18000

∴ Thomas's salary will be equal to the salary of Peter.

16. (i) Wednesday

(ii) Friday

(iii) The total number of text messages received by Keerthi

= 10 + 15 + 5 + 10 + 20 + 30 + 25 = 115

17. To draw bar graph, take subjects along the X-axis and marks along the Y-axis.

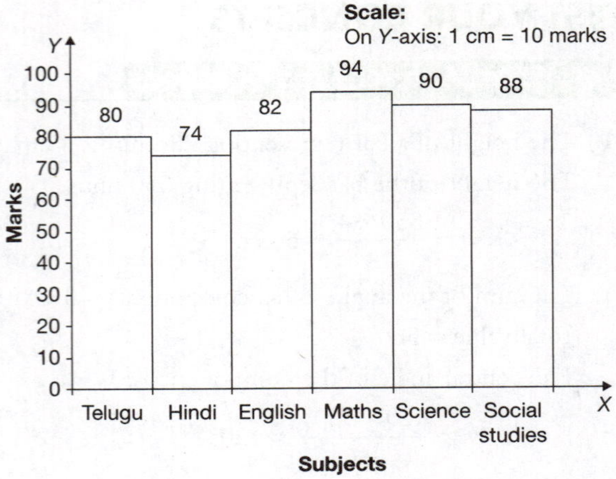

18. Steps:

(1) Draw a circle with suitable radius.

(2) Mark the angles at the centre of the circle and draw the sectors.

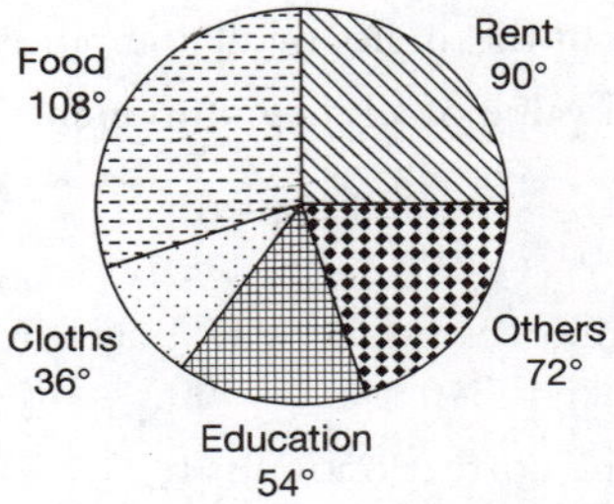

Item	Expenditure	Angle of Sector
Rent	25%	$\frac{25}{100} \times 360° = 90°$
Food	30%	$\frac{30}{100} \times 360° = 108°$
Clothing	10%	$\frac{10}{100} \times 360° = 36°$
Education	15%	$\frac{15}{100} \times 360° = 54°$
Others	20%	$\frac{20}{100} \times 360° = 72°$

19. To draw line graph, take days of a week on X-axis and the number of toys sold on Y-axis.

HINTS AND EXPLANATION

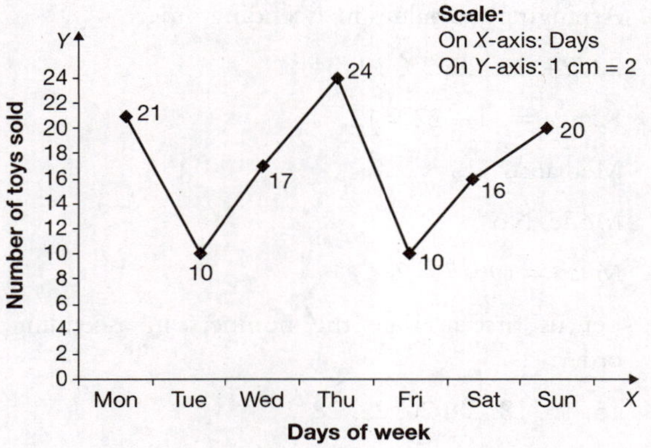

20. (i) Monday

(ii) The number of students present on Thursday = 30

The number of boys present on Thursday = 18

∴ The number of girls present on Thursday = 30 – 18 = 12.

CONCEPT APPLICATION

1. Given, the height of the bar corresponding to football is 13.6 cm.

Then, the height of the bar corresponding to volleyball $= \frac{34}{68} \times 13.6 = 6.8$ cm

The height of the bar corresponding to badminton $= \frac{56}{68} \times 13.6 = 11.2$ cm

Therefore, the required difference = 11.2 − 6.8 = 4.4 cm

Hence, the correct option is (a).

2. For the given data, the total number of students = 27 + 9 + 15 + 21 = 72

Therefore, the central angle of the dancing activity $= \frac{21}{72} \times 360° = 105°$

Hence, the correct option is (c).

3. From the table, we can say that 2 + 5 + 9, i.e., 16 students have secured less than or equal to 30 marks in that test.

Hence, the correct option is (d).

4. From the given data, the age of the eldest teacher is 57 years and the age of the youngest teacher is 22 years.

Hence, the required difference

= 57 − 22 = 35 years.

Hence, the correct option is (b).

5. Among the given numbers, 18 occurs maximum number of times, i.e., thrice. Thus, 18 is having the highest frequency.

Hence, the correct option is (b).

ASSESSMENT TEST

1. The length of a bar representing 450 units is 5.5 cm.

The number of units represented by a bar graph of length 2.2 cm $= \frac{2.2 \times 450}{5.5} = 180$ units

2. The central angle of a component of value 48 is 72°.

The central angle of a component value of 108°

$$= \frac{108° \times 72°}{48} = 162°$$

3. To draw a bar graph, take classes on the X – axis and the number of students on the Y – axis.

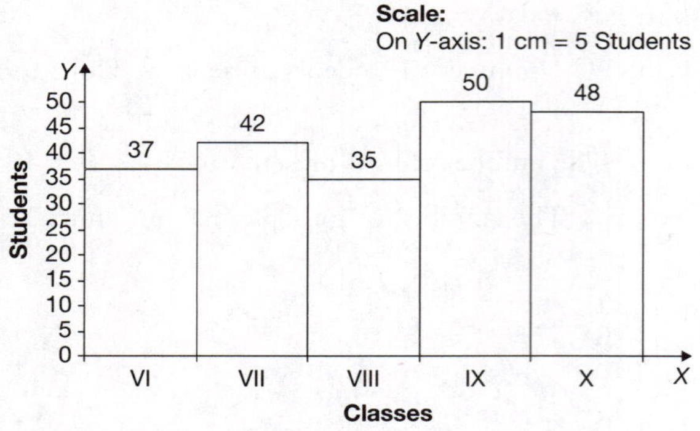

4. Steps:

(1) Draw a circle with suitable radius.

(2) Mark the angles at the centre of the circle and draw the sectors.

Blood Group	% of People	Angle of Sector
A	20	$\frac{20}{100} \times 360° = 72°$
B	45	$\frac{45}{100} \times 360° = 162°$
AB	20	$\frac{20}{100} \times 360° = 72°$
O	15	$\frac{15}{100} \times 360° = 54°$

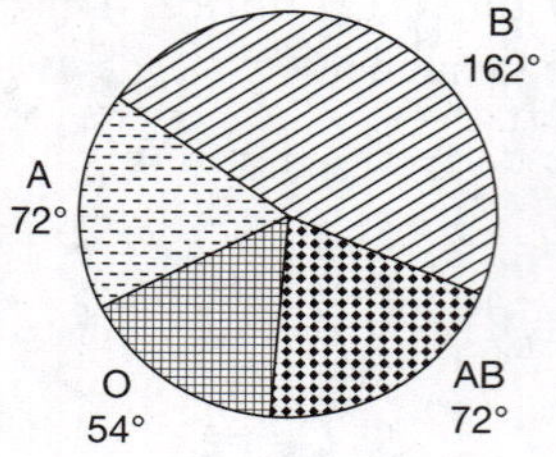

Crossword

5. Arranging the values in ascending order:

22, 24, 26, 28, 30, 32, 34

Range = 34 − 22 = 12

Median: 28

Mode: No

Mean = 196/7 = 28

6. Let us first arrange the numbers in ascending order:

15, 16, 18, 20, 20, 22, 28

As we can see that 20 g appears twice in the data, hence there is one mode viz. 20 g

7. Arranging the data in ascending order:

3, 3, 4, 4, 5, 7, 8

Since the fourth term (i.e., 4) is the middle term, median is 4.

8. Mean = 16

Number of observations = 5

Mean = Sum of observations/number of observations

Hence, sum = 16 × 5 = 80

9. Range = 100 − 70 = 30

Minimum marks obtained = 70

10. Mean = 10

Number of observations = 6

10 = Sum/6

Sum = 60

One of the ways to obtain observations is we can write numeral 10 six times with sum 60.

Hence, the observations are 10, 10, 10, 10, 10, 10

HINTS AND EXPLANATION

Chapter 11

Sets

REMEMBER

Before beginning this chapter, you should be able to:

- Name different types of collections
- Recall different types of numbers and number systems

KEY IDEAS

After completing this chapter, you should be able to:

- Define sets, elements of a set, representation of sets, empty set, singleton set, disjoint sets and subset
- Understand operation on sets
- Understand Venn diagrams
- Learn some formulae on cardinality of sets

INTRODUCTION

In our daily life we, come across different collections of objects.

Example: A cluster of stars, a flock of sheep, a posse of policemen, etc. In Mathematics, we call such collections as 'sets'. The objects are referred to as the elements of the sets.

FIGURE 11.1 Cluster of stars, a flock of sheep and a school of fish

SET

A set is a well-defined collection of objects. Let us understand what we mean by a well-defined collection of objects.

We say that a collection of objects is well-defined, if there is some reason or rule by which we can say whether a given object of the universe belongs to or does not belong to the collection. To understand this better, let us look at some examples.

Examples:

1. Let us consider the collection of even natural numbers less than 10. In this example, we can definitely say what the collection represents. The collection comprises the sequence of even numbers such as 2, 4, 6, 8 and 10.
2. Let us consider the collection of intelligent girls in a class. In this example, we cannot say precisely which girls of the class belong to our collection. So, this collection is not well-defined.

Hence, the first collection is a set whereas the second collection is not a set. From the above example, the set of the first 5 even natural numbers can be represented as $A = \{2, 4, 6, 8, 10\}$

FIGURE 11.2 Universal set of planets

Info Box!

Universal set is a set that is collection of all objects/items of a group in consideration. All sets under this collection are subsets of the universal set. For example, all 8 planets are part of universal set of all planets in the universe.

Elements of a Set

The objects in a set are called its elements or members. We usually denote the sets by capital letters A, B, C or X, Y, Z, etc. If a is an element of a set A, then we say that a belongs to A and we write, $a \in A$. If a is not an element of A, then we say that a does not belong to A and we write, $a \notin A$.

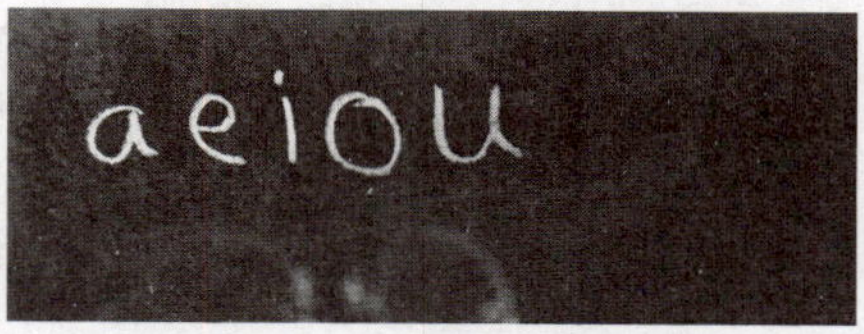

FIGURE 11.3 Elements of the set of vowels in English alphabet

Some sets of numbers and their notations

N = Set of all natural numbers = $\{1, 2, 3, 4, 5, ...\}$

W = Set of all whole numbers = $\{0, 1, 2, 3, 4, 5, ...\}$

Z = Set of all integers = $\{0, \pm1, \pm2, \pm3, ...\}$

Cardinal Number of a Set

The number of elements in a set A is called its cardinal number. It is denoted by $n(A)$.

Example: If $A = \{a, b, c, d\}$, $n(A) = 4$.

NOTE

A set which has finite number of elements is a **finite set** and a set which has infinite number of elements is an **infinite set**.

Examples:

1. Set of consonants in English alphabet is a finite set.
2. Set of all persons living on the earth is a finite set.
3. The set of all integers is an infinite set.

Representation of Sets

We represent sets by the following methods:

1. **Roster method:** In this method, a set is described by listing out all the elements in the set.

   Examples: (i) Let V be the set of all vowels in English alphabet. Then we represent V as, $V = \{a, e, i, o, u\}$.

   (ii) Let E be the set of all odd natural numbers less than 12. Then we represent the set E as, $E = \{1, 3, 5, 7, 9, 11\}$.

2. **Description method:** In this method, the well-defined description of the elements is enclosed in curly brackets.

   Example: $\{1, 2, 3, 4, 5\}$ = {The first five natural numbers}

3. **Set-builder method:** In this method, a set is described by using some property common to all its elements.

   Examples: (i) Let V be the set of all vowels in English alphabet. Then we represent the set V as, $V = \{x : x \text{ is a vowel in English alphabet}\}$

   (ii) Let P be the set of all odd numbers less than 100. Then we represent the set P as, $P = \{x : x \leq 100 \text{ and } x \text{ is an odd number}\}$

TABLE 11.1 Three methods of representation of a set of natural numbers between 5 and 10

Roster Method	Descriptive Method	Set-builder Method
N = {6,7,8,9}	{Natural numbers between 5 and 10}	N = {x : x is a natural number, $5 < x < 10$}

Some Simple Definitions of Sets

Following are definitions of different types of sets.

1. **Empty set or Null set:** A set with no elements in it is called an empty set (or) void set (or) null set. It is denoted by { } or ϕ (read as 'phi').

   Examples: (i) Set of all whole numbers less than 0.
   (ii) Set of all woman Chief Ministers of Andhra Pradesh.

2. **Singleton set:** A set consisting of only one element is called a singleton set.

   Examples: (i) The set of all even prime numbers is a singleton set as 2 is the only even prime number.
   (ii) The set of all the numbers which are neither prime nor composite is a singleton set as 1 is only neither prime nor composite.

3. **Disjoint sets:** Two sets A and B are said to be disjoint, if they have no elements in common.

   Examples: (i) Sets $A = \{0, 5, 6, 7, 12\}$ and $B = \{1, 2, 4, 8, 11\}$ are disjoint as they have no elements in common.
   (ii) Sets $A = \{1, 3, 4, 5\}$ and $B = \{3, 5, 8\}$ are not disjoint as they have some common elements such as 3 and 5.

EXAMPLE 11.1

Are the sets given below equal?

$A = \{x : x \text{ is an even prime}, x > 2\}$

$B = \{\ \}$

SOLUTION

There is no even prime greater than 2.

$\therefore A = \{\ \}$ and $B = \{\ \}$

Hence, A and B are equal sets.

EXAMPLE 11.2

Are the sets given below equal?

$C = \{x : x \in R, 2 < x < 5\}$

$B = \{x : x \in N, 2 < x < 5\}$

SOLUTION

C is an infinite set, since there are infinite real numbers between 2 and 5.

$D = \{3, 4\}$

$\therefore$ C and D are not equal sets.

Operation on Sets

Let us now understand how different types of operations can be performed on sets.

Union of sets

Let A and B be two sets. The union of A and B, denoted by $A \cup B$, is the set of all those elements which are either in A or in B or in both A and B, i.e., $A \cup B = \{x/x \in A \text{ or } x \in B\}$.

EXAMPLE 11.3

Given $A = \{1, 2, 3, 4, 5, 8\}$ and $B = \{2, 4, 6, 8, 9, 11\}$. Find $A \cup B$.

SOLUTION

$A \cup B = \{1, 2, 3, 4, 5, 8\} \cup \{2, 4, 6, 8, 9, 11\} = \{1, 2, 3, 4, 5, 6, 7, 8, 9, 11\}$.

Intersection of sets

Let A and B be two sets. The intersection of A and B, denoted by $A \cap B$, is the set of all those elements which are common to both A and B, i.e., $A \cap B = \{x/x \in A \text{ and } x \in B\}$.

EXAMPLE 11.4

Given $A = \{2, 3, 5, 9\}$ and $B = \{3, 4, 9, 12\}$. Find $A \cap B$.

SOLUTION

$A \cap B\ \{2, 3, 5, 9\} \cap \{3, 4, 9, 12\} = \{3, 9\}$

NOTE

If A and B are disjoint sets, then $A \cap B = \phi$.

Difference of sets

Let A and B be two sets. The difference $A - B$ is the set of all those elements which are in A but not in B, i.e., $A - B = \{x\text{: } x \in A \text{ and } x \notin B\}$.

EXAMPLE 11.5

Given $A = \{1, 2, 4, 5, 6, 8, 20\}$ and $B = \{2, 3, 4, 5, 9, 20\}$. Find $A - B$ and $B - A$.

SOLUTION

$A - B = \{1, 2, 4, 5, 6, 8, 20\} - \{2, 3, 4, 5, 9, 20\} = \{1, 6, 8\}$

$B - A = \{2, 3, 4, 5, 9, 20\} - \{1, 2, 4, 5, 6, 8, 20\} = \{3, 9\}$

NOTE

(a) $n(A \cup B) = n(A) + n(B) - n(A \cap B)$

(b) If A and B are disjoint, then $n(A \cup B) = n(A) + n(B)$

EXAMPLE 11.6

If $n(A) = 10$, $n(B) = 21$ and $n(A \cap B) = 5$, then find $n(A \cup B)$.

SOLUTION

$$n(A \cup B) = n(A) + (B) - (A \cap B)$$
$$= 10 + 21 - 5$$
$$= 26$$

Venn Diagrams

We also represent sets pictorially by means of diagrams called 'Venn' diagrams. In Venn diagrams, the universal set is usually represented by a rectangular region and its subsets by closed regions inside the rectangular region. The elements of the set are written in the closed regions.

Info Box!

Venn diagrams were introduced by John Venn in 1880, but he himself did not use the term Venn. The first person to use the term 'Venn diagram' was Clarence Lewis in 1918.

Examples:

1. Let $\mu = \{1, 2, 3, 4, 5, 6, 7, 8, 9\}$, $A = \{1, 2, 4, 6\}$ and $B = \{2, 3, 4, 5\}$.

   We represent these sets in the form of Venn diagram as follows:

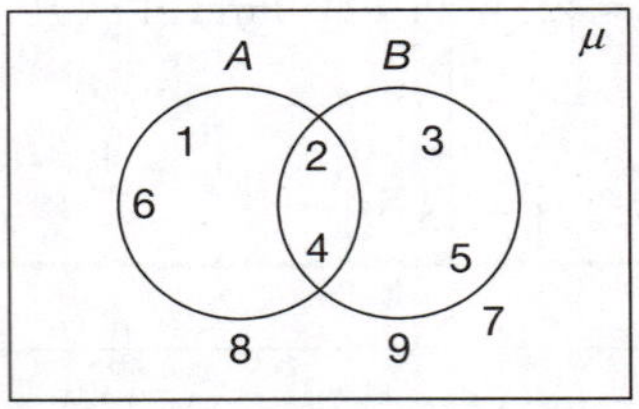

We can also represent the sets in Venn diagrams by shaded regions.

2. Venn diagram of $A \cup B$, where A and B are two overlapping sets, is

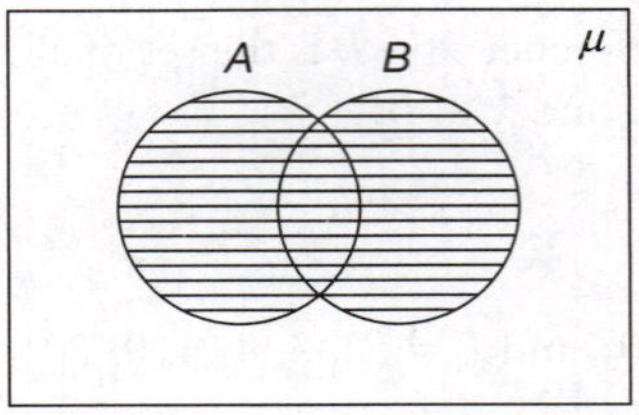

3. Let A and B be two overlapping sets. Then, the Venn diagram of $A \cap B$ is

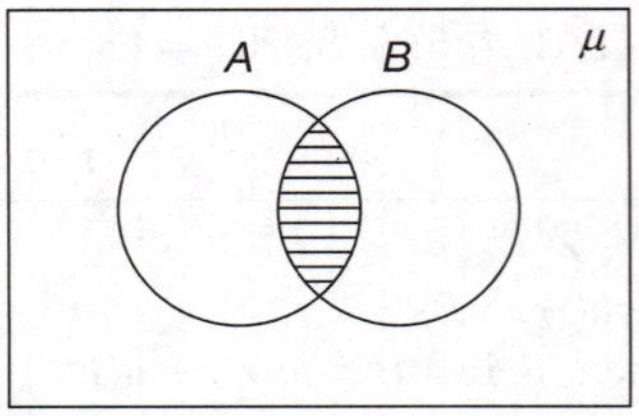

4. For a non-empty set A, the Venn diagram of A' is

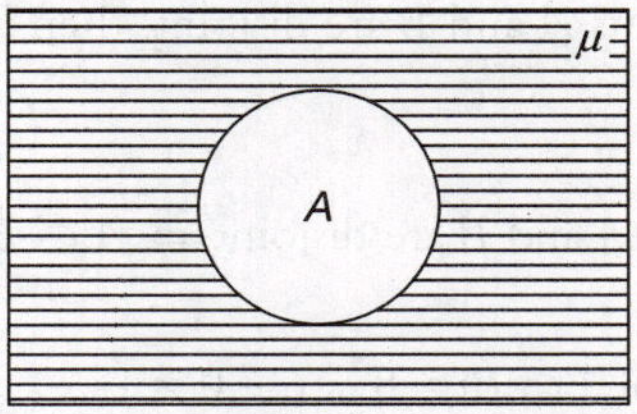

5. Let A and B be two overlapping sets. The Venn diagram of $A - B$ is

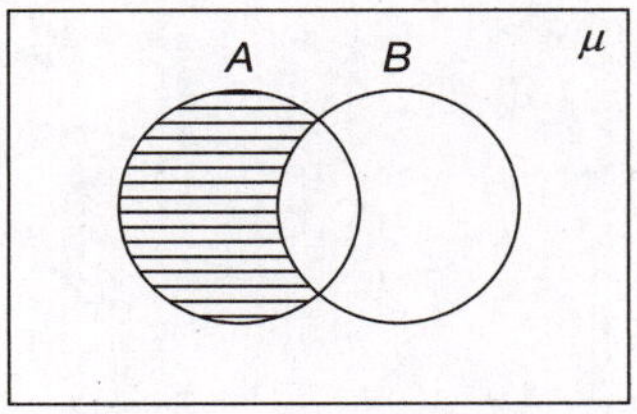

6. Let A and B be two sets such that $A \subset B$. We can represent this relation using Venn diagram as follows.

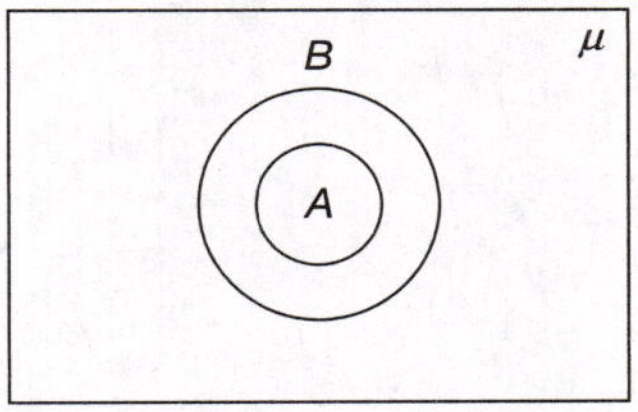

Some Formulae on the Cardinality of Sets

Set $A = \{1, 2, 3, 4, 5, 6, 7\}$ and $B = \{2, 4, 8, 16\}$.

Then, $A \cup B = \{1, 2, 3, 4, 5, 6, 7, 8, 16\}$ and $A \cap B = \{2, 4\}$.

In terms of the cardinal numbers, $n(A) = 7$, $n(B) = 4$, $n(A \cap B) = 2$ and $n(A \cup B) = 9$.

So, $n(A) + n(B) - n(A \cap B) = 7 + 4 - 2 = 9 = n(A \cup B)$.

We have the following formula:

For any two sets A and B, $n(A \cup B) = n(A) + n(B) - n(A \cap B)$.

EXAMPLE 11.7

If $n(A) = 4$, $n(B) = 6$ and $n(A \cup B) = 8$, then find $n(A \cap B)$.

SOLUTION

Given, $n(A) = 4$, $n(B) = 6$ and $n(A \cup B) = 8$

We know that, $n(A \cup B) = n(A) + n(B) - n(A \cap B)$. So, $8 = 4 + 6 - n(A \cap B)$

$\Rightarrow n(A \cap B) = 10 - 8 = 2$

EXAMPLE 11.8

If $n(A) = 8$, $n(B) = 6$ and the sets A and B are disjoint, then find $n(A \cup B)$.

SOLUTION

Given, $n(A) = 8$ and $n(B) = 6$. A and B are disjoint $\Rightarrow A \cap B = \phi$

$\Rightarrow n(A \cap B) = 0$

$\therefore\ n(A \cup B) = n(A) + n(B) - n(A \cap B) = 8 + 6 - 0 = 14$

TEST YOUR CONCEPTS

Very Short Answer Type Questions

Direction for questions from 1 to 5: Fill in the blanks.

1. If $A = \{\phi\}$, then $n(A) =$ ______.
2. The set builder form of $A = \{1, 4, 9, 16, 25\}$ is ______.
3. If A and B are two equivalent sets and $n(A) = 2016$, then $n(B) =$ ______.
4. If ϕ is an empty set, then $n(\phi) =$ ______.
5. The set of prime numbers which are having more than two factors is a/an ______ set (empty/singleton).

Direction for questions from 6 to 10: Select the correct alternative from the given choices.

6. Which of the following is a singleton set?
   (a) The set of all the months in a year having exactly 30 days.
   (b) The set of all the days in a week.
   (c) The set of all the natural satellites of the earth in the solar system.
   (d) The set of all the intersecting points of two parallel lines in a plane.
7. Let A be the set of all triangles in a plane having the sum of three interior angles is greater than 180°, then A is a/an ______set.
   (a) Empty (b) Singleton
   (c) Infinite (d) None of these
8. Which of the following is an infinite set?
   (a) $\{x: x \text{ is a prime}, x < 10\}$
   (b) $\{x: x \text{ is a vowel in the word MATHEMATICS}\}$
   (c) $\{x: x \text{ is a natural number}, 2015 < x < 2016\}$
   (d) $\{x: x \in Z, x \text{ is a non-negative integer}\}$
9. Which of the following is an empty set?
   (a) $\{x: x \in N, x \text{ is divisible by } 2\}$
   (b) $\{x: x \in N, x \text{ is the additive inverse of } 2016\}$
   (c) $\{x: x \text{ is a binary digit}\}$
   (d) $\{x: x \text{ is either prime or composite}\}$
10. Which of the following collections is not a set?
    (a) The colours in RAINBOW.
    (b) All good books in a school library.
    (c) The members of your family.
    (d) The principals of your school.

Direction for question 11: Match Column A with Column B.

11.

	Column A			Column B
(a)	$\{x: x$ is a two digit number, whose units digit is equal to tens digit.$\}$	( )	(p)	Empty set
(b)	The collection of natural numbers each of which is reciprocal of itself.	( )	(q)	Finite set
(c)	The collection of odd numbers which are multiples of 6.	( )	(r)	Infinite set
(d)	The set of straight lines passing through a point in a plane.	( )	(s)	Singleton set

Direction for questions from 12 to 16: Fill in the blanks.

12. If A and B are disjoint sets, then $n(A \cup B) =$ ______
13. If $A = \{x : x \text{ is prime}\}$ and $B = \{x : x \text{ is even}\}$, then $A \cap B =$ ______
14. If $A \cap B = \phi$, then A and B are called ______ sets.
15. If A and B are two non-empty sets, then the minimum number of elements in $A \cap B$ is ______
16. If all the elements of set A are present in set B, then $A \cup B =$ ______.

Direction for questions from 17 to 20: Select the correct alternative from given choices.

17. If $n(A) = 2016$ and $n(B) = 2017$, then the minimum number of elements in $A \cup B$ is ______.
    (a) 0 (b) 1 (c) 2016 (d) 2017
18. If A is the collection of natural numbers which are less than 2 and $B = \{x: x \in N, x \text{ is neither prime nor composite}\}$ then $A \cap B =$ ______.

(a) ϕ (b) $\{1\}$
(c) N (d) None of these

19. If $A = \{x: x \in N, x$ is an additive inverse of $2017\}$ and $B = \{x: x \in N, x$ is a multiplicative inverse of $2017\}$. Then $A \cup B =$ ______.

(a) ϕ (b) $\{-2017, \frac{1}{2017}\}$

(c) 1 (d) $\{2017, \frac{-1}{2017}\}$

20. If $A = \{x: x \in N, 2015 < x < 2017\}$ $B = \{x: x \in N, x + 1 = 2017\}$, then $A - B =$ ______.

(a) ϕ
(b) $\{2016\}$
(c) $\{2015, 2016, 2017\}$
(d) $\{1, 2, 3, . . . 2017\}$

Direction for question 21: Match Column A with Column B.

21.

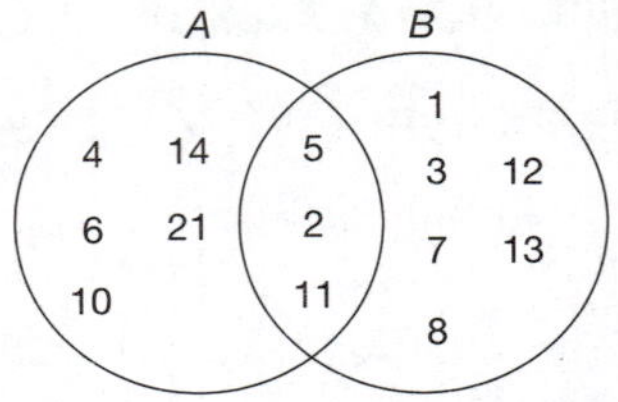

Column A		Column B
(a) $n(A - B)$	( )	(p) 14
(b) $n(A \cup B)$	( )	(q) 3
(c) $n(A \cap B)$	( )	(r) 5
(d) $n(B - A)$	( )	(s) 6

Short Answer Type Questions

22. Let $A = \{x: x$ is the nearest star to the earth$\}$. Find the set A.

23. (a) Describe each of the following sets in the description form.

(i) {A river}
(ii) {Sunday, Monday, Tuesday, Wednesday, Thursday, Friday, Saturday, Sunday}

(b) Describe the following in set builder form.

(i) $\{2, 4, 6, 8\}$
(ii) $\{3, 6, 9, 12, 15, 21.....\}$

24. Check whether the following sets are equivalent?

(i) $A = \{x: x$ is a letter in the word SOLUTION$\}$
$B = \{$P, R, O, B, L, E, M$\}$

(ii) $C = \{x: x$ is either prime or composite, $x < 10\}$
$D = \{1\}$

25. Check whether the following sets are equal?

(i) $A = \{$The set of the first five elements of the periodic table$\}$
$B = \{$H, He, Li, Be, B$\}$

(ii) $C = \{x: x$ is a prime number$\}$
$D = \{x: x$ is an odd number$\}$

26. Classify the following into empty sets or singleton sets.

(i) $A = \{x: x$ is a composite number which is having less than three factors$\}$

(ii) $B = \{x: x \in R, x$ is a multiplicative inverse of $2016\}$

(ii) $C = \{x: x \in N, x$ is neither prime number nor composite number$\}$

27. All equal sets are equivalent. Is the converse true? Support your answer with suitable examples.

28. Let $A = \{x$: x is a letter in the word INDIA$\}$ and $B = \{x: x$ is a vowel in the word EDUCATION$\}$
Verify: $n(A \cup B) = n(A) + n(B) - n(A \cap B)$

29. Let $A = \{x: x \in Z, 2 \le x \le 5\}$ and $B = \{x: x \in Z, -2 \le x < 4\}$. Find the following:

(i) $n(A \cup B)$ (ii) $n(A \cap B)$
(iii) $n(A - B)$ (iv) $n(B - A)$

30. Let $A = \{x: x$ is an even natural number, $x < 10\}$ and $B = \{x: x$ is a factor of $24\}$

(i) Draw Venn diagrams to represent these sets.
(ii) Find: (a) $A \cup B$ (b) $A \cap B$

31. If $n(A) = 20$ and $n(A \cap B) = 5$, then find the value of $n(A - B)$.

32. If $n(A) = x$, $n(B) = 2[n(A)]$, $n(A \cup B) = 2017$ and $n(A \cap B) = 1007$. Find the value of x.

33. If $F(n)$ is the set of all the factors of 'n' excluding 1 and $F(16) \cap F(24) = F(x)$, then find the value of x.

CONCEPT APPLICATION

1. A and B are any two sets, $n(A) = 17$ and $n(B) = 13$. What is the maximum possible value of $n(A \cup B) - n(A \cap B)$?
(a) 4 (b) 13
(c) 17 (d) 30

2. A and B are two equivalent sets, what is the maximum possible value of $n(A \cap B)$?
(a) $n(A)$ (b) $n(A \cup B)$
(c) $n(A) + n(B)$ (d) $n(A) - n(B)$

3. In a class of 25 students, 18 of them passed in Maths, 14 of them passed in Science and 3 of them failed in both the exams. How many students passed in both the exams?
(a) 3 (b) 4
(c) 10 (d) 11

4. A is a set of the factors of 28, B is a set of the factors of 17 and C is a set of the odd multiples of 7 less than 50. Which of the following are singleton sets?
(A) $A \cap B$ (B) $C \cap B$
(C) $A \cap C$
(a) Only (A) and (B)
(b) Only (B) and (C)
(c) Only (A) and (C)
(d) (A), (B) and (C)

5. A is a set of all the prime numbers less than 20, B is a set of all the even natural numbers less than 20 and C is a set of all the odd natural numbers. Which of the following is/are true statements?
(A) $A \cap B$ is a singleton set.
(B) B and C are disjoint sets.
(C) $A \cap C$ is an infinite set.
(a) Only (B) (b) Both (A) and (B)
(c) Both (B) and (C) (d) (A), (B) and (C)

ASSESSMENT TEST

1. Write the set builder form of {January, June, July}.
2. Write the Roster form of $\{x: x \in Z, -3 \le x \le 3\}$.
3. Let $A = \{x: x$ is a factor of 24 excluding 1 and itself, $x \in N\}$.
Write A is in Roster form. Find $n(A)$.
4. Let $A = \{x: x$ is a prime factor of 2016$\}$ and $B = \{x: x$ is a prime factor of 2025$\}$.
Find: (i) $A \cup B$ (ii) $A \cap B$
(iii) $A - B$ (iv) $B - A$
5. If $n(G - H) = 15$ and $n(G \cap H) = 10$, then find the value of $n(G)$.
6. Let $A = \{x^2: x^2 < 50, x \in N\}$ and $B = \{x: x$ is a 2-digit number in which the sum of the digits is 7, $x \in N\}$.
(i) Draw Venn diagram to represent these sets.
(ii) Find: (a) $A \cup B$ (b) $A \cap B$
(c) $A - B$ (d) $B - A$
7. Let $A = \{x: x$ is a multiple of 3, $5 < x < 19\}$ and $B = \{x: x$ is a factor of 18$\}$.
Find: (i) $A - B$
(ii) $B - A$
(iii) What do you notice?
8. Represent the following set in Descriptive and Set-builder forms.
{11, 22, 33, 44, 55, 66, 77, 88, 99}
9. Make a set of all the consonants in the following words: MATHEMATICS, SCIENCE, ENGLISH
10. Which of the following are sets?
(i) A collection of odd numbers
(ii) A collection of small flowers in a garden
(iii) All four-legged animals at Delhi Zoo.
11. If $A = \{4, 8, 12, 16, 20\}$
$B = \{8, 16, 24, 32, 40\}$, then write the correct symbols ($\in$, $\notin$) in the following blanks.
(i) 40 __ A
(ii) 8 __ B
(iii) 44 __ A
12. Can the following be called sets?
(i) Consonants in the word SETS
(ii) Names of days of the week that have at least 4 hours of sunshine.
13. If M = {January, March, May, July} and M = {April, June, September, November}, then write the correct symbols ($\in$, $\notin$) in the following blanks.

February __ M

February __ N

14. What is the cardinal number of the Set N of the natural numbers between 10 and 20?

15. What is the cardinal number of a set with the smallest odd number?

CROSSWORD

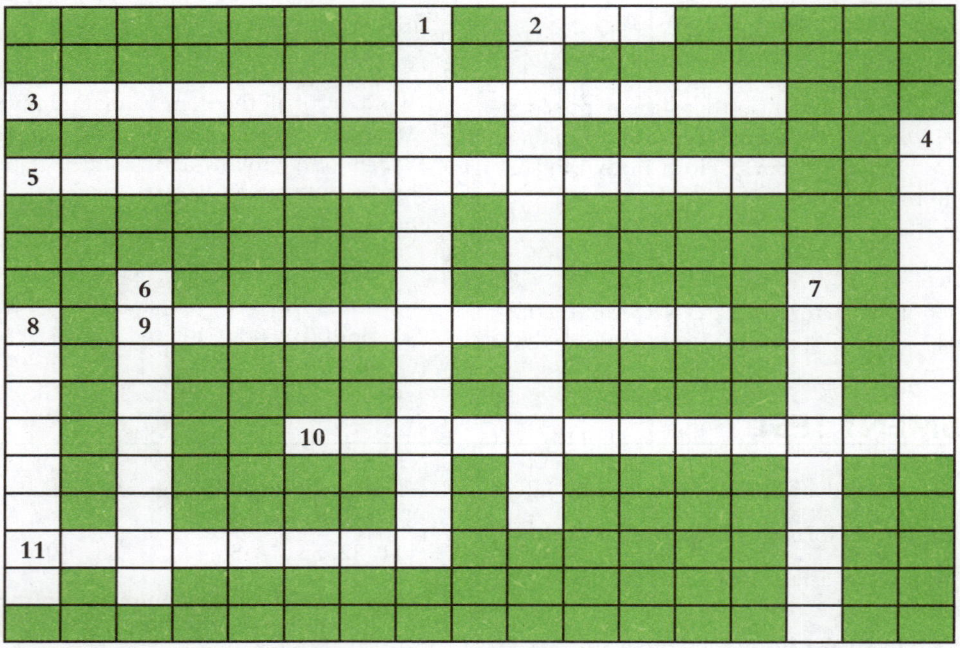

Across

2. A specific collection
3. The set of vowels and the set of first five natural numbers (2 words)
5. How many elements are there in the set? (2 words)
9. You cannot count the elements of this set (2 words)
10. The set of vowels and the set of consonants (2 words)
11. The members of the set

Down

1. These are not disjoint (2 words)
2. Not in the Roster form (no space between the words) (3 words)
4. The set of whole numbers and the set of non-negative integers (2 words)
6. You can find its cardinal number (2 words)
7. Represent a set (no space between the words) (2 words)
8. You cannot find an element in this (2 words)

TEST YOUR CONCEPTS

Very Short Answer Type Questions

1. a
2. $A = \{x^2 : x \in N, x < 6\}$
3. 2016
4. 0
5. empty
6. (c)
7. (a)
8. (d)
9. (b)
10. (b)
11. (a) $\rightarrow$ (q); (b) $\rightarrow$ s; (c) $\rightarrow$ (p); (d) $\rightarrow$ (r)
12. $n(A) + n(B)$
13. {2}
14. Disjoint sets
15. 0
16. B
17. (d)
18. (b)
19. (a)
20. (a)
21. (a) $\rightarrow$ (r); (b) $\rightarrow$ (p); (c) $\rightarrow$ (q); (d) $\rightarrow$ (s)

Short Answer Type Questions

22. {Sun}
24. (i) Yes (ii) No
25. A and B
29. 8, 2, 3, 4
30. (ii) (a) B (b) A
31. 15
32. 1008
33. 8

CONCEPT APPLICATION

1. (d)
2. (a)
3. (c)
4. (c)
5. (b)

ASSESSMENT TEST

2. {–3, –2, –1, 0, 1, 2, 3}
3. 6.
4. (i) {2, 3, 5, 7}
   (ii) {3}
   (iii) {2, 7}
   (iv) {5}
5. 25
6. (ii) (a) {1, 4, 9, 16, 25, 34, 36, 43, 49, 52, 61, 70}
   (b) {16, 25}
   (c) {1, 4, 9, 36, 49}
   (d) {34, 43, 52, 61, 70}
7. (i) {12, 15}
   (ii) {1, 2, 3}
   (iii) $A - B \neq B - A$

CROSSWORD

Across

2. Set
3. Equivalent sets
5. Cardinal number
9. Infinite set
10. Disjoint sets
11. Elements

Down

1. Overlapping sets
2. Set builder form
4. Equal sets
6. Finite set
7. Roster form
8. Empty set

TEST YOUR CONCEPTS

Very Short Answer Type Questions

1. Given $A = \{\phi\}$

   A is a set consisting A of an element ϕ.

   So, $n(A) = 1$.

2. Given $A = \{1, 4, 9, 16, 25\}$

   $A = \{x^2: x \in \text{N}, x < 6\}$

3. A and B are equivalent sets, if $n(A) = n(B)$.

   Given $n(A) = 2016$.

   $\therefore n(B) = 2016$

4. A set having no elements is called an empty set.

   Here, ϕ is an empty set.

   $\therefore n(\phi) = 0$

5. Number of factors of every prime is two.

   There is no prime number having more than two factors.

   $\therefore$ The given set is an empty set.

6. (a) All months in a year having exactly 30 days are April, June, September and November.

   $\therefore$ It is not a singleton set.

   (b) In a week, we have 7 days.

   $\therefore$ It is not a singleton set.

   (c) The natural satellite of the earth in the solar system is moon.

   $\therefore$ It is a singleton set.

   (d) Parallel lines in a plane never intersect.

   $\therefore$ The set of all intersecting points of two parallel lines in a plane is not a singleton set.

   Hence, the correct option is (c).

7. In a plane, there is no triangle, in which the sum of the three interior angles is greater than 180°.

   $\therefore$ A is an empty set.

   Hence, the correct option is (a).

8. (a) $\{x: x \in N, x \text{ is a prime}, x < 10\}$

   $= \{2, 3, 5, 7\}$

   It is a finite set.

   (b) $\{x: x$ is a vowel in the word MATHEMATICS$\}$

   $= \{\text{A, E, I}\}$

   It is a finite set.

   (c) $\{x: x \in N, 2015 < x < 2016\}$

   There is no natural number between 2015 and 2016.

   $\therefore$ It is an empty set.

   $\therefore$ Hence, it is a finite set.

   (d) $\{x: x \in Z, x \text{ is a non-negative integer}\}$

   $= \{0, 1, 2, 3, \ldots\}$

   It is an infinite set.

   Hence, the correct option is (d)

9. (a) $\{x: x \in N, x \text{ is divisible by } 2\}$

   $= \{2, 4, 6, \ldots\}$

   $\therefore$ It is not an empty set.

   (b) $\{x: x \in N, x$ is an additive inverse of 2016$\}$

   Additive inverse of 2016 is but $-2016 \notin N$

   $\therefore$ It is an empty set.

   (c) Binary digits are 0 and 1.

   $\therefore$ Given set is not an empty set.

   (d) Except 1, every natural number is either prime or composite.

   $\therefore$ Given set is not an empty set.

   Hence, the correct option is (b)

10. (a) The collection of colours in a RAINBOW is well-defined. So it is a set.

    (b) We cannot say which books are there in our collection. So it is not a well-defined collection.

    Hence, it is not a set.

    (c) The members of your family is a well-defined collection.

    $\therefore$ It is a set.

    (d) The collection of principals in your school is a well-defined collection.

$\therefore$ It is a set.

Hence, the correct option is (b).

11. (a) {11, 22, 33, 44, 55, 66, 77, 88, 99} is a finite set. $\rightarrow$ (q)

(b) The natural number which is reciprocal of itself is 1.

Given set is a singleton set. $\rightarrow$ (s)

(c) There is no odd number which is a multiple of 6 till now. Given set is an empty set. $\rightarrow$ (p)

(d) There are infinitely many straight lines passing through a point a plane. $\rightarrow$ (r)

Therefore, the correct match is as follows:

(a) $\rightarrow$ (q); (b) $\rightarrow$ (s); (c) $\rightarrow$ (p); (d) $\rightarrow$ (r)

12. Since A and B are disjoint sets, $A \cap B = \phi$

$n(A \cap B) = 0$

$n(A \cup B) = n(A) + n(B) - n(A \cap B)$

$n(A \cup B) = n(A) + n(B)$

13. $A = \{2, 3, 5, 7, \ldots\}$

$B = \{2, 4, 6, 8, \ldots\}$

$A \cap B = \{2, 3, 5, 7, \ldots\} \cap \{2, 4, 6, 8, \ldots\}$

$A \cap B = \{2\}$

14. If $A \cap B = \phi$, then A and B are called disjoint sets.

15. If A and B are non-empty sets, then minimum number of elements in $A \cap B$ is '0'.

16. If all the elements of set 'A' are present in set 'B', then $A \cup B = B$.

17. Given $n(A) = 2016$ and $n(B) = 2017$. The maximum number of elements in $A \cap B = 2016$.

The minimum of $n(A \cup B) = n(A) + n(B) -$ maximum of $n(A \cap B) = 2016 + 2017 - 2016 = 2017$

Hence, the correct option is (d).

18. $A = \{1\}$

$B = \{1\}$

$A \cap B = \{1\}$

Hence, the correct option is (b).

19. Additive inverse of 2017 is -2017 but $-2017 \notin N$

$\therefore A = \{\ \}$

Multiplicative inverse of 2017 is $\frac{1}{2017}$,

but $\frac{1}{2017} \notin N$

$\therefore B = \{\ \}$

$A \cup B = \{\ \}$

Hence, the correct option is (a).

20. $A = \{2016\}$

$B = \{2016\}$

$A - B = \{\ \}$ (or) ϕ

Hence, the correct option is (a).

21. $A = \{2, 4, 5, 6, 10, 11, 14, 21\}$

$B = \{1, 2, 3, 5, 7, 8, 11, 12, 13\}$

(a) $A - B = \{4, 6, 10, 14, 21\}$

$n(A - B) = 5 \rightarrow$ r

(b) $A \cup B = \{1, 2, 3, 4, 5, 6, 7, 8, 10, 11, 12, 13, 14, 21\}$

$n(A \cup B) = 14 \rightarrow$ p

(c) $A \cap B = \{2, 5, 11\}$

$n(A \cap B) = 3 \rightarrow$ q

(d) $B - A = \{1, 3, 7, 8, 12, 13\}$

$n(B - A) = 6 \rightarrow$ s

Therefore, the correct match is as follows:

(a) $\rightarrow$ (r), (b) $\rightarrow$ (p); (c) $\rightarrow$ (q); (d) $\rightarrow$ (s)

Short Answer Type Questions

22. $A = \{x : x$ is the nearest star to the Earth$\}$

$A = \{\text{Sun}\}$

23. (a) (i) {The longest river in India}

(ii) {The days of a week}

(b) (i) $\{x : x = 2n, n \in N \text{ and } n \leq 4\}$

(ii) $\{x : x = 3n, n \in N\}$

24. (a) $A = \{S, O, L, U, T, I, N\}$

$n(A) = 7$

$B = \{P, R, O, B, L, E, M\}$

$n(B) = 7$

Since $n(A) = n(B)$,

$\therefore A$ and B are equivalent sets.

(b) $C = \{x: x \in N, x \text{ is either prime or composite}\}$

i.e., C is the collection of all natural numbers except 1, less than 10.

$C = \{2, 3, 4, 5, 6, 7, 8, 9\}$

$n(C) = 8$

$D = \{1\}$

$n(D) = 1$

Since $n(C) \neq n(D)$,

$\therefore$ C and D are not equivalent sets.

25. (a) A is the set of the first five elements of periodic table.

$A = \{H, He, Li, Be, B\}$

$B = \{H, He, Li, Be, B\}$

$\therefore$ A and B are equal sets.

(b) $C = \{x: x \text{ is prime number}\}$

$D = \{x: x \text{ is odd number}\}$

$C = \{2, 3, 5, 7, 11, \ldots\}$

$D = \{3, 5, 7, 9, \ldots\}$

$2 \in C$ but $2 \notin D$

$\therefore$ C and D are not equal sets.

26. (a) Every composite number has at least three factors. There is no composite number having less than three factors.

$\therefore$ A is an empty set.

(b) The multiplicative inverse of 2016 is $\frac{1}{2016}$.

$B = \left\{\frac{1}{2016}\right\}$

$\therefore$ B is a singleton set.

(c) In a set of natural numbers, 1 is neither prime nor composite.

$C = \{1\}$

$\therefore$ C is a singleton set.

27. All equal sets are equivalent since both the sets have same number of elements. But the converse need not be true since they may not have same elements.

For example: $A = \{1, 2, 3, 4, 5\}$ and $B = \{7, 8, 9, 10, 11\}$ are equivalent sets, since $n(A) = n(B)$.

But A and B are not equal sets, since the elements of A and B are different.

28. $A = \{I, N, D, A\}$

$B = \{E, U, A, I, O\}$

$n(A) = 4$

$n(B) = 5$

$A \cup B = \{I, N, D, A, E, U, O\}$

$n(A \cup B) = 7$

$A \cap B = \{A, I\}$

$n(A \cap B) = 2$

$n(A) + n(B) - n(A \cap B)$

$= 4 + 5 - 2 = 7$

$\therefore n(A \cup B) = n(A) + n(B) - n(A \cap B)$

29. $A = \{2, 3, 4, 5\}$

$B = \{-2, -1, 0, 1, 2, 3\}$

$A \cup B = \{-2, -1, 0, 1, 2, 3, 4, 5\}$

$\Rightarrow n(A \cup B) = 8$

$A \cap B = \{2, 3\} \Rightarrow n(A \cap B) = 2$

$A - B = \{4, 5\} \Rightarrow n(A - B) = 2$

$B - A = \{-2, -1, 0, 1\}$

$n(B - A) = 4$

30. (i) $A = \{2, 4, 6, 8\}$

$B = \{1, 2, 3, 4, 6, 8, 12, 24\}$

It is clear that, every element of A is present in B. So we draw two circles such that one is fully contained in the other.

The Venn diagram is as follows:

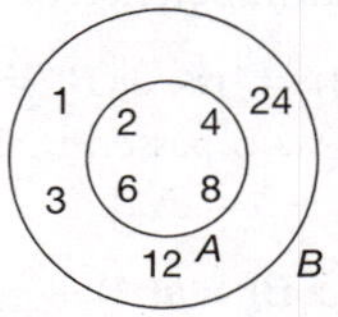

(ii) (a) $A \cup B = \{1, 2, 3, 4, 6, 8, 12, 24\} = B$

(b) $A \cap B = \{2, 4, 6, 8\} = A$

31. Given $n(A) = 20$, $n(A \cap B) = 5$

$n(A - B) = n(A) - n(A \cap B)$

$= 20 - 5 = 15$

32. Given $n(A) = x$, $n(B) = 2[n(A)] = 2x$

$n(A \cup B) = 2017$, $n(A \cap B) = 1007$

$n(A \cup B) = n(A) + n(B) - n(A \cap B)$

$2017 = x + 2x - 1007$

$3x = 3024$

$x = 1008$

33. $F(n)$ is the set of all the factors of n excluding 1.

$F(16) = \{2, 4, 8, 16\}$

$F(24) = \{2, 3, 4, 5, 8, 12, 24\}$

$F(16) \cap F(24) = \{2, 4, 8\} = F(8)$

Given $F(16) \cap F(24) = F(x)$

$\therefore x = 8$

CONCEPT APPLICATION

1. Given that $n(A) = 17$ and $n(B) = 13$.

For the maximum possible value of $n(A \cup B) - n(A \cap B)$, $n(A \cup B)$ should have maximum possible value and $n(A \cap B)$ should have minimum possible value.

Also, $n(A \cup B)$ is maximum, when A and B are disjoint sets.

So, $n(A \cup B) = n(A) + n(B) = 17 + 13 = 30$ and $n(A \cap B) = 0$.

Hence, the maximum possible value of $n(A \cup B) - n(A \cap B) = 30 - 0 = 30$.

Hence, the correct option is (d).

2. Given that A and B are two equivalent sets.

$\Rightarrow n(A) = n(B)$

For the maximum possible value of $n(A \cap B)$, A and B must be equal sets.

When A and B are equal sets, $n(A \cap B) = n(A)$ or $n(B)$.

Hence, the correct option is (a).

3. Let the number of students who passed in Maths be $n(A)$ and that in Science be $n(B)$.

Therefore, $n(A) = 18$, $n(B) = 14$ and the number of students who passed in either of the exams, $n(A \cup B) = 25 - 3 = 22$.

We have, $n(A \cup B) = n(A) + n(B) - n(A \cap B)$.

$\Rightarrow 22 = 18 + 14 - n(A \cap B)$

$\Rightarrow n(A \cap B) = 32 - 22 = 10$

The number of students who passed in both the exams, $n(A \cap B) = 10$.

Hence, the correct option is (c).

4. Given that A is a set of the factors of $28 \Rightarrow A = \{1, 2, 4, 7, 14, 28\}$.

B is a set of the factors of $17 \Rightarrow B = \{1, 17\}$.

C is a set of the odd multiples of 7 less than $50 \Rightarrow C = \{7, 21, 35, 49\}$.

(a) $A \cap B = \{1\}$ is a singleton set.

(b) $C \cap B = \{\ \}$

(c) $A \cap C = \{7\}$ is a singleton set.

Hence, choice (3) follows.

Hence, the correct option is (c).

5. Given that A is a set of all the prime numbers less than $20 \Rightarrow A = \{2, 3, 5, 7, 11, 13, 17, 19\}$

B is a set of all the even natural numbers less than $20 \Rightarrow B = \{2, 4, 6, 8, 10, 12, 14, 16, 18\}$

C is a set of all the odd natural numbers $\Rightarrow C = \{1, 3, 5, 7...\}$

(a) $A \cap B = \{2\}$ is a singleton set.

(b) $B \cap C = \{\ \} \Rightarrow B$ and C are disjoint sets.

(c) $A \cap C = \{3, 5, 7, 11, 13, 17, 19\}$ is not an infinite set.

Hence, choice (2) follows.

Hence, the correct option is (b).

ASSESSMENT TEST

1. Set builder form of the given set {x: x is the name of a month of a year starts with letter 'J'}.

2. The Roster from of $\{x : x \in Z, -3 \leq x \leq 3\}$ is $\{-3, -2, -1, 0, 1, 2, 3\}$

3. The factors of 24 are 1, 2, 3, 4, 6, 8, 12 and 24.

   $\therefore A = \{2, 3, 4, 6, 8, 12\}$

   $n(A) = 6$

4. $A = \{2, 3, 7\}$, since the prime factors of 2016 are 2, 3 and 7.

   $B = \{3, 5\}$, since the prime factors of 2025 are 3 and 5.

   (i) $A \cup B = \{2, 3, 5, 7\}$

   (ii) $A \cap B = \{3\}$

   (iii) $A - B = \{2, 7\}$

   (iv) $B - A = \{5\}$

5. Given $n(G - H) = 15$ and $n(G \cap H) = 10$.

   $n(G) = n(G - H) + n(G \cap H)$

   $= 15 + 10 = 25$

6. (i) $A = \{1, 4, 9, 16, 25, 36, 49\}$

   $B = \{16, 25, 34, 43, 52, 61, 70\}$

   A and B have 16 and 25 as common elements. So, we draw two intersecting circles representing A and B respectively.

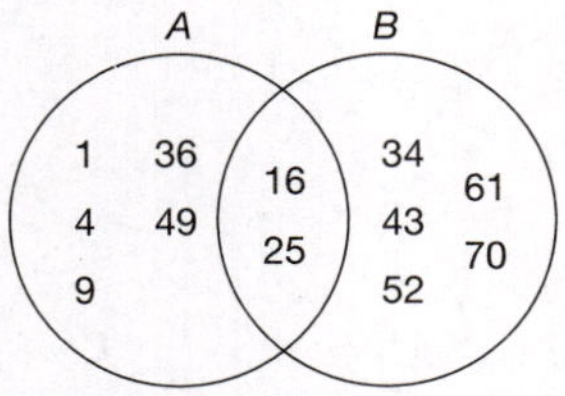

   (a) $A \cup B = \{1, 4, 9, 16, 25, 34, 36, 43, 49, 52, 61, 70\}$

   (b) $A \cap B = \{16, 25\}$

   (c) $A - B = \{1, 4, 9, 36, 49\}$

   (d) $B - A = \{34, 43, 52, 61, 70\}$

7. $A = \{6, 9, 12, 15, 18\}$

   $B = \{1, 2, 3, 6, 9, 18\}$

   (a) $A - B = \{12, 15\}$

   (b) $B - A = \{1, 2, 3\}$

   (c) $A - B \neq B - A$

8. Descriptive: {Two-digit multiples of 11}

   Set builder: {x : x is a two-digit multiple of 11}

9. {M, T, H, C, S}

   {S, C, N}

   {N, G, L, S, H}

10. Collection of small flowers is not a set as there is no reference to measure the size of flowers. Hence, no specific flowers can be grouped to make a set.

11. (i) $40 \notin A$

    (ii) $8 \in B$

    (iii) $44 \notin A$

12. (i) Consonants are S, T, hence, it can be called a set

    (ii) There are no particular days that have four hours of sunshine. Duration of sunshine differs depending on the weather conditions that change daily. Hence, it is not a set.

13. February $\notin$ M

    February $\notin$ N

14. Natural numbers between 10 and 20 are 11, 12, 13, 14, 15, 16, 17, 18, 19. Hence, the cardinal number of this set is 9.

15. The smallest odd number is 1. Therefore, the set with smallest odd number has element 1. Hence, the cardinal number of this set is 1.